Ambition and failure
in Stuart England

MANCHESTER
UNIVERSITY PRESS

Politics, culture and society in early modern Britain

General editors

PROFESSOR ANN HUGHES
DR ANTHONY MILTON
PROFESSOR PETER LAKE

This important series publishes monographs that take a fresh and challenging look at the interactions between politics, culture and society in Britain between 1500 and the mid-eighteenth century. It counteracts the fragmentation of current historiography through encouraging a variety of approaches which attempt to redefine the political, social and cultural worlds, and to explore their interconnection in a flexible and creative fashion. All the volumes in the series question and transcend traditional interdisciplinary boundaries, such as those between political history and literary studies, social history and divinity, urban history and anthropology. They contribute to a broader understanding of crucial developments in early modern Britain.

Ambition and failure in Stuart England

The career of John, first Viscount Scudamore

IAN ATHERTON

Manchester
University Press
Manchester and New York

distributed exclusively in the USA by St. Martin's Press

Copyright © Ian Atherton 1999

The right of Ian Atherton to be identified as the author of this work has been asserted by him in accordance with the Copyright, Designs and Patents Act 1988.

Published by Manchester University Press
Oxford Road, Manchester M13 9NR, UK
and Room 400, 175 Fifth Avenue, New York, NY 10010, USA
http://www.man.ac.uk/mup

Distributed exclusively in the USA by
St. Martin's Press, Inc., 175 Fifth Avenue, New York, NY 10010, USA

Distributed exclusively in Canada by
UBC Press, University of British Columbia, 6344 Memorial Road,
Vancouver, BC, Canada V6T 1Z2

British Library Cataloguing-in-Publication Data
A catalogue record for this book is avalaible from the British Library

Library of Congress Cataloging-in-Publication Data
Atherton, Ian.
    Ambition and failure in Stuart England : the career of John, first
Viscount Scudamore / Ian Atherton.
        p.   cm. — (Politics, culture, and society in early modern Britain)
    Based on the author's thesis (Ph.D.)—University of Cambridge, 1993.
    Includes bibliographical references and index.
    ISBN 0–7190–5091–x
    1. Scudamore of Sligo. John Scudamore, Viscount, 1601–1671.
2. Great Britain—Court and courtiers—History—17th century.
3. Great Britain—Politics and government—1625–1649.
4. Statesmen—Great Britain—Biography. 5. Herefordshire (England)—Biography.
I. Title. II. Series.
DA407.S28A82   1999
942.06'2'092—dc21   99–41573
[B]

ISBN 0 7190 5091 x *hardback*

First published 1999

06   05   04   03   02   01   00   99   10 9 8 7 6 5 4 3 2 1

Typeset in Scala with Pastonchi display
by Koinonia Ltd, Manchester

Printed in Great Britain
by Bookcraft (Bath) Ltd, Midsomer Norton

FOR BAT, MIM, AND WINDY
WHO DIDN'T MAKE IT

Contents

Tables

A note on conventions

All quotations are as they are given in the sources cited, except that abbreviations have been silently expanded.

The old-style or Julian calendar has been retained, except that the new year is taken as beginning on 1 January, not 25 March. In the case of Viscount Scudamore's embassy to France, where the Gregorian or new-style calendar had replaced the Julian and where, consequently, dates were ten days ahead of England, double dating is used, sacrificing elegance for precision. Thus the day that Scudamore left Paris at the end of his embassy, which was Wednesday 2 March 1639 in France but Wednesday 20 February 1638 in England, is rendered in the text as 20 February/2 March 1639.

The first viscount and all his close relations consistently spelled their surname Scudamore, while more distant cousins and others often preferred the usage Skidmore or Skydmore; readers should be aware that Scudamore and Skidmore were the same name and their owners were related. The main subject of this book, John Scudamore of Holme Lacy (1601–71) was created Sir John Scudamore, first baronet, in 1620 and ennobled as the first Viscount Scudamore of Sligo in Ireland in 1628. For clarity, I have occasionally referred to him as Viscount Scudamore before his elevation to the peerage; often, he is simply Scudamore. The Holme Lacy Scudamores used a restricted number of christian names, especially John and James. The first viscount was a John, his father was James (1568–1619), his grandfather (1542–1623) and great-great grandfather (c. 1486–1571) were Johns; his only son to reach adulthood was James (1624–68), whose only son, the second viscount, was another John (1649–97). Possibilities of confusion abound. Where Scudamores other than the first viscount are mentioned, I have tried to make the distinction plain from the context, by including their dates or, in the case of the first viscount's grandfather, calling him Old Sir John Scudamore. I must appeal to the reader's charity if the identification of any Scudamore is not immediately apparent.

Readers should be aware that since my research into the Scudamore papers in the Public Record Office (C115) was completed the arrangement of the bundles has been slightly altered, but the piece numbers remain unchanged and all documents are readily identifiable by their old numbers, which have been retained in this work.

Acknowledgements

The writer of any book incurs many debts, this writer more than most, especially as the present work began as a doctoral dissertation more years ago than is decent to mention. The debts I accrued in my first years of research are mentioned, if not discharged, in the completed dissertation, but since then I have run up many more. I remain indebted to my Ph.D. supervisor, Dr John Morrill, for his continued guidance, for fashioning the best intellectual environment in which to undertake graduate studies, for nurturing and challenging my thinking about all matters relating to the seventeenth century, and for never doubting that the dissertation would, one day, be finished. I must also express my gratitude to the staff of all the libraries and archives in which I have worked for their patience in producing documents and answering queries. My parents, family and friends have continued to provide unstinting support and accommodation as I have travelled to record repositories. Two friends deserve particular mention. Warren Skidmore and John Hunt have earned a special debt of gratitude for their tireless support and unflagging interest in all matters Scudamorean. Their researches have unpicked the genealogy and origins of the Scudamore family and have thereby prevented many a misidentification of one John Scudamore with another.

The transformation of a dissertation into the present work was possible only thanks to the help of many people. The staff of Manchester University Press have been ever patient. Colleagues and students at the Centre of East Anglian Studies at the University of East Anglia, in the Victoria County History and at Keele University have sustained my interest and, often unwittingly, have suggested fresh avenues to explore or approaches to investigate. Dr Jon Finch, Dr Alannah Tomkins, Susie West and Dr Richard Wilson deserve special thanks. Professor Hassell Smith, like others before and since, laboured long and hard to inject precision and rigour into my prose and thoughts, and I am beholden to him even as I demonstrate how far I fall short of his example. Fellow early modernists will not be surprised to learn that Dr Richard Cust, since examining my dissertation, has always been willing to answer my queries, to let me see work in advance of publication and to lend copies of documents. Without the support and encouragement of the three series editors, Professor Ann Hughes, Professor Peter Lake and Dr Anthony Milton (a trinity of editors able to work miracles, to borrow an earlier phrase), this work would never have seen the light of day, and I am indebted to them for their helpful comments, suggestions and guidance, and for much else besides.

Chapter 3 is a much revised and partly rewritten version of I. J. Atherton, 'Viscount Scudamore's "Laudianism": The Religious Practices of the First Viscount Scudamore', *Historical Journal*, 34:3 (1991), pp. 567–96, copyright Cambridge University Press, who are thanked for allowing its use here.

My final, and greatest debt is to Jane Tillier; even she does not know how much both this book and its author owe to her.

I.J.A.
Madeley, All Saints, 1998

Abbreviations

APC   Acts of the Privy Council of England 1542–1631 (46 vols, London, 1890–1964).

Atherton, thesis I. J. Atherton, 'John, 1st Viscount Scudamore (1601–71): A Career at Court and in the Country, 1601–43' (unpublished Cambridge University Ph.D. thesis, 1993).

BL   British Library.

Bodleian   Bodleian Library, Oxford.

CSPD   Calendar of State Papers, Domestic Series, 1547–1685 (75 vols, London, 1856–1939).

CSPV   Calendar of State Papers and Manuscripts, relating to English Affairs, Existing in the Archives and Collections of Venice, and in other Libraries of Northern Italy (38 vols, London, 1864–1947).

DNB   S. Lee and S. L. Leslie, eds, Dictionary of National Biography (63 vols, London, 1885–1900).

FSL   Folger Shakespeare Library.

HCA   Hereford Cathedral Archives.

HCL   Hereford City Library.

HMC   Royal Commission on Historical Manuscripts.

HRO   Hereford Record Office.

LBH   T. T. Lewis, ed., Letters of the Lady Brilliana Harley, Wife of Sir Robert Harley, of Brampton Bryan (Camden Society, 1st series, 58, 1854).

MCW   J. Webb, Memorials of the Civil War between King Charles and the Parliament of England as it affected Herefordshire and the Adjacent Counties, ed. and completed by T. W. Webb (2 vols, London, 1879).

PRO   Public Record Office.

RO   Record Office.

TRHS   Transactions of the Royal Historical Society.

Chapter 1

The rhetorics of
honour and advancement

Ambition will loom large in these pages, and so too will failure, but I hope that readers will see that they come with a twist. On one level, Sir John Scudamore, the first Viscount Scudamore of Sligo (1601–71), was an ambitious politician who sought office at the Stuart court, and failed. Yet his failures were tempered with success, just as his successes bore seeds of failure. He was the leading magnate in his native county of Herefordshire, but his position was rarely unchallenged and he proved unable to pass on to his descendants all the powers he had amassed in his own hands. He was made Charles's ambassador to France in 1635, but he proved an inept diplomat, and much of his time was spent arguing with his colleagues in Paris. He did make himself the leading royalist in Hereford at the beginning of 1643, but much of the blame for the fall of that city to the parliament in April 1643 must be laid at his door, and he spent the remainder of the war a prisoner of the parliament in London. His was not an unblemished career, yet he, his supporters, and later writers managed to turn him into a paragon of all true virtues, 'a Worthy Copy for others to write after'.[1]

There is a second way in which ambition comes with a twist. There was a time when historians were able to present the political aims and prudential calculations of political actors as the products of a heuristically transparent pursuit of power, profit and office. Lewis Namier, whose writings governed much of the way that historians from the 1930s to the 1980s thought about early modern politics, took it as axiomatic that all politicians were engaged in naked desire to acquire and exercise political power. Ambition was, to Namier, the most important of the 'underlying emotions' which governed the course of events and so formed 'the music, to which ideas are a mere libretto, often of a very inferior quality'. Namier pronounced political principles 'irrelevant' and his work ignored them as a distraction from the real business of politics, the struggle for place, power and money.[2] Under this (often unacknowledged)

Namierite tradition the discourse of politics became the discourse of ambition. Thus Barbara Donagan has written of the career of the earl of Holland as a 'courtier's progress' through greed and unprincipled acquisition, comparing him and other courtiers to 'truffle hounds', scavenging for profit. Alison Wall has gone further, and described the pattern of politics in Elizabethan and Jacobean England in terms of competing groups of ambitious county gentry locked into struggles 'for supremacy over any issue which came to hand ... in which the real issues were power and prestige'.[3] Such an approach will no longer suffice, for three reasons. First, it remains possible that some political actors at least were being genuine in articulating their principles. It is simply too cynical to dismiss (as Namier did) all ideology as 'cant'. Second, it is ahistorical merely to assert ambition as an explanation, since many of the objects of ambition, the forms of power, prestige and status available to and pursued by contemporaries, were peculiar to their historical situation and cultural context. Dr Wall's conclusion that 'the ambitions of the gentry were uniform' is both too bland and too bald.[4] Ambition must be understood as being historically conditioned. Third, not only the goals of ambition, but the very means, strategies, devices and rhetorics employed in the pursuit of those goals vary between ages and cultures. It is vital, therefore, to study the discourse, the normative language used, in the pursuit of honour and power, for that normative language will, in part, determine the range of courses available to a political actor.[5] Before recourse can be had to the traditional methodological individualism of the political historian it is necessary to reconstruct the categories and discursive forms within which early modern political actors conceived of themselves, their contemporaries and their environment.

If such a conclusion seems trite and obvious it is nevertheless the case that it has often been ignored, and it has been the field of early Stuart politics which has seen some of the bloodiest battles as historians have tried to listen to what their subjects were doing and saying and how they were so acting, or have ignored contemporary categories and forms altogether. It was the essence of the revisionist attack on the earlier Whig interpretation of the seventeenth century that the categories and assumptions imputed to contemporary actors were anachronistic.[6] Before the 1970s the dominant modes of interpretation of Stuart history tended to seek the origins of key notions of the myth of England (or New England) such as liberty and democracy. Thus we had Wallace Notestein's House of Commons 'winning the initiative' and asserting its self-assurance and power, a view that spawned a whole chamber of followers,[7] and we had puritanism as the torchbearer for modern liberal democracy.[8] Revisionist critiques, notably the work of Conrad Russell and John Morrill,[9] swept away such notions but, it is often assumed, replaced them with a different set of anachronistic assumptions and categories. The triumph of revisionism was seen as the death of ideology.[10] Out went the account of principled differences of view over the means and ends of the political process – the struggle for the constitution that had allegedly taken place in the Commons – and in came an account bristling with the minutiae of daily business in parliament. The fate of Dungeness lighthouse was, the anti-revisionists claimed, privileged over principle, the diurnal over the durable.[11] In the first wave of revisionist writing, localism replaced ideology. In place of political ideology the revisionists put, their detractors said, a simple, straightforward and transparent political narrative in which the motives of political actors in the seventeenth century were in effect obvious to political commentators in the late twentieth, in which the House of Lords of the 1620s and 1640s was described in terms more applicable to the House of Lords in the 1980s and 1990s.[12] Professor Russell's account of Charles I as an essentially unpolitical king, one who refused to acknowledge that politics is the art of the possible, for example, has a certain evident timeless quality, especially in his comparison between Charles in the seventeenth century and William Gladstone in the nineteenth.[13] The stuff of political life was rendered as the pursuit of place, the preservation and furtherance of private, local and corporate interest. Hence the revival of interest in and stress on the role of court factions, usually seen not as groups with a shared ideological viewpoint but as agglomerations that came together to seek their own advancement.[14] The revisionist account did not conceptualise politics within an ideological vacuum, but within an ideological framework dominated principally by the need for consensual decision making, but also by truisms about the equilibrium between prerogative and law, the balance between the rights of the subject and the authority of the monarch, and the need for and content of Protestant orthodoxy. These were nostrums to which nearly all contemporaries assented, and so it was that an emphasis on consensus politics was judged to be the hallmark of revisionism.[15]

Such a stress on consensus is crucial to the revisionist project, for it was not the case that revisionism expelled issues of meaning from politics. What it did do was to discard the notion of ideology as two mutually opposing and exclusive bodies of political ideas and policies, a definition more suited to the conditions of the mid twentieth-century world and the Cold War. In its place revisionism supplied a definition of political culture as congeries of conceptions within which contemporaries viewed political functions. It was a shift of meaning that went largely unnoticed by either the revisionists or their first opponents. The result has been a rather attenuated and partial analysis of the political values and culture of the seventeenth century: analysis has privileged consensus and agreement both as contemporary aspirations and as a social given, as if they were value-free comments on the actual state of Stuart belief and practice.

A number of scholars whom we may term post-revisionist have sought to develop their analyses over and against the revisionist account, but in many areas have deliberately built on the older revisionist version of events rather than rejecting it wholesale.[16] Post-revisionists have embraced the turn to political culture implicit in revisionism, and have accepted much of the revisionist emphasis on the importance to contemporaries of both consensual decision making and the maintenance of broad agreement on the key political and religious issues of the day. They have, however, gone a step further by emphasising that a shared language need not construe a shared meaning. The clichés and platitudes of contemporary political discourse on which almost everybody claimed to be in agreement were not, in fact, always internally coherent or compatible with one another, nor were they always so precisely defined as to exclude the possibilities of shades of meaning, different glosses, or rival appropriations. As Peter Lake has commented, 'revisionist claims about the common languages in which the political was described, organised and manipulated are confirmed, while revisionist conclusions about the extent and nature of ideological division and disagreement in this period are falsified'.[17] The central features of the revisionist account of how the political system and world view worked, and were supposed to work, have been retained, but contemporary disagreement and division have been placed centre stage, a claim signalled in the title of the first post-revisionist manifesto – *Conflict in Early Stuart England*.[18]

One of the most obvious results of such conceptualising and reconceptu- alising of early modern politics has been a renewed interest in the self-image and perceptions of the ruling elite and its dominant notions of power, status and order within which and by which it ruled, maintaining local order, defending its own interests, obeying the crown and upholding the common weal. The prime objects of such research have tended to be persons of a similar cast or ideological stripe – puritan or godly men, and occasionally women and clergy, men prominent in parliament and parliamentarianism, people to whom some of the secular and most of the religious policies of the 1630s were an anathema. We have, for example, studies of the Harley family of Herefordshire, prominent puritans and parliamentarians both locally in the marches of Wales and nationally, and of the Newdigates of Arbury, godly magistrates in Warwickshire; we have editions of the papers of the puritan MPs Sir Richard Grosvenor and Sir Thomas Barrington; we have an account of the self-image of the godly clergy; and where we have more general studies of the gentry we find that it is often those individuals and families of a more godly hue who predominate.[19] Perhaps the main exception to this rule has been the study of the royalists in mid century, but here another single, narrow ideological cast has been to the fore: the moderates or constitutional royalists, those who began in 1640 alienated by Laudianism and prerogative rule but who rallied to the king in 1641–42 under the same banner of the rule of law which had previously led them to oppose Charles's policies.[20]

The biases of recent research are partly the product of its sources, for it was the godly who tended to produce the most self-reflective accounts of attitudes and conduct. The biases are also partly a hangover from pre-revisionist Whiggery which privileged the doings of the puritans and the opponents of the crown, as harbingers and midwives of modern values, over the deeds of the Laudians, conformists and royalists who were seen as standing in the way of progress. Whatever the causes, one of the results of the skewing of modern research has been an impoverished view of the spectrum of contemporary opinion from which the Laudians and those whom Professor Lake calls 'conviction Royalists' have largely been excluded. The figure of Viscount Scudamore allows us to begin to redress this imbalance.

The confined focus of research has allowed revisionists and others to emphasise the essential moderation of contemporary gentry attitudes. The political beliefs of the English before 1640 have tended to be portrayed in revisionist circles as largely consensual. Conflict, therefore, has had to be imported from outside the mainstream political spectrum. Either discord came in the guise of events elsewhere, the so-called 'British problem', with conflict in first Scotland and then Ireland destabilising an otherwise peaceful England,[21] or it arose from the activities of hitherto marginal home-grown groups of religious radicals, the Laudians and the puritans; in some accounts (those of Morrill and Russell) but not in others (Sharpe and Kishlansky) they are twinned with the political incompetence of the king to produce first crisis and then civil war.[22] In the first wave of revisionist writing the sand in the vaseline was Laud, with his followers seen as a predominantly clerical and clericalist group of order-obsessed authoritarians whose views fitted closely with those of the king himself. Here were the real villains of the piece, the true innovators and revolutionaries whose extremism and lack of political tact alienated the moderate majority. Hence Dr Morrill's judgement that 'it is almost impossible to overestimate the damage caused by the Laudians'.[23] Such views were a simple inversion of earlier accounts where the puritans had played a similar role. The puritans were now rescued from the taint of radicalism by a close analysis of their expressed ends and intentions, which turned out, for the most part, to be framed within the established, consensual discourse outlined above.

Reacting against this view of the Laudians a second wave of revisionists, led by Kevin Sharpe, stressed that Charles and Laud also shaped and described their programme in the same rhetorical forms and codes of consensus, and so rescued them too from the charges of innovation and extremism. Charles and Laud were also, it was claimed, moderates, well within the political and religious mainstream, wedded to the rhetoric of the common weal, the preservation of order and consensus, and concerned to strike the proper balance between the prerogatives of the crown and the rights of the subject.[24] The extreme puritans, with their allies the Scots, returned to the centre stage once again playing the role of the villains as incendiaries and provocateurs. Where once historians battled to proclaim their particular heroes revolutionaries, now they struggle to make them moderates.

Some revisionist historians, most notably Glenn Burgess, have taken the attack a step further, claiming that in their search for the political culture and values of the gentry anti- and post-revisionists have succeeded only in using what were in fact mainstream and entirely consensual notions of the commonwealth, service to the country, honour, gentility, of being a patriot or a defender of true religion, to resuscitate inherently Whiggish notions of a puritan opposition to an absolutist and Laudian Caroline regime. Such writing has, in Dr Burgess's view, hidden the massive areas of ideological agreement that not only provided a moderate, Protestant, and constitutionalist case for the crown as well as for the parliament in the 1640s, but also supplied a powerful legitimation for the central policies of the 1630s, one which was accepted by the bulk of the political nation until the dual forces of Scottish crisis and Irish revolt brought meltdown to English politics. Nevertheless, at times Dr Burgess seems to limit his argument for consensus to 'a common set of conventions for the conduct of public political debate', what he calls 'the structure of the discourse', and, as we have already stressed, a shared language did not mean a shared set of meanings. His was a very attenuated consensus.[25]

A case study of just one career cannot hope to adjudicate these disputes or settle all the issues, but Viscount Scudamore does provide a fresh perspective from which to view them. Here we have a lay Laudian, a pillar of local society, an MP, a servant of the crown and a diplomat, an active supporter of the policies of the king and a committed royalist. By studying the crucial elements in his career and world view, by investigating the discursive formations and tropes through which he conceived, presented and sold his many-faceted roles as gentleman, royal servant and Christian, we can gain an insight into the ways in which the consensual cultural and ideological materials by which the gentry understood the political process and their own roles in it could be glossed in a number of different ways – ways that could lead to conflict as well as agreement. For once we can see what the world looked like to an enthusiastic supporter of the Laudian church and of the policies of the personal rule, and to a convinced royalist. Such study is crucial because these people, like Scudamore, have too often been seen as untypical and extreme and, paradoxically, their viewpoint has been marginalised in the historiography of the period even as they have been rendered as causally central in many recent interpretations of the period. Through Scudamore we can gain some sense of how central elements in the mainstream political and social codes of the period could be integrated with and made to serve an aggressively Caroline, Laudian and royalist outlook. This sense is particularly important to the future study of royalism, where a counterbalance is needed to recent accounts which have stressed the experiences and beliefs of men such as Sir Edward Hyde and Sir John Culpepper, men who were opponents of the personal rule but who ended up as royalists. Scudamore reminds us that there were royalists of other hues for whom support for the crown was an unbroken thread and who brought different ideological materials into the royalist synthesis that emerged in the early 1640s.

Historians are slowly waking up to the implications of Stephen Greenblatt's work on 'self-fashioning' and his assertion that in early modern England 'there were both selves and a sense that they could be fashioned'.[26] In particular, work on gentry codes of honour, particularly by Richard Cust, has begun to look at the ways that politicians could fashion positive images from the symbols, discourses and rhetoric of contemporary political culture to present themselves on various stages.[27] There was, indeed, a wide variety of discourses of honour from which contemporaries could fashion their own image in a process that Kevin Sharpe and Peter Lake have called 'creative bricolage'.[28] Mervyn James saw a gradual shift taking place in the image of honour in the late sixteenth and early seventeenth centuries, from a stress on lineage and martial prowess to a more pacific ideal of moral virtue and service to the commonwealth. The change, from Christian knight to godly magistrate, he saw as being brought about by the new ideas of reformers and humanists, and by the failure of noble-led Tudor rebellions. James's view, however, is over-schematic, for there was not one single dominant discourse of honour in the early seventeenth century but a plethora: Cynthia Herrup has written that early modern writings on honour suggest 'multi-vocality, even self-contradiction', not transition.[29]

Echoes of these many voices can be heard by briefly examining what a number of writers said about the source or essence of honour. To Christopher Marlowe the 'virtue is the fount whence honour springs'; to another writer it was the prince who was the 'Fountain of Honour'; that they were contradictory was no bar to such ideas becoming commonplaces.[30] The king, thought Sir John Holles, later earl of Clare, was 'the fountaine, from whence all honor floweth and in that measure, as all light from the sunn'.[31] For some writers honour was no more than reputation: honour, wrote James Cleland in 1607, is 'not in his hand who is honoured, but in the hearts and opinions of other men'.[32] To others, honour was a more tangible quality in and of itself. Honour might reside in lineage: one of the most common symbols of honour was the pedigree, displayed in family trees and coats of arms on parchment, paint, stone and glass, the material culture of nobility. The first Lord Montagu accounted his worthy ancestors 'allways my greatest Glory'; according to Francis Markham, 'blood ... sends out an issue of Honor even to Infinite Generations'.[33] How reverend a thing it is, thought Bacon, 'to behold an ancient noble family, which hath stood out against the waves and weathers of time: for new nobility is but the act of power, but ancient nobility is the act of time'.[34] Often linked with such ideas was the concept of the honour associated with wealth, especially ancient riches. The fifth earl of Huntingdon advised his son that 'without means thy house will looke as naked as trees that are cropped ... riches illustrate honour and set forth the dignity of thy place'. Lord Burghley's dictum that gentility was 'nothing but ancient riches' was much repeated by one generation to the next.[35] Other ideas stressed a link between honour and individual action or merit, rather than inheritance. Service to the king or commonwealth, as commissioner, justice of the peace, member of parliament, ambassador, privy councillor or the like, might confer honour. In Lodowick Bryskett's account, honour was brought by dignities and offices. The earl of Huntingdon, meanwhile, petitioning James I to keep his office of lord lieutenant, distinguished between the honour of a title and the honour of service to the king, and preferred the latter: 'I should professe it as a greater honoure to succeede in your favoure then to inherit an earldom.'[36] Alternatively, elevation to office or title might be seen not as conferring honour itself, but as the public recognition of honour already conferred by virtue; elevation might stipulate or declare virtue, rather than create it. 'Honor is the ensigne of vertue,' wrote Count Annibale Romei; 'the reward of *Vertue* is *Honor*', thought Angel Day, paraphrasing the oft-rehearsed Ciceronian idea.[37] Virtue itself was a multi-faceted concept: education; piety; lordship; service; wealth; lineage; charity; hospitality; justice; temperance; fortitude; prudence; mercy; affability; liberality; mercy – varying ingredients which could be made up to a different recipe each time.

There was no single, prescriptive rule of honour. Internal contradictions within the discourse of honour were rarely played out. Contemporaries saw no necessary contradiction between different elements, such as lineage and virtue, or reputation and worth. A society which held to a humoral theory of the body, a combination of four different elements, was, perhaps, well adapted to the holding of apparently contradictory ideas in creative tension.[38] Contemporaries were capable of picking and mixing from the different varieties in the panoply of honour. James I associated honour as virtue and honour as reputation, making honour the rumour of virtuous action which redounds from the soul to the world and, by reflection, to ourselves.[39] Richard Cust has shown how the earl of Huntingdon was able to manipulate and deploy differing and often contradictory concepts of honour in order to bolster his own position and attack his enemies in a local feud.[40]

Early modern discourses of honour were mutable, adaptable and highly creative. Men could be praised for a particular virtue and for its opposite. The earl of Huntingdon advised his son not only that honour lay in exercising the

Christian duty to reconcile quarrels, but also that honour demanded that no slight could go unchecked and that 'to mainteyne thy reputation unspotted thou must not remayne with an injury offered thee'.[41] The variety of sources from which the code of honour drew vitality – the Bible, classical Antiquity, medieval chivalry, humanism, godly Protestantism – supplied a wealth of images and models which could be used to praise contradictory virtues and actions. Drawing on Renaissance ideas of the court as the epitome of the world, John Cleland idealised the court as 'the principall, and chiefest priuate companie, that anie man can bee in' and advised all men to wait upon the court for 'a man maie learne here within the circuit of their Maiesties pallaces, that which manie men wander through the whole world to see'.[42] A different, biblical topos could be used to honour those who abstained from the court: the image of Barzillai the Gileadite, who refused a place at David's court offered in gratitude for his loyal service. Both Lord Montagu and Sir Fulke Greville were honoured as latter-day Barzillais for preferring life in the country to that at court.[43]

The polyphonic discourses of honour and advancement used many metaphors and similes for preferment and royal bounty. The king's favour might fall like rain, gush forth like water from a fountain, beam down like the rays of the sun, or rise like sap in a tree.[44] All have two features in common worth highlighting here. First, they equate good standing with the monarch and the essentials of life: rain, water, sunshine and food. A gentleman might not flourish – indeed, for him prolonged survival was not possible – without royal favour. To stand in the disfavour of the king was to be under a cloud which it was the duty of the subject to remove.[45] Second, all the metaphors evoked natural processes that occur more or less regardless of the worth of the recipient. God, after all, 'maketh his sun to rise on the evil and on the good, and sendeth rain on the just and the unjust'.[46] So on the one hand, by focusing attention on the king at the centre and the absolutely essential importance of standing in the king's favour, they reinforced the duty of loyal service to the crown, while on the other they suggested that the royal munificence would fall regardless of the service or duty of the subject. Once again we have two apparently contradictory notions of honour. In one, honours were conferred by the king as a reward for loyalty and service to the crown, and not to serve the crown was to stand under a cloud. In the other, honours were conferred as a recognition of pre-existing virtue or birthright, quite possibly already acknowledged by others. In the one, the king's favour led and created honour; in the other, it followed honour.

One way of analysing these two models, a way familiar in Stuart England, was to think in terms of court and country. They were ideological constructs, loci of honour and reputation through service to the crown and service to the commonwealth, rather than distinct and fixed places. Although to reduce matters to a simple opposition is vastly to oversimplify the complexities of politics and honour, seventeenth-century folk were accustomed to thinking in terms of binary opposites.[47] Both court and country had their dangers: the first, that of supporting arbitrary courses and losing the love of the people; the second, that of popularity. Theophilus Downes warned the third Viscount Scudamore against the twin dangers: 'the Ambition of entring into publick Affairs, in which there is hardly one of a hundred that preserves to the last, his Honour and his Innocence', and 'Popularity in the Country, an Advantage of little Moment, and not to be purchased and kept but by perpetual Expence and Slavery'. In the early seventeenth century the same two dangers were recognised, though heightened by the fears of both James I and especially Charles I of the 'itching after popularity'.[48] William Tucker employed the same binary model in his analysis of political motivation:

> In all free monarchies and kingdomes ... some apply themselues to the loue of the prince or head as hauinge the praeminence other to the loue of the people or body of the common wealth some stand aequally some inaequally affected to both prince and people.[49]

Sir Robert Harley, on being elected to parliament for Herefordshire in 1626, was warned of the 'two dangerous temptations between which you now stand, viz. the applause of prince and people', while the monumental inscription of Sir Dudley Digges (died 1639) proudly boasted that he was 'unbiased by popular applause, or court hopes'.[50] Most gentlemen navigated between these two rocks: Harley and Digges, for example, secured both court office and local honour. Except at moments of extreme tension, as happened in some areas over the forced loan in 1627–28, court and country were not in opposition.

Contemporaries rarely saw the two models in conflict. Edward Sherburn, for example, united the two: in 1617 he said that the honour and power of the earl of Pembroke sprang from two well-heads, the king and the people, 'his favour with his Majesty and the good opinion he hath with the subject'. Yet there were also occasions when the two models clashed, particularly when those who held that honour was their birthright felt excluded from the royal bounty: for example, the earl of Essex under Elizabeth or the opponents of the duke of Buckingham in the 1620s.[51] For most of the time, however, the two models were held together in creative tension. One of the great advantages of the two models together was that they could be used to legitimate all sorts of courses of action. When Charles and Buckingham upset the political harmony of the common weal, an alternative source of legitimation was extremely useful. Sir Thomas Wentworth, for example, frequently cast himself before 1627 as the dutiful servant of the king. Faced with the widely unpopular forced loan in 1627, however, Wentworth eschewed the role of the loyal servant of the crown and dutiful commissioner, choosing instead the popular reputation of an honest patriot and friend of the country by refusing the loan, seeking honour from the nation rather than from the king. Thereafter, however, he reverted to the role of the loyal servant through his service on the council of the north and as lord deputy of Ireland.[52] This is not to argue that Wentworth 'changed sides', for as Edward Sherburn recognised the two types of honour and power were intimately linked. Credit with the country and standing in the king's favour were interdependent. Only service to the crown as justice, commissioner or the like conferred the stages on which a local reputation could be won; the good opinion of the country was essential to the sway of a justice or commissioner and the enforcement of the king's rule. The one bolstered the other and, together, might lead to even greater honours. When Henry Sherfield was elected recorder of the borough of Salisbury in 1623, in local recognition of his honour and standing, his brother gleefully advised him that this could be a stepping stone to greater preferment: it would prove 'your strength in your country' which 'will be noted by the rank of great persons'.[53] No politician could risk losing either king or country for long.

The rich textures of the code of honour, drawn from many sources, gave it variety and flexibility; here also, in part, lay the competitiveness of honour. No matter how assiduously a gentleman constructed his own honourable image, a rival could always attempt to re-appropriate the discourse or deploy different tropes to his own ends. Defence of honour demanded self-assertiveness. Sir Francis Hastings was ever vigilant against those who he feared were 'forward enough in willingness to trample upon me if they find even so small stepping stone to lift them up'.[54] 'They that are glorious must needs be factious,' thought Sir Francis Bacon; 'Honour that is gained and broken upon another hath the quickest reflection; like diamond cut with facets.'[55] In Cynthia Herrup's recent judgement, 'Honour was desirable, valuable and never secure.'[56]

The early modern English gentry were born, lived and died in an honour community. Burghley reckoned that 'the gretest possession that any man can have is honor, good name, goodwill of many and of the best sort'.[57] 'Mine honour is my life; both grow in one; / Take honour from me, and my life is done,' says Norfolk in Shakespeare's *Richard II.*[58] Anthony Fletcher has recently argued that the code of honour 'was the nearest that the gentry came at this time to articulating a concept of masculinity'. A gentleman's honour was his manhood.[59] Moreover, a man's honour did not belong to him alone but was held in trust for the benefit of descendants and commonwealth. There was no contracting out of the code of honour. From birth the English gentry had only two options – honour or disgrace.

Locked by an accident of birth into such a competitive system, how were gentlemen to preserve, nurture and pass on their honour, and how were the ambitious to get on in the world? The literature of advice that burgeoned in the sixteenth and seventeenth centuries – the handbooks for courtiers, the precepts handed down from father to son, the institutions for gentlemen – show that these were no idle questions. Indeed, one way of reading the whole corpus is that it was designed to mediate social mobility, simultaneously reinforcing the social and honour hierarchy while displaying the tools and tricks of advancement and social climbing.[60]

Honour was frequently pictured as a prize to be captured or a possession to be demanded.[61]

> By heaven methinks it were an easy leap
> To pluck bright honour from the pale-faced moon,
> Or dive into the bottom of the deep,
> Where fathom-line could never touch the ground,
> And pluck up drownèd honour by the locks

proclaims Hotspur in *Henry IV, Part 1*.[62] 'It lies in himself,' counselled Gervase Holles, 'to become the parent of his own nobility.'[63] Any view that saw honour resting in virtue was bound to proclaim that honour could be seized, whether through martial valour, wisdom, learning, piety or charity. Nevertheless, understandings of honour as based on blood and lineage did not absolutely prevent the winning of honour. It was recognised that family lines failed and new ones rose up to take their place, or that better genealogies might be produced through more accurate and more detailed historical research (or greater fraud).[64] Moreover, most understandings of honour in the early seventeenth century blended ideas of honour as personal virtue with honour as lineage – 'nobility personall ... which wee ourselves acquire by our virtue and well deservinges' and nobility 'which is ... naturall by descent' – into the concept of 'mixed nobleness'. As Sir William Segar explained, 'men may be reputed Noble by three meanes': by descent, by virtue, and 'by mixture of Auntient Noble blood with vertue, which is indeed the true and most commendable kind of Nobilitie'.[65] If honour was virtue, or if honour was held in trust for succeeding generations, a gentleman had a positive duty to care for and maximise his honour. Desire for honour, thought Lodowick Bryskett, is 'worthy high estimation, and necessary for all them that esteeme true honour (as they ought) to be the most excellent good among exteriour things'. Without the desire for honour men became 'insensible and carelesse of their reputation ... like brute beasts'.[66] A desire for honour was thought natural by many writers. Romei thought that men desired honour more than any other outward good, while for Segar it was the desire for honour, rather than mere profit, that distinguished gentlemen from the vulgar.[67]

The danger, however, was in failing to strike a balance between the extremes of carelessness for one's honour on the one side, and of seeking 'by all meanes possible to catch at euery shew of honour, at euery office or degree that is to be gotten ... or to try any base or vnlawfull meanes to compasse the same', which was ambition, on the other.[68] Ambition, the 'licorish after earthly honours', was 'like the Crocodile', advised John Trapp. It 'groweth while it liveth: or like the Ivy which rising at the foot, will over-peer the highest wall. Base it is and slavish.'[69] Ambition, warned James Cleland, 'is an insatiable desire of honour', and he went on to advise 'How yee maie overcome Ambition':[70]

> To subdue this affection you must not mount higher then your wings will permit. Limit your aspiring desires and ambitious thoughts within the compasse of your capacity. Let euer your merits march before your pursuits, and thinke to attaine vnto some honourable charge and office of his Maiestie through your owne deserts, and not by the fauour of your friends, or greatnes of your Pedigree.

From the Roman historian Sallust, or even earlier, there was a literary tradition which saw ambition as the inverse of honour, and Sallust's writings were well known in seventeenth-century England.[71] Ambition was usually cast as an affliction to which the great were prone, the infection of many a state. Ambition had been the downfall of the angels. Ambition was the reason Brutus slayed Julius Caesar.[72] It was boundless ambition that drove Spain and the Habsburgs to aim at world domination.[73] It was 'an ambitious humour of gaining a Reputation among their neighbours', complained the lord keeper in 1602, that was making magistrates more concerned with their own rank and position than with the king's service.[74] Warnings against ambition became a topos of courtly literature. 'Take these instructions with you,' advised Richard Brathwait: 'Doth Ambition buzze in your eare motions of Honour? ... Ambition is the high road which leads to ruine, but Humilitie is the gate which opens unto glory.' Ambition, with its attendants envy and avarice, warned Nicholas Faret, 'make the most flourishing monarchies desolate ... trouble the whole frame of society, and violate the most sacred laws'. Faret took comfort in the face of such grave prophecies, however, from the knowledge that Fortune, 'who takes delight to display ... the most remarkable tricks of her malice and lightness, makes sport at the ruin of a thousand ambitious men'.[75]

More subtle and sophisticated analyses of ambition, however, were sometimes provided by those who had greater practical experience of politics. Sir Francis Walsingham redeemed ambition and saw its place in politics. Ambition in itself was no fault. Though it laid the weak open to fall in other ways, it was a spur to the good to seek honour. 'Ambition by which Men desire Honour the natural way (which consists in doing honourable and good Acts) is the root of the most perfect Commendation that a Morall Man is capable of.' Others were more guarded and traditional in their views but, nevertheless, were prepared to leave a place for ambition in the well ordered common-wealth. Bishop Walter Curle, for example, linked honour, ambition and emulation in a positive sense.[76]

Francis Bacon provided the nicest and most nuanced account in his essay 'Of Ambition'.[77] He recognised ambition as a 'humour that maketh men active, earnest, full of alacrity, and stirring'. The danger lay not in men's ambition, but in the frustration of their ambitious designs, which would make ambition 'malign and venomous'. Princes could, therefore, use men of ambitious natures in certain circumstances: as commanders in war, since a soldier without ambition was like a horseman without spurs, or in toppling overmighty subjects. Bacon went on to acknowledge the inevitability that princes would have to use the ambitious, giving some advice on how best to keep them in check and employ their talents. Finally Bacon, like many other writers, differentiated between ambition and the desire to advance one's honour, which was aspiration: 'Honour hath three things in it: the vantage ground to do good; the approach to kings and principal persons; and the raising of a man's own fortunes. He that hath the best of these intentions when he aspireth is an honest man.' A wise prince would be able to discern an honest aspiration to serve and would employ such a man, someone 'more sensible of duty than of rising'.

Many writers acknowledged that it was legitimate for an honourable man to seek advancement without falling into the trap of ambition, provided he sought only what was commensurate with his own worth, service and merit.[78] The strictures of conduct books moulded the ways in which the ambitious sought advancement: an aspiration to serve and further one's honour was prescribed; ambition was proscribed. Thomas Gainsford advised the hopeful to disavow explicitly any 'dangerous ambition'. Sir Thomas Wentworth, petitioning Buckingham to be allowed to keep his office as *custos rotulorum*, confessed that 'I doe infinittly desire to doe his Majestie service', while promising that he was 'free from ambition to desire places of imployment'.[79]

There was one circumstance where ambition might be admitted: in the desire to do others honourable service. Scudamore himself confessed to Sir John Coke that he had 'ambition' but only such as to 'aspire to make mee no way vnworthy of the free and honorable respect I receiue from you', and in the playful postscript of a familiar letter to Edward Harley accompanying the new year's present of a doe he prayed to be allowed 'the ambition to bee admitted into your Lady's service'. Sir Robert Phelips was prepared to admit to ambition, but by yoking it to the service of the king he removed its negative connotations. Presenting Buckingham with his suit for office ('this suyte ... that by your means I may be brought into his Majestys service') after a period of royal disfavour he wrote, 'I am ambitious by some way of servyce to show his majesty both my penitencye and my gratitude'; 'service' was mentioned no fewer than five times in Phelips's short draft letter.[80] An expression of desire to serve the king, then, was one of the discourses which enabled those who sought advancement to escape the taint of ambition. There were other 'tropes of personal promotion' which avoided the odour of ambition. Advancement, as Sir Walter Raleigh recognised, might say nothing about the person advanced and everything about that person's affiliates: the preferment of a client might reflect glory to the patron; the advancement of a client might be read as the reward of the patron or as a check to another. As John Hassall explained, thanking his patrons for the favours he received from them, when an object shines in the sunshine, 'to the sunne alone belonges all the honor of it'.[81] What we may see as self-advancement and ambition, to the early seventeenth century may have been 'a vertuous man ... seek[ing] at the hands of fortune, the honor he deserueth' so that he 'may be known to be' the man he truly was.[82] In part, success or failure depended on the manipulation of the discourses and images of political culture, weaving together some of the many strands of the code of honour to one's own ends so that one was not entirely at the mercy of the interpretations of a hostile world and the constructions of others.

We should be careful of imputing inherently cynical and exclusively manipulative motives to the political actors of the early seventeenth century. Politicians could not simply adopt a discourse at will. The very act of creating an image was also limiting: politicians shaped their images which, in turn, shaped them. Most discourses are both creative and restrictive, opening up some possibilities of action while closing down others. Language and action are not separate entities, but interdependent, constantly shaping one another. Moreover, as Richard Cust has suggested, it is not just the actions and responses, but the very thought patterns, of political agents which are structured by discourses and tropes. The codes and discourses of honour and political action could not be donned and doffed like a cloak. They were a part of the gentry's understanding of themselves and their place in the universe. 'I hold my reputation much dearer to me than my life,' said Henry Sherfield in 1633, shortly before he lost first his reputation as a loyal, godly magistrate, and then, broken, his life.[83]

Magistrates and politicians were not simply rummaging in the bag of legitimations hoping to justify a series of inherently prudential and self-seeking political manoeuvres. Contemporaries certainly recognised the possibility of such deception. They were frequently concerned with rhetorical artifice and artificiality. Both popery and puritanism were branded, by their opponents, as a veneer of piety masking self-seeking and ambition. The poet George Wither denounced 'Hypocrites' with 'Double-hearts' and 'counterfeited Graces' who, dissembling, 'make themselves appeare unto the State / Good Patriots' despite being, behind their masks, 'scarce so honest men as go to hell'.[84] Contemporary concern with rhetorical artifice and hypocrisy helps to explain Charles I's concern with trust and loyalty. He considered that he had been the victim of duplicity when he had accepted the 'mask' of the 1624 parliament men and believed their rhetoric in favour of war, only to find the reality in 1625–26 when they refused to grant sufficient subsidies to support the war effort. 'Disaffected persons' had, so Charles believed, manipulated political discourse in two ways in the period 1623–29 'to mask and disguise their wicked intentions': first, they had deployed anti-Spanish and pro-war rhetorics to urge him into war with Spain, then 'turbulent and ill-affected spirits' had sought to misrepresent him and the duke of Buckingham to the public and 'wound [his] honour'. Charles convinced himself that, while posing as 'honest patriots' they courted 'popularity' and aimed 'to erect an universal over-swaying power to themselves'.[85] In consequence Charles was determined not to be duped again, and to test any professions of loyal service to ensure that they were backed up with deeds Nathaniel Tomkins advised Sir Robert Phelips late in 1626 that he had consulted several courtiers who had all told him that 'at the present it is hardly possible to procure any Act of Favour towards you from his majestie, but ex post facto, they seem all hopeful and to thinke it feasable'; the earl of Holland in particular had said that he would 'vndertake vpon your meriting of his Majestie in this busines [the forced loan]'.[86] Charles was determined that rhetoric must be linked with action.

Even without Charles's extravagant demands of unswerving loyalty, any image had to rest on a degree of fact to remain credible. A politician risked exposure, disgrace and loss of honour and power if it was thought that the legitimating images and rhetoric he deployed were a sham. The long-running feud between Lord Poulett and Sir Robert Phelips in Somerset provides an interesting example of the manipulation of rhetorics and the dangers therein. Phelips laboured long and hard to fashion a series of images for himself on various stages. To the privy council he presented himself as a diligent subsidy commissioner working 'for the advauncement of this service and for the raysing of the subsedyes in this our division'. To Archbishop Laud he endeavoured to show himself concerned for the success of the collection for St Paul's Cathedral. In and out of parliament in the 1620s he cultivated the reputation of an honest patriot, the 'countries only freinde'.[87] In a remarkable manuscript tract of late 1623 Phelips sought to present himself as a country gentleman, the defender of parliament, and the defender of the common-wealth, upholding the traditional unity of king and people in parliament for the supply of the former and the protection of the latter.[88] In the mid 1620s Phelips was aiming for high office: petitioning the duke of Buckingham for the office of master of requests; hoping for appointment to the privy council. He was also seeking to bolster his local position against Lord Poulett.[89] The care of an ambitious politician for his own honour and reputation is most clearly shown in a letter from Nathaniel Tomkins to Phelips about the forced loan. Charles's extra-parliamentary financial expedients presented local magnates like Phelips with acute problems of maintaining their credit: never before had the choice between favour with the king and reputation among the people been so stark or the division so wide. Tomkins advised Phelips at length on the best course to follow:

> I may erre, and doe submitt vnto you, but I should not in this case judge the middle way a good way: if you ... are not a leader of those who shall refuse, you will hardly be held a meriter among them: if you doe not avowedly declare your self to advance the work, you shall haue no thanks from the King

The difficulty of meeting the competing claims of loyalty to the king, maintaining reputation, and avoiding the pains of punishment, is exemplified by Tomkins's decision to follow the middle way himself and pay the loan quietly, despite his advice to Phelips to do otherwise.[90]

Phelips was an adroit politician, yet the way he presented himself and the rhetoric he used were frequently attacked by his local enemies. Poulett in particular sought to manipulate and re-appropriate the images to undermine his rival's power and reputation. In the 1620s, Phelips remembered, Poulett spread the rumour 'that I had forsaken the country was turnd Courtyer and such lyke phrases vppon design to withdraw the good opinion of the country from me'.[91] A decade later Poulett and others tried to overturn Phelips's image as a diligent and effective deputy lieutenant, accusing him to the lord lieutenant of negligence and attempting to expose him as a hypocrite and double dealer:[92]

> What his Ends are herein may bee probably coniectured, which is to gayne a double reputacion to himselfe One aboue by pretendinge good Affeccions to the Seruice, another here by shewinge his dislikes against itt ... Besides some vse itt seemes he intends to make of giuinge ill representacions to your lordship of our Carriage, as if itt had a byas of Envy or some other vnworthy respect towards him

Political rhetoric and images were constantly being shaped and reshaped as politicians and local magnates sought to increase their own credit and undermine their rivals'. The case of Sir Robert Phelips shows such strategies at work, but it also shows some of their limitations, how contemporaries attempted to look beyond the artifice of carefully constructed political identities. The higher honours Phelips sought never did come his way.

One of the aims of this study is to consider one particular aspiring county magnate and politician, John, first Viscount Scudamore, and to examine how he sought honour, and office, in seventeenth-century England and, as Charles I's ambassador to Louis XIII, France: how far he succeeded and the extent to which he ultimately failed. We shall need to examine how, from the material available within contemporary political culture, he attempted to construct various self-images and present himself to the world on different stages. But we shall also have to look at the nitty-gritty details of early modern politics and diplomacy to see on what those images were based. The two main sources will be Scudamore's own papers, mostly in the British Library and Public Record Office in London, and the state papers, both domestic and foreign, also in the Public Record Office. Despite the large quantity of remaining Scudamore papers, little of the first viscount's outgoing correspondence seems to have survived; he seems to have kept out-letter books only while an ambassador in Paris, for example.[93] Lacunae in the evidence mean that no complete or continuous biography of Viscount Scudamore is possible: little is known, for example, of his movements in the period between his return from Paris early in 1639 and the outbreak of war in the summer of 1642. The raw materials being somewhat episodic, we will proceed thematically in the hope that the greater light shone on areas of interest will more than compensate for any necessary repetition or lack of chronological coherence.[94] The relative absence of private correspondence or other personal materials written by Scudamore also means that some of his intentions will have to be inferred from his actions and how their outcomes were viewed by others.[95]

Viscount Scudamore's inheritance of power, reputation and honour, wealth and family background, and particularly the careers of his father and grand-father, both Elizabethan courtiers, will be examined in chapter 2. Chapter 3 will explore Scudamore's religious and intellectual views, for these not only helped to shape his political views and his work on local, national and inter-national stages, they were a further part of his image of honour. Chapter 4 will explore Scudamore's work as a local politician and county magnate in Herefordshire, examining his activities as magistrate, deputy lieutenant and commissioner for subsidies, the forced loan and the repair of St Paul's Cathedral. Chapter 5 will concentrate on his search for preferment, intimately linked with his quest for office and higher honour. Chapter 6 will look at the fruits of his quest for office, his service as ambassador in France in the 1630s. Finally, chapter 7 will deal with the outbreak of the civil war, the nature of Scuda-more's royalism, and his nemesis in defeat and capture in 1643. Through an examination of this one 'second division' politician and his presentation to the world, the book will attempt to illuminate three central issues. First, it will be a case study of how an ambitious gentleman sought to forge a political career on a variety of levels – in his county, at court and as an ambassador. It is hoped that Scudamore's failures will be as illuminating as his successes, echoing the successes and much greater failings of the king whom he served. Second, it will seek to examine religion, divisions at court, and foreign policy in the 1620s and the personal rule, all of which have recently been radically reassessed, particularly by Kevin Sharpe.[96] Finally, it will attempt to under-stand a zealous supporter of royal policy and government, a lay Laudian and a supporter of the duke of Buckingham, all phenomena which historians have tended to depict as rare, or even overlook, in their rush to portray the critics of royal policy and zealous puritans. Where historians have turned to royalists and the lay supporters of Charles, those studied have tended to be the moderates and the constitutionalists, despite the clear immoderation and unconstitutionality of both King Charles and Archbishop Laud.

Viscount Scudamore the man may have been the generous, heroic and charitable figure depicted by his many admirers, 'good and wise' in the words of one early nineteenth-century panegyric,[97] but as a politician he was a much more human mixture of failure and success. For more than a decade he sought high office but when finally given the opportunity he proved unequal to it: in the opinion of his colleagues he lacked the tact and diplomacy needed in an ambassador; as a royalist leader his first instinct was to run away, and he must shoulder much of the blame for the loss of the king's garrison of Hereford in 1643. It is as a flawed character that he is so interesting. Historians have begun again to stress the failings and shortcomings of Charles I as king as the most important dynamic between 1625 and 1641. If the mixture of political skill and ineptitude in my portrait of Viscount Scudamore finds echoes in Charles's own political management and mismanagement, if Scudamore's religious views parallel those of the king, then perhaps this study may shed a little light on the Stuart political scene. In any case, Scudamore the failure seems to me a much more real and human figure than Scudamore the heroically virtuous. Previous writers have tended to see in the viscount reflections of themselves. Only time and the reader will be able to tell whether I have fallen into the same trap.

NOTES

1 W. Carpenter, *Jura Cleri: or An Apologie for the Rights of the long-despised Clergy* (Oxford, 1661), p. 11; below, appendix.

2 L. B. Namier, *Personalities and Powers* (London, 1955), pp. 3–4, 6; L. B. Namier, *The Structure of Politics at the Accession of George III* (2nd edition, London, 1957), p. ix; Q. Skinner, 'The Principles and Practice of Opposition: The Case of Bolingbroke versus Walpole', in N. McKendrick, ed., *Historical Perspectives: Studies in English Thought and Society in Honour of J. H. Plumb* (London, 1974), pp. 100–1; J. Brooke, 'Namier and Namierism', *History and Theory*, 3 (1963–64), pp. 340–1.

3 B. Donagan, 'A Courtier's Progress: Greed and Consistency in the Life of the Earl of Holland', *Historical Journal*, 19 (1976), pp. 317–53; A. Wall, 'Patterns of Politics in England, 1558–1625', *Historical Journal*, 31 (1988), pp. 947–63, especially p. 950.

4 Wall, 'Patterns of Politics in England', p. 963.

5 Skinner, 'Principles and Practice', pp. 103–8, 127–8; Q. Skinner, *The Foundations of Modern Political Thought* (2 vols, Cambridge, 1978), I, pp. xi–xiii.

6 The terms revisionism and revisionist, though sometimes ambiguous, are retained here to describe a trend rather than a school; they have become an accepted label and self label. See: G. Burgess, 'On Revisionism: An Analysis of Early Stuart Historiography in the 1970s and 1980s', *Historical Journal*, 33:3 (1990), pp. 609–27; G. Burgess,

'Revisionism, Politics and Political Ideas in Early Stuart England', *Historical Journal*, 34:2 (1991), pp. 465–78; S. Adams, 'Early Stuart Politics: Revisionism and After', in J. R. Mulryne and M. Shewring, eds, *Theatre and Government under the Early Stuarts* (Cambridge, 1993), pp. 29–56; R. P. Cust and A. Hughes, 'Introduction: After Revisionism', in R. P. Cust and A. Hughes, eds, *Conflict in Early Stuart England* (Harlow, 1989), pp. 1–46. I am extremely grateful to Professor Peter Lake for his help in developing my thoughts about revisionism and post-revisionism.

7   W. Notestein, *The Winning of the Initiative by the House of Commons* (London, 1924); K. Sharpe, 'Parliamentary History 1603–1629: In or Out of Perspective?', in K. Sharpe, ed., *Faction and Parliament: Essays on Early Stuart History* (Oxford, 1978), pp. 1–3.

8   A. S. P. Woodhouse, ed., *Puritanism and Liberty: Being the Army Debates (1647–49) from the Clarke Manuscripts* (London, 1938); W. Haller, *Liberty and Reformation in the Puritan Revolution* (New York, 1955).

9   C. Russell, *Parliaments and English Politics, 1621–1629* (Oxford, 1979); J. S. Morrill, *The Revolt of the Provinces: Conservatives and Radicals in the English Civil War, 1630–1650* (London, 1976); and their principal essays now republished as C. Russell, *Unrevolutionary England* (London, 1990), and J. S. Morrill, *The Nature of the English Revolution* (Harlow, 1993).

10   T. K. Rabb, 'The Role of the Commons', *Past and Present*, 92 (August 1981), pp. 55–78; D. Hirst, 'The Place of Principle', *Past and Present*, 92 (August 1981), pp. 79–99.

11   For Dungeness lighthouse see D. Hirst, *The Representative of the People? Voters and Voting in England under the Early Stuarts* (Cambridge, 1975), pp. 161, 179; Russell, *Parliaments*, pp. 37–8, 399.

12   See C. Russell, *The Fall of the British Monarchies, 1637–1642* (Oxford, 1991), p. x.

13   C. Russell, *The Causes of the English Civil War* (Oxford, 1990), ch. 8, especially p. 198.

14   K. Sharpe, 'Faction at the Early Stuart Court', *History Today*, 33 (October 1983), pp. 39–46; D. Starkey, ed., *The English Court: From the Wars of the Roses to the Civil War* (Harlow, 1987); Wall, 'Patterns of Politics in England'.

15   M. Kishlansky, 'The Emergence of Adversary Politics in the Long Parliament', *Journal of Modern History*, 49 (1977), pp. 617–40; M. Kishlansky, *Parliamentary Selection: Social and Political Choice in Early Modern England* (Cambridge, 1986).

16   P. Lake, 'Retrospective: Wentworth's Political World in Revisionist and Post-revisionist Perspective', in J. F. Merritt, ed., *The Political World of Thomas Wentworth, Earl of Strafford, 1621–1641* (Cambridge, 1996), pp. 270–8.

17   Lake, 'Revisionist and Post-revisionist Perspective', p. 276.

18   R. P. Cust and A. Hughes, eds, *Conflict in Early Stuart England: Studies in Religion and Politics, 1603–1642* (Harlow, 1989).

19   J. Eales, *Puritans and Roundheads: The Harleys of Brampton Bryan and the Outbreak of the English Civil War* (Cambridge, 1990); V. Larminie, *Wealth, Kinship and Culture: The Seventeenth-Century Newdigates of Arbury and their World* (Woodbridge, 1995); V. Larminie, *The Godly Magistrate: The Private Philosophy and Public Life of Sir John Newdigate, 1571–1610* (Dugdale Society, occasional papers, 28, 1982); R. P. Cust, ed., *The Papers of Sir Richard Grosvenor, 1st Bart. (1585–1645)* (Record Society of Lancashire and Cheshire, 134, 1996); A. Searle, ed., *The Barrington Family Letters 1628–1632* (Camden, 4th series, 28, 1983); T. Webster, *Godly Clergy in Early Stuart England: The Caroline*

Puritan Movement, c. 1620–1643 (Cambridge, 1997); F. Heal and C. Holmes, *The Gentry in England and Wales, 1500–1700* (Basingstoke, 1994).

20 D. L. Smith, *Constitutional Royalism and the Search for Settlement, c. 1640–1649* (Cambridge, 1994).

21 C. Russell, 'The British Problem and the English Civil War', *History*, 72 (1987), pp. 395–415; Russell, *Causes*; Russell, *Fall*.

22 Morrill, *Nature*; K. Sharpe, *The Personal Rule of Charles I* (New Haven and London, 1992); M. Kishlansky, *A Monarchy Transformed: Britain, 1603–1714* (Harmondsworth, 1996), chs 5–6.

23 Morrill, *Nature*, p. 52.

24 Sharpe, *Personal Rule*; K. Sharpe, 'Archbishop Laud', *History Today*, 33 (August 1983), pp. 26–30.

25 G. Burgess, review in *History*, 82:267 (1997), p. 499; G. Burgess, *Absolute Monarchy and the Stuart Constitution* (New Haven and London, 1996); the quotations come from p. 208.

26 S. Greenblatt, *Renaissance Self-fashioning from More to Shakespeare* (Chicago and London, 1980), p. 1.

27 R. P. Cust, 'Wentworth's "Change of Sides" in the 1620s', in J. F. Merritt, ed., *The Political World of Thomas Wentworth, Earl of Strafford, 1621–1641* (Cambridge, 1996), pp. 63–80; Cust, *Papers of Sir Richard Grosvenor*; R. P. Cust, 'Honour, Rhetoric and Political Culture: The Earl of Huntingdon and his Enemies', in S. D. Amussen and M. Kishlansky, eds, *Political Culture and Cultural Politics in Early Modern England* (Manchester, 1995), pp. 84–111.

28 K. Sharpe and P. Lake, 'Introduction', in K. Sharpe and P. Lake, eds, *Culture and Politics in Early Stuart England* (Basingstoke, 1994), p. 15.

29 M. James, *English Politics and the Concept of Honour, 1485–1642* (*Past and Present Supplement*, 3, 1978); C. Herrup, '"To Pluck Bright Honour from the Pale-faced Moon": Gender and Honour in the Castlehaven Story', *TRHS*, 6th series, 6 (1996), pp. 137–40.

30 C. Marlowe, *Tamburlaine the Great*, ed. U. Ellis-Fermor (2nd edition, London, 1951), part I, act 4, scene 4, p. 155; *An Essay of a King* (London, 1642), p. 3; the attribution to Francis Bacon is doubtful.

31 Quoted in L. L. Peck, *Court Patronage and Corruption in Early Stuart England* (London, 1993), p. 213.

32 J. Cleland, *The Institvtion of a Yovng Noble Man* (Oxford, 1607), p. 179.

33 E. S. Cope, *The Life of a Public Man: Edward, First Baron Montagu of Boughton, 1562–1644* (Memoirs of the American Philosophical Society, 142, Philadelphia, 1981), p. 8; Heal and Holmes, *Gentry*, p. 31.

34 F. Bacon, *The Essays*, ed. S. H. Reynolds (Oxford, 1890), pp. 92–3.

35 Cust, 'Honour, Rhetoric and Political Culture', p. 91; Heal and Holmes, *Gentry*, p. 98.

36 L. Bryskett, *A Discovrse of Civill Life* (London, 1606), p. 241; Cust, 'Honour, Rhetoric and Political Culture', p. 93.

37 A. Romei, *The Courtiers Academie*, trs. I. K. ([London, 1598]), p. 114; A. Day, *The English Secretorie* (London, 1586), p. 110; W. Segar, *Honor Military, and Ciuill* (London, 1602),

p. 208; F. Whigham, *Ambition and Privilege: The Social Tropes of Elizabethan Courtesy Theory* (London, 1984), p. 73.

38 For humoral theories see A. J. Fletcher, *Gender, Sex and Subordination in England, 1500–1800* (New Haven and London, 1995), pp. 30–59.

39 K. Sharpe, 'Private Conscience and Public Duty in the Writings of James VI and I', in J. S. Morrill, P. Slack and D. Woolf, eds, *Public Duty and Private Conscience in Seventeenth-Century England* (Oxford, 1993), p. 89.

40 Cust, 'Honour, Rhetoric and Political Culture'.

41 Cust, 'Honour, Rhetoric and Political Culture', pp. 92–3.

42 Cleland, *Institvtion*, pp. 172–3.

43 II Samuel 19:31–9; Cope, *Montagu*, p. 3; R. P. Cust, 'Humanism and Magistracy in Early Stuart England', p. 30 (unpublished paper), citing Warwickshire RO, CR136, B701. (I am grateful to Dr Cust for allowing me to read this paper.)

44 Peck, *Court Patronage*, pp. 1, 47, 213–14; Sharpe, *Personal Rule*, p. 177; A. Wilson, *The Life and Reign of James, the First, King of Great Britain*, in J. Hughes, ed., *A Complete History of England* (3 vols, London, 1719), II, p. 747.

45 J. Cuming, ed., 'Mr. Henry Yelverton (afterward Sir Henry) his Narrative of what Passed on his being Restored to the King's Favour in 1609', *Archaeologia*, 15 (1806), p. 27.

46 Matthew 5:45.

47 D. Underdown, *A Freeborn People? Politics and the Nation in Seventeenth-Century England* (Oxford, 1996), pp. 30–1; Cust and Hughes, 'After Revisionism', pp. 19–21.

48 T. Downes, *Mr Downs's Letter to Lord Scudamore* in *Plain Truths: or, A Collection of Scarce and Valuable Tracts* ([?Edinburgh, ?1716]), p. 62; Underdown, *Freeborn People?*, p. 25.

49 BL, Harl. MS 188, fol. 6v.

50 Eales, *Puritans*, pp. 5–6.

51 Peck, *Court Patronage*, p. 63; R. C. McCoy, 'Old English Honour in an Evil Time: Aristocratic Principle in the 1620s', in R. M. Smuts, ed., *The Stuart Court and Europe: Essays in Politics and Political Culture* (Cambridge, 1996), pp. 133–55.

52 J. P. Cooper, ed., *Wentworth Papers 1597–1628* (Camden, 4th series, 12, 1973), p. 101; S. R. Gardiner, ed., *The Fortescue Papers* (Camden Society, 2nd series, 1, 1871), p. 26; Cust, 'Wentworth's "Change of Sides"'.

53 P. Slack, 'The Public Conscience of Henry Sherfield', in J. S. Morrill, P. Slack and D. Woolf, eds, *Public Duty and Private Conscience in Seventeenth-Century England* (Oxford, 1993), pp. 165–6.

54 Quoted in Fletcher, *Gender, Sex and Subordination*, p. 147.

55 Quoted in Whigham, *Ambition and Privilege*, p. 49.

56 Herrup, 'Gender and Honour', p. 139; see also James, *Concept of Honour*, pp. 5, 88.

57 Quoted in F. Heal, 'Reputation and Honour in Court and Country: Lady Elizabeth Russell and Sir Thomas Hoby', *TRHS*, 6th series, 6 (1996), p. 161.

58 Act I, scene i, lines 182–3.

59 Fletcher, *Gender, Sex and Subordination*, p. 126.

60 Whigham, *Ambition and Privilege.*

61 Romei, *Courtiers Academie*, pp. 114–16.

62 Act I, scene iii, lines 201–5.

63 G. Holles, *Memorials of the Holles Family 1493–1656*, ed. A. C. Wood (Camden, 3rd series, 55, 1937), p. 4.

64 Heal and Holmes, *Gentry*, pp. 20–47.

65 Holles, *Memorials*, p. 4; Segar, *Honor Military, and Ciuill*, p. 113; Cust, 'Honour, Rhetoric and Political Culture', p. 92.

66 Bryskett, *Discovrse of Civill Life*, pp. 241–2.

67 Romei, *Courtiers Academie*, p. 90; Segar, *Honor Military, and Ciuill*, 'To the Reader' and pp. 209–10.

68 Bryskett, *Discovrse of Civill Life*, p. 242.

69 J. Trapp, *Mellificium Theologicum, or the Marrow of Many Good Authors* (London, 1647), pp. 646, 652.

70 Cleland, *Institvtion*, pp. 242–4.

71 D. C. Earl, *The Political Thought of Sallust* (Amsterdam, 1966); see, for example, Ben Jonson's *Catiline* (1611).

72 W. Shakespeare, *Henry VIII*, III.ii.441–2; *Julius Caesar*, III.ii.27–30; R. Younge, *Philarguromastix, or, The Arraignment of Covetouseness, and Ambition* (2 vols, London, 1653); Trapp, *Mellificium Theologicum*, pp. 646–57.

73 Somerset RO, DD/PH/227/26, fol. 5v; [J. Reynolds], *Vox Coeli, or Newes from Heaven* ('Elisium', 1624), t.p., pp. 2–3, 8, 19, 44, 54, 67.

74 Heal and Holmes, *Gentry*, p. 168.

75 W. Paulet, *The Lord Marqves Idlenes* (London, 1586), p. 7; R. Brathwait, *The English Gentleman* (London, 1630), pp. 34–9, 339–40, 371; N. Faret, *The Honest Man or the Art to Please in Court* (1630), quoted in M. L. Kekewich, ed., *Princes and Peoples: France and the British Isles, 1620–1714* (Manchester, 1994), p. 30.

76 F. Walsingham, *Sir Francis Walsingham's Anatomizing of Honesty, Ambition, and Fortitude. Written in the Year 1590* (London, 1672), pp. 336–7; Hampshire RO, MS 21M65/A1/31, fol. 14r.

77 Bacon, *Essays*, pp. 264–7.

78 F. O. Wolf, ed., *Die neue Wissenschaft des Thomas Hobbes* (Stuttgart, 1969), p. 143; Brathwait, *English Gentleman*, p. 37.

79 T. Gainsford, *The Secretaries Stvdie* (London, 1616), pp. 90–2; Gardiner, *Fortescue Papers*, p. 26.

80 BL, Add. MSS 64890, fol. 48r, 70123, Scudamore to Harley, 2 January 1656; Somerset RO, DD/PH/221/18.

81 Whigham, *Ambition and Privilege*, pp. 49–50, 131 and ch. 4; PRO, SP84/121, fol. 53r.

82 Romei, *Courtiers Academie*, p. 115.

83 Slack, 'Henry Sherfield', p. 169.

84 Quoted in T. Cogswell, *The Blessed Revolution: English Politics and the Coming of War,*

1621–1624 (Cambridge, 1989), pp. 84–5. For this and the preceding paragraph see Cust, 'Wentworth's "Change of Sides"', pp. 79–80, and Sharpe and Lake, 'Introduction', p. 16.

85 M. B. Young, *Charles I* (Basingstoke, 1997), p. 67; R. P. Cust, 'Charles I and a Draft Declaration for the 1628 Parliament', *Historical Research*, 63:151 (June 1990), pp. 143–61.

86 Somerset RO, DD/PH/219/35.

87 Somerset RO, DD/PH/223/112, DD/PH/223/114, DD/PH/221/33(ii); T. G. Barnes, *Somerset 1625–1640: A County's Government during the 'Personal Rule'* (London, 1961), pp. 281–98.

88 Somerset RO, DD/PH/227/16; Cogswell, *Blessed Revolution*, pp. 157–9.

89 Somerset RO, DD/PH/221/18, DD/PH/219/33; Cogswell, *Blessed Revolution*, p. 153.

90 Somerset RO, DD/PH/219/35; for Wentworth's dilemma over the loan see Cust, 'Wentworth's "Change of Sides"', pp. 74–6.

91 Somerset RO, DD/PH/222/53.

92 Somerset RO, DD/PH/222/19.

93 BL, Add. MSS 35097, 45142.

94 Readers wanting a more chronological approach may turn to Atherton, thesis.

95 In 1896 Sotheby's sold what was described as Scudamore's 'Original Autograph Diary'; I have been unable to trace the present location of this manuscript, which was most probably not a diary at all but Scudamore's official 'relation' summarising his service as ambassador on his return in 1639. Sotheby's, *Bibliotheca Phillippica. June 1896* (London, 1896), lot 1052; Bodleian, MS Phillipps-Munby d.16, no. 3.

96 Sharpe, *Personal Rule*.

97 O. Y., 'Memoir of John first Viscount Scudamore', *Gentleman's Magazine*, 87:1 (January–June 1817), p. 99; see appendix below.

Chapter 2

An inheritance of honour

In 1639 Viscount Scudamore had penned a short account of his ancestors, 'A Catalogve of the trulie Auntient and Honorable Familie of Scvdamore', emphasising his ancient and honourable lineage. It claimed to prove Scudamore's descent from Richard, first duke of Normandy, and King Harold II, along with 'Aliances with diuers Honorable Families', the whole 'Justified by venerable Testimonies, Records and other Euidences'.[1] By no means as openly mendacious as some lineages concocted by other families at the same time, it did distort the truth somewhat. Nevertheless, its claim that the Holme Lacy Scudamores could trace descent from Walter de Scudamore, beneficiary of Dore Abbey, in 1149, has been supported by modern research.[2] In fact, it is now believed that the Scudamores were Normans or Bretons who first settled in the Dore or Golden Valley in western Herefordshire, along the wild frontier with Wales, during the reign of Edward the Confessor.[3] In the early seventeenth century the Scudamores of Holme Lacy were recognised as having an honourable and ancient pedigree, to which others were eager to claim a relation.[4]

In the last quarter of the fourteenth century Philip Scudamore, alias Ewyas, a younger son of the Scudamores of Rowlstone, Herefordshire, settled at Holme Lacy, on rising ground on the right bank of the river Wye five miles south-east of Hereford.[5] There he founded a family of minor gentry. In the late fourteenth century, and throughout the fifteenth, it was, however, the Scudamores of Kentchurch, cousins of the Holme Lacy branch, who were the more important in the Welsh marches. Jenkin Skydmore of Kentchurch (died *c.* 1407) was acknowledged by the Holme Lacy Scudamores in the sixteenth century to have been 'a stout fellow and had all the rule of the county thereabouts'. His son, Sir John Skydmore (died 1435), extended his power across South Wales by both vigorously suppressing the revolt of Owain Glyndwr and marrying Glyndwr's daughter and heiress, Alice. Sir John was sheriff of Herefordshire three times and MP six times, steward of various Welsh castles and deputy justiciar of South Wales. In the later fifteenth century the Kent-church Scudamores' support for the Lancastrian cause weakened their power somewhat.[6] They suffered almost total eclipse in the sixteenth century, however, when the head of the family died in 1522, leaving as his heir a grandson not yet one year old, and when that one-year-old, John Scudamore of Kentchurch (1522–93/94), and his son Thomas (*c.* 1543–1606) adhered to the Roman Catholic faith. Although the family conformed to the church of England after 1606 they were not again important within Herefordshire until the 1640s and 1650s when the parliamentarianism of John Scudamore (1600–69) was his *entrée* to county office. His eldest son John (1624–1704) was strongly anti-Catholic and played a leading role in igniting the tinders of the Popish Plot: in November 1678 he raided the Jesuit seminary at Cwm in southern Herefordshire, leading to the execution of five Catholic priests. The Scudamores of Kentchurch remained important in Herefordshire into the nineteenth century.[7]

The real founder of the fortunes of the Holme Lacy branch was John Scudamore (*c.* 1486–1571), who amassed power, prestige and wealth through court service, friendship with Thomas Cromwell and Sir Richard Rich, and from the dissolution of the monasteries. As receiver of the court of augmentations for Herefordshire, Worcestershire, Shropshire and Staffordshire, he was well placed to acquire some of the choicest pickings for himself, especially land around Holme Lacy such as Bolstone, and estates from Dore Abbey. With his new riches he rebuilt Holme Lacy House in brick in the 1540s. From 1514 or 1515 until 1537 he was a gentleman usher at Henry VIII's court, after which he may have been an esquire for the body. Combined with his service as a courtier was great power within Herefordshire and the Welsh marches. He was sheriff of Herefordshire four times, MP for the shire at least once, a JP in Herefordshire by 1528 and *custos rotulorum* there by 1561, a JP in Worcester-shire from 1532, and in Shropshire and Gloucestershire from 1554, steward for life of various duchy of Lancaster manors, member of the council of Wales from 1553, and steward of Hereford for many years. He was, acknowledged Richard Willison in 1570, one of those who had 'woon unto them ... the hartes of theire cowntrie'. Despite his religious conservatism, exemplified in his will, drawn up in July 1570, which asked for the prayers of the Virgin and all the saints and left a bequest to the poor to pray for his soul, he maintained his power until his death in 1571.[8]

The duality of service at court and power within the southern marches of Wales was a legacy and a pattern to the Holme Lacy Scudamores for the next century. Bill Tighe notes this as the '"compenetration" of court influence and country authority', the reciprocal relationship and mutual reinforcement of courtiership and country status.[9] John Scudamore engineered court offices for two of his sons. Richard Scudamore (died *c.* 1586) was a yeoman of the toils from 1539 until *c.* 1556 and London agent and secretary to Sir Philip Hoby, ambassador at the court of Charles V. Philip Scudamore (died 1602) was a gentleman usher to Queen Elizabeth.[10] John's eldest son William predeceased him in 1560, after which the preferment of William's eldest son, John Scudamore the younger (1542–1623), was overseen by John Scudamore the elder and Sir James Croft (1517/18–90). Croft, heir of one of the leading Herefordshire families, had already experienced several turns of Fortune's wheel. He had risen under his patron John Dudley, duke of Northumberland, to become lord deputy of Ireland (1551–53) and gentleman of the privy chamber to Edward VI, but was condemned to death in 1554 for his part in Wyatt's rebellion. Spared, he was rehabilitated at the beginning of Elizabeth's reign. Appointed governor of Berwick in 1559, he was made the scapegoat for English military failings against the Scots and retired to Herefordshire in disgrace the following year. Croft was granted the wardship of the younger John Scudamore in 1561 in order to secure the marriage between John and Croft's daughter Eleanor.[11]

Despite Sir James Croft's disgrace, it was an advantageous marriage, for Croft retained the favour of Robert Dudley, son of his former patron and soon to be earl of Leicester. More important for the young John Scudamore, the marriage cemented a close friendship between him and his father-in-law which survived the death of Eleanor in 1569 and lasted until Croft's death in 1590. Consequently, it was entirely natural that, when Croft was returned to the queen's favour in 1569 through the good offices of Robert Dudley, earl of Leicester, and appointed comptroller of the household early in 1570, Scudamore should follow him to court. By January 1570 Scudamore's friends were addressing him as 'Mr Cowrtier' and expecting his imminent promotion; in July the queen was asking for Scudamore's attendance at court; by early 1572 Scudamore had been made a gentleman pensioner, one of the fifty elite royal guards.[12]

Scudamore had now to seize his chance, to grasp the honour that was his – he had, in Bill Tighe's phrase, 'to match *fortuna* with his *virtù*' – especially as Croft and Leicester were soon to split acrimoniously.[13] Probably in January 1574 he secretly married Mary Shelton, daughter of Sir John Shelton of Norfolk, a member of the queen's privy chamber and second cousin to Elizabeth. It was a bold move, for Elizabeth was habitually opposed to the marriage of her maids, withholding her permission from those who sought it and holding in high dudgeon those who did not. When the marriage was revealed the enraged queen attacked Mary with a candlestick, breaking one of Mary's fingers. By October 1574, however, Mary had been forgiven by the queen. The marriage, which had so nearly been the ruin of John Scudamore, became instead the foundation of his political success. Mary became a lady of the privy chamber and mistress of the robes. It has been suggested that the privy chamber declined in importance under Elizabeth, but it continued to provide the all-important access to the royal ear, so essential in maintaining credit with the queen and obtaining favours for friends while blocking them for rivals. To her enemies at court Lady Scudamore was 'a barbarous brazen-faced woman', but to her friends she formed, with Lady Blanch Parry and Ann Russell, countess of Warwick, 'A Trinity of Ladies able to worke miracles'.[14]

With the support of Sir James Croft in Herefordshire and at court, and with guaranteed access to the queen through his wife, John gradually rose as a courtier and local magnate through the 1570s and 1580s. He was on the Herefordshire commission of the peace by November 1569. Croft had assumed the office of *custos rotulorum* in 1571, but he passed it on to Scudamore in 1574. The following year Scudamore was a deputy lieutenant of Herefordshire. In 1571, 1572, 1584, 1586 and 1589 he was returned to parliament as the junior knight for Herefordshire, with Croft as the senior knight. In 1581–82 Scudamore was sheriff of Herefordshire.[15] Although he probably spent less time at Holme Lacy than at court (he had a house at the tiltyard at Greenwich), Scudamore's position in Herefordshire appeared secure.[16]

Scudamore's local standing in the later 1580s is all the more remarkable because the years from 1583 saw bitter rivalry between Sir James Croft and Sir Thomas Coningsby and a struggle for power within the shire which erupted into bloodshed. For a generation Crofts and Coningsbys and their respective allies fought each other in faction fight and street battle in Leominster, London and Hereford.[17] The experience of this contest was to colour much of the local politics of Herefordshire throughout the early seventeenth century. Scudamore showed himself a master of political adeptness. He remained largely aloof from many of the seamier details of this contest, at least until Croft's death in 1590, and for a long time held together the seemingly irreconcilable, the patronage of Croft and the respect of Coningsby.[18] From 1590, however, Scudamore's position became much harder to maintain: Sir James Croft died in October and the earl of Essex saw this as his chance to strengthen his power base in the southern marches by intervening decisively on the side of Coningsby. Scudamore lost out to Essex in the contest for the stewardship of Hereford in 1590. In 1593 and 1601 Scudamore stepped aside to allow Sir James Croft's grandson Herbert to serve in parliament as junior knight for Herefordshire (in 1597 Scudamore was junior knight); on each occasion Coningsby was senior knight.

Throughout the 1590s Scudamore was partially eclipsed in Herefordshire by the Coningsby–Devereux interest. He did not, however, lose out at court, for he and his wife retained the favour of the queen. In the autumn of 1592 he was knighted.[19] In 1599 he was made standard bearer of the gentleman pensioners, third in rank of the band's chief officers.[20] Perhaps the most valuable prize won in the 1590s, however, was the close friendship of John and

Mary Scudamore with the seventh earl and countess of Shrewsbury. John became steward of the Shrewsburys' Herefordshire manors of Archenfield and Goodrich, conducting much of their business in the southern Welsh marches. In return the Scudamores received their backing in the country and at court.[21] Sir John Scudamore, with his usual adroitness, also attempted to open a channel of communication to the earl of Essex through his son, James Scudamore (1568–1619). In 1596 James accompanied Essex on the attack against Cadiz and was there knighted, probably by Essex; the following year he joined the ill-fated Islands voyage.[22] Sir James Scudamore continued his attempts to remain within the Essex circle. In March 1597 he married Mary, daughter and co-heiress of Peter Houghton, alderman of London; Essex attended the wedding banquet.[23] She died in August 1598 and in the summer of 1599 Sir James remarried, again within the Essex circle. His second wife was Mary, widow of Sir Thomas Baskervile; both she and her infant son Hannibal had been in Essex's care since her first husband's death.[24] Probably at about the same time Sir James Scudamore acquired the Suffolk manor of Drinkstone from the earl of Essex.[25]

The disgrace and execution of the earl of Essex in 1601 destabilised the uneasy truce that had prevailed in Herefordshire for the previous decade. In the scramble for place and office that ensued Sir James Scudamore lost out to Coningsby in the elections to parliament, but Sir John Scudamore did obtain the stewardship of Hereford after a long and dirty fight against Coningsby and his allies. Moreover, in the parliaments of 1604 and 1614 Sir James Scudamore was the senior knight of the shire with Sir Herbert Croft the junior. The Scudamores' eventual success was exemplified by Sir John's appointment to the council in the marches of Wales in May 1602; Coningsby did not receive this honour until 1617.[26]

Sir John and Lady Mary Scudamore lost their court offices on the dissolution of Elizabeth's household after her funeral in April 1603. Lady Mary herself died the following August.[27] Sir John retired to Herefordshire, where Scudamores and Coningsbys governed in relative harmony until the 1620s.[28] The energies of Sir Herbert Croft were absorbed by his increasingly desperate attempts to find money, and his leadership of the campaign to exempt the four English shires (Herefordshire, Worcestershire, Gloucestershire and Shropshire) from the jurisdiction of the council in the marches of Wales, a move designed, in part, to win back for his family his grandfather's former pre-eminence in the southern marches. It was a contest in which most of the other marcher gentry were content to play second fiddle lest it failed, as proved the case: on the collapse of the campaign Croft fled to the Continent, bankrupt, where he converted to Catholicism and died a lay brother at Douai.[29]

Without the enmity of Coningsby and Croft destabilising Herefordshire, the Scudamores were free to get on with the business of governing the country and securing their reputation. Sir John Scudamore was acknowledged as 'a very great man in our Cuntrye'.[30] There is no better witness to the power of the Scudamores in the first two decades of the seventeenth century than the ease with which they cast off, disowned and crushed Sir James's second wife Mary and her son by her first marriage, Hannibal Baskervile, when the marriage turned sour after 1604. Mary turned to her relations and, with their support, spent two decades seeking relief in turn from the bishop of London, the privy council, the archbishop of Canterbury, the prerogative court of Canterbury, the court of arches and, finally, parliament, all with very little success. The Scudamores perverted legal process with relative impunity.[31] Moreover, despite warnings to the Scudamores that their treatment of Mary would cause scandal and 'thereby work the ruyne of your house and posteritie', there is no evidence that the case tarnished their reputation or honour one jot.[32] Sir John Scudamore, noted Rowland Vaughan in 1610, 'hath alwayes beene to the comfort of the country: Nurse to the Infancie of many young Gentlemen bred therein, and cherisher of the rest'. Consequently, according to William Higford, Sir John's 'trayne and equipage was comparable to the greatest Earles of Englande' and Holme Lacy 'seemed not onely an Academy, but even the very Court of a Prince'.[33]

Into this academy or court, in February 1601, John Scudamore (the first viscount) was born, the eldest child of Sir James and his second wife, Mary.[34] The reputations of Sir John, his grandfather, 'the goodliest personage ... in the Courte of Englande', and his 'thrice noble' father, Sir James, were an invaluable asset for the young John Scudamore.[35] To this inheritance of honour three further assets were added by his grandfather and father: a good education, a good marriage and a good estate.

From the little that can be pieced together, the young John Scudamore's education seems to have been entirely conventional. Family tradition, recorded in the early eighteenth century, says that he was educated under a domestic tutor at Holme Lacy, although his youngest brother Barnabas (1609–52) went to school in Hereford.[36] In November 1616 he matriculated at Magdalen College, Oxford. Here his short career was unremarkable. Within a month he was finding his annual allowance of £50 insufficient for the student life. He (or perhaps, as so often in such cases, his tutor) penned a short Latin verse on the death of Anne of Denmark, wife of James I, published in one of those collections so beloved of the early seventeenth century.[37] In December 1617 he entered the Middle Temple, by the favour of the family's neighbour and legal adviser Walter Pye, the reader-elect there.[38] Eleven months later he went to France accompanied by one servant, with a pass for three years' travel, and he was still in France in April 1619. It was a typical upper gentry education in law, rhetoric and practical virtues.[39]

What distinguished John's education was the atmosphere into which he was born at Holme Lacy. His father, and especially his grandfather, were great patrons of learning and friends to the learned. One W. Phillip dedicated his translation of a Dutch description of the East Indies to Sir James because of Scudamore's 'good disposition to the fauouring of trauell and trauellers'.[40] Sir John was a patron of the Bodleian Library, giving £40 in 1603, with which one manuscript (a twelfth-century commentary on the Apocalypse) and about 114 books were bought.[41] Both Sir John and Sir James were intimate friends with Sir Thomas Bodley. They exchanged gossip, news, metheglin and medicaments, and Bodley seems to have visited Holme Lacy in the first years of James I's reign.[42] The mathematician Thomas Allen was another learned guest at Holme Lacy: on one visit Sir John's maids, hearing the ticking of Allen's watch, then a great rarity, and believing it to be a devil, threw it into the moat.[43] A third friend of Sir John Scudamore, and also of his second wife Mary, was John Dee, the astrologer, alchemist and mathematician, who was held in high regard during his life. In 1581 Mary Scudamore was godmother to Dee's daughter Katharine.[44] Sir John was also a patron of music.[45]

That some of this atmosphere of learning, and especially mathematics, rubbed off on the young John Scudamore is suggested by his later erudition, patronage and friendships in various fields including philosophy, theology and mathematics.[46] Samuel Hartlib in 1648 reckoned him 'A great schollar' and one who was 'studying hard continually'.[47]

Grandfather and father carefully arranged an advantageous marriage for John. On 12 March 1615, less than a month after reaching the legal age, he was married to the young heiress Elizabeth Porter, a year his senior, in the chapel of Holme Lacy House.[48] Elizabeth, the only child of Sir Arthur and Lady Anne Porter of Llanthony, Gloucestershire, was the sole heiress of the Porter estates, lying just beyond the walls of Gloucester. The marriage articles were very favourable to the Scudamores: Sir John was given the power to determine Elizabeth's jointure should his grandson predecease her without issue.[49] The early marriage was designed to be politically advantageous, but it was not so much the Porters as their cousins who were valuable to the Scudamores. Lady Anne Porter was the sister of Henry, Lord Danvers (later earl of Danby). Indeed, the impetus for the marriage may have come from Danvers himself: he was seen as the key figure in the marriage negotiations, while the Scudamores and the Danvers family already had links, perhaps formed when Sir James Scudamore and the brothers Charles and Henry Danvers had been, to different extents, within the circles of the earl of Essex.[50] The Porters counted among their kin and friends several important marcher gentry, such as Sir Richard Welsh of Worcestershire, Sir Henry Poole of Sapperton (Gloucestershire) and Sir William Cooke of Highnam (Gloucestershire).[51] These were useful contacts within the wider circles of gentry sociability and the honour community, and the links between the Scudamores and some of these families were maintained.[52] Lord Danvers and his brother Sir John Danvers both became friends of the first viscount. He would pay Lord Danvers visits at Cornbury in Oxfordshire and exchange news, cider and horses with Sir John Danvers; his son James was a beneficiary of Danby's will.[53] The Cookes of Gloucestershire in particular became close associates of the Scudamores over several generations, lending one another money, settling disputes and intermarrying: in 1676 Dennis Cooke of Highnam married the first viscount's granddaughter Mary.[54] Although little is known about the marriage of John and Elizabeth, it gives every indication of having been happy: in a letter of 1650, after thirty-five years of marriage, Elizabeth addressed her husband as 'Sweet hart'.[55]

If the marriage of John and Elizabeth was designed to reinforce the ties of the Holme Lacy Scudamores with important marcher families, it was also intended to bring substantial wealth to the Scudamores. The Porter estates lay in the parish of Hempsted, just to the south-west of Gloucester but in sight of the city walls and within the inshire of Gloucester. They included the site of Llanthony Priory,[56] with a mansion house made from some of the claustral buildings, another house at Newark, half a mile away, and good grazing meadow along the banks of the river Severn, highly prized for the production of cheese. It is difficult to determine the size of the estate, for it was variously reckoned at 350 acres and 910 acres;[57] estimates of its annual value varied between £426 and £763.[58] None of these lands, however, was to pass into Viscount Scudamore's hands until December 1632, after the deaths of Sir Arthur and Lady Anne Porter.[59]

Much greater wealth already lay in the hands of the Scudamores. They were probably the richest family in Herefordshire, a county with no resident peer, although their wealth paled beside that of the Somersets of Raglan, just over the border in Wales, perhaps the wealthiest family in the kingdom. The Scudamores, nevertheless, held a very substantial estate. At Holme Lacy they held approximately 3,000 acres of arable and meadow; elsewhere they held land in approximately fifty places, mostly in southern Herefordshire, but also in Worcestershire and elsewhere.[60] The very stylised feodary's survey on the death of Sir James Scudamore gives figures for his lands of 13,600 acres in Herefordshire and 1,840 acres in Worcestershire.[61] The value of the Scudamores' lands is unknown, for the first surviving Scudamore account books belonged to the first viscount and date from the 1630s; they suggest an annual income of about £3,500.[62] This is perhaps an underestimate of the Scudamores' income in the first two decades of the seventeenth century, for the first viscount had not inherited all the family estates and had disposed of some outlying properties in the later 1620s. Not only did this great wealth bring worth and honour to the Scudamores in itself, further honour was brought to the family by the spending of Sir John and Sir James on public works in the county of Hereford. They built Wilton Bridge across the river Wye near Ross and gave land to found a hospital in Hereford.[63]

On 13 April 1619, when young John Scudamore was but eighteen years old and still in France, his father died, possibly from complications arising from the gammy leg for which he had previously been treated at Bath.[64] The aged Sir John Scudamore quickly purchased his grandson's wardship and oversaw his entry to local office and politics.[65] John, 'though as yet he be but yonge and unexperienced', quickly stepped into his father's place as captain of the county horse at the creation of the lord lieutenant and lord president of the council of Wales and the marches, the earl of Northampton, 'out of the good respect I beare to his famyly'.[66] It was a mark of honour to be so appointed; lack of military experience did not matter. As Gervase Markham explained, training and martial exercise were the muster master's duties while captains should be 'men of honorable woorthie, and vertuous Disposition, such as their Contries loved to followe both for their bloods and vertues sakes', with sufficient estate to uphold the honour of their place without taxing the country or the soldiers.[67] John Scudamore's preferment bore witness to the respect and honour in which his father and grandfather were held, especially by Northampton, who had known Sir James at Elizabeth's court in the 1590s. Most of the overt opposition to the council's jurisdiction in Herefordshire had died down before Northampton was made lord president in 1617, since when the Scudamores had rendered dependable service to the lord lieutenant and to the council. Sir John and Sir James were both members of the council; Sir James was also a deputy lieutenant; Sir John's brother Rowland Scudamore of Sellack held the office of porter of the council.[68]

The honour, reputation, power and wealth of the Holme Lacy Scudamores were a great inheritance for the young John. Through them, and under the careful guidance of his grandfather, his *entrée* into local politics and office was secure. His inheritance was the bedrock of all his later success. It was, however, much more than that. The careers and reputations of his grandfather and particularly of his father were animating spirits shaping his self-image and helping to determine the patterns into which he would attempt to mould his own career. In no area is this more clear than in Viscount Scudamore's military self-image.

Military traditions and chivalric display loomed large in the careers of the Holme Lacy Scudamores in the sixteenth century, even though their power at court and locally was based on the more mundane routine of local office-holding and ready access to the royal ear. John Scudamore (c. 1486–1571) had begun his long court career as one of the eight gentlemen attending Henry VIII on foot at a tournament at Greenwich in 1516.[69] Sir John Scudamore's duties, as a gentleman pensioner to Queen Elizabeth, may have been largely ceremonial, but they sustained traditions of military service to the crown. These traditions were further developed by the first viscount's father, Sir James Scudamore. As a youth he attached himself to Sir Philip Sidney, the greatest courtier knight of the Elizabethan age, elevated to the status of hero and pattern for all to follow by his early death. James Scudamore, then aged only eighteen, bore the pennon of arms at Sidney's funeral in 1587.[70] In the mid 1590s Sir James emerged as one of the greatest courtier knights within the Spenserian tradition at Elizabeth's court. He was Edmund Spenser's model for Sir Scudamore, the 'gentle knight', the pattern and type of chivalry, in the *Faerie Queene*.

> I hauing armes then taken, gan auise
> To winne me honour by some noble gest,
> and purchase me some place amongst the best

announces Sir Scudamore in book four, in a case of life and art mirroring one another.[71] In 1595 James Scudamore emerged as one of the main knights at the Ascension Day tilts. That year he bore the motto 'L'escu d'amour' as a pun on his name. It was, versified George Peele,

> ... the arms of loyalty
> ... and on he came,
> And well and worthily demeaned himself
> In that day's service: short and plain to be,
> No lord nor knight more foreard than was he.

He took part in each year's tilt until 1600. The cost of appearing each year was very great, and Sir James probably spent most of the £12,000 fortune that his first marriage brought him maintaining the display.[72] He had himself painted as a knight of the crown, wearing his best suit of Greenwich armour adorned with velvet, lace and silver, bearing an orange scarf (the colours of the earl of Essex) like a lady's favour, and carrying a lance, the whole composition set in a romantic sylvan setting like an arcadian pastoral scene.[73] His stance reflected the image of Sir Philip Sidney, the shepherd knight, the manly military champion of Elizabethan England.

Sir James Scudamore retired from tilting and from court in 1600, 'cuming best at Tilt' that year.[74] He did not, however, abandon his chivalric image, for at Holme Lacy he and his father continued to train horses. The image of Sir James Scudamore at the tiltyard, and later at Holme Lacy, were a potent force, exercising a particular fascination over many who saw them or heard of his exploits, long after his death. William Higford's 'Institutions', written as advice to his grandson in the later 1640s or early 1650s, bear ample witness to the didactic power of Sir James's image, encouraging others to emulate his virtues. William Higford's son John had married Sir James's daughter Frances in 1626; in his treatise of advice to John's son John, William reminded his grandson of his 'thrice noble grandfather', Sir James Scudamore, recalling in great detail the magnificence of his display.[75]

> A knightt on horseback is the goodliest sight the worlde can presente to viewe; and is not lesse then a Prince ... mee thinkes I see sir James Scudamore ... a brave man att Armes, both att Tiltes, and Barriers after the voyages of Cales, and the Canara Ilandes. wherein he performed verie remarkable signall service ... enter the Tilte yarde in an handsome equipage all in compleate Armor, embelished with plumes, his beaver close, mounted vppon a verie highe boundinge horse. I haue seene the shoes of his horse glister aboue the heades of all the people. and when hee came to the encounter or shocke, brake as manie speares as the beste, Her majestie Queene Elizabeth with a trayne of ladies like the starres in the firmamente, and the whole Courte lookinge vppon him with a verie gratious aspecte. and when hee came to reside with sir John Scudamore his father (two braver gentlemen shall I neuer see togeather att one time, much more a sonne and a father). himselfe and other brave Cavalers and some of their meniualls and of his suite to manage euerie morninge 6 or more brave well ridden horses. euerie horse broughte forthe with his groome in such decencye, order and honour that Holme Lacie att that time seemed not onlie an Academia, but euen the verie Courte of a Prince.

The passage is important, revealing the awe in which a courtier knight was held, and disseminating the military honour of the Scudamore family: manuscripts of Higford's treatise, including this paean, seem to have circulated outside the family; moreover, it was printed in 1658, with a second edition, dedicated to Viscount Scudamore, two years later.[76]

That Sir James's image was a living inheritance, held up within the Holme Lacy family as well as beyond, is suggested by the careers of his two surviving younger sons, James (1606–c. 1631) and Barnabas (1609–52), both of whom followed military careers, living and dying within the tradition of martial honour. James, while a student at the Middle Temple in 1623, challenged Sir Simonds D'Ewes to a duel, although the two would-be combatants made their peace with one another before coming to blows.[77] By the autumn of 1626 James Scudamore had gone to the Low Countries to seek his fortune in the wars. It proved elusive. Serving under Sir Charles Morgan he had the misfortune to kill one Captain Kay, a Scotsman, in another duel in 1631. James himself died soon after and was buried at The Hague.[78] Barnabas's early years are very sketchy. He was in Ireland in the summer of 1631, but his money ran out and he was sent home by the earl of Cork with £20 and an errand to perform. At the end of the year he crossed over to the Low Countries, perhaps to follow in his brother's footsteps, but he was back in England four years later, again working for Cork, and in March 1636 he went to France as an attendant on the earl's sons Lewis, Viscount Kinalmeaky, and Roger, Lord

Broghill.[79] In 1640 Barnabas joined Colonel Sir Charles Vavasour's regiment as a captain and saw action in the bishops' wars at the battle of Newburn in August, and was still with the remnants of the English army the following March when he joined forty or so officers in defending the army's conduct to the earl of Northumberland.[80] The outbreak of fighting in England in the summer of 1642 was to provide him with further opportunities for military glory.[81]

The first viscount cut a much less dashing figure than his two younger brothers; nevertheless, the military glory of his father exercised a pull over him too. By his will Sir James left John 'my Armor which I used to weare'; the survival of parts of two suits (now in the Metropolitan Museum of Art, New York), one illustrated in his portrait, the other drawn in an armourers' pattern book, show that his armour was of the very finest Greenwich work.[82] The gesture was the passing down of the mantle of military honour from father to son.

The decline of tilting at the Stuart court closed down one avenue of possible chivalric display, while Viscount Scudamore's duties as head of a great house and local governor restricted his ability to chase martial honours overseas. Nonetheless, there were opportunities at home to seek to cover oneself with the glory of military virtues by manipulating the imagery and rhetoric of chivalry, for the exercise of arms remained an essential part of gentry culture.[83] Scudamore's duties as captain of the county horse and, from 1622, deputy lieutenant of Herefordshire, were the stage on which he could project his military self-image and his chivalric inheritance.[84]

Viscount Scudamore refashioned the chivalric ideals he had inherited from his father and manipulated the rhetoric of nobility from contemporary political culture to project an image of military honour. So much is clear from a speech he wrote for the assembled Herefordshire gentry on the need to improve the county troop of horse. The speech is undated but must have been written early in the reign of Charles I.[85] Scudamore had three main thrusts. The first was on the need for the effective training of the militia, illustrated by a story from the days of the Spanish Armada. In Scudamore's tale, when the news of the Spanish fleet's approach reached court in 1588, Lord Burghley rushed into the presence chamber, clapped his thighs and exclaimed to the 'braue yong gallants' that thronged the court, 'If I had a sonne which would not presently put himself into the Queenes navy to fight with this Spanish fleete, I should bee glad to see him hang'd at the Court-gate.' Lashed by the old man's tongue, the brave courtiers 'put on wings and flew in all hast to the Queens navy'. Once they got to the coast they pestered the navy for an opportunity to fight the Spanish. The result, however, was not what they intended, for they nearly wrecked the war effort through lack of training. 'Spiritts and Sinews they wanted not; The Ignorance of handling their armes, of order, of discipline did the hurt'. Scudamore drew the obvious moral: 'Bee then our affections and armes and hands never so strong, wee shall receiue inconvenience rather then profitt, if some paynes bee not taken to haue our abilities regulated by the rule of discipline.' However unlikely the story may seem, the viscount's father, grandfather and step-grandmother were all at court in 1588 and may have heard the tale then, if not actually witnessed the scene itself.

Scudamore's second thrust concerned the role of martial courage in the code of honour. According to Scudamore, military valour was an essential virtue for any gentleman. Without it, not only would the blood honour of a noble ancestry be stained, but the coward's very masculinity would be called into question. Manhood and military honour were, in Scudamore's eyes, inseparable.

> I will say, and I dare say, that hee which is a gentleman and hath a lusty body, doth degenerate from the virtue of his auncestors and is vnworthy the name of a man, if through feare, covet[ousness] pride or sloth he refuseth to bestow time and paines to indue himself with a qualitie necessary to the preservation of country and posteritie in such estate of libertie as by his predecessors himself had the happiness to be left in.

In other words, the survival of free-born Englishmen depended not only on the exercise of martial valour by gentlemen seeking to live out their masculinity within the precepts of the code of honour, but on training and practice in arms. The code of honour, the concept of chivalric virtue, demanded regular training in arms, not just the display of military prowess in exceptional times of war.

Finally, Scudamore had a vision of the well ordered commonwealth founded on the exercise of the virtues he had outlined to the assembled gentry. All men were bound, 'by nature and gratitude', to preserve the country 'from which they did first draw breath'; no one could be excused. Men and horse in the trained bands, he said, were 'designed to the service of the King' and had been 'dedicated so to the interest of the King' that they 'must alwayes bee in reddiness at the call of the Kin[g's] officers'. His was a highly structured and hierarchical vision. He saw the code of honour as prescribing different roles for different sorts of people, all united in the service of the king. The foot companies of the county trained bands were for the yeomen; the county horse was reserved for gentlemen. Scudamore was most concerned to keep the social distinction within the trained bands. Such ideas were commonplace in the early seventeenth century. Gervase Markham, for example, writing a popular military manual, divided the cuirassiers, carbiners and dragoons by social rank, the cuirassiers to be 'of the best degree', the carbiners to be the best yeomen.[86] Scudamore, however, went further than most, attempting to enforce a strict separation between gentry and yeomen. He was particularly anxious that the gentlemen charged with maintaining a horse in the county troop should serve themselves, rather than procuring a deputy (often of lower status) to ride in their place. By deploying the rhetoric of the nobility of armed service, he persuaded forty of the principal gentlemen of the troop to ride their own mounts in the troop themselves or, at the very least, to procure only gentlemen as their deputies, on the condition that 'they may not bee consorted with groomes or market-men or the like'. Furthermore, to ensure that the gentlemen of the troop did not face the indignity of being trained in military discipline by a muster master who was their social inferior, Scudamore promised that he would undertake the burden of training the troop himself. To this end Scudamore went to great pains to obtain details of drill and strategy. He swopped with his great friend at court Sir Henry Herbert a fine horse from the Holme Lacy stables for details of Dutch military methods. He secured further information about tactics from his younger brother James, serving as a soldier in the Low Countries. By such means he obtained many papers detailing military training, such as 'Rules to order a horse Troope' explaining how to 'Diuide your Troopes into two diuisions and scarmach on against another with false powder'.[87] Scudamore's vision was of his troop composed only of the most honourable and ancient county families, fully trained in military virtues, ready to serve the king and defend the liberties of England.

Scudamore should not be thought of as articulating a comprehensive and entirely coherent account of military honour, however. Like most contemporary accounts of honour it contained what may seem to the external reader internal contradictions. In Scudamore's vision, military prowess was vital to the possession of honour, and without it no one was fit to be called a gentleman. Nonetheless, Scudamore did not open the gates of honour to any who could seize the prize by feats of martial bravery. His stress on the rigidities of the social structure and concern to keep the county horse untainted from association with 'groomes and market-men' were explicitly anti-egalitarian, resting on ideas of the fixed association of honour with blood, lineage and time. Second, although the whole tenor of the speech stressed military service as the true path to honour, Scudamore allowed one exception. Justices of the peace were excused service in the trained bands. When the militia was sent out of the county the JPs must remain behind to keep the peace, 'that lewd persons apt in such times to committ insolencies, may bee held in awe and order'. Service to the crown in the commission of the peace provided the one other route, apart from military employment, to an honourable reputation.

Scudamore did seek honour by serving the crown as a JP, and in many other fields, but he also attempted to act out his own rhetoric and present himself as a man of martial virtue. When, for example, he had his portrait painted in 1642 by Edward Bower, he chose to wear a suit of armour, just as his father had done.[88] In the 1620s Scudamore matched his actions to his rhetoric. By May 1627 he had formed his own company of trained men: twenty-four household servants and twenty-one retainers, with a further eighteen retainers whom he noted as untrained. Barely any of the male servants at Holme Lacy, except perhaps the fool, can have escaped the military training. It was apt, therefore, that Higford later described the viscount's household as 'Like an Army drawn up in battle array'.[89] Such private companies were by no means unknown. Sir Thomas Cornewall, a deputy lieutenant in neighbouring Shropshire, formed a voluntary company of gentlemen at about the same time, which he entertained at his own cost and encouraged in the use of arms. In 1627 the duke of Buckingham was reported to be raising a horse troop from among his friends and followers 'to ease his Majesties charge'.[90] The example of the earl of Northampton, lord president of the council in the marches of Wales and lord lieutenant of the marcher counties, was important. He was known for his 'ardent zeale ... vnto Military discipline'. In 1618 he had proposed to all the deputy lieutenants of his lieutenancy the creation of an academy of horsemanship at Ludlow, seat of the council, and the following year it was noted that not only had he drawn his gentlemen and the council clerks into a trained company, but that he also had eighteen horses trained in the castle yard at Ludlow every day, rather as the viscount's father and grandfather had done at Holme Lacy.[91]

In addition to such private companies formed by the leadership of one man, such as Scudamore, Cornewall or Northampton, the early seventeenth century saw the formation of a plethora of more public artillery companies and artillery gardens for military exercises. London had its by the 1580s (refounded in 1610), followed by many other towns, including Coventry in 1616 (encouraged by the earl of Northampton), Bristol in 1625, and Gloucester and Chester in 1626.[92] Scudamore himself, who from 1640 had a house in Westminster, was one of sixty-one men who leased the Artillery Ground in Tuthill Fields, Westminster, from the dean and chapter of Westminster in 1664 so that it could be used for military exercises.[93] Such artillery companies seem to have been relatively open, at least to adult male householders: the London Artillery Company mustered 6,000 men in 1616.[94] There are, then, a number of potential sources within contemporary culture for Scudamore's actions and the formation of his image as a gentleman of martial virtues and chivalric honour. His rhetoric, the stress on regular military training and the importance of martial prowess in a gentleman's honour, should be set in the context of a continuing, perhaps even increasing concern for chivalric virtues within the political culture of early Stuart England: William Hunt has written of the attempted 'remilitarization of English society' in response to the Habsburg victories of the 1620s.[95] The examples of the earl of Northampton and other marcher gentry were important to Scudamore. Wales and the marches, with their histories as contested and border zones and traditions of lawlessness persisting long into the sixteenth century, retained a strong sense of the importance of the greater gentry as war leaders like the former marcher lords.[96] Scudamore's inheritance and family traditions were also important in defining his self image. The Holme Lacy stables retained their reputation for fine horses under the first viscount, and the gift of a horse from Scudamore was highly prized.[97]

Scudamore's speech has a number of implications for the study of the Stuart chivalric ethos. Much of the military and chivalric rhetoric of the 1620s was explicitly anti-Spanish and often puritan or aggressively Protestant.[98] Scudamore's speech drew on this Hispanophobia to encourage his auditors to hone their military prowess. In an interpolation to the speech he added: 'Is there any man that would not rather chuse, to thrust himself into the mouth of a Cannon, then to liue and to bee put into fetters vnder the wand of an intollerable tyrannizing Spaniard?'[99] Scudamore was not, however, a natural Hispanophobe and was in the 1630s, as we shall see, linked with the pro-Spanish faction at court.[100] His anti-Spanish rhetoric in the mid 1620s was probably an example of the malleability of political imagery and the desire to mine a popular vein during the war with Spain. It should stand as a warning, both against taking political rhetoric at its face value, and to those historians who see chivalric culture and martial imagery as inherently anti-Spanish and implicitly critical of the policies of James I and Charles I.[101]

While Scudamore posed, a little unconvincingly, as an anti-Spanish hero in the mid 1620s, following the lead of Charles and Buckingham, he did not link his martial image with zealous Protestantism as others did. His guiding principles were not the link between chivalry and godliness made by some writers, such as John Reynolds and Samuel Ward but, as we have seen, the intimate connection between martial honour and gentility.[102] This bond made by Scudamore is important in two respects. First, it explicitly rejected the more egalitarian implications in some chivalric rhetoric. Many of the sermons delivered to artillery companies sought, for example, through the honour of the military vocation open to all, to ennoble the citizens and merchants who joined the urban artillery companies. Thomas Adams, for example, tried, through a linguistic sleight of hand and by straightforward mistranslation, to assert that 'captain' and 'duke' were the same term and that *miles* meant both knight and common soldier to the ancient Romans. Virtue, preached Adams, depended on courage, not wealth and social status: 'Honour should go by the Banner, not by the Barne: and Reputation be valued by valour, not measured by the acre.'[103] Indeed, one of the paradoxes of the chivalric tradition was the populist strand which it contained. Tales of knights errant were among the staple reading of the middling sort: the admission of John Bunyan, the tinker's son, that he grew up reading of Bevis of Southampton and St George and not the more improving works of pious divines, is well known.[104] Scudamore's concern that his horse troop should not have to mix with 'groomes or market-men', and his acknowledgement that service in the county trained bands was limited to 'Men of the better Ranke – Gentlemen and Yeomen', seemed to suggest that the gates to the fields of martial glory should be narrow and the fame of military honour restricted by birth.[105] Nevertheless, his actions – forming even his household servants into a private military company, and sponsoring the Westminster Artillery Ground – tempered his rhetoric somewhat.

If Scudamore's vision of the role of military glory, as set out in his speech, was socially exclusive, it did encompass the lesser or 'parish gentry'. This is the second important point to be made about his stress on the bond between chivalry and gentility, for it provides an important corrective to the emphasis in recent work by John Adamson, where the study of the political culture of chivalry looks only at the greater nobility.[106] Scudamore was concerned to show that there was a route to honour available to all 'Men of the better Ranke' – yeoman, gentry and justices – through service in the foot, horse or commission of the peace.

At the head of this pyramid or hierarchy of honour in Herefordshire Scudamore offered himself in the classic topos of self-advancement clothed as service to the commonwealth: 'The labour in disciplining' the gentry horse troop 'will be more then little' he warned, yet he confessed that he would be 'contented to bestow' that labour, 'so it may bee vpon men not vncapable or of too meane condition'. He would undertake the role himself. The 'academy' of martial horsemanship, which his father and grandfather had created at Holme Lacy, was to be revived. Anthony Fletcher sees in Scudamore's speech the 'unbounded confidence' of Stuart local governors.[107] We may also see in it the ambition and drive of a local magnate and son of a leading local family seeking to emulate his forefathers, prove worthy of his inheritance and carve out for himself an even greater honour and prestige. For at Easter 1623, only a few years before this speech, Scudamore's grandfather, old Sir John, had died. Young John Scudamore was not the legal heir of the estate: that was old Sir John's eldest surviving son, another John (1567–?1625). This John had, however, been ordained as a Roman Catholic priest in 1592, although he converted to Protestantism in the early seventeenth century and was taken into the household of the archbishop of Canterbury. Old Sir John, however, disinherited his son John in favour of his grandson John; fortunately for the grandson, the son did not contest the will.[108]

In a culture as obsessed by lineage and honour as that of the gentry of early modern England, it is clear that the honour and reputation of one's ancestors could be as an important an inheritance as a large estate. It could be a galvanising example to inspire emulation and central to one's self definition. We have seen the process at work on the first viscount; in turn, his example worked on his descendants. The first viscount's 'Piety, Loyalty, and other eminent Vertues' were, his great-grandson the third viscount was told, 'left as a Model to his Posterity, and belong to you as your peculiar Inheritance'; Theophilus Downes expected the third viscount to follow what he saw as the path of the first in loyalty to the Stuarts.[109]

If Viscount Scudamore inherited a particular concern for a military self-image from his family's tradition, the way he chose to act it out, in service as a deputy lieutenant and captain of the county horse, were partly dictated by his inheritance of the gentry code of service to crown and commonwealth. It was an early modern commonplace that the gentry were born to serve the kingdom. The inscription which ran around the town hall in Leominster, erected in 1633, trumpeted the proper place and duty of the gentry: 'Where Justice Rvle, There Virtu Flow ... Like as Collvmns doo Vpprop the Fabrik of a Bvilding, so Noble Gentri doo Svpport the Honor of a Kingdom'. The Ciceronian precept, endlessly repeated by gentry father to gentry son, was that 'We are not borne to ourselves but others'; by birth the gentry were public persons who could expect some call to government.[110] It was a message that Viscount Scudamore, like so many other gentry, wholeheartedly accepted. He monitored the education of his grandson Jack (later the second viscount) very carefully, ensuring that he studied Aristotle, Euclid, geography, Justinian and the common law while at Oxford, in order, he told Jack, to 'make you that are an Englishman fitt for employment'. The upbringing of his son James had been as carefully supervised, with the same end of fitting him for service to the commonwealth. In 1661 the viscount put James forward, in his first major role on a public stage, for election to parliament as knight of the shire for Herefordshire, explaining to the voters:

> whatsoeuer abilities hee is in possession of ... I know nothing that hee can imploy them in which can bring me equall ioy, as to imploy them in the service of his naturall Soveraigne the King, and of this particular County where he drew in his first Breath. And as this ioynt end, the serving the King and this countrey, was the obiect of my endeauours in his education, so I doe now heere offer and deuote him therunto next to the serving of God.

The viscount was here using the word 'country' in the same way that others, such as Sir John Newdigate and Sir Richard Grosvenor did, as a blend of commonwealth and shire, with overtones of sentimental attachment and patriotism, and as a body to which the gentry owed a debt of service.[111] If Viscount Scudamore was to match *fortuna* with his *virtù* as his father, grandfather and great-great-grandfather had, then service to the country was one stage to which he was fitted by birth, education and inheritance.

In 1623 Scudamore assumed the mantle of the head of the Holme Lacy family. He was 'the Flourishinge Braunche of so Renowned an Offspringe'. He had a long and worthy pedigree; he had the lives of his great-great-grandfather, grandfather and father to emulate, with their traditions of chivalric honour and service to the crown; he had wealth, education and local standing. Yet these were, as he was reminded by John Gwillim junior (whose father, John Gwillim senior, had carried out genealogical and heraldic research for old Sir John Scudamore), only 'the Sparkes of Honor' which had yet to 'burste forthe into Flames'.[112] Scudamore was also, like all his contemporaries, born into a gentry culture which demanded great care of one's own honour, which had to be nurtured, defended and extended. In other words, the task before Scudamore was now, as it was to be for the rest of his life, to match both fortune and virtue with his blood. 'Sir, you may not boast your self to descend from such Auncestors,' warned William Higford to his grandson John Higford, having described at length the worthiness of Sir John and Sir James Scudamore, 'unless also you have an earnest emulation to succeed them in their virtues.'[113] William's advice was directed to his grandson John Higford; how much more appropriate was it for Viscount Scudamore. How he sought to do this, and the measure of his success, will form our theme in the following pages.

NOTES

1 PRO, C115/C13/1263.

2 F. Heal and C. Holmes, *The Gentry in England and Wales, 1500–1700* (Basingstoke, 1994), pp. 34–7; W. Skidmore, *The Scudamores of Upton Scudamore: A Knightly Family in Medieval Wiltshire, 1086–1382* (2nd edition, Akron, 1989); W. Skidmore, *Thirty Generations of the Scudamore/Skidmore Family in England and America* (Akron, 1991).

3 Skidmore, *Scudamores of Upton Scudamore*, pp. 1–8.

4 F. W. Steer, *A Catalogue of the Earl Marshal's Papers at Arundel Castle* (Harleian Society, 115–16, 1964), p. 2; G. D. Squibb, *Reports of Heraldic Cases in the Court of Chivalry 1623–1732* (Harleian Society, 107, 1956), pp. 30–2.

5 Skidmore, *Thirty Generations*, pp. 47–8.

6 Skidmore, *Thirty Generations*, pp. 88–92; G. Williams, *Renewal and Reformation: Wales c. 1415–1642* (Oxford, 1993), pp. 167, 181, 183, 191, 194; J. S. Roskell, L. Clark and C. Rawcliffe, eds, *The House of Commons 1386–1421* (4 vols, Stroud, 1992), IV, pp. 391–4.

7 Skidmore, *Thirty Generations*, pp. 92–9; G. E. McParlin, 'The Herefordshire Gentry in County Government, 1625–1661' (University College of Wales, Aberystwyth, Ph.D. thesis, 1981), pp. 247–51, 255–8, 264–5, 268, 277; G. H. Jenkins, *The Foundations of Modern Wales: Wales 1642–1780* (Oxford, 1993), pp. 143–4, 189–90.

8 W. J. Tighe, 'The Gentleman Pensioners in Elizabethan Politics and Government' (Cambridge University Ph.D. thesis, 1984), pp. 264, 438; W. J. Tighe, 'Country into Court, Court into Country: John Scudamore of Holme Lacy (c. 1542–1623) and his Circles', in D. Hoak, ed., *Tudor Political Culture* (Cambridge, 1995), pp. 158–60; S. T.

Bindoff, ed., *The House of Commons 1509–1558* (3 vols, London, 1982), III, pp. 284–5; C. J. Robinson, *A History of the Manors and Mansions of Herefordshire* (London and Hereford, 1873), pp. 32–3, 139, 185.

9 Tighe, 'John Scudamore and his Circles', pp. 157, 176.

10 Skidmore, *Thirty Generations*, pp. 49–50; S. Brigden, ed., 'The Letters of Richard Scudamore', *Camden Miscellany XXX* (Camden, 4th series, 39, 1990), pp. 67–148.

11 Skidmore, *Thirty Generations*, pp. 50–1; Tighe, 'John Scudamore and his Circles', pp. 160–1; W. J. Tighe, 'Courtiers and Politics in Elizabethan Herefordshire: Sir James Croft, his Friends and Foes', *Historical Journal*, 32:2 (1989), pp. 257–79.

12 Tighe, 'John Scudamore and his Circles', pp. 157–8, 161–3.

13 Tighe, 'John Scudamore and his Circles', pp. 159–60, 162.

14 Tighe, 'John Scudamore and his Circles', pp. 163–4; P. Wright, 'The Ramifications of a Female Household, 1558–1603', in D. Starkey *et al.*, eds, *The English Court* (Harlow, 1987), pp. 150, 161–2, 166–7; A. Collins, ed., *Letters and Memorials of State* (2 vols, London, 1746), I, p. 67, II, pp. 97, 174; R. Vaughan, *Most Approved, and Long Experienced Water-workes* (London, 1610), sigs. Hv–H2r. Mary's portrait is reproduced in R. C. Strong, *The English Icon* (London, 1969), p. 292.

15 Tighe, 'Gentlemen Pensioners', p. 268; Tighe, 'John Scudamore and his Circles', p. 165.

16 Tighe, 'John Scudamore and his Circles', p. 164; BL, Add. MS 11053, fol. 40; HMC, *A Calendar of the Shrewsbury and Talbot Papers* (2 vols, London, 1966–71), I, p. 60.

17 For the Croft–Coningsby feud see: Tighe, 'Gentleman Pensioners', pp. 268–90; Tighe, 'Courtiers and Politics in Elizabethan Herefordshire'; Tighe, 'John Scudamore and his Circles', pp. 167–74; A. J. Fletcher, 'Honour, Reputation and Local Officeholding', in A. J. Fletcher and J. Stevenson, eds, *Order and Disorder in Early Modern England* (Cambridge, 1985), p. 102.

18 BL, Add. MS 11042, fols 16, 29–30.

19 Atherton, thesis, p. 45 n. 9.

20 Tighe, 'John Scudamore and his Circles', p. 157.

21 HMC, *Shrewsbury and Talbot Papers*, I, pp. 60, 77, 89, 108, 150, 154, 170, II, pp. 166, 173, 176, 255, 263, 265, 329; PRO, C115/N2/8508, C115/N2/8513, C115/N2/8519.

22 BL, Add. MS 5482, fol. 116v; W. Higford, *The Institution of a Gentleman* (London, 1660), pp. 69–70.

23 Skidmore, *Thirty Generations*, p. 53; Collins, *Letters*, II, pp. 28, 97.

24 HRO, AL17/1, 16 August 1598; Skidmore, *Thirty Generations*, p. 53; BL, Harl. MS 4762, fol. 52; PRO, PROB11/90/71, fol. 106; HMC, *De L'Isle and Dudley* (6 vols, London, 1925–66), II, pp. 314, 323.

25 W. A. Copinger, *The Manors of Suffolk: Notes on their History and Devolution* (7 vols, privately printed, 1905–12), VI, p. 263; PRO, STAC8/181/13. In 1610 Sir James sold the manor to Sir Arthur Ingram: A. F. Upton, *Sir Arthur Ingram c. 1565–1642: A Study of the Origins of an English Landed Family* (Oxford, 1961), p. 45.

26 Tighe, 'John Scudamore and his Circles', pp. 170–4; PRO, C115/I16/6191.

27 Tighe, 'John Scudamore and his Circles', p. 174; HRO, AL17/1, 15 August 1603.

28 BL, Add. MS 11050, fols 81–6; HRO, AL19/16, fols 52–62.

29 PRO, C115/N2/8507; R. E. Ham, 'The Career of Sir Herbert Croft' (University of California at Irvine Ph.D. thesis, 1974); R. E. Ham, 'The Four Shire Controversy', *Welsh History Review*, 8 (1977), pp. 381–400; P. Williams, 'The Attack on the Council in the Marches', *Transactions of the Honourable Society of Cymmrodorion*, 1 (1961), pp. 1–22.

30 HMC, *Shrewsbury and Talbot*, I, p. 108.

31 Atherton, thesis, pp. 49–67.

32 PRO, C115/N2/8510.

33 Vaughan, *Water-workes*, sig. G3v; Society of Antiquaries, London, MS 790/7, William Higford's 'Institutions', p. 40; Higford, *Institution*, pp. 70–1.

34 HRO, AL17/1, 22 March 1601; Atherton, thesis, p. 68; Skidmore, *Thirty Generations*, p. 53.

35 Society of Antiquaries, MS 790/7, William Higford's 'Institutions', pp. 12, 40.

36 M. Gibson, *A View of the Ancient and Present State of the Churches of Door, Home Lacy, and Hempsted* (London, 1727), p. 63; B. Scudamore, *Sir Barnabas Scvdamore's Defence*, ed. I. J. Atherton (Akron, 1992), pp. 3, 55.

37 J. Foster, *Alumni Oxonienses: The Members of the University of Oxford, 1500–1714* (4 vols, Oxford, 1891–92), IV, p. 1327; Bodleian, MS Rawl. D.859, fols 73-4; [Oxford University], *Academiae Oxoniensis Fvnebra Sacra aeternae Memoriae serenissimae Reginae Annae* ([Oxford], 1619), sig. H1r.

38 H. A. C. Sturgess, *Register of Admissions to the Honourable Society of the Middle Temple*, vol. I *1501–1781* (London, 1949), 1 December 1617; C. T. Martin, *Minutes of Parliament of the Middle Temple* (3 vols, London, 1940–45), II, p. 624; BL, Add. MS 11042, fols 83–6.

39 FSL, Vb 2(9); *APC 1617–19*, p. 253; PRO, WARD9/217, fol. 254v.

40 B. Langenes, *The Description of a Voyage made by Certaine Ships of Holland into the East Indies*, trs. W. Phillip (London, 1598), sig. A2.

41 W. D. Macray, *Annals of the Bodleian Library* (2nd edition, Oxford, 1890), p. 421; F. Madan *et al.*, *A Summary Catalogue of the Western Manuscripts in the Bodleian Library* (7 vols, Oxford, 1895–1953), II, pp. 360–1; the manuscript is now MS Bodley 352.

42 PRO, C115/M20/7591–5, printed in H. R. Trevor-Roper, 'Five Letters of Sir Thomas Bodley', *Bodleian Library Record*, 2 (1941–49), pp. 134–9.

43 J. Aubrey, *Brief Lives*, ed. A. Clark (2 vols, Oxford, 1898), I, pp. 27–8.

44 J. Dee, *Private Diary*, ed. J. O. Halliwell (Camden Society, 1st series, 19, 1842), pp. 7–8, 11, 50–1; I. Seymour, 'The Political Magic of John Dee', *History Today*, 39 (January 1989), pp. 29–35.

45 R. Alison, *An Howres Recreation in Musicke* (London, 1606), sig. A2r. Sir John's eldest son John (1567–?1625) was friendly with the composer John Dowland: Skidmore, *Thirty Generations*, p. 52; G. Anstruther, *A Hundred Homeless Years: English Dominicans 1558–1658* (London, 1958), pp. 25–6.

46 See below, pp. 51–4.

47 Sheffield University Library, Hartlib Papers, 31/22/19B, 'Ephemerides', 1648.

48 HRO, AL17/1, 12 March 1615; Gloucestershire RO, PMF 173, 13 May 1600.

49 PRO, C115/C9/1137.

50 PRO, C115/H25/5439; HRO, AL17/1, 1605; H. Spurling, *Elinor Fettiplace's Receipt Book* (Harmondsworth, 1987), p. 16; F. N. Macnamara, *Memorials of the Danvers Family* (London, 1895), pp. 102–3, 284–6, 291–2. Charles Danvers was executed after Essex's rebellion. James I returned the family lands to Henry and gave him a barony; Charles I created him earl of Danby.

51 PRO, IND1/23396, fols 109v–110r, C115/E13/2414; J. Maclean and W. C. Hearne, eds, *The Visitation of the County of Gloucester* (Harleian Society, 21, 1885), pp. 126–7; A. T. Butler, ed., *The Visitation of Worcestershire 1634* (Harleian Society, 90, 1938), p. 98; W. P. W. Phillimore and G. S. Fry, eds, *Abstracts of Gloucestershire Inquisitiones Post Mortem. Part I. 1625–1636* (British Records Society, London, 1893), pp. 128–9; Gloucestershire RO, D3117/1.

52 PRO, PROB11/133/50, fol. 402, C115/B1/518.

53 PRO, C115/M24/7772; BL, Add. MSS 11042, fols 71–3, 11043, fol. 69, 11044, fols 5–7; House of Lords RO, Box 181/23.

54 PRO, C115/I1/5542, C115/I19/5230; BL, Add. MS 11047, fols 226–7; HRO, BE7/1, fol. 38r.

55 PRO, C115/I3/5677.

56 This was Llanthony *secunda*. The first Llanthony Priory, an Augustinian foundation, was near Abergavenny in south-east Wales, but in 1136 the canons had removed themselves to the security of Gloucester to escape the depredations of the Welsh.

57 Phillimore and Fry, *Gloucestershire Inquisitiones Post Mortem*, pp. 128–9; PRO, C115/C9/1145; PRO, WARD7/80/12, WARD5/15/part 2/2783; J. Leland, *Itinerary*, ed. T. Hearne (2nd edition, 9 vols, Oxford, 1744–45), IV, p. 79.

58 PRO, C115/I1/5553, C115/I18/6214–21, C115/I19/6225, C115/M14/7283.

59 Gloucestershire RO, PMF 173, 20 March 1630; PRO, C115/G8/3608; J. V. Kitto, ed., *The Register of St. Martin-in-the-Fields London 1619–1636* (Harleian Society, Register Section, 66, 1936), 15 December 1632.

60 PRO, C115/E1/2151, C142/404/114, C142/374/85, WARD7/68/122.

61 PRO, WARD5/16, Sir James Scudamore, 1619.

62 HCL, L.C.647.1, 'Scudamore MSS: accounts 1635–37'.

63 J. Gwillim, *A Display of Heraldrie* (London, 1611), p. 272; Commissioners for Inquiring Concerning Charities, *Reports* (32 vols in 40, London, c. 1818–40), XXXII, part ii, p. 21.

64 HRO, AL17/1, 14 April 1619; PRO, C142/374/85, C115/M18/7524.

65 PRO, WARD5/16, 18 August 1619, WARD9/217, fol. 254v, WARD9/205, fol. 224v, WARD9/93, fol. 417.

66 BL, Add. MSS 11050, fol. 98, 11044, fol. 3r.

67 G. Markham, 'The Muster-Master', *Camden Miscellany XXVI* (Camden, 4th series, 14, 1975), p. 57.

68 R. C. Strong, *The Cult of Elizabeth: Elizabethan Portraiture and Chivalry* (London, 1977), pp. 209–11; Williams, 'Attack on the Council in the Marches', p. 15; BL, Egerton MS 2882, fols 20v, 52r, 78r, Add. MS 11050, fols 83, 87–8.

69 *Letters and Papers, Foreign and Domestic, of the Reign of King Henry VIII*, II, part 2, p. 1507.

70 K. Duncan-Jones, *Sir Philip Sidney: Courtier Poet* (London, 1991), p. 320; B. H. Newdigate, 'Mourners at Sir Philip Sidney's Funeral', *Notes and Queries*, 180 (January–June 1941), p. 398.

71 E. Spenser, *Faerie Queene*, ed. J. C. Smith (2 vols, Oxford, 1909), III.xi.14, IV.x.4, vols. I, p. 494, II, p. 122. Linda Galyon, in A. C. Hamilton, ed., *The Spenser Encyclopedia* (Toronto, Buffalo and London, 1990), pp. 634–5, thinks Sir Scudamore represents rather a special compliment to Sir John Scudamore, Sir James's father, but the figure of the chivalrous knight fits James better than it does his father.

72 Strong, *Cult of Elizabeth*, pp. 138, 156, 209–11; Collins, *Letters*, II, p. 28; J. Chamberlain, *Letters*, ed. N. E. McClure (2 vols, Memoirs of the American Philosophical Society, 12, 1939), I, p. 43.

73 Strong, *Cult of Elizabeth*, pp. 158–9. For orange as Essex's colour see: G. B. Harrison, *The Life and Death of Robert Devereux Earl of Essex* (London, 1937), p. 34; [P. V. Cayet], *Chronologie Novenaire, contenant l'Histoire de la Guerre, sous le Regne du ... Henri IIII* (3 vols, Paris, 1608), II, fols 464v–5r. I am grateful to Dr Paul Hammer for advice on this point.

74 Bodleian, MS Rawl. D.859, fol. 36r.

75 Society of Antiquaries, MS 790/7, William Higford's 'Institutions', p. 40; HRO, MS AL17/1, 10 June 1626.

76 W. Higford, *Institutions or Advice to his Grandson* (London, 1658); Higford, *Institution*. The printed version was abridged and published by Clement Barksdale: Bodleian, MS Tanner 41, fol. 182v. What appear to be other manuscript versions of William Higford's treatise were Phillipps MSS 11587, 13098, and 18412.

77 Martin, *Parliament of the Middle Temple*, II, pp. 677, 679, 696; S. D'Ewes, *Diary*, ed. E. Bourcier (Paris, [1974]), pp. 169–70. (Bourcier misidentifies D'Ewes's opponent, 'one Scidmor', as the first viscount.)

78 Bodleian, MS Rawl. D.859, fols 24v, 73v, 92r; PRO, SP84/142, fols 6v–7r.

79 A. B. Grosart, ed., *The Lismore Papers (first series)* (5 vols, privately printed, 1886), III, p. 90; PRO, E157/15, fol. 41v, SP16/318/21, SP78/100, fol. 256r.

80 E. Peacock, *The Army Lists of the Roundheads and Cavaliers* (2nd edition, London, 1874), p. 82; PRO, C115/M13/7267; BL, Harl. MS 476, fols 91v–2v.

81 See below, pp. 243–4.

82 PRO, PROB11/133/50, fol. 402r; B. D., 'The Armor of Sir James Scudamore', *Bulletin of the Metropolitan Museum of Art*, 8:6 (June 1913), pp. 118–23.

83 J. S. A. Adamson, 'Chivalry and Political Culture in Caroline England', in K. Sharpe and P. Lake, eds, *Culture and Politics in Early Stuart England* (Basingstoke, 1994), pp. 164–5; W. Segar, *Honor Military, and Ciuill* (London, 1602), especially p. 60.

84 Scudamore was a deputy lieutenant by 18 May 1622: BL, Add. MS 11050, fol. 104v.

85 FSL, Vb 2(24).

86 G. Markham, *The Souldiers Accidence, or An Introduction into Military Discipline* (London, 1625), pp. 37–46.

87 PRO, C115/N3/8537–8, C115/M13/7271; BL, Add. MS 11050, fols 176–7, 217–38r.

88 M. Whinney and O. Millar, *English Art 1625–1714* (Oxford, 1957), p. 79 n. 7; R. Ormond and M. Rogers, *Dictionary of British Portraiture* (4 vols, London, 1979–81), I, p. 123.

89 FSL, Vb 3(2); BL, Add. MS 45714, fol. 67v; for the fool see F. C. Morgan, ed., 'The Steward's Accounts of John, First Viscount Scudamore of Sligo (1601–1671) for the Year 1632', *Transactions of the Woolhope Naturalists' Field Club*, 33 (1949–51), pp. 164–6.

90 PRO, SP16/41, fol. 44; SP16/63/33, fol. 43r.

91 HMC, *Tenth Report, Appendix, Part iv. The Manuscripts of the Earl of Westmorland ... and Others* (London, 1885), pp. 367–8; E. Davies, *Military Directions, or The Art of Trayning* (London, 1618), sig. A2r; E. Davies, *The Art of War, and Englands Traynings* (London, 1619), 'To the Reader'.

92 W. Hunt, 'Civic Chivalry and the English Civil War', in A. Grafton and A. Blair, eds, *The Transmission of Culture in Early Modern Europe* (Philadelphia, 1990), pp. 213–18; A. Hughes, 'Politics, Society and Civil War in Warwickshire 1620–1650' (Liverpool University Ph.D. thesis, 1979), p. 116 n. 2.

93 Westminster Abbey Library, Lease Register 1662–66, fols 142B–143B. The Artillery Ground is shown on R. Morden and P. Lea, *A Prospect of London and Westminster* (London, 1682).

94 Hunt, 'Civic Chivalry', pp. 217, 219.

95 Adamson, 'Chivalry and Political Culture'; Hunt, 'Civic Chivalry', p. 218.

96 Williams, *Renewal and Reformation*, pp. 346–74.

97 PRO, C115/N3/8537–8; BL, Add. MS 11049, fols 16–17.

98 Hunt, 'Civic Chivalry', pp. 220–9; Adamson, 'Chivalry and Political Culture', pp. 166–9.

99 FSL, Vb 2(24).

100 See below, pp. 181, 189.

101 William Hunt, for example, thinks 'civic militarism' made 'civil war possible' and that 'the ideal of "citizen honour" ... played a significant role in the catastrophe of the Stuart monarchy': 'Civic Chivalry', pp. 231, 233.

102 [J. Reynolds], *Vox Coeli, or Newes from Heaven* ('Elisium', 1624), p. 53; S. Ward, *Woe to Drvnkards* (London, 1622).

103 Hunt, 'Civic Chivalry', pp. 223, 225; T. Adams, *The Sovldiers Honovr* (London, 1617), sig. B2, pp. 30–1.

104 R. Thompson, ed., *Samuel Pepys' Penny Merriments* (London, 1976), pp. 24–64; M. Spufford, *Small Books and Pleasant Histories: Popular Fiction and its Readership in Seventeenth-Century England* (London, 1981), p. 7.

105 FSL, Vb 2(24).

106 J. S. A. Adamson, 'The Baronial Context of the English Civil War', *TRHS*, 5th series, 40 (1990), pp. 93–120; Adamson, 'Chivalry and Political Culture'.

107 A. J. Fletcher, *Reform in the Provinces: The Government of Stuart England* (New Haven, 1986), p. 367.

108 Skidmore, *Thirty Generations*, p. 52; G. Anstruther, *The Seminary Priests* (4 vols, Ware, Ushaw and Great Wakering, 1969–77), I, pp. 304–5; Anstruther, *A Hundred Homeless Years*, pp. 24–7; PRO, SP14/61, fol. 39r.

109 T. Downes, *Mr. Downs's Letter to my Lord Scudamore* ([?Edinburgh, ?1716]), p. 61.

110 G. F. Townsend, *The Town and Borough of Leominster* (Leominster and London, 1863), p. 329; Huntington Library, H.A. Personal Box 15, no. 8, fol. 13 (a reference I owe to Dr Richard Cust); Heal and Holmes, *Gentry*, pp. 178–84, 190.

111 BL, Add. MS 11044, fols 244r, 253v–4r; R. P. Cust, 'Humanism and Magistracy in Early Stuart England' (unpublished paper); R. P. Cust and P. Lake, 'Sir Richard Grosvenor and the Rhetoric of Magistracy', *Bulletin of the Institute of Historical Research*, 54 (1981), pp. 48–50.

112 Beinecke Library, Osborn MS b.28, dedicatory epistle (composed between 1623 and 1628); PRO, C115/H25/5427, C115/M18/7514.

113 Higford, *Institution*, p. 70.

Chapter 3

The intellectual and religious world of Viscount Scudamore

To a late twentieth century audience, accustomed to the media representation of leading political figures, familiar with the manipulation of their
public images through 'spin doctors', cynical of the presentation of such
figures, and adept at seeking out the 'reality' behind the image, the idea of self-
fashioning in a politician, even in the seventeenth century, is not startling. But
the suggestion that a religious image could be fashioned and deployed is
perhaps more surprising, or if not, carries overtones of insincere (at least to a
British audience) American telly-evangelists, deluding their naïve public behind
a web of self-serving deceit and hypocrisy. Even if the idea can be swallowed
without its twentieth-century coating, the idea of self-fashioning in a religious
sphere throws into sharp relief a number of interesting questions about the
relationship between image and reality. Presentation is often considered an
ephemeral matter, a mask to be adopted or discarded at will, while religious
belief is a matter of deep-seated conviction, the very antithesis of image. If
religious belief was a matter of conviction, how could it be manipulated into
an image? If fashionable, how could it be anything more than a matter of
hypocrisy?

Such questions strike at the heart of the whole notion of self-fashioning, of
deploying cultural images and rhetorics to form an identity. At one level they
are unanswerable: can we ever be certain of the 'sincerity' of a political agent?
And in part such issues rest on a bogus dichotomy. Image and reality are not
two separate spheres, linked only by the guile and cunning deceit of the
scheming politician. An image is itself creative and limiting, opening up
certain avenues of action, closing off others. An image helps mould and
determine the very action or person it seeks to represent. Self-fashioning was
about moulding the person as well as the perception of that person in the
world. The question of image and reality rests on a distinction between the
two which is inherently untenable. It suggests that there is a reality hiding

behind and distinct from the image, a single 'self' known to the individual and which we as historians can uncover and know for ourselves too. Real life is, alas, far more complex.

A number of studies have show how religion was a key factor in public image and self-fashioning, and how a reputation as a 'pillar of religion' (as Sir Robert Harley was described) was important in the construction of an honest magistrate. Accounts of Sir Richard Grosvenor in Cheshire and Sir Robert Harley in Herefordshire have shown how important their reputations as *godly* magistrates were in gaining them honour and credit. Meanwhile, it has been suggested that one of the main determinants in deciding who was elected to parliament in the 1620s was the electorate's desire to choose MPs who could present the staunchest Protestant and the truest anti-popish credentials.[1] Such studies have concentrated on godly or puritan magistrates; much less attention has been focused on the image of gentlemen who were undoubtedly pious and upholders of religion but who assuredly were not puritans. Viscount Scudamore is just such a gentleman.

It is with Scudamore's learning, however, that we shall start, for it too had a place in the reputation of a gentleman and politician. Ever since King Solomon prayed for an understanding heart to judge the Israelites (I Kings 3:5–14), the virtues of wisdom and learning have been upheld as essential for the good magistrate. As Sir John Newdigate of Arbury in Warwickshire rhetorically asked about 1600, 'the judge which never readeth, the judge which never studieth, the judge which never openeth a booke ... how is it possible he executeth true justice?'[2] Scudamore was widely praised for his learning. Although the earl of Leicester, in a sustained campaign designed to discredit the viscount, castigated him as 'a formal Pedante ... a very simple Man', many more commended his erudition. In 1648 Samuel Hartlib described him as 'A great schollar' who was 'studying hard continually'; fifteen years later the Herefordshire clergyman, theologian, philosopher and horticulturalist John Beale called him 'a person learned and greate fautor of sound learning'.[3] Rowland Watkyns linked Scudamore's qualities of piety, learning and justice as a magistrate:

> Who knows his pious mind, or spirit; knows
> A sea of vertues, which nere ebbe, but flows.
> Justice, Religion, wisdom in his breast
> As in their center fixt, do safely rest.[4]

Scudamore's learning encompassed various fields. He was in contact with the antiquaries Sir Robert Cotton and Ralph Starkey. He indulged in a bit of manuscript collecting for himself – he was given 'Geffrey Chaucer in a faire auncient written hand' as a New Year's gift in 1626, which he promised to lend to Cotton – and, while he was ambassador, for William Laud.[5] Scudamore was a keen classical scholar who was said to have 'naturalized' the Latin tongue.[6] Another of the viscount's interests was mathematics, a passion he perhaps inherited from his grandfather. He patronised the mathematician John Newton, rector of Ross after the restoration, who in return praised him for understanding the importance of arithmetic and geometry. William Higford upheld Scudamore as 'in an extraordinary measure versed' in the 'rare faculty' of mathematics and accountancy.[7]

Divinity, of which he was a great reader, was the greatest of Scudamore's intellectual accomplishments. George Wall praised his 'affection to Divine knowledge' and 'good proficiencie in it'. His study was so intense that Laud had to warn him to 'Booke it not to much'; William Higford advised his grandson to ask the viscount, 'a great lover of learning and very learned', to guide his own study.[8] The viscount lent Henry Rogers, a Herefordshire minister, theological works in the early 1630s so that Rogers could complete a treatise on the visibility of the church, and he read a version of the book in draft. He recommended Jeremy Taylor's *Holy Living* and *Holy Dying* to his son, and he consulted Laud and Henry Hammond for his own reading. Hammond directed him to Augustine, Aquinas, Peter Lombard, Suarez and Grotius; clearly he was no beginner, and he had already purchased part of Aquinas's works.[9] When, in 1653, Jeremy Stephens wanted to thank Scudamore for his bounty to him, he could think of no better way than allowing Scudamore to have the pick of his theological papers.[10] In the early eighteenth century Matthew Gibson, Scudamore's first biographer, was astonished at the amount of theological notes among the first viscount's papers. These, however, have all but disappeared, leaving only Gibson's word that Scudamore

> applied himself very strictly to his Studies; marking every Day, how much he read, and making out at one time what he lacked at another ... How much he booked it, to my Admiration I have seen by his Remarks upon, and his Extracts out of so many Authors of all Sorts, that I cannot but think he must needs have taken old Pliny's Rule, Nihil legit, quod non excerperet [he read nothing without making extracts].

Such a picture fits what we already know of Scudamore from other sources; it fits, too, with what we know about early modern reading practices. We are indebted to Gibson for preserving this account of Scudamore's reading, but at Gibson's hands may well lie the reason why none of Scudamore's notes survives today. He discovered a letter from Hammond to the viscount, and noted that 'In the same bundel that I found this Letter, I have all the reason in the World to beleeve there had been several more of the same sort. But assoon as I touched them, they crumbled all to pieces in my hands'.[11]

In the later 1630s and early 1640s Lord Scudamore stood on the borders of that republic of letters which had gathered around Marin Mersenne; he was friendly with the philosophers Thomas Hobbes, Charles du Bosc and Hugo

Grotius. Later he would stand on the edge of the circles of Samuel Hartlib and the Royal Society (without ever being a member himself).[12] Hobbes and Scudamore probably met in Paris in 1635 or 1636, when Scudamore was ambassador and Hobbes was tutor to the earl of Devonshire, who was on an extended grand tour. Only one letter survives to testify to their friendship: from Hobbes in April 1641, excusing his sudden departure to France without first seeing the viscount.[13] Scudamore was friendly with the Norman philosopher and minister of the French crown Charles du Bosc, who acted as one of his contacts with the French court after 1638. Du Bosc was also a good friend of Hobbes, a key member of the Mersenne circle and an important link between English and French scientific and philosophic circles.[14] In Paris Scudamore met another of Mersenne's correspondents, Sir Kenelm Digby and, in Hartlib's phrase, grew 'very intimat' with him.[15]

A third philosophical friendship from his years in Paris was with the Dutch thinker Hugo Grotius, who was in France as the Swedish ambassador. A real friendship struck up between the two, within the limits of diplomatic protocol. They had extensive discussions about uniting the Scandinavian Lutheran churches with the church of England, one of Grotius's pet projects but an idea that did not appeal to Scudamore. Nonetheless, the viscount tried to arrange for Grotius's reception into the church of England. But for the English civil war Grotius could have become the most notable convert to the English church in the seventeenth century; it would have been a great propaganda coup for Laud and Scudamore. In 1638 Hugo Grotius's wife was godmother to the Scudamores' last child, the short-lived Charles, while one of the viscount's chaplains, Matthew Turner, also struck up a friendship with the Swedish ambassador.[16] We may presume that Scudamore did more than regale such philosophers with a glass of his famous cider, and that conversation turned to deeper matters than the latest gossip, but the details are lost. Frustrating as it is, all we have left is the superficial evidence of Scudamore's association with these thinkers, and we can do little more than point out the obvious differences of opinion between Scudamore and his learned friends.

Scudamore's interest in philosophy continued long after he had left Paris. In 1659 he asked William Ogstone, a Scots minister who was attacked and ejected by the Covenanters and who then took a Gloucestershire living and served as chaplain in the royalist army, to find a young man 'skilled in Philosophy and well approved for his lyfe and orthodox Religion' to be his chaplain and teach him philosophy. Peter Gunning had already refused the post, for which the viscount was offering £40 a year, preferring instead the same role in Sir Robert Shirley's household, which carried the better stipend of £100 a year. Ogstone suggested one John Fork, master of arts, of 'civill and religious Carriage' and 'well approved for his learning and skill of Philosophy, Latin and Greek toungs', versed in logic, ethics, physic and metaphysics too.

There is, though, no evidence of any John Fork ever taking such a position in Scudamore's household.[17]

In addition to furthering his own learning, Scudamore took a keen interest in the education of his children, even his daughter Mary. His unusual concern for a daughter's schooling drew the attention of Hartlib, who noted, 'Lord Scudamore seems to be bent for Andvancem[ent] of learning and a lover of education. For hee hath given his daughter to Dr. Coursel to teach her languages etc.' Her teacher was probably Pastor Etienne de Cursol, a former French monk who joined the church of England, was briefly pastor of the Franco-Dutch community on the Isle of Axholme, was entrusted by Laud and Neile with enforcing conformity to the church of England and, in the early 1640s, was pastor of a church that met in Sir Arthur Haselrig's house, having broken away from the French church in London.[18] Scudamore had employed French servants at Holme Lacy in the 1620s, was fluent in French himself, and after his embassy even his menial servants were reported to be able to speak French. Higford advised his grandson to learn French from Viscount Scudamore and his household. Nonetheless, Mary's education must surely have included more than French to excite Hartlib's attention, for daughters of the nobility habitually learnt French as an essential skill in polite society.[19]

More is known about the education of the viscount's son James, who accompanied his father to Paris. His governor there was Michael Branthwaite, who had been employed by Sir Henry Wotton as tutor, secretary and agent in Germany and Venice in the 1620s; Wotton praised his 'judgement and fidelity and erudition' highly.[20] When the viscount returned to England early in 1639 James, aged fourteen, remained in Paris at Beauvais College, in the care of Matthew Turner and Mons. Dupont. Lord Scudamore's letters to them are full of concern, even interfering meddling, for the minutiae of James's education, prescribing the choice of his tutor and dancing master, how he should avoid English company and go to the English embassy as infrequently as possible (but at least three times a year for communion), how he was to 'continue in classe till hee hath done Lucian' and study Greek and swordplay, what French grammar he was to use, even how his day was to be divided. Apart from the cost, Lord Scudamore was particularly concerned that his son should 'dwell in the vniversity' to be 'neare all exercisses of Learninge and conferrence with Learned men'.[21] From Paris James went at Christmas 1639 to St John's Oxford, Laud's old college, and took a room in the new Canterbury Quadrangle, recently built at the archbishop's expense. He matriculated in March 1640 and stayed until midsummer 1641. Even after he left he promised to follow his father's commands to study logic.[22] Lord Scudamore took a similar interest in the education of his grandson Jack (the second viscount), first at Westminster School, then at Christ Church Oxford.[23]

Viscount Scudamore saw the object of Jack's education as practical, to

'make you that are an Englishman fitt for employment'.[24] He was also concerned to apply his own learning to practical ends, especially in the field of
agricultural innovation. It was the first viscount who discovered, grafted and
developed the redstreak apple from a wilding, producing the best cider crab of
the seventeenth century. It was a hard apple, reddish-yellow to purple in
colour, late ripening, and astringent, even inedible as a fruit, but it made an
excellent drink. Unlike common or 'small' cider, which was gaseous, cloudy
and weak, and was reserved for the lower orders, Scudamore's redstreak cider
was clear, with a reddish-yellow tinge, flat and strong, a drink of distinction for
the discerning. Scudamore had elegant, tall and thin soda-glass flutes engraved
with both his arms and the royal arms, for such a drink; one survives in the
Museum of London. By the development of the redstreak, Scudamore was
credited by Beale in helping to turn 'an unreguarded Windy drinke fit only for
clownes, and day labourers', into a drink for kings, princes and lords. In the
tradition of Baconian science Scudamore tested various ways of improving his
cider, experimenting (but failing) with preserving cider in oil. Scudamore was
an exception to the rule that cider was not kept in cellars. Recognising that the
best way of keeping cider was in a cool and dark place with an even
temperature, such as a cellar under sand or spring water, he developed at
Holme Lacy 'rare contrived sellers in his park for the keeping of sider, with
springs of water running into them'. Holme Lacy also had, in 1632, its own
'sydar house' with a lockable door. Moreover, it was probably Scudamore who
introduced the technique of bottling the cider, rather than leaving it in barrels
like 'small cider', thereby stopping it clouding and further improving its
keeping qualities. Beale reckoned that Scudamore's cider was best kept a year
or two before drinking.[25]

Scudamore was by no means alone in attempting to improve Herefordshire cider. In the 1650s an annual competition was held in Hereford, judged
by Scudamore's friend Dr Roger Bosworth, to see who could produce the best
cider; Beale, for one, reckoned that Scudamore's cider was 'safely of the best
sort' and that top-quality cider came from only a few estates, including Holme
Lacy.[26] By the 1660s cider production at Holme Lacy was a large-scale
enterprise. A single tree at Holme Lacy, it was said, could produce 300 gallons
of cider a year; in addition, fruit was sometimes brought in from elsewhere.
Towards the end of 1667, for example, 253 bushels of redstreak apples were
bought in at a cost of £25 12s. to supplement those grown on the estate, and
ten boxes of cider weighing over 55 cwt were sent to London, the carriage alone
costing more than £16.[27]

Converts to redstreak cider could hardly praise it highly enough. Blind
tastings were held at which it was proclaimed to be as good as the finest of
French wines. Walter Chetwynd of Staffordshire, having ordered 720 bottles
of Herefordshire cider in 1689, invited his friends together over a bottle to

'compare cider with claret, as the Ancients did Homer with Virgil, and put it to the question ... [which] shall have the preheminence'. To the *cognoscenti* the bouquet and taste of redstreak cider were reminiscent of peaches and angelica root. In addition, it was believed to have important medicinal properties. Since cider was a 'cold' and 'wet' drink, it was thought good for 'hot' and 'dry' diseases like fevers and hot agues. As an aid to digestion Scudamore drank his cider mulled with sugar and ginger, and he supplied Sir Robert Harley the younger with bottles for his ailments.[28] The redstreak was ineluctably linked with Viscount Scudamore, and his fame spread with that of the apple, often called the 'Scudamore crab', and the cider, allegedly pronounced 'vin de Scudamore' by an Italian prince visiting Oxford. In addition, Scudamore's hospitality was famed for his custom of offering his guests a taste of his cider. Poems were written praising the redstreak. Principally through Scudamore's efforts, it was claimed, 'all Herefordshire is become, in a manner, but one intire Orchard'.[29]

Lord Scudamore's agricultural expertise was in great demand. Beale sought his help for schemes to propagate fruit trees and mulberries (the bushes could be used for sericulture, the fruit could be added to cider to make a punch). Scudamore was as liberal in sending out grafts and seeds to order as he was in giving tastings of his cider, and was reputed to have enough apple pips for an entire province. At one stage it was hoped that he would help in preparing Beale's notes for publication. Such was Lord Scudamore's fame as a patron of agricultural improvement that if his support for Beale's mulberry scheme could be procured, it was believed, 'His example would be leading to all Herefordshire and much further.'[30]

Scudamore's experimentation stretched beyond cider to other areas of agricultural improvement. Beale for example lauded him for 'always keeping able servants to promote the best expediences of all kinds of Agriculture'.[31] Tradition credits Scudamore with importing seven white-faced red cattle from the Low Countries, probably through the agency of members of the Hereford family, merchants at Dunkirk and relatives of Scudamore's estate steward in the 1660s, John Hereford. Whether or not these were the ancestors of the famous white-faced Hereford cattle, Scudamore was consciously trying to improve the local breed (perhaps extending various techniques employed at Holme Lacy for three generations in the breeding of horses).[32] Finally, Scudamore was probably one of the first to take up Rowland Vaughan's innovations in the floating of meadows, digging networks of trenches and sluices to flood grassland in a controlled manner, so providing better grazing for cattle and sheep. In Mayling Stubbs's recent verdict, Scudamore 'was a paragon among improving landlords'.[33]

Scudamore's agricultural interests may, however, have sprung from a deeper concern than improving yields. In the early and mid seventeenth century many feared a serious timber shortage. One possible solution advocated by some was the planting of fruit trees which, it was hoped, would have a triple benefit. The wood could be used for fuel and joinery, the cider and perry from apples and pears would mean less beer was consumed, so saving the wood and grain used in brewing, and the fruit would be a good source of income for the poor.[34] Whether this was Scudamore's intention or not, it was in this context, of concern for timber, for agriculture and for the poor, that his work was praised by Beale: Scudamore was one of the 'admirable Contrivers for the publick good' and 'a great preserver of Woods against the Day of England's need'. Beale devoted much of his life to the promotion of cider and orchards. He was a friend of Hartlib, Boyle and Evelyn and had connections with many of the Herefordshire gentry, particularly the Pyes and the Scudamores, having grown up in the house of the viscount's cousin William Scudamore of Ballingham. Beale's father Thomas may have helped Scudamore in his apple growing before the civil war.[35] Beale was Scudamore's main link first with the Hartlib circle and then with the Royal Society, relaying details of Scudamore's developments and experiments in cider production to Hartlib and others. His other link with the Royal Society was through his godson John Hoskins (1634–1705), who was to be its president in 1682–83, long after the first viscount's death.[36] Scudamore was in many ways just the sort of man envisaged by Bacon, Beale and Hartlib, possessing a wide knowledge, from theology to husbandry, mathematics to philosophy and languages, put to practical use, whether it be agricultural improvement or church restoration. He accorded well with Robert Boyle's desire to see an active nobility, actually gardening, actually experimenting, not for money but to avoid idleness and to engage with nature.[37] Scudamore, however, lay on the outer edges of the circles of Hartlib and the Royal Society, connected with them by ties of friendship and acquaintance, rather than being a wholehearted follower of their ideals. The traffic was probably one-way, and the ideas of the Hartlibians and Royal Society may not have been communicated back to Scudamore. Beale's cherished plans for fruit trees and mulberry bushes, in which he tried to involve Scudamore and others, for example, never came to fruition.

There is a further possibility for the springs of Scudamore's interest in cider and cattle, one that links them with his piety. Seventeenth-century English horticulturalists rediscovered the figures of God and Christ the gardeners, and practical husbandry was intimately linked with the spiritual contemplation of the divine. Ralph Austen stressed both the spiritual and the temporal benefits of planting fruit trees, remarking that the similitudes between fruit trees and the garden of Eden, the church, and the Messiah, meant that orchards 'doe truely (though without an articulate voyce) Preach the Attributes and perfections of God to us'. This belief that the divine could be approached through the investigation and appreciation of the natural world, axiomatic among Hartlibians, was by no means confined to them.[38] John Sommerville has argued that early modern England saw a decisive turn from immanence to transcendence, but the examples of divines and poets like George Herbert, Henry Vaughan and Thomas Traherne suggest otherwise.[39] Such men shared a sense of the physical world and the English landscape as manifestations of God.[40] As we shall see, Scudamore's religious practices were sacramental, focusing on physical objects, in contrast to the religion of many Protestants that focused on the word and was less concerned with, or even rejected, the material as a means to God. He stood within the trend of men like Andrewes and Laud, concerned for the beauty of holiness (the right use of material objects and the physical world to glorify God), and its obverse, or flip side, sacrilege (the wrong use of physical things). Within these contexts, esteeming the countryside 'becaus it is the Theatre of GODs Righteous Kingdom', in Traherne's phrase, and contemplating the church's fabric, as in Herbert's *The Temple*, Scudamore's interest in cider apples, in cattle, in husbandry in general, and in church restoration, may perhaps be tentatively placed, as means of seeking and contemplating God within the natural and physical world.[41] Scudamore's three great passions, God, cider and cattle, would then form a neat trinity. It is to God, and to divinity more generally, that we must now turn.

The loss of Scudamore's theological notes means that it is no longer possible to construct a complete system of divinity for the viscount, if he had ever worked out a comprehensive theological position. Perhaps, like his friend William Laud, he preferred to leave off the deeper points of divinity. In the absence of what Scudamore wrote, we must concentrate on what he did, and the best manifestations of his piety and divinity are the churches he rebuilt and restored, principally Abbey Dore. The loss of Scudamore's once voluminous theological papers is not, however, limiting; paradoxically, had they survived, they might have proved distracting, for the essence of the Laudian project was on getting externals right, both as a sign of the rightness of inward devotion, and as a means of structuring the religion of the heart. Laud himself stressed the importance of the visible signs of a true inward piety – 'the Externall worship of God in his Church is the Great Witnesse to the World, that Our heart stands right in that Service of God' – and he described ceremonial and practice as 'the Hedge that fence the Substance of Religion from all the Indignities, which Prophanenesse and Sacriledge too Commonly put upon it'.[42] The approach adopted in the study of the viscount's religious views will echo that followed by Peter Lake and Sears McGee in concentrating on outward worship and external practice,[43] rather than on soteriology and doctrines of grace. The argument that there was a distinct 'Laudian style', of which Scudamore was a leading lay exponent, is, I think, more fruitful than discussions of predestination which have recently sidetracked the historio-graphical debate.[44] At no point is such an approach intended to deny, however, that there was a distinctly different theological element to the Laudian program-me, as a number of writers have recently, and misguidedly, attempted to do.[45]

Viewed from the perspective of his actions, and in the context of a Laudian style, Scudamore's piety appears to have been built around two main pillars: the special or sacred nature of the church and all things dedicated to it, including the clergy; and the importance of the sacraments, especially the eucharist, in his devotions. He appears as a ritualist with a well developed sense of the sacrilegious. Central to the Laudian programme was an attempt to reposition the boundary between the sacred and the profane. The border guard policing this redrawn boundary was the concept of sacrilege, which Laudians placed at the centre of their religious concerns.[46]

The Scudamores acquired the site of the former Cistercian abbey of Dore in 1540, and the rectory of the church later in the sixteenth century. By the early seventeenth century the abbey lay in ruins and the curate, John Gyles, was forced to read services from the shelter of an arch to protect his prayer book from the rain.[47] Between 1632 and 1635 Lord Scudamore rescued what he could of the old abbey, creating the parish church from the ruins of the crossing and choir, and adding a new roof, south porch, tower, belfry, a new bell, and a churchyard wall. The church was also fitted out inside, with an altar, new woodwork (rails, screen, pulpit, reading desk and pews) and stained glass. The total cost was over £425.[48]

In his will Sir John Scudamore (1542–1623) left half the profits of the impropriate rectory of Dore for ten years to repair Dore church,[49] but what was probably a more important motivation to his grandson was the Laudian campaign to repair churches, of which the soliciting of contributions for the repair of St Paul's Cathedral (which the viscount wholeheartedly supported) was only a part.[50] Viscount Scudamore's repair of Dore came just at the same time as Charles and Laud were restoring St Paul's, while his speech on the necessity of repairing churches commending the repair of St Paul's in 1633 applied equally to his work at Dore.[51] Scudamore clearly felt that it was his duty to God to repair churches and dedicate them to God's service. At the consecration of Dore church in March 1635, Scudamore expressed the hope that by the repair and reconsecration 'Gods Holy and euer blessed name maye herein be Honoured and calld vppon', and that 'God may be glorified in the service and ministration' of the priest. The ruins of the abbey had been 'altogeither prophaned and applied to secular and base vses', which 'did much redound to the dishonor of Almightie God and the contempt of his holy worshipp'; the consecration symbolically re-enacted God's decree whereby the church was 'severed from all former prophane and common vses'.[52] By the rebuilding and reconsecration, Scudamore was restoring the proper boundary between the sacred and the profane, and so preventing sacrilege. Walter Stonehouse, writing in 1636, thought that failure either to repair, or to beautify churches was a form of church robbery and so sacrilegious.[53]

Scudamore's restoration of Dore is the outstanding example of his religious views, showing a joint concern to avoid sacrilege and to worship the Lord in the beauty of holiness (Psalm 96:9). The altar was the centrepiece of the church. It was the original marble altar of the Cistercian abbey, twelve feet long, four feet wide, and three inches thick, set on three stone pillars, which had been discovered during the rebuilding in profane use for the salting of meat and making of cheese, and which Scudamore, ever vigilant against the sin of sacrilege, ordered to be restored. A somewhat improbable story reached William Blundell in Lancashire of the terrible events surrounding the earlier misuse of the altar. One of Scudamore's servants who tried to carry it away was killed and another had his leg broken. It was used for pressing cheeses but they ran with blood, whereupon it was moved to the laundry, but all night long it emitted the din of laundry being battered against it. Only when it was returned to the church did it fall silent. In this unlikely story we can perhaps detect a distant echo of Scudamore's fears of committing sacrilege.[54]

Sanctity radiated from the altar and around it were created a series of hallowed spaces, declining in their intensity of holiness with distance from the altar. The altar rails marked off the first space. Under the altar Scudamore replaced some of the medieval green glazed tiles. Behind it, according to Gibson, was set a 'carved Altar-piece very suitable, and proper', which has unfortunately since disappeared. Carved altarpieces were very rare in the seventeenth century; if a reredos was set up it was usually a tapestry or the decalogue.[55] Above, in the east window, Scudamore had stained glass set at a cost of £100. The centre light depicts the ascension of Christ, with St John the Baptist and Moses above. In the side lights stand apostles and evangelists with inscriptions beneath.[56]

The next sanctified space was delimited by the chancel screen which separated the chancel (made from the crossing of the abbey church) from the nave. The oak screen itself was carved by John Abel of Herefordshire in a Renaissance style with Ionic columns. It carries three cartouches bearing coats of arms (those of Charles I in the centre, Scudamore to the north, and the see of Canterbury impaling Laud to the south) and, on its west face, the Latin inscription 'Live as acceptable to God, as dead to the world, as free from crime, as prepared to pass away'. East of the screen, in the chancel, stood only the minister's seat and reading desk; the pulpit and all the pews stood in the nave to the west of the screen (although they were moved into the chancel at the beginning of the twentieth century).[57] The chancel formed not only a separate communion room but a clerical space into which the laity were invited on the clergy's terms.

The nave formed the next space. Here stood font, pulpit and pews. On the walls were painted instructive texts including the Ten Commandments and the Lord's Prayer; the image of Time and the skeleton with the inscription 'Memento Mori' still to be seen in the church may also date from Scudamore's restoration.[58] By the way that Dore was furnished Scudamore stressed the higher nature of the eucharist, clergy and divine service of the common prayer, the latter especially in relation to the role of preaching reflected in the position of the pulpit. This was classic Laudianism. Laud stated that 'the touchstone of religion was not to hear the word preached, but to communicate'; others commented that the placing of the pulpit below the altar in churches symbolised that the word was merely a means of preparation to the sacrament, just as the texts painted on the walls at Dore could also be used in preparation for moving towards communion.[59] The final, and least hallowed, ground, was the churchyard, divided from the profane world outside by a stone wall.[60] The consecration was the symbolic act whereby the church was separated from the world and the order of hallowed spaces created. At divine service the whole Christian community was thus assembled and ordered in sacred time and sacred space, the living in their pews, the dead buried in church or churchyard, all arranged around the altar with the minister near by.

Dore was not the only one of Scudamore's churches to benefit from his edification. In the 1660s the floor of Holme Lacy church was paved, the roof ceiled, the chancel wainscotted; the churchyard, previously only railed, was walled; and new seats, pulpit and reading desk were installed.[61] Scudamore also contributed to the repairs of Hereford, Bristol and St Paul's Cathedrals.[62]

The fear of committing sacrilege was certainly one that frightened Scudamore. Warnings about the imminent punishment of sacrilege were not unique to Laudians (they even feature in handbooks for gentlemen), but the Laudians did pronounce them more shrilly than others, and they formed a Laudian parallel to the better known puritan examples of God's vengeance against sabbath breakers. Alongside warnings against those who withheld tithes was a developing concern that it was sacrilege to hold lands which had once belonged to the dissolved monasteries, for, as Edward Brouncker put it, 'whatsoever is once dedicated and freelie bestowed to a holie vse, can never, with out the guilt of sinne, bee taken a way or imployed to any other vse then what is holy'.[63] Thomas Bayly, in a sermon in Sussex in 1640, warned that those who held former abbey land were guilty of sacrilege and would not prosper; others warned that the sacrilegious would be punished by the extinction of their family line.[64] Scudamore was clearly concerned. Much of his estate was in impropriations and abbey lands, the legacy of his great-great-grandfather John Scudamore, who had used his position as receiver of the court of augmentations to enrich himself with monastic spoils. Moreover, Scudamore may have been worried about the extinction of the Scudamore line. On two recent occasions, in 1571 and 1623, the inheritance of the family's patrimony had, through premature death, skipped a generation, from grandfather to grandson; in addition, Scudamore's first three children all died in their first few weeks.[65] On top of all this, in 1626–27 Scudamore was facing a financial and political crisis: his local power was under threat and he was desperately short of money, having to sell land to pay his sister's marriage portion. Perhaps he feared all this was God's judgement on his sacrilege: his personal straits certainly seem to have produced a spiritual despair that worked some kind of conversion in him. He wrote to Laud in January 1627, asking whether he could keep his family's impropriations without sin or, if not, whether selling them but keeping the money himself would absolve him. Laud suggested that if tithes were due to the priest by divine law, then obviously Scudamore as a layman had no right to them or any profits arising from their sale; no act of parliament could dispense with this moral law of God.[66]

Probably at the same time Scudamore drew up a list of six questions concerning the lay receipt of tithes as they applied to his own estates, wanting to know whether he, as a layman, could receive impropriate tithes; whether he should enjoy the lands of Holme Lacy which had formerly belonged to a company of clerics, or lands in Sellack which were given for alms; whether he had any right to the lands of the dissolved monastery of Dore, since they had originally been given to the church; and whether it was right for him to exploit section seventeen of the act for the dissolution of the monasteries, 31 Hen. VIII c. 13, which had freed all former monastic land from the payment of tithes. In the midst of his crisis he was in two minds about what to do. He pointed to a passage in Hooker arguing that there might be cases in which it was legitimate for lay persons to hold church property, but admitting that under colour of this the church had been robbed. On the other hand he also noted down the possibility that by the act of donation to the church the lands 'remaine the proper possession of God till the worlds end, unless himself renonce or relinquish it'. Through his own reading, and under Laud's gentle prompting, Scudamore soon answered all six questions to his own satisfaction. Church land seized at the reformation could be kept in lay hands, but it had to be subject to the payment of tithes; tithes themselves could not be owned by the laity, but those tithes, 'the inheritance being in a Bishop', could be leased from the church.[67] Scudamore's may not have been the most radical or far-reaching solution, but few were more zealous in returning impropriations or paying tithes than he. Perhaps the timorous viscount really believed that like Jehoram he too would suffer divine evisceration if he did not pay his tithes.[68] Soon Scudamore was held up by others as a glorious example against the sacrilegious, 'a Worthy Copy for others to write after'. George Wall senior claimed that the viscount made a 'publicke protestation' that he 'would not hold a foote of that land, nor retaine that to ... [him]selfe, which should not pay Tithes to the Minister'.[69]

Scudamore threw himself into the divine duty of paying and restoring tithes with all the zeal of a new convert. He began to act under the authority of a licence of mortmain obtained in 1631, but it was a task not completed until the 1660s. He helped John Newton, the minister at Ross, to bring in the tithes of Ross, Brampton Abbotts and Weston-under-Penyard.[70] He had inherited two-thirds of the impropriated tithes of Holme Lacy; these he returned in October 1632. To Holme Lacy he annexed the parochial chapel of Bolstone in 1634, where the minister previously had no income but what he could get by illegally marrying couples who had no licence. The manor of Temple Court or Upledon, previously exempt, was charged with the payment of tithes (about £10 annually) to the vicar of Bosbury, at that time the same George Wall who praised the viscount's munificence to the church. This was a considerable augmentation when the tithes previously amounted to only £12 a year. As well as rebuilding the church at Dore, he endowed it with the manor house and lands, the impropriate rectory and all the tithes from the hitherto exempt site and demesne of the abbey. He endowed the church of Bredwardine with the tithes of Robert's Meadow and the church of Little Birch with those of Ayleston's Wood, previously exempt as formerly held by the nunnery of Aconbury.[71] He also held the site of Llanthony Priory, near Gloucester, likewise exempt from tithes. On these lands too he levied tithes and annexed them to Hempsted. The glebe, advowson and impropriated tithes of Hempsted he bought from Henry Powle for £376 in January 1662 and returned to the church, saving only the advowson for himself. For many years the impoverished church of Hempsted had been supplied only by a poorly paid curate; Scudamore installed George Wall junior as the first rector there. Scudamore had transformed the annual value of the living from £9 10s. to £80.[72] In order to remove any doubts about the validity of these endowments, and to settle them on the church for ever, in 1662 Scudamore had an act passed confirming them, 'An Act for the Endowment of several Churches by the Lord Viscount Scudamore of Sligo in the Realm of Ireland', 13 & 14 Car. II c. 12.[73]

Making amends for what his ancestors had seized from the church was not enough; Scudamore was interested in other aspects of sacrilege. 'Sacrilege of time', particularly by profaning the sabbath, was a common topic in works on sacrilege. Scudamore was especially concerned by one example of the separation of sacred and profane in temporal terms – the hallowing of the time of Lent. He was particularly diligent in securing licences to eat flesh in Lent on account of his sickness and infirmities. That he was motivated by more than the fear of being caught by the renewed drive to enforce such licences in the 1630s is suggested by his concern with the issue in 1620, 1632, 1633, 1641, 1642, 1643, 1650 and 1661. Laud regretted the general neglect of fasting in Lent.[74] Moreover, in order to ensure a strict separation between sacred and profane time, Scudamore was insistent that his son, while continuing his education in France, should rest only on 'those Holly dayes which our church appoints to bee kept Holly'. There is no suggestion that Scudamore was a strict sabbatarian, but it is instructive, nonetheless, that, for all Laud's concern for Scudamore's reading, we know of only one book that he gave Scudamore: 'Bryerwoods Saboths', which he sent the viscount in 1632, either *A Learned Treatise of the Sabbath* (Oxford, 1631) or *A Second Treatise of the Sabbath* (Oxford, 1632), both by Edward Brerewood. Unfortunately, there is no indication of what either Laud or Scudamore thought of the book. John Gregory, whom Scudamore presented as rector of Hempsted, wrote a *Discourse of the Morality of the Sabbath* suggesting a shared interest with Scudamore in the problem of sacrilege, and drawing a parallel between his patron's rescue of revenues dedicated to God's worship and his own attempted rescue of the seventh day similarly dedicated to God's worship.[75]

Scudamore was a wholehearted supporter of the clerical estate. In 1624 he claimed that both he and Sir Robert Harley had a continual 'care to mainteyne the reuerence and dignity of the Ministry'. At a surface level such an identification was accurate: Harley wanted to augment clerical stipends and, in the 1630s, was thought by the bishop of Hereford to be one of the few gentlemen in the county likely to take the church's side in a dispute; he was not opposed to episcopacy until about 1641.[76] At a deeper level, however, Scudamore's attitude to the ministry differed greatly from Harley's. As Andrew Foster and Peter Lake have made plain, the claims and pretensions of the Laudian clergy had a theological basis rooted in their sacrament-centred world view and their attempt to redefine the sacred and the profane.[77] Many divines were at pains to point out that the sin of sacrilege included not only despoiling the church and withholding tithes, but also failure to respect the clergy. In the words of Gryffith Williams, 'it is sacrilege any waies to abuse Gods Ministers ... not only those men which spoile Churches and rob God himselfe, but those also which scorne and deride the Ministers and Preachers of Gods Word, are to be deemed sacrilegious persons'. Sacrilege was a public sin against the whole body of religion, far worse than idolatry or murder, opening the way to atheism and all corruptions.[78]

Scudamore's concern for the clergy extended to their housing. He gave Dore manor house to the rector as a parsonage house, and when that proved unsuitable (it was frequently flooded) he had it pulled down and rebuilt. He also had the parsonages of Holme Lacy and Hempsted rebuilt in stone at his expense.[79] In addition, he was careful to protect the rights of his clergy and see them set apart from the laity. At the consecration of Dore he charged the parishioners never to burden the rectory 'with any charges, payements, contributions, or duties whatsoeuer, otherwise then according to the Lawes Ecclesiasticall of this Kingdome'. His assertion of ecclesiastical over temporal law is noteworthy; the 1601 poor law act had specifically stated the liability of rectors, vicars and impropriators to payment of the poor rate. Moreover, where he often took his cue from Laud, here he exceeded what the archbishop dared: at his trial Laud denied the charge that he had intended to make clergy free of all local rates.[80] At the Restoration Scudamore's charge caused a complete breakdown of relations between the rector of Dore, James Bernard and his parishioners. Scudamore's intervention in this dispute clearly showed his favouritism for the clergy above the laity. The problem had begun somewhat farcically with the restoration of prayer book services at Dore about 1658. Bernard was so short that he could not be heard clearly above the top of the reading desk, but he refused to stand on the stool used by his equally short predecessors. For two years Scudamore, through his steward William Vaughan, forced the parishioners to bear this and keep silent. When the underlying cause of the animosity, Bernard's refusal to pay the poor relief, finally surfaced, Scudamore sought legal and ecclesiastical advice. Sir Geoffrey Palmer, the attorney general, and Sir William Turner, DCL, both advised that the parishioners were not bound in law to free their parson from levies such as the poor relief which were directed by act of parliament to be paid by all people according to the value of their estate. Contrary advice was given by Bishops Wren of Ely and Croft of Hereford, who believed that the parishioners were bound in conscience to keep the promise made on their behalf thirty years earlier. Scudamore showed where his sympathies lay by accepting the advice of the two bishops. He directed the parishioners to 'forbeare to charge' their rector, who in return had merely to thank them 'and take it kindly'.[81]

Still Scudamore's interest in sacrilege was unsated. He discussed the sacrilege of others with Jeremy Stephens, sending Stephens a comment he had heard Cardinal Richelieu make on England's troubles with the Scots, 'that now the time has come that our kingdome should suffer for their sacrilege'. He wanted to prevent other lay persons from holding tithes. Some of the parishes encompassing Llanthony land were impropriate in lay hands; he wanted to ensure that the lay impropriator was 'debarred, from the right of those Tythes', which should only be 'payable to him, that celebrateth diuine offices'.[82] The fear of sacrilege continued to haunt Scudamore, all the way to his grave. By his will he left £20 to the vicar of Holme Lacy 'for my Tythes forgotten'.[83]

Both Wall and Gibson praised the strict account Scudamore kept of his tithes, ensuring none of his lands were exempt and that not a penny went unpaid.[84] Before his act of 1662 Llanthony was extra-parochial and Hempsted, the nearest living, unsupplied. Scudamore, therefore, charged himself with the tithes, reckoned at £64 a year, and kept an account of the arrears in the hope that one day he could apply them to the church. By 1652 he had accumulated £1,200. This he started to use as a fund for helping orthodox clergy, some sequestered, some beneficed, during the 1650s. By 1662, when the tithes of Llanthony were settled on Hempsted by act of parliament, over £1,650 had been dispensed to more than eighty clergy. Of these I have been able to identify over fifty.[85] Most received a single payment, usually £5 or £10, but a few received a regular pension, such as Morgan Godwin, son of Bishop Francis Godwin of Hereford and archdeacon of Salop, who fell 'into great want and mysery' and had £20 a year from Scudamore from 1652 until his death in 1657, or Walter Carwardine, a former vicar choral of Hereford, who received £6 in 1653 and 1656, and £4 in 1654 and 1655.[86] More than half of Scudamore's identifiable beneficiaries were local men from Herefordshire or the neighbouring counties, or men closely linked with the viscount: patronage after all had usually been distributed locally since the Middle Ages.[87] Perhaps his favourite priest was Matthew Turner. Turner had been linked with the Scudamores since 1630 or even earlier; the viscount presented him to Dore in 1635, took him to Paris, where he had charge of the education of the viscount's son James, gave him a small pension from 1653 to 1655 and employed him at Holme Lacy as vicar in the 1650s.[88] Another local man aided by the viscount was John Taylor, sequestered from Upton Bishop and Moccas; according to John Walker he would have perished in the 1650s but for the viscount's regular pension. Scudamore 'tooke so great a likeing' to Taylor that after the Restoration he entertained him as his domestic chaplain, willing him £10.[89] Twelve of the beneficiaries were Hereford Cathedral clergy. Scudamore had close and long-established links with the cathedral of Hereford: like his great-great-grandfather, grandfather and father before, and his grandson after him, he was chief steward of the dean and chapter.[90] The college of vicars choral of Hereford Cathedral considered him an 'Honorable friend to this place', and he contributed to the repair of their roof.[91] His kindness also benefited the dean and chapter, for as well as contributing liberally to their repairs he kept their act book safe and hidden from the sacrilegious hands that seized all their other records during the years of turmoil; he returned the act book in 1660.[92] Much, then, of the viscount's munificence was an example of charity beginning at Holme.

The other half of those ministers identified spanned the country from Cheshire to Kent and Devon. Some are obscure figures, such as Richard Leak, vicar of Ampleforth, but many others were well known figures connected to Charles I, Laud or other members of the episcopal bench, or men castigated by their opponents as theological and ceremonial innovators, such as Edward Boughen (who received £10 in 1652), Bishop John Bramhall (£10 in May 1659), Richard Dukeson (£10 in 1656), William Fuller (£10 in 1656) and Richard Sterne (£20 a year, 1652–56).[93] The greatest beneficiary was Matthew Wren, who received at least £220 as he lay in the Tower, far more than anyone else. Possibly Scudamore's friendship with one of the most hated men in England, 'little Pope Regulus', stretched back to Wren's short episcopate in

Hereford, 1634–35. In his will Wren described Scudamore as 'my truely noble friend and ancient patron', directing that, should his theological notes be published by his executors, Scudamore and four others, all bishops (Gilbert Sheldon, Humphrey Henchman, John Cosin and Sterne), 'worthy friends [in] ... very good esteeme for their worth', were to receive special presentation copies.[94] Scudamore does seem to have sought out such Laudian clerics, but he also poured out his bounty on many clergy not associated with the changes of the 1630s and even on one opponent of the Laudian regime. Thomas Warmestry had publicly attacked images, the 1640 canons and the etcetera oath; he received £5 in 1658, possibly because he was then lecturer at St Margaret's Westminster, where Scudamore worshipped when he was in London.[95]

The money given to local clergy in Herefordshire was usually distributed at Scudamore's direction by his trusted servant John Crumpe, but in most cases beyond the southern marches we do not know how Scudamore distributed the money, or how deserving cases came to his attention. The viscount's charity could, however, respond quickly to an immediate need: Mr Roch, 'a countrey minister lying sick', was sent £2 on 6 April 1655.[96] One way that distressed divines could have come to Scudamore's attention was by means of public appeals, which were not unknown in the 1640s and 1650s. One likely example was the petition, probably from 1643, of sequestered ministers imprisoned in London, who appealed for money to be sent to a named lawyer of Holborn, London. Of the eight signatories, certainly four and possibly six received money from Scudamore over a decade later, suggesting that the viscount had a long memory. Another example was the appeal circulated in 1655 on behalf of Charles I's former domestic servants; of the twenty-four clergymen who signed the petition testifying to the sad condition of the appellants, three were soon to be beneficiaries of Scudamore's bounty. A counter-example, however, is supplied by Charles I's appeal to the London clergy in November 1648 on behalf of Bishop Robert Maxwell of Kilmore; a copy of Charles's entreaty exists among Scudamore's papers, but there is no evidence that the Irish bishop received anything from the viscount.[97]

Another means that Scudamore used was to distribute his money via other ejected clergy. Four men are known to have acted as his almoners in this way: Jeremy Stephens, Timothy Thurscrosse, George Benson the younger and Henry Hammond. Stephens (1591–1665) had been Sir Henry Spelman's coadjutor in work on sacrilege, a subject on which he corresponded with Scudamore, and had been ejected from his Northamptonshire livings by 1645. He was a recipient of Scudamore's bounty himself, as well as occasionally distributing it to others. Thurscrosse (died 1671), formerly prebendary of York Minster, and also archdeacon of Cleveland until he resigned in 1638, troubled that he had obtained preferment through simony, was one of those Anglican clergy who conducted clandestine prayer book services in Interregnum

London. In 1655 he received £10 from Scudamore for himself; in 1658 he distributed twelve sums, each of £5, from Scudamore.[98] Benson (c. 1613–93), the son of a canon of Hereford, had been a ejected from his Shropshire living; his father-in-law was Samuel Fell, dean of Christ Church Oxford, who was also known to Scudamore.[99] Hammond was a link between ejected divines and operated a kind of clerical employment agency, seeking patronage for the orthodox. He tried to encourage well-affected gentry to support pious and learned youths at university, 'upon the sober principles and old establishment of the Anglican Church' in the words of his biographer John Fell (son of Scudamore's acquaintance Samuel Fell); Scudamore sent Hammond at least £100 via Benson.[100]

Scudamore's scheme was but one among many to relieve distressed divines, but his charity was on a far wider and more organised scale than all the others, bar one. Only Bishop John Warner of Rochester exceeded him, giving £8,000 to distressed divines.[101] Despite Robert Bosher's argument that such charity should be placed within the context of a 'clear cut policy' which 'prepared the way for the Laudian triumph in the future settlement', the element of party in Scudamore's bounty can easily be overdrawn. The key point in determining his beneficiaries was that all (bar one) were Anglicans who, whether they officiated in the 1650s or not, also served the episcopal church of England before 1642 or after 1660.[102] Though many were beneficed during the later 1640s and 1650s only one is known to have actively supported the parliamentary or Interregnum regimes and that one, George Durant, a county committeeman in Worcestershire, was suspected of royalism.[103] Perhaps the most illustrative case is John Tombes, vicar of Leominster, who was supported by Scudamore in the 1630s but received nothing from him in the 1650s. In 1641 Tombes had thanked the viscount for a 'noble favour by which your Honour hath beene pleased to cheare me in this very great, and very poore Cure'; presumably Scudamore had augmented Tombes's living out of the impropriate tithes of Leominster, which he leased from the bishop of Hereford. In the 1640s and 1650s, however, Scudamore gave Tombes nothing, and the committee for plundered ministers had to order an augmentation of his living out of Scudamore's sequestered estate. The key is that Tombes, in the 1630s a conforming minister with a gift for preaching, became after 1640 an increasingly radical Baptist and an opponent of episcopacy who refused to observe the established rites and ceremonies of the pre-civil war church.[104]

Analysis of the nine clergymen whom Scudamore employed – seven ministers presented to the four livings in his gift (Holme Lacy, Brobury and Dore in Herefordshire and Hempsted in Gloucestershire) and a further two who served as his chaplains without further preferment from the viscount – reveals a similar pattern. Apart from Thomas Lockey, appointed by Scudamore on Laud's recommendation as one of his three chaplains during his embassy in

Paris, none was a major figure or had any known links with the archbishop or other Laudian figures. They were predominantly local, and obscure, figures.[105] Some, however, must have shared the viscount's ceremonial passions: it would have been difficult for Thomas Lockey, Thomas Manfeild and Matthew Turner to have conducted the services in Scudamore's embassy chapel, kitted out, as it was, with full Laudian trappings, if they were opposed to the pro-gramme of the beauty of holiness. Manfeild and Turner presumably also carried out their ministry in Herefordshire, at Holme Lacy and Dore, in enthusiastic Laudian style, but since they provoked no adverse comment no hard evidence has survived.[106]

A further link between many of these clergymen was that they were learned. We have already seen how Scudamore attempted to appoint a household chaplain in the 1650s who would teach him philosophy, and Scudamore seems to have preferred a learned clergy, especially one skilled in classical learning. Lockey was reckoned the best classicist in Oxford and became Bodley's librarian at the Restoration.[107] Turner wrote all his sermons in Greek and was a skilled Hebraist.[108] It was said of John Gregory, whom Scudamore presented to Hempsted in 1669, that he 'became famous in Greek by reading all Authors prose and verse, occasioned by his being overdone once by an Antagonist in Greek'. Gregory was an accomplished linguist who knew Latin, Greek, Hebrew, Italian, Anglo-Saxon and Arabic, and who boasted that 'no man loves those Holy Fathers of the Church more than my self (they being part of the greatest pleasure of my life)'.[109]

If it is not possible to argue that Scudamore appointed only Laudians to his livings, his Laudianism had an important 'negative' influence on his patronage. In presenting ministers he shared none of the puritan concern for a preaching ministry; in this he was the exact opposite of his cousin and neighbour Sir Robert Harley, and was unswayed by the claims that Herefordshire was destitute of preaching.[110] Despite even Laud's opposition to pluralism, he presented non-preaching, pluralist, non-resident and absentee ministers. Turner was already rector of Dinedor when he was presented to Dore in 1635, and he would stay in Dore only on Saturday and Sunday nights once a fortnight. Later that same year he went to Paris while still holding these two benefices.[111]

Few people can have been as zealous as Lord Scudamore in avoiding the sin of sacrilege, whether in rebuilding and endowing churches, returning tithes or supporting the clergy. White Kennett claimed that in total Scudamore spent £50,000 on church and clergy, but that is the wild exaggeration of a later age determined on eulogising the viscount. On another occasion he gave a more restrained estimate that Scudamore's bounty 'amounted at a moderate com-putation to at least £10000', a figure that agrees with Gibson's appraisal that the viscount spent £4,200 on charity, gifts and building, and returned to the church lands worth £350 a year (which at fifteen years' purchase would have been valued at £5,250). Even these lower, and more realistic judgements represent a sizeable sum.[112] George Wall preached that a treble honour was due to the minister: obedience to his doctrine; reverence to his person; maintenance for his life. Viscount Scudamore paid that honour to the full. It was no surprise that Wall dedicated his sermon, a plea for the rights of the clergy, to Scudamore. He told the viscount that he was 'a true Nehemiah' who had not only shown munificence to the church in re-edifying Dore and 'reconsecrating what had beene long neglected and prophaned' but had also 'strengthened the weake hands of the spirituall builders', the clergy of the church of England.[113]

The other principal pillar of Scudamore's faith was the decent and reverent celebration of divine service, and especially the eucharist, according to the rites of the church of England. Rather than receiving the minimum three times a year enjoined in the book of common prayer, by the late 1650s he tried to receive communion monthly, following the exhortations of divines such as Hammond, Andrewes and Cosin for more frequent communion. Scudamore's parishioners and household servants did not, however, share the viscount's zeal for the eucharist, and he had difficulty finding at least two other communicants. The benefits of frequent communion were not confined to the receiving of the consecrated elements. Central to the practice was the great preparation that Christians were to make beforehand, examining themselves to ensure that they were worthy to receive. Scudamore took such advice very seriously, for had not St Paul warned that anyone who received unworthily ate and drank damnation to himself (I Corinthians 11:29)? Many seventeenth-century divines stressed the importance of proper preparation for the eucharist.[114] Scudamore fretted over his own 'sinns of frailty' – 'Vagatis mentis, drowsines, infervencie, in prayer' – and the consequences of receiving whilst still so suffering. Communion was to be taken only in the right state of mind: he was concerned that 'for a scruple of Conscience' he should decline that sacrament even at Easter, even though he was not convinced that what his conscience stumbled at was indeed a sin.[115]

Exhortations to frequent communion and warnings about the proper preparation for it led to a rediscovered stress on auricular confession. The book of common prayer held the congregation's general confession to be sufficient, but urged private confession in the visitation of the sick, and to those who could not quiet their own conscience. Beyond this the issue of auricular confession was generally ignored, or denounced as pure popery. In the early seventeenth century, however, sacramentalists such as Richard Mountagu, John Cosin, Herbert Thorndike and Scudamore's friend Matthew Wren began to encourage its resumption (usually only on an individual basis) while continuing to condemn the Roman church for enforcing it as absolutely necessary. Scudamore, worried about his unworthiness to receive the eucharist, was one of those few of the laity to confess their sins privately; perhaps this was one of the reasons he appointed his own domestic chaplain. In addition he urged its restoration on others: in the service of consecration of Dore auricular confession and spiritual guidance are mentioned along with other more conventional items such as communion, baptism, marriage and catechising as the uses of the newly repaired church. Scudamore, though, seems to have gone further than many who advocated the restoration of auricular confession for mortal sins only. He wondered whether he was bound to confess privately even venial and dimly remembered sins (which Cosin, for example, believed need not trouble the conscience of Christians). The viscount's belief in the benefits of communion, and his sense of his own failings, led him straight into the arms of the clergy as his spiritual guides.[116]

In addition to tying communion to its proper preparation, there was a tendency for divines to couple receiving with liberality and charity, not only at the offertory, but as a pledge of the leaving of all sins. Scudamore was remembered for his many acts of charity: his nephew recalled that the viscount 'alwaies had his purse open to the poore; and particularly to the indigent Clergy'.[117] He allowed the poor of Holme Lacy, Bolstone and Little Dewchurch three bushels of corn or rye a week and, at St Thomas's day (21 December) and Good Friday, 40s. a year. He allegedly aided royalist prisoners.[118] By his will he left £400 to buy stock to set the poor of the city to work, aiming to fulfil a long-standing desire of the Hereford citizens that some means should be found to find work for the poor.[119] Carrying out the wishes of his late wife Elizabeth in 1652, he gave £200 to the city of Bath to create Lady Scudamore's Charity, under which a physician was paid to give free advice to all the poor who came to the spa to be cured.[120] He was famed, both in his lifetime and after, for his hospitality, at a time when fears were being expressed for the decline of the old hospitable traditions.[121]

Not all this charity was tied to the eucharist, but one example clearly was. Each year Scudamore allowed 17s. 6d. for the custom of 'Cakebreade' on Palm Sunday in three Herefordshire parishes: Sellack, Hentland and King's Caple. The cakes were small buns distributed to the people with the greeting 'Peace and good neighbourhood' (hence their other name of 'pax cakes'). They were, doubtless, derived from the late medieval tradition of distributing cakes or unconsecrated wafers among the people during the Palm Sunday processions.[122] Scudamore's continuation of the custom was double-barrelled. One the one side the cakebread symbolised reconciliation and the forgiving of old grudges in preparation for the Easter communion. On the other it was a means of structuring the ideal Christian community of good neighbourhood beyond the church door.

The importance to Scudamore of the proper celebration of the eucharist is further shown by his frequent gifts of altar plate and eucharistic implements. At the consecration of Dore he gave a purse of gold, with which a silver flagon, chalice and paten were bought.[123] For Holme Lacy he consulted Laud about the design of the plate, spending over £47 on two flagons, two patens and a chalice, all of silver gilt, with leather cases and an iron chest to keep them in. These he gave to the church in April 1626. To save them from the hands of the sacrilegious they were all were entrusted to the churchwardens during the civil wars, but one of them stole the plate instead and fled to France, where he met an instructively miserable end. Scudamore left £45 in his will for new plate for Holme Lacy, with which a flagon, two chalices, two patens and a leather case were bought.[124] Most interesting, however, are the gifts at Sellack almost certainly from the viscount for the service of the altar: as well as a silver chalice and cover he gave a silver flagon and a paten, inscribed 'D[at,] D[icat,] D[edicat,] Peccatorum humillimus I.S.'. The further gift of a viatic paten specially for giving the blessed bread to the dying suggested a strong belief in the necessary benefits of the grace thereby received through the sacrament.[125]

In addition to plate Scudamore gave other items for the celebration of the eucharist. As well as 'one large Damaske cloth to Couer the high altar' Holme Lacy received a smaller damask napkin and six 'framed formes', presumably to support a houseling cloth. He was probably the donor of the corporal, pall and damask rail cloth also given to Sellack.[126] The corporal is a napkin placed under the vessels as they stand on the altar, the pall a second corporal which lies folded on the chalice until the prayer of consecration and then after communion is spread over any remaining consecrated elements. Their use suggested a feeling that communion should be celebrated with great solemnity. The gift of a rail cloth, or houseling cloth, is even more indicative of the way in which Scudamore expected the Lord's supper to be celebrated. This was a towel held before the communicants or spread over the altar rails as they knelt to receive, designed to catch any crumbs of the blessed bread dropped during the administration, perhaps implying a strong belief in the real presence, but certainly indicating a degree of ceremonial uncommon even in cathedrals: its use outside the royal chapel in the seventeenth century was extremely rare.[127]

We cannot know what the chapel of Holme Lacy House looked like, as it was swept away with the rest of the house in the rebuilding conducted by the second viscount. What we know of the embassy chapel under Scudamore when he was ambassador to France, 1635–39, however, reinforces the impression of Scudamore as a Laudian ceremonialist. Before he left he obtained a description of Lancelot Andrewes's private chapel and the celebration of communion there from Stephen Boughton, sub-dean of the chapel royal.[128] It is not known how far Scudamore arranged his chapel in Paris to conform to this plan, but certainly its furnishing caused a storm of protest. Previously, English ambassadors had ordered their chapel to placate the Huguenots; the French Protestants were scandalised by Scudamore's insistence on the full Laudian ritual. He set up an altar upon which burned candles, and to which his chaplains used to bow, 'after the usuall forme of the Church of England', it was disingenuously added; the practice of standing candlesticks on the communion table, though allowed by Edward VI's 1547 injunctions, was rare, usually limited to cathedrals and the chapels of royalty, bishops and colleges, and the continual burning of tapers even rarer. Despite the protests – the Huguenots accounted the ceremonies in the embassy chapel 'a great superstition' – Scudamore 'was resolud not to alter it'. It was later claimed that Scudamore's chapel was 'adorned according to the newe devise, so that manie Papists there said they were at the English masse'.[129]

The importance to Scudamore of the sacraments, the offices of the book of common prayer and Laudian ceremonial is reinforced by the order of consecration of Dore. Among Scudamore's papers is a copy of the order of consecration used by William Barlow, bishop of Lincoln, at Fulmer in 1610, but this was not the order used at Dore. It may be that it was rejected as insufficiently elaborate: the form used at Dore was both much longer and much more ceremonial.[130] The day chosen was itself thrice significant. First, it was a Sunday, 22 March 1635. Second, it was Palm Sunday, the Sunday of preparation for Easter. Although the comparisons were not made explicit, the procession around the church and churchyard, and the entry of bishop, priests and people into the temple, had echoes of both the late medieval Palm Sunday processions and Jesus's entry to Jerusalem and the Temple.[131] Third, it was the thirty-fourth anniversary of Scudamore's own baptism, the day on which he was admitted into the church, when, as the order of consecration described baptism, he had been 'baptized in this Laver of the newe birth' and 'sanctified and washed with the Holie Ghost', delivered from God's wrath, 'recieved into the Arke of Christs Church', and had received 'the fulnesse of grace' and thereby ever remained 'in the nvmber of Thy faithfull and elect Children'.[132] It was envisaged that all the sacraments and divine offices of the church of England should be performed at the consecration: baptism, marriage, burial, the churching of women, confirmation and communion. In the event only the last two took place: suitable volunteers could not be found for the others.[133] The day-long service of consecration, church in the morning, churchyard in the afternoon, was the visible expression to the parishioners of how, and with what due reverence, Scudamore expected Dore to be used.

Theophilus Field, bishop of St David's, deputising for Matthew Wren, bishop of Hereford (who was detained at court), began at 8.00 a.m. with a procession round the church, then moved to the church door, where Scudamore's schedule (explaining his actions) was read and prayers were said.

The bishop, his chaplain, the rector and the founder then processed inside. The bishop, like the Christian soul on its Laudian pilgrimage from entry to the church door through reception into the church (baptism), instruction (pulpit) and prayer (reading desk) to the remission of sins and fulfilment with divine grace at communion, processed from font to pulpit to reading desk, chancel screen and altar before retracing his steps, signing the building and all the pews with the sign of the cross. At this point the congregation entered and the service proceeded with adapted forms of morning prayer and the litany, a sermon, and communion. Thus ended the morning's proceedings. At 2.00 p.m. the congregation reassembled for the consecration of the churchyard, beginning outside before moving into the church and laying the consecration act and Scudamore's deed of conveyance on the altar, and concluding with a sermon, evening prayer and confirmation.[34] Throughout, the Laudian understanding of ceremonial and the purpose of the church was insisted upon. The parishioners were reminded that neither church nor churchyard was ever to be used for profane purposes, for by the consecration they had been set apart. The church was 'gods house' and 'an Holie Habitation for ever' and as such must always be repaired, adorned and 'decentlye furnished', and they must act accordingly with due reverence and 'demeane themselues in all occasions'. The message that the church was a house of prayer was reinforced at several points in the service. Full Laudian ceremonial and bodily gestures were insisted on: kneeling for prayers and kneeling at the altar to deliver oblations, bowing to the altar, facing east at critical points such as the creed, the use of the corporal. The church building was 'to vs the Gate of Heaven', and the bishop prayed that all those who entered it might be made sacred. The whole consecration was, thus, a sermon in stones, ceremonies and divine offices, an exposition of the Laudian church and its understanding of God's grace and our place in the divine order.

Gibson summed up Scudamore's churchmanship, in Paris and Hereford-shire, as ritualist: 'The Publick Service was allwaies performed with great Solemnity and Devotion; and such an Order observed, as might in some measure have become that of a Cathedral Church. His Excellency indeed carried things of this kind to the highest pitch.'[35]

It was partly on the grounds of ceremony in worship that Scudamore distanced himself from the French Protestants. He refused to attend their services at Charenton and, in Clarendon's words, was 'careful to publish upon all occasions by himself, and those who had the nearest relation to him, that the Church of England looked not on the Huguenots as part of their communion'.[36] He disapproved of the Huguenots' different ceremonies: they received standing, Scudamore and the church of England kneeling. 'Voila vn grande difference ... dans le point de respect,' agreed the prince of Condé in conversation with

Scudamore.[137] Scudamore may also have cavilled at the Huguenots as a non-episcopal church; his judgement on the reformed episcopal churches of northern Europe, with which he was prepared to countenance union, was less harsh. Lay elders were to him an innovation, and he defended Laud's attack on 'those Puritans that would lay a necessitie vpon all churches to receiue Lay-Elders', even personally translating Laud's speech at the trial of Burton, Bastwick and Prynne into French and having it published in Paris.[138]

Scudamore was a firm believer in episcopacy. He was the first to sign (as precedence dictated) the Herefordshire petition in favour of episcopacy in January 1642. Initially he refused the solemn league and covenant for its opposition to bishops, an office which had, he wrote in his notes as he justified his refusal of the oath, the authority 'of longest continuance', was legally established, and was 'Eminent in Martyrs, and reformers'. It was 'sound doctrine, that doctrine which hath been universally taught and receiued in all churches from the beginning'. Most important, Scudamore revealed a belief in *iure divino* episcopacy: the office of bishop 'great Divines hold to bee Iure Divino', and was 'according to the word of God'. The Herefordshire petition was more muted in its support for episcopacy, making no reference to claims of divine right; presumably the viscount's own more extreme beliefs made poor propaganda in 1642.[139] For a believer in *iure divino* episcopacy the Huguenots' lack of bishops may have been sufficient reason to unchurch the French Protestants. More usually, though, even believers in episcopacy by divine right shrank from unchurching the non-episcopal Continental Protestant churches, allowing them the plea of necessity, the fiction that they were forced to do without bishops through historical circumstance.[140] Nonetheless, sixty years later it was recalled that 'many priests and divers English divines resorting much to the Lord Scudamore and the Earl of Leicester when ambassador at Paris' said 'daily that the Protestants in France had no true ministers or sacraments etc. because they had no bishops'.[141]

Scudamore did have a higher opinion of the episcopal Lutheran churches. He participated in talks with his friend Hugo Grotius aimed at reuniting the Protestant episcopal churches of northern Europe: Sweden, Denmark, Norway and the British Isles. (The Calvinist churches were excluded.) Nonetheless, the viscount held out little hope for the success of the plan, owing to the practical difficulties, and advised Laud rather to concentrate on what he called 'the better half of that Vnion', which would be effected 'when you haue finished the victorie which you haue fought for so stoutly and wisely in settling the Church of England to the principles of her first Reformation, and conforming to her Ireland and (if please God) unhappy Scotland'.[142]

The viscount's attitude to Catholicism is much harder to determine. In conversation with Condé he seemed to imply that union was more likely with the Gallicans in France than with the Scandinavian churches: if the point of respect and the like were all the difference in the Church of Christ, it mought bee easily hoped that a Vnion of all parts, euen of those of the church of Rome, might bee effected. But that particular interests vnder the name of Religion kept all assunder. This same vniuersalitie of Jurisdiction was the hard point to bee departed from.

He went on to suggest that Richelieu could do nothing greater 'then to bee a means to heale the wounds that the body of Christ suffers under'. This may have been no more than diplomatic small talk, but it does echo the attempts by several Laudian divines to represent separation from Rome in jurisdictional rather than doctrinal terms, without necessarily hoping for imminent reunion.[143] Gregorio Panzani, the papal agent whose gullibility and optimism in the case of English sympathy for Rome knew no bounds, described Ambassador Scudamore as surrounded by men 'very moderate' towards Catholicism. Nonetheless, in Paris the embassy chaplains were keen to defend their church against the attacks of the papists. If the Catholic priest Richard Lassels is to be trusted, however, these chaplains were likely to end up disagreeing amongst themselves about what they did hold.[144] Scudamore was no particular favourer of Catholics. Although he received Bishop Richard Smith of Chalcedon and other Catholic priests in Paris 'very kindly', so did the earl of Leicester, the extraordinary ambassador.[145] The story that on his return from Paris Scudamore filled Llanthony House with French papists was no more than anti-Catholic hysteria and exaggeration at the outbreak of the civil war; perhaps he had acquired some French servants and hangers-on from his embassy.[146] Gunning, whom Scudamore sought in vain as his private chaplain, was famous above all for his set disputations with papists.[147] In his objections to the solemn league and covenant the viscount defined the 'common enemies' of true religion as 'papists and such as oppose things werein wee haue communion and are one.'[148]

Scudamore remained loyal to the episcopal church of England. Scudamore was one of that growing number who cherished the rhythms of the Anglican year and the prayer book, and who really cared for the church of England.[149] But he was also a sacerdotalist; a sacramentalist who insisted on decorous services; one who encouraged Laud in his reforms; one who tried to give practical expression to ideas of the beauty of holiness, the sacred nature of church property and reverence for the priesthood; and a close friend of many linked with the religious changes of the 1630s.

Throughout his rebuilding and his practice, though he sometimes turned to figures such as Hammond and Wren for advice, Scudamore principally drew his inspiration from the example set by three others: Lancelot Andrewes, William Laud and Charles I. Andrewes's practice was a direct influence on Scudamore. It was he who popularised the idea of donating a whole set of communion plate at a time, an example Scudamore followed at Dore and

Holme Lacy, and it was Andrewes's order which formed the basis of the consecration service of Dore. In 1635 Scudamore obtained an account of the proceedings and furnishings in Andrewes's chapel, and his purchase of linen and 'framed forms' for Holme Lacy copied Andrewes's use of a houseling cloth resting on forms outside the altar rails. Scudamore obtained as separates copies of Andrewes's will and two of his letters. Andrewes, like Scudamore, was concerned at the spread of sacrilege. John Buckeridge remembered how Andrewes 'did find much fault and reprove three sinnes, too common, and reigning in this later age': usury, simony and especially sacrilege, 'which he did abhorr ... and he wished some man would take the paines to collect, how many Families, that were raised by the spoyles of the Church, were now vanished, and the place thereof knowes them no more'.[150] Moreover, Andrewes was a more general influence on all Laudians. When Andrewes died in 1626 Laud bemoaned to Scudamore the extinction of 'the great light of the Christian world'.[151] Peter Lake, while seeing Andrewes as one of the key early 'avant-garde conformists', thinks that Richard Hooker 'invented the style of piety' associated with Laudianism almost single-handed; Diarmaid MacCulloch, meanwhile, has suggested that it was primarily Andrewes, not Hooker, who launched 'the catholic sacramentalist adventure'. Scudamore should not be read as normative for all Laudians, but it is clear that, though he had read Hooker, he owed much more, and more directly, to Andrewes.[152]

The second principal influence on Scudamore was Charles himself. Some of the viscount's practices seem to have been modelled on the royal chapel, most notably the burning of candles on the altar during the daytime, which Scudamore adopted in Paris. Others of his practices and beliefs, such as auricular confession and episcopacy by divine right, were shared by Charles if not copied from him. In the ordering of his embassy chapel Scudamore acted with the full support of the king.[153] For Scudamore, the royal supremacy was a cornerstone of the English church. One of his reasons for refusing the covenant and negative oath was that they had been condemned by Charles: 'That which the King forbids is unlawfull because hee [is] the supreme gouernour ... There is no law to alter Religion against the will of the King' he concluded.[154]

Laud was the greatest influence: a cleric to be honoured; a spiritual counsellor and adviser to be guided by; a metropolitan to be obeyed; a model to be copied. The restored church of Dore resembled elements of the archbishop's chapel at Lambeth. There Laud set the communion table altarwise, railed it in and placed a tapestry reredos of the Last Supper behind. It is likely that the Ascension painted in glass at Dore was copied from the same theme in the windows at Lambeth repaired, if not actually put up, by Laud.[155] Scudamore professed himself a supporter of his friend's ecclesiastical policies in strong terms, rejoicing that Laud continued 'vnmooud and resolute to stand the

Storme to the utmost', anticipating the time when their success would win Laud that 'crowne of glory' laid up for him

> I cannot but hope that God will yet bless with success the pious endeavours of his Hezekiah and you the chiefe Instrument: and for those that oppose, may th[eir] conceptions bee chaff, and their fruite stubble, and the fire of their own breath their devourer, if they will not returne and seeke the churches peace.

'God make all that oppose you, Seekers of you,' he concluded.[156]

It is difficult to tease apart the influences of Laud and Charles on one another and on third parties. Kevin Sharpe feels that it was Charles rather than Laud who was the prime initiator of the liturgical changes of the 1630s. Julian Davies has gone further, demoting the whole concept of Laudianism to the subsidiary role of a mere handmaid to what he styles 'Carolinism'.[157] There are a number of problems with both these readings of Laudianism. Sharpe sees Laud as little more than a conservative bureaucrat imposing no more than conformity and order, and with no distinctive theological underpinnings to his position. Such a view is deeply problematic, and flies in the face of Laudian attitudes to the sanctity of church buildings, or to the return of impropriations, for example. Davies, meanwhile, sees Laud as often powerless, a view that few in the 1630s could have accepted. Both Sharpe and Davies take at face value Laud's defence of his actions (when he was on trial for his life) that he was merely copying the king's chapel at Whitehall. It was an easy defence, but in many ways groundless, for Laud had been sworn dean of the chapel royal in 1626 and so could be held responsible for the innovations there.[158]

The case of Scudamore's relationship with Laud highlights three further areas where, I believe, Dr Davies has misunderstood, and so underestimated, Laud's role. One of the key elements in Davies's whole thesis of 'Carolinism' (Charles's 'notion of sacramental kingship' or 'caesaro-sacerdotalism') is the role of the chapel royal, both as an exemplar for parish churches and as a culture to be diffused throughout the realm. One of his examples of these processes in action is Viscount Scudamore's rebuilding at Dore, which Davies thinks was based upon the chapel royal.[159] On the contrary, however, Scudamore did not obtain a description of the chapel royal until June 1635, three months after Dore was finished.[160] As we have seen, Dore was inspired by a desire to separate the sacred and profane, and elevate the former over the latter, and not by the specific example of the king's chapel. Scudamore's ambassadorial chapel, however, may have been modelled on the chapel royal, but two further points need to be made here. First, the embassy chapel was a special case because, as we shall see, as ambassador Scudamore was acting as Charles's representative and so was careful to take his cue in so many of his actions from the king.[161] Second, the model that Scudamore obtained in June 1635 was of the chapel royal under Lancelot Andrewes, who had died in 1626, making the influence of Andrewes at least as important as that of Charles in this respect. Should historians, then, add 'Andrewesianism' to their list of ways of describing the ecclesiastical policies of the period 1625–41? I think not.

Dr Davies's second misrepresentation of Laud lies in seeing his primary motivation as economic. He acknowledges that as early as April 1626 Charles asked Laud to advise about impropriations, but Davies assumes that the king's actions meant that Laud's role in 1626 was restricted to 'economic problems'.[162] Although it is clear that Laud was concerned to see poor clergy relieved, the underpinning of his concern about impropriations was not economic but a desire to separate the sacred and the profane, and to stress that the retaining of impropriations in lay hands was sacrilege; it was in such terms that Laud advised Scudamore concerning impropriations in 1627.[163] Once Laud's desire to redefine the boundary between the sacred and the profane is stressed, his actions can be understood in a very different light from that portrayed by Dr Davies.

Thirdly, Julian Davies seems to think that Laud cannot have inspired anyone who went further than himself. Since Davies sees Laud as essentially conservative, even moderate in some areas such as the altar policy (a claim which is itself controversial, although Davies has conducted more local research in diocesan archives than anyone so far), the more rigorous or extreme policies of other bishops, such as Wren, are evidence for Dr Davies of the Laud's lack of influence and his secondary role to the king.[164] Acceptance of Davies's model would mean that few movements in history should bear the name of their founder. Davies has highlighted important differences in attitude between major figures like Laud and Wren, but there is no evidence that Scudamore, for example, saw any contradiction in his relations with these two prelates. Scudamore went further than Laud publicly dared or managed on issues such as freeing clergy from secular rates or restoring impropriations, but there is no doubting that he drew his inspiration and guidance from the archbishop.[165] Not everything that Scudamore did can necessarily be described as 'Laudian', but it is clear that until the 1640s the viscount was inspired, guided and directed by Laud, and that thereafter he remained true to Laud's vision of a church of England restored, repaired, reverenced, respected, ritualist and renowned. There is no need to abandon the term 'Laudian' either in the individual case of Viscount Scudamore or in the collective case of Caroline England.

We have considered Viscount Scudamore's religious and intellectual worlds partly because it was his religious self-presentation which underlay so much of his political career and the successes he had. The 'good opinion' that, according to Laud in 1627, King Charles had of Scudamore, and which Laud himself shared, was in part founded on a shared religious vision for the church of England. It was partly Scudamore's reputation in religious matters which brought him preferment as an ambassador in 1635, as George Wall noted.[166] Scudamore, of course, used his religious reputation for his own ends and was adept at shaping his image to suit the occasion. He did not, for example, always present himself as the pupil of William Laud. In 1642, in signing the Herefordshire pro-episcopacy petition, his public image was of a non-Laudian defender of moderate episcopacy. In 1660 he stressed that he was a loyal Anglican, horrified at the religious experimentation of the previous two generations. This was not a deceiving mask: the image worked precisely because it was true. In the charged atmosphere of the Restoration Scudamore hoped to use it to seize the political initiative. In a speech in the spring of 1660 at the Herefordshire election to the Convention Parliament he viewed with horror the experiments of the 1640s and 1650s and outlined the all too obvious consequences of laying aside episcopacy and the book of common prayer. The restoration of the church of England would, he said, be a means of obtaining a settlement:

> the Godhead of the Sonne, the procession of the Holy Ghost the Licence of these times haue emboldened some to dare to question. This settlement, comprehends in it the Conseruation of the church, which is the Spouse of our Sauiour; for the mission by which men are impowered to preach the saving word, is disvalued: the Sacraments ordained by christ himself, the one Baptisme hath receiued a wound and the Supper of the Lord, is in many places laid aside: the Comandments which direct vs what to doe, the Beliefe which instructs vs what to beleiue, the Lords prayer which teacheth vs how to pray, are in many places slighted and not vsed, and the power of ordaining and the iurisdiction of the Church, are fallen into distractions and sidings.

The restoration of church and crown would be a means to protect and conserve the 'glory of the very trinity itself'. Scudamore was making a bid for the leadership of the county based on the restoration of the church of England and his credentials as an Anglican. In April 1660 he was not entirely successful. His candidate, Sir John Kyrle, second baronet, was forced to withdraw in favour of Thomas Price, who had the support of a group of ultra-royalists led by Sir Henry Lingen. Moreover, Scudamore's position and image were undermined somewhat by the royal court: almost on the eve of the election Scudamore received letters from Sir Philip Warwick, Sir Orlando Bridgeman and Sir Geoffrey Palmer intimating Charles's support for Edward Harley, despite Harley's Presbyterian views. Only days after the Declaration of Breda, Scudamore discovered the limitations of posing as an Anglican loyalist.[167]

Publicly Scudamore could present himself as a defender of the church of England and, when necessary, dissociate himself from the Laudian innovations. Privately he seems not to have defined himself as an innovator at all. Like his mentor William Laud, he saw the Laudian project in terms of returning the church of England to what he saw as the true Elizabethan settlement, before it was hijacked by Calvinists. Writing to Laud in 1637–38, Scudamore wished Laud well 'for so stoutly and wisely' striving for so long to settle 'the Church of England to the principles of her first Reformation', deliberately echoing Laud's claim that he was endeavouring to settle the church 'to the Rules of its first Reformation'. A few years later, agonising over the solemn league and covenant, Scudamore defined his 'Place and Calling' as 'a Christian, and as a subiect (and no innovator)'.[168]

Scudamore's successes in trading on his reputation for piety and support of the church were helped by the nature of the Herefordshire environment. The county was recognised by many as being conservative in religion and an area where, except for a few pockets such as Leominster and the extreme north-west around Brampton Bryan, home of the Harleys, puritanism had found few converts. Sir Robert Harley is said to have described 'his owne Country' in 1604 as 'the most Clownyshe Countrye of Inglond'. Welsh influences were strong in Herefordshire and Welsh could be heard spoken in the streets of its towns. Parliamentary observers in the civil war described the citizens of Hereford in terms which suggested that godly reform had made little headway. Festive culture, especially morris dancing and maypoles, remained strong in the county.[169] Much work on the religious image of gentlemen has so far been concerned only with the godly, men like Sir Richard Grosvenor and Sir Robert Harley, and has rested on the assumption that the image of the godly magistrate had force and power because it was popular. That popularity may not have rested in the magistrate's puritanism or attacks on tippling and alehouses, but it did trade on his anti-Catholicism and anti-Laudianism. The successful image of Scudamore as a 'truly Noble, *Relligious*, Generous, Learned, and most Accomplisht Gentleman' challenges some of these assumptions.[170] It may be that in Herefordshire Laudianism was more popular than historians have allowed, and the discovery of three Laudian gentlemen (Scudamore, Coningsby and Brabazon) in one county – a very high number in what is a small corner of England – might lend some support to this, but much more work would need to be done on the county before such a judgement could be accepted, and this is not the place for that investigation.[171] Against such a view it could be countered that all three of these men had to pose as non-Laudians in 1642. What can be suggested is that Scudamore's image as a religious gentleman and defender of the church was more successful in conservative Herefordshire than it might have been in more puritan areas.

Among Scudamore's papers is an essay, 'De Jure Patronatus', on the causes and effects of patronage.[172] Three causes induced the church to approve of lay patronage: lords, 'out of their devotion and charitable bountie', gave some of their land to holy uses, dedicating it 'everlastingly to the Lord', and making 'God himselfe the owner thereof'; on that ground the lords built churches and houses for the clergy; and from their lands the lords allowed yearly maintenance for the minister. From these three causes arose three effects of patronage: 'Honos, Onus, et Utilitas', the honour of presenting the minister, and of precedence among the pews; the burden of protecting and defending the church; and the profit of being a patron. Much of Scudamore's life was a fulfilment of these causes and effects.

NOTES

1 R. P. Cust, *The Papers of Sir Richard Grosvenor, 1st Bart. (1585–1645)* (Record Society of Lancashire and Cheshire, 134, 1996); R. P. Cust and P. Lake, 'Sir Richard Grosvenor and the Rhetoric of Magistracy', *Bulletin of the Institute of Historical Research*, 54 (1981), pp. 40–54; J. Eales, *Puritans and Roundheads: The Harleys of Brampton Bryan and the Outbreak of the English Civil War* (Cambridge, 1990), especially p. 194; R. P. Cust, 'Politics and the Electorate in the 1620s', in R. P. Cust and A. Hughes, eds, *Conflict in Early Stuart England* (Harlow, 1989), pp. 134–67. This chapter is a revised and much expanded version of my 'Viscount Scudamore's "Laudianism": The Religious Practices of the first Viscount Scudamore', *Historical Journal*, 34:3 (1991), pp. 567–96.

2 R. P. Cust, 'Humanism and Magistracy in Early Stuart England' (unpublished paper), citing Warwickshire RO, CR/136, B/3475.

3 A. Collins, ed., *Letters and Memorials of State* (2 vols, London, 1746), II, p. 387; Sheffield University Library, Hartlib papers, 31/22/19B; H. Oldenburg, *Correspondence*, ed. A. R. and M. B. Hall (13 vols, Madison and London, 1965–86), II, p. 11; M. Stubbs, 'John Beale, Philosophical Gardener of Herefordshire', Part I, 'Prelude to the Royal Society (1608–1663)', and Part II, 'The Improvement of Agriculture and Trade in the Royal Society', *Annals of Science*, 39 (1982), pp. 463–89, and 46 (1989), pp. 323–63.

4 R. Watkyns, *Flamma sine Fumo*, ed. P. C. Davies (Cardiff, 1968), p. 24.

5 BL, Cotton MS Julius CIII, fols 336–7; PRO, C115/N4/8575–9; below, p. 208. Unfortunately the Chaucer MS can no longer be traced.

6 F. Godwin, *Annales of England*, trs. M. Godwin (London, 1630), sig. A3v; T. Farnaby, *Florilegium Epigrammatum Graecorum* (London, 1629), dedication.

7 E. G. R. Taylor, *The Mathematical Practitioners of Tudor and Stuart England* (Cambridge, 1954), pp. 170–2, 225, 351, 361, 363, 369, 376, 394, 408. J. Newton, *The Compleat Arithmetician* (London, 1691), sig. A3v; W. Higford, *The Institution of a Gentleman* (London, 1660), p. 82.

8 G. Wall, *A Sermon at the Lord Archbishop of Canterbury his Visitation Metropoliticall* (London, 1635), sig. A2v; PRO, C115/M24/7768; Higford, *Institution*, p. 45.

9 H. Rogers, *The Protestant Church Existent* (London, 1638), sig. Av; Arundel Castle Archives, 'Howard Letters and Papers 1636–1822 II Various', Viscount Scudamore to James Scudamore, 19/29 January 1657, and reply, 26 January/5 February 1657; BL, Add. MS 11689, fols 51v, 52v; HCL, 'Scudamore MSS: Accounts 1635–37[8]', MS L.C. 647.1, fol. 44; HCA, MS 6417, fol. 27r.

10 BL, Add. MS 11044, fol. 233r.

11 M. Gibson, *A View of the Ancient and Present State of the Churches of Door, Home Lacy, and Hempsted* (London, 1727), p. 64; Pliny the younger, *Letters*, trs. J. D. Lewis (London, 1879), p. 80 (book 3, no. 5); Cust, 'Humanism and Magistracy'; Balliol College, Oxford, MS 333, fol. 67r.

12 Q. Skinner, 'Thomas Hobbes and his Disciples in France and England', *Comparative Studies in Society and History*, 8 (1965–66), pp. 153–67; Sheffield University Library, Hartlib papers, 31/22/14A, 15B, 19B; T. Birch, *The History of the Royal Society* (4 vols, London, 1756–57), I, p. 179.

13 T. Sorrel, ed., *The Cambridge Companion to Hobbes* (Cambridge, 1996), p. 23; BL, Add. MS 11044, fols 180–1, also in P. Zagorin, 'Thomas Hobbes's Departure from England in 1640: An Unpublished Letter', *Historical Journal*, 21 (1978), pp. 157–60.

14 PRO, C115/N9/8873, C115/M24/7780; BL, Add. MS 11044, fols 180–1; Zagorin, 'Hobbes's Departure', pp. 158–60; R. Pintard, *Le Libertinage érudit* (Paris, 1943), p. 334; S. Sorbière, *A Voyage to England* (London, 1709), p. 66; M. Mersenne, *Correspondence*, ed. C. de Waard *et al.* (12 vols, Paris, 1932–72), VIII, p. 359 n. 1; T. Hobbes, *The Correspondence*, ed. N. Malcolm (2 vols, Clarendon Edition of the Works of Thomas Hobbes, 6–7, Oxford, 1994), II, pp. 795–7.

15 PRO, SP78/104, fol. 15, C115/M13/7264; Sheffield University Library, Hartlib papers, 31/22/19B.

16 BL, Add. MS 11044, fols 92–105; H. Grotius, *Epistolae* (Amsterdam, 1687), p. 626; PRO, SP78/105, fol. 134v; *Notes and Queries*, 1st series, vol. 8, no. 207, 15 October 1853, p. 367; W. J. Tighe, 'William Laud and the Reunion of the Churches: Some Evidence from 1637 and 1638', *Historical Journal*, 30 (1987), pp. 717–27; C. Barksdale, *Memorials of the Life and Death of H. Grotius* (London, 1654); H. Grotius, *The Truth of the Christian Religion*, ed. J. Le Clerc (London, 1711), pp. 332–5; T. Pierce, *The New Discoverer Discover'd* (London, 1659), p. 12.

17 PRO, C115/M13/7231–2; Atherton, thesis, p. 469; BL, Harl. MS 7039, fol. 199; T. Baker, *History of the College of St John the Evangelist, Cambridge*, ed. J. E. B. Mayor (Cambridge, 1869), pp. 235–6. John Fork was perhaps John Ford, fellow of Exeter College 1656–64, and vicar of Totnes 1664–71: Atherton, thesis, p. 351.

18 Sheffield University Library, Hartlib papers, 31/22/14A; B. Cottret, *The Huguenots in England* (Cambridge and Paris, 1991), pp. 115, 132–3, 144, 147; *CSPD 1635–36*, pp. 60–1.

19 PRO, E179/119/462, E179/118/432, PROB11/159/21, fol. 161v; Higford, 'Institutions', Society of Antiquaries, MS 790/7, p. 48; K. Lambley, *The Teaching and Cultivation of the French Language in England during Tudor and Stuart Times* (Manchester, 1920).

20 L. P. Smith, *The Life and Letters of Sir Henry Wotton* (2 vols, Oxford, 1907), II, pp. 364, 464–5; J. M. French, *The Life Records of John Milton* (5 vols, New Brunswick, 1949–58), I, pp. 361–2.

21 PRO, C115/M24/7779–80; Arundel Castle Archives, 'Howard Letters and Papers 1636–1822 II Various', Scudamore to Dupont and Turner, 5 September and 23 November 1639; BL, Add. MS 11044, fol. 86r.

22 J. Foster, *Alumni Oxonienses 1500–1714* (4 vols, Oxford, 1891–92), IV, p. 1327; H. R. Trevor-Roper, *Archbishop Laud 1573–1645* (London, 1940), pp. 32, 42, 57–8, 285–6; PRO, C115/N10/8897; details kindly supplied by the Keeper of the Archives of St John's College.

23 Atherton, thesis, pp. 326–7.

24 BL, Add. MS 11044, fol. 244r.

25 R. K. French, *The History and Virtues of Cyder* (London, 1982), pp. 3, 13–15, 81–2, 103–4, 126; Sheffield University Library, Hartlib papers, 31/1/56B, 52/44B–45A, 52/137A–138B; J. Hayes, *The Garton Collection of English Table Glass* (London, 1965), p. 12; HMC, *The Manuscripts of his Grace the Duke of Portland* (10 vols, London, 1891–1931), II, p. 292; R. Vaughan, ed., *The Protectorate of Oliver Cromwell* (2 vols, London, 1838), II, p. 475; F. C. Morgan, ed., 'The Steward's Accounts of John, First Viscount Scudamore of Sligo (1601–1671) for the Year 1632', *Transactions of the Woolhope Naturalists' Field Club*, 33 (1949–51), p. 178; Oldenburg, *Correspondence*, II, p. 11.

26 Sheffield University Library, Hartlib papers, 52/138B, 51/105A; Birch, *Royal Society*, I, pp. 149–50; Oldenburg, *Correspondence*, II, pp. 11–12; BL, Add. Charter 1953; PRO, C115/E6/2244, C115/13/5682.

27 Sheffield University Library, Hartlib papers, 52/49B; HCL, MS 631.16, 'Scudamore Papers. Farm Accounts of Holm Lacy', 1667–68, 14 November and 5 December 1667.

28 Sheffield University, Hartlib papers, 52/44B, 52/141A; Vaughan, *Protectorate*, II, pp. 440–1; M. W. Greenslade, *The Staffordshire Historians* (Collections for a History of Staffordshire, 4th series, 11, Staffordshire Record Society, 1982), p. 39; French, *Cyder*, pp. 51–69, 82; BL, Add. MS 70010, fol. 204r.

29 Bodleian, MS Don. f.5, fols 36–7; HMC, *Portland*, II, p. 292; Sheffield University Library, Hartlib papers, 51/97A; J. Philips, *Cider: A Poem in Two Books*, ed. C. Dunster (London, 1791), I, lines 501–11; Oldenburg, *Correspondence*, I, p. 479; J. Evelyn, *Sylva ... to which is annexed Pomona* (2nd edition, London, 1670), pp. 2, 8.

30 Oldenburg, *Correspondence*, II, p. 11, VII, pp. 439–40; Vaughan, *Protectorate*, II, pp. 440–1; Sheffield University Library, Hartlib papers, 52/56A, 52/63B, 51/63B, 51/97A; Stubbs, 'Beale', I, p. 339; Birch, *Royal Society*, I, p. 146; Evelyn, *Pomona*, p. 31; French, *Cyder*, p. 133; Royal Society, *Philosophical Transactions*, 2:27 (July–September 1667), p. 501.

31 J. Beale, *Herefordshire Orchards, a Pattern for all England* (London, 1724), p. 22.

32 H. G. Bull, 'A Sketch of the Life of Lord Viscount Scudamore', in H. G. Bull, ed., *The Herefordshire Pomona* vol. I (Hereford, 1876–85), p. 84; J. MacDonald and J. Sinclair, *History of Hereford Cattle* (London, 1886), pp. 24–5; E. Heath-Agnew, *A History of Hereford Cattle and their Breeders* (London, 1983), p. 12; R. Trow-Smith, *A History of British Livestock Husbandry* (London, 1957), pp. 208–9; G. E. Fussell, *The English Dairy Farmer* (London, 1966), p. 22; Higford, *Institution*, pp. 70–1; PRO, C115/I14/6077.

33 Stubbs, 'Beale', II, pp. 344–5; E. Kerridge, *The Farmers of Old England* (London, 1973), pp. 112, 131; R. Vaughan, *Most Approved, and Long Experienced Water-workes* (London, 1610); M. Delorme, 'A Watery Paradise: Rowland Vaughan and Hereford's "Golden Vale"', *History Today*, 39 (July 1989), pp. 38–43; Atherton, thesis, p. 331.

34 L. Sharp, 'Timber, Science and Economic Reform in the Seventeenth Century', *Forestry*, 48 (1975), pp. 55–86; J. Thirsk, *The Agrarian History of England and Wales*, vol. V.ii, *1640–1750. Agrarian Change* (Cambridge, 1985), pp. 309–10; C. Webster, *The Great Instauration* (London, 1975), pp. 546–8; R. Austen, *A Treatise of Frvit-Trees* (Oxford, 1653), 'The Epistle Dedicatory'; S. Hartlib, ed., *A Designe for Plentie, by an Vniversall Planting of Frvit-Trees* (London, [1652]).

35 Beale, *Herefordshire Orchards*, p. 22; Atherton, thesis, p. 328; J. Thirsk, ed., *The Agrarian History of England and Wales*, vol. V.i, *1640–1750. Regional Farming Systems* (Cambridge, 1984), p. 162.

36 Oldenburg, *Correspondence*, I, p. 479, II, pp. 11–12, VII, p. 440; Birch, *Royal Society*, I, pp. 146, 149–50, 179; PRO, PROB11/336/96, fol. 331v.

37 M. Oster, 'The Scholar and the Craftsman Revisited: Robert Boyle as Aristocrat and Artisan', *Annals of Science*, 49 (1992), pp. 255–76.

38 T. Raylor, 'Samuel Hartlib and the Commonwealth of Bees' and M. Leslie, 'The Spiritual Husbandry of John Beale', both in M. Leslie and T. Raylor, eds, *Culture and Cultivation* (Leicester and London, 1992), pp. 91–129, 151–72; Austen, *Frvit-Trees*, especially 'To the Reader' and pp. 12–17, 32–3; R. Austen, *The Spiritvall Vse, of an Orchard* (Oxford, 1653).

39 C. J. Sommerville, *The Secularization of Early Modern England: From Religious Culture to Religious Faith* (New York and Oxford, 1992).

40 R. Askew, 'Faith in the Theological Countryside', *Theology*, 94:759 (May/June 1991), pp. 195–8; T. Traherne 'Thanksgivings for the Glory of God's Works' in T. Traherne, *Centuries, Poems, and Thanksgivings*, ed. H. M. Margoliouth (2 vols, Oxford, 1958), I, *passim*, II, pp. 244–56; G. Herbert, *The Temple* in G. Herbert, *Works*, ed. F. E. Hutchinson (Oxford, 1941), pp. 1–89. There is no direct evidence that Scudamore met either George Herbert or Thomas Traherne, but he was distantly related to the former and, more important, George Herbert's brother Sir Henry was one of Scudamore's closest friends, while Scudamore had links with the Traherne family and was a close friend of Thomas Traherne's patron Sir Orlando Bridgeman. See Atherton, thesis, p. 333.

41 Traherne, *Centuries*, 2.97, I, p. 107; Herbert, especially 'The Altar', 'The Church-floore', 'Church-lock and Key', 'The Windows', in *Works*, pp. 1–189.

42 W. Laud, *A Relation of the Conference betweene William Lawd … and Mr. Fisher the Jesuite* (London, 1639), sig. *3.

43 P. Lake, 'The Laudian Style: Order, Uniformity and the Pursuit of the Beauty of Holiness in the 1630s', in K. Fincham, ed., *The Early Stuart Church, 1603–1642* (Basingstoke, 1993), pp. 161–85; J. S. McGee, 'William Laud and the Outward Face of Religion', in R. L. DeMolen, ed., *Leaders of the Reformation* (Selinsgrove, 1984), pp. 318–44.

44 N. Tyacke, *Anti–Calvinists: The Rise of English Arminianism c. 1590–1640* (Oxford, 1987); P. White, 'The Rise of Arminianism Reconsidered', *Past and Present*, 101 (1983), pp. 34–54; N. Tyacke and P. White, 'Debate: The Rise of Arminianism Reconsidered', *Past and Present*, 115 (1987), pp. 201–29; P. White, 'The *Via Media* in the Early Stuart Church', in Fincham, *Early Stuart Church*, pp. 211–30.

45 For example G. W. Bernard, 'The Church of England, *c.* 1529–*c.* 1642', *History*, 75 (1990), pp. 181–206; K. Sharpe, *The Personal Rule of Charles I* (New Haven and London, 1992), ch. 6; C. Hill, *A Nation of Change and Novelty: Radical Politics, Religion and Literature in Seventeenth-Century England* (1990), ch. 4.

46 A. Milton, *Catholic and Reformed: The Roman and Protestant Churches in English Protestant Thought, 1600–1640* (Cambridge, 1995), pp. 71, 198.

47 Deputy Keeper of the Public Records, *Tenth Report* (London, 1849), appendix II, no. II, p. 267; Northamptonshire RO, Temple (Stowe) Box 40/11; PRO, E134/4W&M/Easter 16; Gibson, *View*, pp. 25–7, 36.

48 PRO, C115/D19/1907–16, C115/D19/1924; BL, Add. MS 11044, fols 267–9; H. M. Colvin, 'The Restoration of Abbey Dore Church in 1633–34', *Transactions of the Woolhope Naturalists' Field Club*, 32 (1946–48), pp. 235–7; M. Neville, 'Dore Abbey, Herefordshire, 1536–1912', *Transactions of the Woolhope Naturalists' Field Club*, 41 (1975), pp. 312–17; E. Sledmere, *Abbey Dore, Herefordshire, its Building and Restoration* (Hereford, 1914); R. Shoesmith and R. Richardson, eds, *A Definitive History of Dore Abbey* (Little Logaston, 1997), pp. 163–72, 177–200; Gibson, *View*, p. 41. The rebuilding cost at least £326, the glass £100.

49 PRO, PROB11/142/84, fol. 137v.

50 A. Foster, 'Church Policies of the 1630s' in R. P. Cust and A. Hughes, eds, *Conflict in Early Stuart England* (Harlow, 1989), pp. 200–4; below, pp. 110–18.

51 BL, Add. MS 11044, fols 247–9.

52 J. W. Legg, *English Orders for Consecrating Churches in the Seventeenth Century* (London, Henry Bradshaw Society, 41, 1911), pp. 146–91 especially 149–51, transcribing BL, Add. MS 38915, a draft of what was intended to be done on the day. The record of what was actually done (which differs only in a few minor details) is in the bishops' register, HRO, MS AL19/18, fols 71r–94r, a certified transcript of which is BL, Add. MS 15645. This last has been printed, but with many passages missing, in J. F. Russell, ed., *The Form and Order of the Consecration and Dedication of the Parish Church of Abbey Dore* (London, 1874). Scudamore's schedule only is printed in W. Kennett, *The Case of Impropriations* (London, 1704), appendix XII, pp. 30–5.

53 Magdalen College, Oxford, MS 350, cols. 418–19.

54 Gibson, *View*, pp. 40–1; Shoesmith and Richardson, *Dore Abbey*, p. 155; T. E. Gibson, ed., *Crosby Records: A Cavalier's Note Book, being Notes, Anecdotes and Observations of William Blundell* (London, 1880), pp. 170–1.

55 Shoesmith and Richardson, *Dore Abbey*, p. 160; Gibson, *View*, p. 38; G. W. O. Addleshaw and F. Etchells, *The Architectural Setting of Anglican Worship* (London, 1948), pp. 139 n. 3, 157–62.

56 Gibson, *View*, p. 41; Royal Commission on Historical Manuscripts for England, *An Inventory of the Historical Monuments in Herefordshire* (3 vols, London, 1931–37), I, p. 7 and plate 79; Shoesmith and Richardson, *Dore Abbey*, pp. 188–94; Tyacke, *Anti-Calvinists*, p. 219.

57 PRO, C115/N9/8875; Shoesmith and Richardson, *Dore Abbey*, pp. [ii], 41, 178–9; G. F. Townsend, *The Town and Borough of Leominster* (Leominster and London, 1863), pp. 328–9: the same inscription is on the old town hall of Leominster, built by Abel in 1633.

58 Shoesmith and Richardson, *Dore Abbey*, pp. 181–3.

59 W. Laud, *Works*, ed. W. Scott and J. Bliss (7 vols, Oxford, 1847–60), IV, p. 284; W. Laud, *A Speech Ddelivered in the Starr-Chamber* (London, 1637), p. 47; Lake, 'Laudian Style', pp. 174–5.

60 PRO, C115/N9/8874.

61 Gibson, *View*, p. 126; HCL, 'Scudamore Papers. Farm accounts of Holm Lacy', MS 631.16, 25 June and 2 July 1668; BL, Add. MS 11044, fols 270–3.

62 HCA, 2382, and dean and chapter act book, vol. 3, 1600–1712, p. 237; Bristol RO, DC/F/1/1; Guildhall Library, London, MS 25475/1, fol. 2r.

63 K. Thomas, *Religion and the Decline of Magic* (Harmondsworth, 1982), pp. 103–21; R. Brathwait, *The English Gentleman* (London, 1630), pp. 214–16; H. Spelman, *De Non Temerandis Ecclesiis* (2nd edition, London, 1616); H. Spelman, *The Larger Treatise Concerning Tithes*, ed. J. Stephens (London, 1647); [E. Udall], *Noli Me Tangere is a Thinge to be Thought on* (London, 1642); W. Walker, *A Sermon Preached in St Pavls-Church* (London, 1629); R. Mountagu, *Diatribae vpon the First Part of the late History of Tithes* (London, 1621), pp. 388–9; E. B[rouncker], *The Cvrse of Sacriledge* (Oxford, 1630), p. 11; Bodleian, MS Add. A.40, fols 21r, 114r.

64 Milton, *Catholic and Reformed*, p. 333; Bodleian, MS Add. A.40, fols 11v, 125r, 131r–2r; J. Buckeridge, *A Sermon Preached at the Fvneral of ... Lancelot late Lord Bishop of Winchester* (London, 1629), p. 21, in L. Andrewes, *XCVI. Sermons* (London, 1629); Greenslade, *Staffordshire Historians*, p. 75.

65 W. Skidmore, *Thirty Generations of the Scudamore/Skidmore Family in England and America* (Akron, 1991), p. 55.

66 PRO, C115/M24/7773, C115/M24/7758; below, pp. 142–4.

67 PRO, C115/D19/1901; R. Hooker, *Of the Lawes of Ecclesiastical Politie* (London, 1622), book 5, chapter 79, p. 431.

68 II Chronicles 21:12–19, repeated in H. Spelman, *The History and Fate of Sacrilege* (London, 1698), p. 14, a book originally written in 1632 and circulated widely in manuscript. In 1725 the library at Holme Lacy had a manuscript copy which must have been acquired by the first viscount: it was written in the hand of his friend Jeremy Stephens, who had sent at least one chapter of the book to Scudamore in 1653: T. Hearne, *Remarks and Collections*, ed. C. E. Doble *et al.* (11 vols, Oxford Historical Society, Oxford, 1885–1921), VIII, p. 353; BL, Add. MS 11044, fol. 233r.

69 W. Carpenter, *Jura Cleri: or An Apology for the Rights of the long-despised Clergy* (Oxford, 1661), p. 11; Wall, *Sermon*, sig. A3r.

70 PRO, E371/818/256, IND1/4224, fol. 17v, IND1/6747, November 1631, SO3/10, November 1631; Newton, *Compleat Arithmetician*, sigs. A2v–A4r; Gibson, *View*, pp. 123–5, 131–4, 169–72, 190–7, 206–24, 229–30, 235–8; BL, Lansdowne MS 989, fol. 31.

71 BL, Add. MS 11044, fols 265–6; HRO, AT24/1, p. 101, AO28, AL19/18, fols 191v–2r; F. C. Morgan, 'Bosbury Tithes and Oblations', *Transactions of the Woolhope Naturalists' Field Club*, 38:2 (1965), pp. 140–8; Gibson, *View*, pp. 132–4, 229–30; PRO, C115/D21/1921, C115/D21/1962, C115/I13/6055, C115/A2/29, C115/I1/5587.

72 Gibson, *View*, pp. 169–72, 235–6. R. Bigland, *Historical, Monumental and Genealogical Collections, Relative to the County of Gloucester* (3 vols, London, 1786–1838), II, pp. 65–6; PRO, C115/M24/7783; Gloucestershire RO, PMF 173, *sub* 1662; B. S. Dawson, 'Notes on the Manor and Church of Hempsted', *Transactions of the Bristol and Gloucestershire Archaeological Society*, 13 (1888–89), pp. 150–1; HRO, AA20/x/010/A, 1641 no. 101; N. M. Herbert, ed., *A History of the County of Gloucester*, vol. IV: *The City of Gloucester* (Victoria County History of Gloucestershire, Oxford, 1988), p. 427; Bodleian, MS Top. Glouc. c.3, fol. 197v.

73 House of Lords RO, 13 & 14 Car. II no. 44; Gibson, *View*, pp. 206–24; HRO, AT24/1, pp. 127–35.

74 Spelman, *Sacrilege*, pp. 15–16; PRO, C115/G23/3887, C115/I26/6519, C115/I26/6522–3, C115/M24/7751, C115/M35/8393, C115/M35/8398, IND1/23396, fols 374v–5r; BL, Add. MS 11055, fol. 120; HRO, BE7/1, 16 November 1632; Birmingham City Archives,

Coventry MS 602725, no. 100; Westminster City Archives, E154, E156; J. F. Larkin and P. L. Hughes, eds, *Stuart Royal Proclamations* (2 vols, Oxford, 1973–83), II, pp. 354–5; Laud, *Speech*, pp. 24–5.

75 Arundel Castle Archives, 'Howard Letters and Papers 1636–1822 II Various', Scudamore to Dupont, 5 September 1639; HCA, 6417, fol. 27r; J. Gregory, *A Discourse of the Morality of the Sabbath* (London, 1681), sig. A2.

76 BL, Add. MS 70001, fol. 156r; PRO, SP16/374/51, fol. 102r; HMC, *Twelfth Report. Appendix, Parts I–III. The Manuscripts of the Earl Cowper* (3 vols, London, 1888–89), II, pp. 172–3; Eales, *Puritans*, pp. 12–13, 37–9, 47, 53, 66, 111–16, 180–4.

77 A. Foster, 'The Clerical Estate Revitalised', in K. Fincham, ed., *The Early Stuart Church, 1603–1642* (Basingstoke, 1993), pp. 139–60; Lake, 'Laudian Style', pp. 176–7.

78 G. Williams, *The True Church* (London, 1629), p. 436; Spelman, *Sacrilege*, p. 16.

79 Gibson, *View*, pp. 42–3, 128–9, 173–5; PRO, C115/A2/29, C115/D19/1917–18, C115/D19/1923, C115/D21/1962, C115/I13/6055, C115/N9/8875; HCL, MS 631.16, 'Scudamore Papers. Farm Accounts of Holm Lacy', 1667–68, *sub* 28 May–17 September 1668.

80 Legg, *English Orders*, p. 152; C. Hill, *The Economic Problems of the Church from Archbishop Whitgift to the Long Parliament* (Oxford, 1956), pp. 134, 197.

81 PRO, C115/D19/1919–22, C115/D21/1964.

82 BL, Add. MS 11044, fols 233–4; PRO, C115/I19/6232.

83 PRO, PROB11/336/96, fol. 330r.

84 Wall, *Sermon*, sig. A3r; Gibson, *View*, pp. 166–7.

85 Gibson, *View*, pp. 110–12, 166–8, 179; PRO, C115/N9/8877–9, C115/E5/2206–39, C115/I10/5879. For these ministers see Atherton, thesis, appendix III; Scudamore usually gave only their surname, making identification difficult.

86 Atherton, thesis, pp. 436, 459.

87 R. O'Day and F. Heal, eds, *Continuity and Change* (Leicester, 1976), pp. 68–73.

88 Atherton, thesis, pp. 477–8.

89 Bodleian, MS J. Walker c.2, fol. 177v; A. G. Matthews, *Walker Revised* (Oxford, 1948), p. 196; PRO, PROB11/336/96, fol. 331v. Taylor, however, predeceased his patron by about a month.

90 Bodleian, MS Top. Herefs. d.2, p. 137 no. 1148; HCA, 2761–2, and dean and chapter act book, vol. 3, 1600–1712, pp. 1, 24–5, 188, 320; PRO, C115/F9/2985, C115/I4/5690, C115/I4/5706.

91 F. C. Morgan, 'Hereford Cathedral Vicars Choral Library', *Transactions of the Woolhope Naturalists' Field Club*, 35 (1955–58), p. 238; R. Rawlinson, *The History and Antiquities of the City and Cathedral-Church of Hereford* (London, 1717), p. 57; FSL, Va 147, fols 36r–38v.

92 HCA, 2382; BL, Add. MS 11044, fol. 295r; HRO, Hereford City Records, vol. VII, fol. 46r.

93 Atherton, thesis, pp. 458–9, 461–3, 474.

94 PRO, PROB11/324/80, fol. 179. None of Wren's notes were in fact published.

95 Atherton, thesis, p. 479.

96 PRO, C115/E5/2206–39, C115/N9/8877; Atherton, thesis, p. 472.

97 Matthews, *Walker Revised*, p. 59; Bodleian, MS Tanner 60, fol. 55; *The Humble Representation of his late Majesties and Princes Domestick Servants* ([London, 1655]); PRO, C115/ F14/3140; Atherton, thesis, appendix III.

98 Atherton, thesis, appendix III.

99 Matthews, *Walker Revised*, p. 303; Atherton, thesis, pp. 64–5.

100 H. Hammond, *The Miscellaneous Theological Works*, ed. N. Pocock (3 vols, Oxford, 1847), I, pp. lvii, lxii; BL, Harl. MS 6942, especially fols 18r, 31r, 35r, 36r, 83r, 88r, 91r, 93r–93*r, Add. MS 11044, fols 231–2.

101 E. Lee-Warner, *The Life of John Warner Bishop of Rochester 1637–1666* (London, 1901), pp. 56, 58–9; Bodleian, MS Eng. hist. b.205, fols 3–12, 15–20, 25v; Atherton, thesis, pp. 347–8.

102 The exception was Julius Spinula, archbishop of Laodicea, who received £10 in May 1659: PRO, C115/N9/8879.

103 Matthews, *Walker Revised*, p. 384.

104 J. Tombes, *Christs Commination against Scandalizers* (London, 1641), sig. *4r; PRO, C115/G25/3922–3, C115/G25/3925, C115/D13/1723; Bodleian, MS Bodley 323, fols 140v, 141v; J. Aubrey, *Brief Lives*, ed. O. L. Dick (Harmondsworth, 1976), p. 455; Atherton, thesis, p. 350.

105 PRO, SP16/397/57, PC2/49, fol. 182/p. 367, Bishops' institution books, series A, (1556–1660), vol. I, fol. 99r, Bishops' institution books, series B (1660–1721), vol. I, pp. 137, 141; Lambeth Palace Library, COMM.XIIa/10, fol. 175r; HRO, AL19/18, fols 186–7, 198r, 223Ar; A. T. Bannister, *Diocese of Hereford. Institutions, etc. (A.D. 1539–1900)* (Cantilupe Society, Hereford, 1923), pp. 31, 33, 37; Corpus Christi College, Oxford, C206, fols 3–4; Gibson, *View*, pp. 170–2; Bigland, *Collections*, II, p. 66; Bodleian, MS J. Walker c.2, fol. 177v; Atherton, thesis, p. 349.

106 See below, pp. 72–3 for the embassy chapel. The 1641 puritan survey of the Herefordshire ministry, Corpus Christi College, Oxford, C206, passed no comment on Manfeild and Turner except to say that the former 'preacheth seldome' and the latter was a non-resident at Dore who employed a non-preaching curate (fols 3, 4r).

107 *DNB*; A. Wood, *Fasti Oxonienses*, ed. P. Bliss (2 parts in 1, London, 1815–20), II, p. 242; BL, Lansdowne MS 987, fol. 12r.

108 Wood, *Fasti*, I, p. 407; Pierce, *New Discoverer*, p. 12.

109 Bigland, *Collections*, II, p. 66; Bodleian, MS Rawl. D.191, fol. 8r; Gregory, *Morality of the Sabbath*, pp. 29–30, 34, 46.

110 J. Eales, 'Sir Robert Harley, K.B. (1579–1656), and the "Character" of a Puritan', *British Library Journal*, 15:2 (1989), pp. 134–57; Vaughan, *Water-workes*, sigs. Fv, F2v–F4r; Corpus Christi College, Oxford, MS C206.

111 Laud, *Works*, VI, p. 354; PRO, E134/4W&M/Easter 16; Corpus Christi College, Oxford, MS C206, fols 1r, 4r.

112 BL, Lansdowne MS 989, fol. 31r; Hill, *Economic Problems*, pp. 271–2; Kennett's own interleaved copy of his *Case of Impropriations*, with his MS additions, Bodleian, Gough Eccl. Top. 47–8, II, appendix, facing p. 31; Gibson, *View*, p. 180; A. Collins, *The Baronetage of England* (2 vols, London, 1720), II, p. 176, repeated Kennett's lower estimate.

113 Wall, *Sermon*, sigs A2v–A3r. Nehemiah was an Old Testament leader who reformed Jewish religious practice, including payment of the tithe: see especially Nehemiah 13.

114 BL, Add. MS 11689, fols 51–2; Hammond, *Works*, I, pp. 386-8, 399; L. Andrewes, *Ninety-six Sermons* (5 vols, Oxford, 1851–53), V, p. 67; J. Cosin, *Works* (5 vols, Oxford, 1843–55), V, pp. 94, 124, 130, 132–4; J. Spurr, *The Restoration Church of England, 1646–1689* (New Haven and London, 1991), pp. 17–18, 294–5, 348–51; Lake, 'Laudian Style', p. 170. Interestingly, Scudamore only insisted on communion three times a year for his son in Paris in 1639: Arundel Castle Archives, 'Howard Letters and Papers 1636–1822 II Various', Scudamore to Dupont, 5 September 1639.

115 BL, Add. MS 11689, fols 51–2.

116 H. B. Porter, *Jeremy Taylor, Liturgist* (Alcuin Club collections, 61, 1979), pp. 97–100; J. Taylor, *The Whole Works*, ed. R. Heber (15 vols, London, 1828), XIV, pp. 503–4; R. Mountagu, *A Gagg for the New Gospell?* (London, 1624), pp. 83–7, and *Appello Caesarem* (London, 1625), pp. 297–302; Cosin, *Works*, V, pp. 163–4; H. Thorndike, *The Theological Works* (6 vols, Oxford, 1844–56), IV, pp. 258–9, V, p. 610; M. Wren, *Articles to be Inquired of within the Diocesse of Hereford* (London, 1635), sig. Br; Tyacke, *Anti-Calvinists*, pp. 116, 222; Milton, *Catholic and Reformed*, pp. 69–70, 72–5, 472–3; Legg, *English Orders*, pp. lvi, 172–3; BL, Add. MS 70086, no. 74, sequestration of Richard Sterne, Add. MS 11689, fols 51–2.

117 Hammond, *Works*, I, p. 387; BL, Add. MS 11054, fol. 26r.

118 PRO, C115/M14/7281, C115/R4, C115/R6, nos. 1–20; Balliol College MS 333, fol. 57r; HCA, MS 6417, fol. 19r.

119 HRO, Hereford City Records, law day papers, 1655–71, presentation of the third inquest, 19 October 1658, misfiled under April 1659; F. C. Morgan, 'Local Government in Hereford', *Transactions of the Woolhope Naturalists' Field Club*, 31 (1942–45), p. 50; Gibson, *View*, p. 114; PRO, PROB11/336/96, fol. 332r; HCL, MS L.C.929.2, 'Webb MSS: Pengelly and Scudamore Papers', p. 100. The money was allowed to be used for educating poor children by the acts 14 Geo. III. c. 38 and 3 & 4 Vict. c. 125, and there is still a primary school in Hereford named 'Lord Scudamore's School'.

120 PRO, C115/I3/5682–3; Bath City Archives, Furman Cat., p. 641 item 14; T. Dingley, *History from Marble*, ed. J. G. Nichols (2 vols, Camden Society, 1st series, 94, 97, 1867–68), I, p. xlix; Balliol College, MS 333, fol. 56r.

121 Sheffield University Library, Hartlib papers, 51/97A; Beale, *Herefordshire Orchards*, p. 22; Birch, *Royal Society*, I, p. 146; Collins, *Baronetage*, II, p. 176; Sharpe, *Personal Rule*, p. 417; F. Heal, *Hospitality in Early Modern England* (Oxford, 1990).

122 HCL, MSS 647.1, 'Scudamore MSS: Accounts 1640–42', fol. 76r, 'Scudamore MSS: Accounts 1641–42', fol. 3r, and 'Scudamore MSS: Accounts 1635–37[8]', MS L.C.647.1, fol. 98r; J. M. Simpson, *The Folklore of the Welsh Border* (London, 1976), p. 142; R. Hutton, *The Rise and Fall of Merry England: The Ritual Year 1400–1700* (Oxford, 1994), pp. 20–1, 52; E. Duffy, *The Stripping of the Altars: Traditional Religion in England 1400–1580* (New Haven and London, 1992), pp. 24–5.

123 Gibson, *View*, p. 41; B. S. Stanhope and H. C. Moffatt, *The Church Plate of the County of Hereford* (London, 1903), p. 1.

124 PRO, C115/M24/7760, C115/M24/7765, PROB11/336/96, fol. 332r; HRO, AL17/1, 1626, 1671, Holme Lacy Bishops' Transcripts, Box 221, *sub* 1671; Gibson, *View*, pp. 128–9.

125 Donations to St Tysilio's, Sellack, recorded in the church on a board of 1825; Stanhope and Moffatt, *Church Plate*, pp. 154–5. I am indebted to the Revd Maurice Woodward for showing me see the remaining plate at Sellack.

126 HRO, AL17/1, 1626; Sellack donations.

127 F. G. Lee, *A Glossary of Liturgical and Ecclesiastical Terms* (London, 1877), pp. 98, 258–9; P. Dearmer, *Linen Ornaments of the Church* (Alcuin Club tracts, 17, Oxford and London, 1929), pp. 7–8, 14–20; V. Staley, *The Ceremonial of the English Church* (Oxford and London, 1899), pp. 129–31.

128 PRO, C115/N9/8848–9.

129 PRO, SP78/98, fols 307r, 308r; Bodleian, MS Clarendon 7, no. 541, fol. 145r; *Gentleman's Magazine*, 25 (1755), pp. 70–1; HMC, *Report on the Manuscripts of the late Reginald Rawdon Hastings* (4 vols, London, 1928-47), IV, pp. 291–2; E. Hyde, earl of Clarendon, *The History of the Rebellion and Civil Wars in England*, ed. W. D. Macray (6 vols, Oxford, 1888), II, pp. 418–19; V. Staley, ed., *Hierurgia Anglicana* (3 parts, London, 1902–04), I, pp. 56–7, 69–107; D. R. Dendy, *The Use of Lights in Christian Worship* (Alcuin Club collections, 41, 1959), pp. 152–63; R. N. Worth, ed., *The Buller Papers* (privately printed, 1895), p. 128.

130 PRO, C115/N9/8876; Legg, *English Orders*, pp. 9–16, 146–91.

131 The New Testament reading chosen, John 1:13 ff, lays more stress on Jesus's cleansing of the Temple as a sacred place than on his entry into Jerusalem. For the pre-Reformation Palm Sunday see Hutton, *Merry England*, pp. 20–1, and Duffy, *Stripping of the Altars*, pp. 23–7.

132 HRO, AL17/1, 22 March 1601; Legg, *English Orders*, p. 161.

133 Legg, *English Orders*, pp. xxxiii, 164, 166–7, 175–9, 188.

134 Wren had at least a hand in the devising of the consecration order (PRO, C115/N9/8875), and so the preaching of a sermon in the afternoon is noteworthy, because Dr Davies thinks that Wren was one of the few bishops to attempt to suppress all afternoon sermons when he was later bishop of Norwich: J. Davies, *The Caroline Captivity of the Church: Charles I and the Remoulding of Anglicanism 1625–1641* (Oxford, 1992), pp. 139–41.

135 Balliol College, MS 333, fol. 11r.

136 R. W. Blencowe, ed., *Sydney Papers* (London, 1825), pp. 261–2; Clarendon, *Rebellion*, II, pp. 418–19.

137 BL, Add. MS 11044, fol. 83r.

138 BL, Add. MS 11044, fol. 83v; W. Laud, *Harangve Prononcee en la Chambre de l'Estoille* ([Paris], 1637[8]), p. 6; PRO, SP78/104, fols 403r, 430r, 464v; SP78/105, fols 81r, 115r, 134r, 178r.

139 BL, Add. MS 70003, fol. 195v; [T. Aston], *A Collection of Svndry Petitions* ([London], 1642), pp. 39–40; PRO, C115/M14/7312-14, SP23/198, p. 771.

140 N. Sykes, 'The Church of England and Non-episcopal Churches in the Sixteenth and Seventeenth Centuries', *Theology* occasional papers, new series, 11 (London, 1948); Tighe, 'Laud and the Reunion'.

141 HMC, *Portland*, III, p. 584.

142 BL, Add. MS 11044, fols 92–5; PRO, C115/M12/7223; Tighe, 'Laud and the Reunion'.

143 BL, Add. MS 11044, fol. 83; Milton, *Catholic and Reformed*, pp. 345–73.

144 PRO, PRO31/9/17B, a reference I owe to Dr Anthony Milton; E. Chaney, *The Grand Tour and the Great Rebellion* (Geneva, 1985), p. 98.

145 Westminster Diocesan Archives, MSS XXVIII, nos. 81, 206, pp. 325, 643, XXIX, nos. 3, 9, 15, pp. 5, 19, 31.

146 Bodleian, MS Top. Glouc. e.1, fol. 25v; the story was told to Archdeacon Richard Furney in 1717 by 'Welch Thomas', who as a teenager had been one of the royalist soldiers sent to besiege Gloucester in 1643.

147 Cambridge University Library, Add. MS 41, fol. 127.

148 PRO, C115/M14/7313.

149 J. S. Morrill, 'The Church in England, 1642–49', in J. S. Morrill, ed., *Reactions to the English Civil War* (London, 1982), pp. 89–114.

150 C. Oman, *English Church Plate 597–1830* (London, 1957), pp. 145–7; PRO, C115/N9/8849; HRO, AL17/1, 1626; BL, Add. MS 11055, fols 9–12; Buckeridge, *Sermon*, p. 21. Laud had another account of Andrewes's chapel: W. Prynne, *Canterburies Doome* (London, 1646), pp. 120–4.

151 P. A. Welsby, *Lancelot Andrewes 1555–1626* (London, 1964), pp. 129–32, 193, 255, 263, 274; PRO, C115/M24/7772; Atherton, thesis, p. 371.

152 P. Lake, 'Lancelot Andrewes, John Buckeridge, and Avant-garde Conformity at the Court of James I', in L. L. Peck, ed., *The Mental World of the Jacobean Court* (Cambridge, 1991), pp. 113–33; Lake, 'Laudian Style', p. 181; D. MacCulloch, 'The Impact of the English Reformation', *Historical Journal*, 38:1 (1995), p. 152; PRO, C115/D19/1901.

153 Prynne, *Canterburies Doome*, pp. 62–3, 189; PRO, SP78/98, fols 307r, 308r; C. Russell, *The Causes of the English Civil War* (Oxford, 1990), p. 197; *Gentleman's Magazine*, 25 (1755), p. 70.

154 PRO, C115/M14/7312.

155 Prynne, *Canterburies Doome*, pp. 59–62, 466; Atherton, thesis, p. 373.

156 PRO, C115/M12/7223, fol. 65; BL, Add. MS 11044, fol. 93r. Scudamore was paraphrasing Isaiah 33:11. Hezekiah was a pious Old Testament king who purged Judaism of many corruptions: II Kings 18:1–6; II Chronicles 29–31.

157 K. Sharpe, 'The Image of Virtue: The Court and the Household of Charles I, 1625–1642', in D. Starkey *et al.*, eds, *The English Court* (Harlow, 1987), p. 241 n. 88; K. Sharpe, 'The Personal Rule of Charles I', in H. Tomlinson, ed., *Before the English Civil War* (London, 1983), pp. 62–3; Davies, *Caroline Captivity*.

158 Prynne, *Canterburies Doome*, pp. 62–3; W. Laud, *The History of the Troubles and Tryal* (London, 1695), p. 313; E. F. Rimbault, ed., *The Old Cheque-book, or Book of Remembrance, of the Chapel Royal* (Camden Society, 2nd series, 3, 1872), p. 126.

159 Davies, *Caroline Captivity*, pp. 15, 20–1, 213 n. 33.

160 PRO, C115/N9/8848–9.

161 See below, pp. 176, 180–1, 190.

162 Davies, *Caroline Captivity*, pp. 24–5, 44, 84–5.

163 PRO, C115/M24/7758.

164 Davies, *Caroline Captivity*, especially chs 4–6.

165 Atherton, thesis, pp. 373–5.

166 PRO, C115/M24/7758. Wall, *Sermon*, sig. A3r.

167 BL, Add. MSS 11044, fol. 250v, 11051, fols 229–31; B. D. Henning, ed., *The House of Commons 1660–1690* (3 vols, London, 1983), I, pp. 261–2; HMC, *Portland*, III, p. 220; A. Browning, ed., *English Historical Documents 1660–1714* (London, 1953), pp. 57–8.

168 PRO, C115/M12/7223, C115/M14/7313; Laud, *Works*, VI, p. 42.

169 BL, Egerton MS 2714, fol. 363v; J. N. Jackson, 'Some Observations upon the Herefordshire Environment of the Seventeenth and Eighteenth Centuries', *Transactions of the Woolhope Naturalists' Field Club*, 36:1 (1959), pp. 36–7; I. J. Atherton, ed., 'An Account of Herefordshire in the First Civil War', *Midland History*, 21 (1996), pp. 142–3, 149–50; PRO, SP16/492/32; Hutton, *Merry England*, pp. 165–6; *LBH*, p. 167.

170 Beinecke Library, Osborn MS b.28 (the emphasis is mine).

171 For Coningsby and Brabazon see below, chapter 6.

172 BL, Add. MS 11055, fols 182v–3r. For a similar view of patronage see J. Doddridge, *A Compleat Parson* (London, 1630), pp. 5–8.

Chapter 4

Scudamore as a local governor

In October 1625 Roger Palmer sent a long letter to Scudamore with titbits of court news and gossip. Palmer was one of Scudamore's more distant relations but one of his key contacts at court who, through his office as cup-bearer to the king, had immediate access to the royal ear, and in the letter he also detailed how, while waiting upon the king's table, he had bent Charles's ear in favour of Scudamore. The letter is worth quoting extensively.[1]

> I must acquaint you that I tooke occasion vpon speach to the king to speake of the trayned souldiers horse and foote I saw in hereforshire, whereby I spake of the foote beeing well armed theare, and of the good horse vnder your leading for the whole shire, to be as good or better then in kent or middlesex or any I had seene elswhere. And wayghting in my place att the chayr I acquainted his majestie that as you wear his zealously deuoted in the late Parlaments and therein by all dutifull meanes exprest it by your selfe and all you could procure by frendes, you wear in all other services in the country solicitous to doe him service, as in subsedye busines, to aduance it as farr as formerly it euer had beene att least, and in musters you did the like whose power and loue in your country is such that all men weare the more willing and forward to be well accommodated, in his majesties service, for the honor of theyr Captayne.

The letter, and Palmer's efforts on Scudamore's behalf, neatly encapsulate some of the main themes of Scudamore's activity as a local governor from his entry to county politics in 1620 to his appointment as ambassador to France in 1635: the crown's demands for money and an 'exact militia', particularly to enable Charles to cut a grander figure on the European stage; Charles's growing fear from 1625 to 1629 of being betrayed by a populist plot stirred up by some members of the House of Commons; and Scudamore's response to these and his attempts to seek further honour and preferment from the king. Charles and some of his closest advisers clearly linked taxation, the 'exact militia', and responses to government policy, with their fears of populist subversion of legitimate monarchical rule. Charles detected an anti-monarchical spirit at work in commissioners who connived at low subsidy assessments.[2] Lord Keeper Williams declared that inaccurate assessments were a sin against the Holy Ghost, the eternal sin against the divine order that could never be forgiven.[3] William Tucker, who wrote a treatise on how to raise the subsidy, complained of fellow commissioners who 'gather applause of their owne frendes and the common people' in order to 'affect popularitie in all their actions'.[4] Sir Robert Phelips was accused of courting popularity rather than seeking strictly to perfect the trained bands.[5] Privy Council orders concerning subsidies and the militia regularly warned the commissioners and deputy lieutenants that their implementation of crown policies would be monitored and that laxity would not go unpunished. Throughout his reign Charles warned deputies, justices, commissioners and taxpayers that he would regard their enforcement of his policy as a sign of their loyalty to the crown and to him.[6] Palmer's letter, then stands as an introduction to this chapter and the next.

The bedrock of Scudamore's work as a local politician was his service as a JP for Herefordshire, first appointed in February 1622, and his position as *custos rotulorum* of the county, assumed the following May.[7] The patchy survival of evidence makes a complete assessment of Scudamore's work on the commission of the peace elusive, but where evidence remains, for parts of the 1620s and 1660s, he appears as a fairly active justice. Between his appointment to the Herefordshire bench in February 1622 and his elevation to the Irish peerage in July 1628, Scudamore attended thirty of the forty-six session days and chaired eight of the twenty two-day sessions (more than anyone else). In the mid 1660s Scudamore was even more active as a JP, chairing seven of the ten sessions between October 1665 and January 1668. The nature of the evidence means that it is not possible to assess Scudamore's attendance at quarter sessions from his elevation to the peerage in July 1628 until 1665, when the first surviving quarter sessions records begin, but it is known that he attended the assizes in Hereford in 1632, and that he provided sixty-six dinners there for his servants.[8]

Scudamore's attendance at sessions was not, however, vital to the maintenance of his reputation and authority, for networks of friendship and clientage on and below the bench ensured his position and power. He had a number of allies among the senior justices who also acted as chairmen of the sessions,[9] such as Bishop Francis Godwin of Hereford (1562–1633), who wrote a history of England which was dedicated to Scudamore by his son Morgan,[10] his brother-in-law and friend Sir Giles Bridges (*c.* 1573–1637),[11] and his cousin and business partner in an ironworks on the river Wye, Sir John Kyrle, first baronet (1568–1650).[12] Other friends and allies on the bench included his cousin and associate in many estate and business ventures,

William Scudamore of Ballingham (1579–1649),[13] and Dr William Skinner, chancellor of the diocese of Hereford.[14] Moreover, Scudamore kept a firm grip on the machinery of quarter sessions. All the clerks of the peace and deputy clerks of the peace from 1618 to 1642 were closely linked with Scudamore as friends, relatives, associates or servants.[15] For example, in July 1629 Scudamore secured the appointment of his servant the lawyer Richard Seaborne as a JP. Seaborne immediately assumed the clerkship of the peace, and was later appointed by Scudamore as his deputy steward of both Hereford city and the dean and chapter of Hereford.[16] For most of the two decades before the civil war the deputy clerk was John Wilcocks, one of Scudamore's servants who regularly carried messages to London for him and performed many other essential errands.[17] Scudamore had other allies and dependants in key positions in the county's administration. The county treasurer in 1642, for example, was Philip Trehearne, one of his most valued clients and a key ally on the corporation of Hereford.[18] By such means Scudamore ensured his influence over the bench and its work even during his absence in Paris in the later 1630s.

The loss of the quarter sessions and assize papers before the 1660s inevitably circumscribes what can be known about Scudamore's work as a JP and focuses attention on his other responsibilities as a subsidy commissioner, deputy lieutenant and MP, but it was precisely these areas that Palmer chose to highlight in his praise of Scudamore to the king in 1625.[19]

Roger Palmer's claim that Scudamore had advanced the subsidy in Herefordshire 'as farr as formerly it euer had beene att least' was both bold and astute.[20] From 1624 to 1630 the most pressing problem facing the English crown was war finance. The earl of Clarendon opened his *History of the Rebellion and Civil Wars* with the death of James I, leaving Charles 'engaged in a war with Spain, but unprovided with money to manage it'. Within weeks of coming to the throne Charles was committed to spending nearly £500,000 a year on a European land war: £20,000 a month pledged to Count Mansfeld and an equivalent sum to the Danes.[21] The yield of the subsidy had been in steep decline since the early years of Elizabeth's reign: king and privy council were alive to the problem, blaming low assessments which bore little or no relation to the taxpayer's actual wealth. In February 1626, for example, the privy council informed all subsidy commissioners of the true extent of the collapse in subsidy yields since 1559 and demanded that the commissioners 'assess men at higher values than of latter times hath been used'.[22]

Scudamore was closely involved in the collection of the subsidies of 1624, 1625 and 1628 as a subsidy commissioner and, as *custos rotulorum*, had the duty of comparing the new assessment with earlier ones.[23] He cannot, therefore, have been unaware of the decline in the value of the subsidy in Herefordshire.

Table 1 Net sums collected of individual subsidies in Herefordshire, 1621–28

Year	Subsidy	Net total collected £	s.	d.	Index
1621	First	862	2	9	100.0
1621	Second	857	16	8	99.5
1624	First	795	1	4	92.5
1624	Second	786	5	4	91.2
1624	Third	Figures incomplete			
1625	First	784	5	7	91.0
1625	Second	780	0	6	90.5
1628	First & Second	1,482	16	4	86.0
1628	Third	725	3	0	84.1
1628	Fourth	714	15	1	82.9
1628	Fifth	706	9	4	81.9

Sources. The totals collected for Herefordshire subsidies are calculated from the following, all held in the PRO: books and rolls of collectors, E179/283; enrolled accounts, pipe office, accounts of subsidies, 1621–28, E359/62–3, 65–8, 70; pells receipt books, 1621–29, E401/1906–15; abbreviates of pells receipt books, 1622–29, E401/2313–26. These have been compared with the original assessments for Herefordshire, 1621–28, E179/118 and E179/119. Norfolk and Cheshire figures have been extracted and computed from M. J. Braddick, *Parliamentary Taxation in Seventeenth-Century England: Local Administration and Response* (Woodbridge, 1994), appendix 2. The inaccuracies of seventeenth-century accounting mean that the figures can be only approximate. For the procedure of subsidy accounting at the exchequer see R. S. Schofield, 'Parliamentary Lay Taxation 1485–1547' (Cambridge University Ph.D. thesis, 1963), pp. 388–97. Hundreds were grouped variously for collection of the subsidy; I have combined only those most usually (but not always) partnered for collection of the subsidy.

Between 1621 and 1629 there was a fall of more than 18 per cent in the net yield of an individual subsidy collected in Herefordshire (Table 1). These Herefordshire figures can be compared with the Norfolk and Cheshire totals compiled by Mike Braddick (Table 2). Whilst the yield of a subsidy in Norfolk declined by nearly 30 per cent in the 1620s, more than in Herefordshire, the return of the subsidy held steady in Cheshire, showing that decline was not inevitable. Indeed, in the early seventeenth century subsidy yields in Flintshire and southern Gloucestershire actually increased modestly.[24] Nevertheless, in Herefordshire, as in most of England, decline was the order of the day, with each fresh subsidy grant bringing in less than the previous one. Nationally, it was the multiple grants under Elizabeth which had caused the most serious collapse in the subsidy, to which the grants of the 1620s were but a coda.[25] An examination of the returns for Herefordshire from the 1620s, however, can

Table 2 Changing subsidy yields in Herefordshire, Norfolk and Cheshire, 1621–28

Year	Subsidy	Herefordshire index	Norfolk index	Cheshire index
1621	First	100.0	100.0	100.0
1621	Second	99.5	101.5	n/a
1624	First	92.2	90.4	99.7
1624	Second	91.2	87.1	99.2
1624	Third	n/a	86.2	98.0
1625	First	91.0	n/a	102.5
1625	Second	90.5	90.4	103.6
1628	First & Second	86.0	76.7	100.5
1628	Third	84.1	72.0	100.2
1628	Fourth	82.9	70.1	98.7
1628	Fifth	81.9	70.4	98.4

Sources. As Table 1.

illuminate some of the reasons for its continued decline. In Herefordshire as a whole the sharpest decline came with the five subsidies of 1628, although the steepest drop between individual subsidies was from the second subsidy of 1621 to the first one of 1624. The figures suggest very clearly that the paramount principle was precedent, with each subsidy raising slightly less than the last. When, however, the yields from individual hundreds or divisions are analysed, the picture becomes slightly less clear, with greater fluctuation between individual subsidies and some occasions of later subsidies actually raising slightly more than previous ones (Table 3). There were two main reasons for the fall in subsidy returns. The first was inaccurate and low valuations, with the rich especially escaping with low subsidy valuations that bore little relation to their true wealth.[26] The second was that large numbers of subsidy payers simply slipped off the assessments, so that the declining burden was shouldered by an even faster declining number of taxpayers. In 1599, for example, the hundred of Webtree had been assessed for one subsidy by Sir James Scudamore at £99 5s. 4d., laid on at least 229 individual taxpayers. The fifth and final subsidy of 1628, by comparison, was assessed at £61 5s. 3d., borne by 140 named individuals.[27]

The returns by hundreds and divisions suggest that, although individual commissioners were clearly aware of the general situation in other hundreds and divisions, they were not co-ordinating their efforts and there was no overall central control of the subsidy within the county, a role that the privy

Table 3 Net sums collected of individual subsidies in Herefordshire, by hundreds and divisions, 1621–28

Year	Subsidy	Net total collected			Index	% of total collected in county
		£	s.	d.		
(a) Broxash						
1621	First	157	15	10	100.0	18.3
1621	Second	154	3	4	97.7	17.9
1624	First	142	13	8	90.4	17.9
1624	Second	139	5	8	88.3	17.7
1624	Third	135	14	6	86.0	n/a
1625	First	135	8	4	85.8	17.3
1625	Second	135	2	8	85.6	17.3
1628	First & Second	229	15	2	72.8	15.5
1628	Third	110	6	10	69.9	15.2
1628	Fourth	104	15	6	66.4	14.7
1628	Fifth	103	4	2	65.4	14.6
(b) Huntington						
1621	First	27	2	2	100.0	3.1
1621	Second	[88	3	2	with Grimsworth]	
1624	First	27	10	0	101.4	3.5
1624	Second	26	14	0	98.5	3.4
1624	Third	26	6	6	97.1	n/a
1625	First	26	15	2	98.7	3.4
1625	Second	27	18	0	103.9	3.6
1628	First & Second	52	13	2	97.1	3.6
1628	Third	26	13	6	98.4	3.7
1628	Fourth	[81	3	11	with Stretford]	
1628	Fifth	26	5	0	96.8	3.7
(c) Stretford						
1621	First	62	2	2	100.0	7.2
1621	Second	[132	1	6	with Wigmore]	
1624	First	54	16	0	88.1	6.9
1624	Second	54	16	0	88.1	7.0
1624	Third	56	3	0	90.2	n/a
1625	First	58	13	4	94.3	7.5
1625	Second	57	7	8	92.2	7.4
1628	First & Second	111	13	0	89.7	7.5
1628	Third	55	1	4	88.5	7.6
1628	Fourth	[81	3	11	with Huntington]	
1628	Fifth	[142	18	4	with Wolphey]	

Year	Subsidy	Net total collected £	s.	d.	Index	% of total collected in county
(d) Wolphey						
1621	First	127	19	10	100.0	14.8
1621	Second	125	14	4	98.3	14.7
1624	First	123	16	6	96.8	15.6
1624	Second	121	18	2	95.3	15.5
1624	Third	119	15	0	93.6	n/a
1625	First	120	19	0	94.5	15.4
1625	Second	117	5	4	91.7	15.0
1628	First & Second	195	14	8	76.5	13.2
1628	Third	92	11	8	72.4	12.8
1628	Fourth	91	0	2	71.1	12.7
1628	Fifth	[142	18	4	with Stretford]	
(e) Wigmore						
1621	First	65	4	4	100.0	7.6
1621	Second	[132	1	6	with Stretford]	
1624	First	62	5	10	95.5	7.8
1624	Second	62	9	4	95.8	7.9
1624	Third	[Figure missing]				
1625	First	64	4	2	98.5	8.2
1625	Second	61	16	6	94.8	7.9
1628	First & Second	121	17	6	93.4	8.2
1628	Third	63	0	8	96.7	8.7
1628	Fourth	60	13	0	93.0	8.5
1628	Fifth	61	3	7	93.8	8.7
(f) Hereford city						
1621	First	63	4	5	100.0	7.3
1621	Second	62	16	10	99.4	7.3
1624	First	56	11	0	89.4	7.1
1624	Second	55	6	8	87.5	7.0
1624	Third	53	16	6	85.1	n/a
1625	First	52	7	11	82.9	6.7
1625	Second	51	5	4	81.1	6.6
1628	First & Second	95	15	2	75.7	6.5
1628	Third	48	19	8	77.5	6.8
1628	Fourth	48	10	2	76.7	6.8
1628	Fifth	47	16	0	75.6	6.8

Year	Subsidy	Net total collected £	s.	d.	Index	% of total collected in county
(g) Grimsworth						
1621	First	61	8	6	100.0	7.1
1621	Second	[88	3	2	with Huntington]	
1624	First	53	3	8	86.9	6.7
1624	Second	51	2	0	83.2	6.5
1624	Third	51	13	6	84.1	n/a
1625	First	[118	3	6	with Webtree and Ewyas Lacy]	
1625	Second	[115	0	2	with Webtree and Ewyas Lacy]	
1628	First & Second	99	6	10	80.9	6.7
1628	Third	46	11	2	75.6	6.4
1628	Fourth	45	15	8	74.5	6.4
1628	Fifth	45	15	8	74.5	6.5
(h) Webtree and Ewyas Lacy						
1621	First	81	3	3	100.0	9.4
1621	Second	76	13	10	94.5	8.9
1624	First	66	18	0	82.4	8.4
1624	Second	65	18	6	81.2	8.4
1624	Third	64	3	0	79.1	n/a
1625	First	[118	3	6	with Grimsworth]	
1625	Second	[115	0	2	with Grimsworth]	
1628	First & Second	155	2	2	95.7	10.5
1628	Third	75	3	6	92.6	10.4
1628	Fourth	76	18	4	94.8	10.8
1628	Fifth	74	12	8	92.0	10.6
(i) Wormilow, Greytree and Radlow						
1621	First	216	0	2	100.0	25.1
1621	Second	218	3	8	101	24.4
1624	First	207	6	8	96.0	26.1
1624	Second	208	15	0	96.9	26.6
1624	Third	208	19	9	96.7	n/a
1625	First	207	14	2	96.2	26.5
1625	Second	214	4	10	99.2	27.5
1628	First & Second	420	13	10	97.4	28.4
1628	Third	206	14	8	95.7	28.5
1628	Fourth	205	18	4	95.3	28.8
1628	Fifth	204	13	6	94.8	29.0

Sources. As Table 1.

council expected Scudamore, as *custos*, to play. Just as central government surrendered control over assessment to the counties in order to win compliance with the tax, so counties seem to have surrendered control to individual commissioners and collectors for the same reason.

It is necessary, therefore, to consider Scudamore's efforts as a subsidy commissioner. He cannot be accused of indolence: in 1624 he slaved night and day over the assessments, for which he was gently reproved by Laud, but it was to little effect.[28] Far from advancing the subsidy as far as it ever before had been, virtually the only assessment he managed to increase was his own, from a valuation of his Holme Lacy lands of £20 p.a. in 1625 to £100 in 1628, but this was connected with his ennobling, and was on an estate worth about £2,500 a year.[29] The privy council repeatedly exhorted commissioners to set an example to others by raising their own valuations, 'not only [to] show a good demonstration of your zeals to further his Majesty's service but thereby [to] draw others the more willingly to come up to larger taxations'.[30] While Scudamore may have shown his zeal for Charles's service in his own assessment, he failed rather signally in others. He connived at the widespread evasion of the statutory and conciliar demands that justices and subsidy commissioners should be assessed at no less than £20. The lands of Herefordshire justices, commissioners and deputies such as John Hoskins and Roger Vaughan were regularly valued at only £10 by Scudamore and the other commissioners.[31] Such under-assessment was by no means unusual in Norfolk and elsewhere, reflecting what Dr Braddick calls a kind of 'moral arithmetic', whereby subsidy assessments might be discounted against service to the commonwealth, for example as a justice, or in the militia.[32]

As a commissioner, Scudamore was generally allotted to the hundreds of Wormilow, Greytree and Radlow (usually considered as one division), Webtree and Ewyas Lacy (almost always partnered together), and Grimsworth.[33] These were the areas where his estates were concentrated; in these six hundreds, plus Hereford city, which made up the southern half of the county, his power was strongest. Here, then, is where Scudamore had the greatest opportunity to arrest the slide. Analysis of the subsidy returns in these areas reveals a mixed picture (Table 3). In Hereford city and in Grimsworth the decline was more marked than in the county as a whole, with yields falling by a quarter between 1621 and 1628. In Wormilow, Greytree, Radlow, Webtree and Ewyas Lacy, however, the fall was much less marked, with yields down no more than 8 per cent over the same period. The pattern is instructive, for it follows the distribution of Scudamore's estates in the shire: he owned little land in Grimsworth and Hereford, lots in Wormilow, Webtree and Greytree. The social, economic and political power conferred by these estates gave Scudamore considerable leverage over the lower rungs of subsidy administration – the assessors in each parish (probably the constables) and the collectors for each hundred or division. Indeed, a number of historians have suggested that patronage lay at the heart of the early Stuart taxation system.[34] Although it has not been possible to study the assessors, it can be shown that Scudamore and a number of the high collectors were bound by ties of friendship, patronage and economic dependence. Toby Payne, high collector of the first subsidy of 1624 in Wormilow, Radlow and Greytree, had long-established links with the Holme Lacy Scudamores. He was a friend, client and servant of Scudamore himself, his grandfather, father and great-uncle, and was to go on to be the viscount's steward for a number of manorial courts; he also lent the viscount money.[35] Four high collectors, Richard Hall (first subsidy of 1621 for Wormilow, Greytree and Radlow), Henry Melling (first subsidy of 1624 for Hereford), James Barroll (first and second subsidies of 1628 for Hereford) and Rowland Eckley (fifth subsidy of 1628 for Grimsworth) had direct links with Scudamore as servants, retainers or tenants, while a further three, William Apperley (second subsidy of 1621 for Greytree and Radlow), Abel Carwardine (second subsidy of 1624 for Webtree), Richard Colloe (fourth subsidy of 1628 for Wormilow), acknowledged themselves the viscount's clients in 1639 by sending him presents at Christmas that year. Apperley was also distantly related to Scudamore, having married Joan Scudamore of Ballingham.[36]

Scudamore's achievement over the subsidy, then, was distinctly limited and fell far short of Palmer's bravura. Nevertheless, Scudamore was certainly alive to the crown's desperate need for money. He lamented the dissolution of the 1626 parliament for losing the king £500,000, and in 1628 supported a failed motion to lay down a minimum £50 subsidy valuation on himself and the other English baronets.[37] Why, then, did he fail to translate his views into higher assessments on his neighbours? The answer lies with the traditions and requirements of subsidy brokerage and assessment. Notions of equity rather than accuracy lay behind the assessments that commissioners and taxpayers expected. Even the privy council, despite its pressure for higher yields, bowed to reality and told commissioners in 1626 that it did 'not expect ... that ... all men should be taxed at their just and true values either in lands or goodes', just that men should be rated 'neerer to their abilities and liveing'.[38] Because subsidy valuations were often used to determine liability for other rates, such as for the militia, this notion of equity extended far beyond the immediate payment of a particular subsidy, and an individual's assessment was, therefore, the product of a complex series of calculations in 'moral arithmetic', tradition and the power relationship between taxpayer, assessor, collector, commissioner and crown. Raising any person's assessment was fraught with difficulty. Tucker explained that his attempts as a commissioner to increase subsidy yields had provoked the 'cankered malice of some either open or secret enemies' and complained that 'To raise any man rich or potent whosoever, is not only matter of vnkindnesse, but action of iniurie and reuengeable iniury also'. It was not merely attempts to increase assessments that might be met with determined opposition. When, early in Charles I's reign, Humphrey Morrice tried to distrain for non-payment of the second subsidy of 1625 in London the victim's father-in-law prevented the distraint with the words 'You are very busy in your office, and more busy than you need to be ...' and by gathering an angry crowd. The constable had to come to Morrice's aid and lead him away. Had Scudamore tried seriously to carry out his boast to the king, he would have courted political disaster. In Hampshire the only reward for Thomas Milward's attempts at reform of subsidy assessments was the loss of the support of his fellow commissioners, who procured his removal from the subsidy commission.[39]

Given the near impossibility of reforming the subsidy, recognised by the crown in its abandoning of directly assessed taxes after the Restoration, and given Scudamore's very limited success, Palmer's claim on his friend's behalf that Scudamore had advanced the subsidy 'as farr as formerly it euer had beene att least' was a particularly brazen bit of spin doctoring.[40] Sensitive to the privy council's warnings that their zeal over the subsidy was being watched, commissioners elsewhere were content with more modest claims while covering themselves with excuses about the poverty of their area, the 'deadness and damp of commerce', or the heavy burden of recent taxation.[41] First the Elizabethan and then the early Stuart crown bought acquiescence to royal taxation by surrendering the mechanism of assessment wholly into local hands. The price to the crown was a collapse in the yield of an individual subsidy; the benefit to the commissioners was, as Roger Schofield has commented, 'the local political capital they could make from favourable assessments'.[42] As Dr Braddick has stressed, it was not the nexus of the centre–locality relationship that shaped the collection of the Elizabethan and Jacobean subsidy so much as the interplay between competing interests within the locale; often it was a case of 'pure country to pure country: the interest of the national government appears nowhere in the equation'.[43] What Scudamore seems perceptively to have realised as early as the autumn of 1625 was that Charles was a king who was no longer prepared to pay such a high price for a smooth-running taxation system. Charles, with the financial expedients of the later 1620s and 1630s – privy seals, the forced loan, knighthood fines and ship money – was attempting to wrest the reigns of control back for the crown, first by greater cajoling and threatening of the local gentry charged with collecting the taxes, second, in the case of ship money, by returning to a quota-based assessment. That he failed is a measure both of the magnitude of the task and of his own political ineptitude. While Charles's policies undoubtedly made political life much less comfortable for local governors, they also gave the ambitious a greater opportunity to seek preferment from the crown in return for a job well done. It was this moment that Scudamore was trying to seize.

Whereas previous historians have understood taxation in terms of the local patronage that subsidy commissioners could accrue and dispense by manipulating assessments,[44] the case of Scudamore and the Caroline subsidy suggests that there is a story to be told of the national political capital that might be made from the service of the subsidy.

As the council threatened local governors that their activities in the subsidy were being watched, so even more did king, favourite and council supervise the financial expedients of the early years of Charles's reign, viewing them very much as tests of loyalty for the county gentry;[45] yet from Scudamore and Herefordshire they drew a very qualified response. There could be no opposition to the statutory basis of the subsidy, merely complaints about the levels of assessment or evasions and under-assessment, but the authority of financial expedients such as the forced loan could be and was questioned, making the lot of the commissioners even more difficult, for their response could be, and indeed was, interpreted in ideological terms. Scudamore's main concern in response to the privy seal loan of 1625–26 was to protect himself from all sides. A copy of the king's letter of 17 September 1625 to the earl of Northampton, lord president of the council in the marches and lord lieutenant of Herefordshire, ordering a return of the names of those fit to lend to the crown 'with in the Counties of our principallity of wales' arrived at Holme Lacy on 14 October, with a covering note from the earl. At first, Scudamore and the other local governors, still busy with the first subsidy granted earlier that year, did nothing; ignoring the crown's demand for loans on privy seals was almost a national sport, the first response in other counties too, such as Warwickshire. On 24 November 1625 John Rudhall wrote to Scudamore to admit that 'In the business of the Priuy seales wee haue done nothinge, but left euery man to make his owne excuse'. However, Rudhall and Scudamore then set about organising a programme of meetings to assess the loan in six hundreds.[46] Nonetheless, they did not immediately inform the lord president of their action. Northampton, reprimanded by the privy council for not returning the expected list of those fit to pay, was still complaining to the Herefordshire deputies about their lack of co-operation on 7 January 1626.[47] Instead, Scudamore and ten other justices, but interestingly not Rudhall, wrote to Northampton refusing to do anything about the loan on the grounds that the king's letter authorised them to act only in Wales, and Herefordshire was no part of the principality. They were using the old arguments about the jurisdiction of the council of Wales from the four shires controversy to evade unpopular instructions. Six days after the justices sent their letter, however, Northampton returned to the privy council a list of those able to lend in Herefordshire. It looks as if Scudamore and Rudhall had sent him their returns compiled seven weeks earlier.[48] The privy seal loan, as an unparliamentary way, had been unpopular: Scudamore and the other JPs had previously, in 1622, expressed their preference for parliamentary taxation, although this was mainly a delaying tactic.[49] National resistance to the privy seal loan was no doubt compounded by the fact that it was set in motion in between the first and second subsidies of 1625. The project was revitalised by the privy council in April 1626, with Rudhall as collector in Herefordshire, but he brought in less than £400. The privy seal loan had met with foot-dragging across the country and was finally abandoned in the summer of 1626.[50] Scudamore's response was a bold, imaginative and disingenuous attempt to satisfy all sides.

Scudamore was well prepared for the biggest of Charles's financial expedients of the 1620s, the forced loan. Early in 1626 he borrowed a book from the antiquary and newsmonger Ralph Starkey which showed how English kings 'have Releeved their estates without parleament'. Scudamore's close friend and court confidant Sir Henry Herbert forewarned him about the loan on 29 September 1626, placing the importance of his response in a European context, 'this [is] not to make him out of loue with Parlaments ... Giue freely and then will be mony enough to maintaine 10000. for the king of Denmark'. The importance placed by the king on a right response was further reinforced to Scudamore by Laud in January 1627: 'attend the seruice of his Maiestye in the loane, and nourishe that good opinion he hath of you'.[51] From the announcement of the loan in the autumn of 1626 to the following February Scudamore was kept informed of the progress of the loan in other counties, from a standpoint broadly sympathetic to the king's aims, by Amerigo Salvetti, the Tuscan resident whom Scudamore employed as a newsfactor.[52]

The Herefordshire commissioners for the loan first met at Hereford on 13 February 1627, in the presence of the earl of Northampton. Out of the twenty-five Herefordshire gentlemen named to the commission, only Scudamore and nine others were present.[53] Despite the low turn-out, the city and seven of the eleven other hundreds subscribed or consented to the loan before Northampton departed. The king and council seemed well pleased and praised the commissioners' care and diligence. In neighbouring Gloucestershire, by comparison, twelve of the twenty-five commissioners openly refused both payment and subscription just three days after the meeting at Hereford. In Herefordshire only one commissioner, John Rudhall, is recorded as having refused to pay. Having been so active in the privy seal loan, but with so little success, he was perhaps a little piqued at this fresh imposition.[54]

Scudamore's position as the leading magnate in Herefordshire with an influence stretching across the southern marches, the most powerful of the loan commissioners, and as a potential patriot who, on his past record, may be thought not to have been entirely in support of the loan, was recognised by John Burgoyne, minister of Cirencester in Gloucestershire. Burgoyne preached against the loan and sent letters to a number of leading figures in the southern marches, including Scudamore, urging opposition to it. In Scudamore in 1627, however, he picked the wrong man. Scudamore tried to nourish the king's good opinion of him by reporting Burgoyne to the privy council. Burgoyne was arrested and threatened with a show trial in star chamber for sedition. There was, no doubt, an element of self-preservation in Scudamore's response. Mr Dutton of Gloucestershire received a similar letter, which he burned instead of disclosing to the government; for this he was imprisoned by the privy council.[55]

By the summer of 1627 the privy council's initial pleasure at the commissioners' progress in Herefordshire had turned sour as the commissioners delayed and dragged out the collection of the loan. The commissioners began to show a distinct lack of enthusiasm for the service. They applied only the minimum of pressure to those who refused to pay, merely calling defaulters before them; they explained their laxity to the privy council with the disingenuous excuse that this was 'as much as We cann performe in the execucion of this service'.[56] Their lack of zeal is shown best in the sums raised for the loan in Herefordshire. Nationally the loan was a striking financial success, raising £267,064 15s. 11d. (if the amount collected but paid in the shires, spent on billeting and supplying the army, is included). This compares with the £275,000 raised by the five subsidies of 1628; in other words the forced loan raised nearly 97 per cent of the five subsidies it was supposedly equal to.[57] In Herefordshire, however, the loan raised £2,704 16s., or just 75 per cent of the £3,628 14s. 8d. raised by the five subsidies in the county.[58]

In all hundreds except Broxash the response to the loan, compared with the sums raised by the five subsidies of 1628, was disappointing, but the poorest response was in three of the hundreds where Scudamore's power was strongest and in which he usually acted as a subsidy commissioner: Grimsworth, Webtree and Ewyas Lacy. Scudamore and the other commissioners had disguised their intentions, balancing responsibilities to crown and county. They had not openly refused, but had hidden behind a façade of work whilst taking the sting out of the loan's tail, producing a low return in the county, particularly by certifying that a large number of subsidy payers were too poor to contribute to the loan; a similar course was pursued by the diligent commissioners in Hampshire.[59] In so doing they probably helped to defuse the forced loan, for there is no evidence of it becoming politically charged as it did in neighbouring Gloucestershire and elsewhere. Across the country the elections to parliament in 1628 saw the return of loan refusers in large numbers, but not in Herefordshire: two of the county's MPs (Scudamore for the city and Sir Giles Bridges for the shire) had been active as commissioners and none was recorded as a non-payer.[60]

Scudamore's response to two more of Charles's financial expedients and demands, knighthood fines and the commission for the repair of St Paul's

Cathedral, can be examined for further evidence of his reaction and the ways he sought to balance local reputation and credit with the king.

By a precedent originating from the twelfth century, all men who had for three years held freehold land worth more than £40 a year had an ancient duty to present themselves for knighthood at the coronation. In the early years of Charles's reign some creative archival research in the Tower led to the rediscovery of this long-disused right. After nearly three years of wondering how best to exploit this particular feudal due, in the summer of 1630 the crown sent out a knighthood commission to every county. Over the next two years the commission was renewed three times. The crown's proceedings were both novel, since earlier commissions had been restricted to London, and purely fiscal in intent. There was no question of creating more knights (on coming to the throne Charles was convinced that there were already more knights than necessary), simply of fining those who had failed to appear at the coronation as an excuse to raise money.[61] Scudamore headed the commission in Herefordshire and was appointed collector.[62] Distraint of knighthood was legal but unpopular. Secretary Dorchester dubbed it 'the business of no knights', adding that it was 'lawful' but 'extraordinary', 'no man disputing the legality of it in general'. Clarendon noted afterwards that 'though it had a foundation in right, yet, in the circumstances of proceeding, was very grievous, and no less unjust'.[63] The response of Scudamore and the Herefordshire commissioners showed a nice sense of these competing tensions, the legality of the commissions and the desire to serve the king and fulfil their duty, coupled with the realisation that the manner of proceeding might be seen as grievous and unjust.

Scudamore and his fellow commissioners made the business of the knights a comparative success in Herefordshire. On the first commission sixty men paid a total of £677; the names of a further forty-nine were returned to the exchequer as refusers. Although this is not a particularly high proportion of payers, it compares very favourably with neighbouring Gloucestershire, where only twenty-eight of 300 persons compounded on the first commission.[64] By the close of the fourth commission thirty-two of these forty-nine in Herefordshire who had refused on the first commission had been prevailed upon – ground down, mostly, by repeated summons – to compound. In total £1,558 10s., the equivalent of two subsidies at the 1628 rate, was raised from 129 Herefordshire men, a considerably better return than from many counties.[65]

The Herefordshire commissioners had performed a difficult balancing act. They had learnt the lessons of the forced loan, perhaps better than their counterparts elsewhere. They acted jointly: of the seven commissioners only Rudhall, named to the third commission, does not seem to have acted.[66] Furthermore, they did not stall, as the justices and deputies had done over the privy seal loans, but acted promptly. Each commission was executed within two months of its receipt (saving the paying in of all the money), no mean feat considering the work involved. In this the Herefordshire commissioners contrast sharply with their counterparts in other counties. Commissioners in Cornwall, Norfolk and Kent were all unenthusiastic and unco-operative. Lord Montagu was apprehensive about the legality of the powers conferred on him by the royal instructions, and wanted to seek further advice from the council; his doubts probably increased the number in Northamptonshire who refused to compound, forty-three out of fifty-seven by November 1630.[67] In Sussex Anthony Fletcher found that there was no serious attempt to execute the commission fully. The magnates, he concluded, 'merely dipped into the pool' of the large numbers eligible 'to provide a respectable showing'. In contrast the Herefordshire commissioners certainly did more than pick upon a few names to fend off the privy council.[68] Scudamore and his colleagues cast their net wide, and then let many through the holes. Under the third commission, for example, at least 246 persons were summoned by the commissioners; of these, twenty-four compounded and seventeen were returned into the exchequer with their various excuses. The other 200 or so must have been let off, the commissioners presumably convinced by their pleas of poverty or exemption.[69]

The commissioners acted to ease local resentment in other ways. Scudamore responded to the inevitable complaints from the mayor of Hereford that he, as steward, should be more jealous of the city's liberties and involve the corporation more closely in the business, by bringing in Philip Trehearne, one of his clients in the corporation, to lend his support. At least ten men in the city then compounded.[70] Second, despite the tenor of Charles's instructions, the commissioners could act with tactful leniency, accepting compositions below the official minimum rates.[71] Justice John Abrahall, for example, rated at £10 in the 1628 subsidy, escaped from the first commission with a fine of only £20. His strong links with the Scudamores may have helped lessen his fine, for he could hardly plead poverty: a few years later he was able to lend the viscount £1,300.[72] Usually they were content with £10, a sum small enough to ensure reluctant payment by most after they had failed to secure exemption from the commissioners. The privy council was far less lenient than the Herefordshire commissioners: the largest fine, £100 paid by Francis Smallman, was levied by the board, not by the county commissioners.[73] Finally, however, persistent determination was usually sufficient to evade payment to the county commissioners. Eleven persons who refused on the first commission were still being returned as refusers on the fourth commission. By then, Scudamore and his fellows had adopted the expedient of pleading their own ignorance, merely returning the excuses to the exchequer with the comment 'wee Cannot informe ourselves whether the same be true or nott'.[74] After four commissions Scudamore and the others, Pilate-like, were washing their hands of the business, signalling to the council that there were limits to their co-operation. As with the forced loan, Scudamore and his fellow commissioners acted to minimise local resentment at the crown's demands by interpreting the council's instructions leniently. They spread the net wide to raise greater revenue, but softened their approach by accepting the pleas of perhaps most of those whom they summoned. The contrast with the commission for collections towards the repair of St Paul's Cathedral could hardly be greater.

On Wednesday 4 June 1561 the spire of St Paul's Cathedral in London was struck by lightning, and the spire and part of the roof were destroyed by fire. Only the roof was subsequently repaired. Thenceforth the state of St Paul's, the City's most important church, was regarded as a national disgrace, but the monarch and privy council showed only spasmodic interest, never sustained for long enough to achieve much. James I had seemed poised to spearhead a rebuilding, but the initiative quickly lapsed.[75] He was said to have vowed to fast on bread and water until the church was repaired,[76] but his promise was soon forgotten and he built the Banqueting Hall instead for richer fare.

Only Charles, who, in Clarendon's judgement, 'had already discover'd an Activity, that was not like to suffer him to sit still',[77] with the backing of Laud, had the energy to sustain the necessary momentum to see the repairs through to their completion. They made St Paul's a central plank in their campaign to repair and beautify churches throughout the land, a visible assertion of their belief in the church of England as both catholic and reformed, a church with a history, but a church revived and purified. As Edmund Waller versified of the king's intent, St Paul's was 'an earnest of his grand design, / To frame no new church, but the old refine'. Charles and Laud attempted to make commitment to the restoration of St Paul's a measure of commitment to their ideology. (We shall see later how difficult it is to judge most people's reactions in this way.) Writing to the inns of court in 1638 for subscriptions to the repair, Charles stated boldly that 'wee shall take notice of ther seuerall expressions as a signe of ther zeale to religion and conformity to our Royall example'. This was a dangerous line to take if the collection was not as successful as expected.[78]

After failing to raise sufficient money from London and surrounding areas, Charles turned to the whole of England and Wales for support. County commissions, issued to all justices, were sent out in September 1632, too late for anything to be done that year.[79] Scudamore, who as *custos* headed the commission, had been forewarned by John Pory, one of his newsletter writers, in May that county commissions were imminent.[80] The following spring, Scudamore threw himself into his duties with great energy. He addressed the assembled gentry, probably at the Easter sessions of 1633, on the subject.[81] The viscount concentrated on persuading the assembled company of their God-given duty to repair and beautify churches. His speech was peppered with biblical allusions yet reason was his main text. 'Vse your reason,' he urged his auditors, 'Reason being that instrument which the Creator of all things hath graciously bestowd vpon reasonable creatures, to the end wee should vse it when wee would discerne good from evil.' Mere reason showed the necessity of worship, from which followed the need for churches: 'the very light of nature doth cleerly discover that there is not only an inward reasonable worship belonging vnto god, but also a solemne outward serviceable worship, wherunto convenient place is necessary'. Such places ought to be as 'magnificall and great' as the 'almightiness and incomparable greatness' of God Himself, 'for whose service they were set apart'. The light of reason urged the necessity of magnificent adornment of the places of divine worship so strongly that the very heathen obeyed its dictates. It was, thought Scudamore, 'a vniforme example' of the heathen to honour their gods 'with the best of their wealth'. Reason pressed so hard on King David that, despite the Lord's command not to build the temple, he felt aggrieved that his own house was of cedar while the ark of God had only a tent. 'In the eye of reason it appear'd greiuous to him that the habitation of the most high, should be inferiour to the dwelling of a mortall creature.' Reason even worked on God, who was swayed by David's argument and approved of his desire to build a temple.[82]

In addition to reason, Scudamore had three further examples to persuade each of his countrymen to 'fill his hand to day vnto the Lord'. The first was the example of former ages, not just the Israelites but the more recent times of the great cathedral builders. So generous were the people then, marvelled Scudamore, that proclamations were needed to stop them from giving any more, lest too much be collected. The

> time hath beene, when for a worke of this nature the tender women did not only offer all their Jewells and other ornaments of their bodyes to the worke but did cary out even in their bosomes the very dust and earth which was digg'd out, not regarding the costliness of theire apparell, or the tenderness of their bodies.

How much less was asked now, when Scudamore merely hoped for the price of a bushel or two of grain from 'any man heere that keeps a plow and looks to reape the benefitt of a good Harvest'.

Second, Scudamore warned his audience with reminders of God's vengeance on the Israelites when they repaired and beautified their own houses but neglected the house of the Lord. Any who cast a mocking eye on those who gave generously to the repair of churches, he counselled, should 'take heede lest the ravens of the valley pluck it out, and the yong eagles eat it'. Bitter experience had taught the Israelites that when they had power and opportunity 'by plentie and peace' to look after their own houses, that was the time 'wherin gratitude expected the house of the Lord should not lye wast'. Under the peace of Solomon the Jews had built their temple; now was that time, promised Scudamore, when England, with 'the peace which wee enioy vnder our Salomon', should repair St Paul's, 'this principall ornament of the land'.

Scudamore's final argument was the example set by Charles himself. 'Our gracious vnspotted Soveraigne leads the way,' having given order for the payment of a 'great summe' of his own wealth. If the people 'offred willingly vnto the Lord with a perfite heart', then the king would rejoice 'with great joy'.

Scudamore's speech ploughed many of the same furrows as other exhortations to contribute to the repair of St Paul's. The attempt to embarrass the present age by comparison with earlier, more generous times was almost universal. Bishop Walter Curle of Winchester, in a letter to his clergy in 1634, contrasted the present day with 'former times when Religion was in life' and the people gave with alacrity, 'noe cost spared, nothing too good, noe thing too much for God and his Church'.[83] Bishop Richard Corbet, in a speech to the clergy of Norwich diocese in April 1634 that circulated widely, used the same story as Scudamore of the charity of former times being given so fast that it had to be stopped by order.[84] While there was nothing new in using the example of medieval generosity to beat contemporary Protestant parsimony, such language was often more politically charged in the 1630s. Previously, these arguments had been cast within a wider context of criticism of Romish abuses, of censure of the time of popery. During the Laudian campaign to repair St Paul's and re-edify other churches, by contrast, such caveats were often dropped, and the rhetoric of Laud and his followers looked to their enemies like unqualified admiration of the piety of the Roman church.[85] In this context it is worth noting that, while Scudamore's speech praised the generosity of the past but made no reference to any abuses of the church at that time, the warrant from the Herefordshire commissioners to church-wardens ordering a collection to be taken noted what a 'Scandall' it would be if St Paul's, 'raised in the times of Superstition and ignorance', should go unrepaired and so fall down 'nowe in the dayes of Godes true worshippe'.[86]

Just as common as arguments about the munificence of earlier ages were the biblical examples of David and Solomon.[87] Graham Parry and Julian Davies have suggested that Charles I attracted neither the biblical parallels associated with his father, 'Great Britain's Solomon', nor any consistent religious imagery, until after his martyrdom.[88] The propaganda in favour of St Paul's suggests otherwise. Scudamore was not alone in praising Charles as 'our Salomon'. Bishop Curle drew the distinction further. James I, who wished to see St Paul's restored but who did little, was David, while Charles was David's son Solomon, blessed by God with the glory of effecting the rebuilding.[89] The analogy with Solomon was significant for two reasons. First, he was the biblical exemplar of both wisdom and temple building. Second, Solomon's temple was widely regarded as the origin of the classical orders of architecture, expressing the universal and fundamental harmonies. By repairing St Paul's in classical style, Charles was not merely following the latest architectural fashion, he was echoing the wisdom of Solomon and the structured hierarchies of the divinely ordered commonwealth that so many of his other projects, such as his reform of his own household or the court masques, sought to promote.[90]

Charles himself was central to all the arguments in favour of giving to the repairs; his was the royal example to follow. The king's promise to pay for the west end himself was much repeated, as was his desire to have undertaken the whole work himself, had the cost been not so great. The king was explicitly identified as the 'Author' of the project by Giles Fleming. Since the person of the king was bound up with the project, so the honour of the king became dependent on its success.[91] The irony is that in a book which attempts to argue that the church policies of the 1630s were the initiative of the king, and not the archbishop of Canterbury, 'Carolinism', not 'Laudianism', Julian Davies sees the restoration of St Paul's as one of the few 'authentically Laudian projects' of the decade.[92] The propaganda of the project suggests otherwise, that the campaign was a genuinely royal enterprise among a whole host of plans that are otherwise best described as Laudian.

Scudamore had shown why the folk of Herefordshire should repair and adorn churches; that he felt it necessary to explain from first principles suggests, perhaps, that he thought they needed heavy prompting. What he did not do, however, was to demonstrate why they should pay for the repair of St Paul's Cathedral in far-away London. This was a theme of much of the arguments in favour of St Paul's, but not Scudamore's. Others contended that St Paul's embodied the religion of England, that it was 'the mother church of the kingdome in a sort ... the most magnificent church of churches', or '*Cathedram Cathedrarum*, The mother of all our Cathedrals'. It was held to be a 'speciall ornament' not only to London but to the whole kingdom, even (with some exaggeration) held up as the eighth wonder of England, 'whose lyke for greatnes is not in Christendome'. As such, it bore witness to the world to the state of the church of England and the Protestant religion.[93] Of all this, Scudamore said nothing. He attempted to show that repairing and beautifying churches was a God-given duty, but he did not explain why it should be the subsidymen of Herefordshire who should pay for St Paul's. He embraced the project enthusiastically and set an early example to the people of Hereford-shire. As soon as Charles had launched the appeal for money, Scudamore responded. On 14 November 1631 he gave 100 marks towards the repair, only the twenty-sixth person in the country to contribute since the first commission was issued.[94] Meanwhile, to borrow another of the viscount's phrases, the people of Herefordshire remained more 'like the Crampe fish', cold in their devotions.

With the launch of the county commission, Herefordshire was divided in two. Wallop Brabazon took charge of the four northern hundreds of Wolphey,

Wigmore, Stretford and Broxash; Scudamore took the southern seven. These he split, appointing his servant and clerk of the peace Richard Seaborne collector of Grimsworth, Webtree, Ewyas Lacy, Huntington and the city of Hereford, and his cousin Sir John Kyrle collector of Greytree, Radlow and Wormilow.[95] The southern commissioners met in mid April 1633 to summon all the subsidymen and others before them to take subscriptions and receive monies. Refusers were summoned three further times, in July, in August and again the following summer after the commission had been renewed. Following their instructions from the privy council, the commissioners encouraged those of lesser abilities to contribute towards parish collections made in church, a way of proceeding similar to that used for church briefs. Monies collected were delivered to the chamberlain of London (appointed to receive all monies), a task which continued until February 1636.[96] No doubt animated by Scudamore's zeal, the justices of the seven southern hundreds went through the form of joining in the service. Of the seventeen justices resident in Hereford and these seven hundreds, at least twelve were involved in executing the commission.[97] The driving force, nonetheless, was Viscount Scudamore. William Scudamore of Ballingham noted that his cousin the viscount 'did take great care and paines for the advancement of that service'. With the viscount's appointment as ambassador to Paris in 1635 the effort virtually ceased. When in mid 1637 the privy council tried once more to reinvigorate the collection, the Herefordshire commissioners replied lamely that they had not met again.[98]

Scudamore's vigour met none in return. Only his energy rescued the collection from complete failure. Under the first commission £216 5s. 6d. was collected in the seven southern hundreds and Hereford city, while over £184 remained assessed but unpaid. Scudamore had assessed his division of the county for the equivalent of one whole subsidy, but had been able to collect only just over half that. The second commission raised a mere £30 17s., and with the viscount's departure to Paris none was paid to London. The story in the four northern hundreds, untouched by Scudamore's zeal, was even more disappointing. Here only £38 5s. 6d. was collected, compared with an assessment of well over £300 in each of the 1628 subsidies.[99] Elsewhere rates for contributions to the repairs were based on the subsidy, as in Staffordshire, on purveyance, as in Hampshire, or the poor rate, as in York.[100]

One way of assessing reactions to the project across England and Wales is to compare the sums demanded on the ship money writs of 1635 (to give an approximation of each county's wealth, as perceived by the privy council) and the sums collected for the repair of St Paul's between 1632 and Michaelmas 1640.[101] Nationally, the county collections raised £21,283 17s. 6¾d., or just under 10.3 per cent of the £202,500 levied in ship money in 1635. In Herefordshire the proportion was 6.4 per cent. Wide variation across the kingdom is noticeable in the returns. Distance from St Paul's itself was a key factor, for the most generous counties (Middlesex, Sussex and Hertfordshire, contributing 37 per cent, 21.4 per cent and 20.4 per cent of their 1635 assessments, respectively) were all in or not far from the diocese of London, while some of the least generous (such as Cornwall, Montgomeryshire and Northumberland, where the proportion was less than 4.5 per cent) were far removed from the cathedral. Distance, however, was not all. Buckinghamshire, for example, in the diocese of Lincoln, was the second least generous county of all, at only 2.5 per cent. Widely recognised as a crucial factor in soliciting contributions was the attitude of the commissioners themselves.[102] In southern Herefordshire Scudamore raised the equivalent of just over half a subsidy, whereas nationally county collections raised less than four-tenths of a subsidy. The other commissioners utterly failed to give Herefordshire a stirring lead. Sir John Kyrle was active as a collector but declined to add any money to the time he contributed. He was followed by several other commissioners: John Hoskins, Sir Walter Pye (probably the elder), Sir Richard Hopton and John Vaughan declined to contribute, even though the sums involved were paltry.[103]

Overall, the repair of St Paul's was a success for the Caroline regime. Over £101,000 was raised in ten years. By comparison, when the restoration commission was relaunched in 1663 it gathered only £14,728 in ten years; after the Restoration it took nearly twenty years to raise what Charles and Laud had managed in ten, and that was achieved largely by an imposition on coal. By September 1642 the choir had been repaired, the nave and transepts recased in classical style, a west portico added, and the buildings which had crowded against the cathedral swept away; work was about to commence on the tower when the upheaval of the civil war brought everything to a stop.[104] The county collections, however, bore little of the credit for the success. Only just over £21,000 was raised by the county commissions, despite years of appeals, threats and cajoling; much more important were the contributions of a few individuals, such as Charles himself, who gave over £8,000, and Sir Paul Pindar, who donated £9,000, and the diversion of all fines levied by high commission to the repairs.[105]

There is a variety of reasons for the failure of the county commissions. Opposition to the rebuilding of St Paul's as a part of the Laudian programme of the beauty of holiness cannot be ruled out: John Bastwick denounced the whole project as 'making a seat for a priest's arse'.[106] Nevertheless, it is hard to detect puritanism behind responses to the commissions. Strongholds of puritanism such as Bristol were relatively generous, while some puritan gentry, such as Sir Thomas Barrington in Essex, were active in soliciting contributions.[107] A number of historians have tried to read responses to the collection as a straightforward index of attitudes to Laudianism; it cannot be done.[108]

A far more important ideological response to the collection revolved around the issue of compulsion. The collection was a benevolence, strictly voluntary, and all the propaganda reflected the free and voluntary nature of the contributions as gifts. The pro-forma acquittances which the privy council ordered to be printed stressed that the monies received were 'freely giuen'. Laud advised the bishops of his province to summon the clergy to exhort non-payers, but counselled them against 'pressing any man beyond that which he shall please voluntarily and cheerfully to give'.[109] Nevertheless, the machinery of summoning those deemed able to pay and, as in Herefordshire, resummoning those who refused to give a further three times, smacked of compulsion. Further pressure was applied to those judged able to contribute. The privy council warned that notice was taken of those who had refused to pay, and the board carefully scrutinised the lists of those who had contributed. The insistence was on very careful record keeping, with, for example, two lists of those who contributed to the parochial collections drawn up, one for the commissioners, the other to be kept in the parish chest. Such strict accounting was double-edged. On the one hand it was in the tradition of medieval benefactors' rolls and was to ensure that there was a record 'to remayne for a testimony of their good devotion'; on the other, it was a way of checking up on non-contributors.[110]

The question of enforcement was a lively issue. One writer, probably Bishop Richard Mountagu of Chichester, thought that, though the collection was voluntary, by both the laws of the land and the canons of the church it would have been lawful for the king to impose it as a compulsory 'Exaction'. The powers of the commissioners were not clearly defined and much depended on individual initiative. While some went through the motions of the service and returned the small sums collected with excuses about the poverty of their area or hollow assertions that the monies promised were a fair reflection of people's ability to pay, others returned the names of the refractory to the board and even asked for exemplary punishment against constables who were deemed negligent and niggardly in the collection.[111]

The methods of commissioners and council backfired in many instances and stirred up resentment against the collection. In Dorset Denis Bond noted that 'some men [were] inforced to give, by the active clergy then put in justices of the Peace'.[112] The Herefordshire commissioner James Tomkins was prepared to invite contributions in Greytree hundred but, finding 'a certaine Cohersion or Compulsion in the later perte' of a warrant summoning refusers in Grimsworth, refused to sign it, despite pressure from Scudamore.[113] Bartholomew Garwell, a Lincolnshire yeoman, threatened to prosecute any commissioners with *praemunire* if they sent summons to refusers.[114] Other ideological responses to the collection in Herefordshire also turned on this principle of coercion. Henry Rogers preached in the cathedral that the collection was justified by the royal prerogative, suggesting that he believed that the commissioners had the power to force people to contribute. The sermon provoked the notorious James Clarke, who had already refused to pay both the forced loan and his knighthood fine.[115] Clarke was reported to have denied that the king or the commissioners had any such power of compulsion, allegedly calling the collection 'contrary to the petition of Right an extorting and exacting of the subiects and that the proiectors of such businesses in other Countreys had their skinnes flayed of their heads'.[116] The petition of right had asked

> that no man hereafter be compelled to make or yield any gift, loan, benevolence, tax, or such like charge without common consent by Act of Parliament, and that none be called to make answer ... or to give attendance or be confined or otherwise molested or disquieted concerning the same or refusal thereof;

Clarke seems to have had some grounds for his grievance.[117]

Others feared that the contributions for St Paul's would become an annual levy. The privy council, rather like a modern-day charity seeking donations by deeds of covenant, pushed the commissioners hard to encourage people to make an annual contribution to the repairs and follow the lead of Charles and Laud. Some of the commissioners responded to this prompting. In 1633, in Basingstoke town and the six hundreds that made up Basingstoke division in Hampshire, for example, 385 people promised to contribute: 262 for one year only, nine for two years, forty-seven for three years and sixty-seven for four years, 'so long as the work continew and they live soe long'. The four people who promised to contribute nothing until 1636, when they would each give 6*d.*, may have gambled that the work would be finished or the project long forgotten by then. The pressure for regular giving, however, brought pleas from various parts of the country that the contributions should not be made annual. Such complaints parallel the criticisms of ship money when what people expected was an extraordinary levy turned into a regular exaction.[118] Interestingly, in Herefordshire Viscount Scudamore and the other commissioners seem not to have applied pressure to anyone to promise an annual contribution, perhaps out of sensitivity to the popular concern that the collection might become an annual levy.[119]

It is not possible to show a principled response to the collection in most cases. Refusers were not generally inspired by hatred of Laudianism, they merely wished to protect their pockets; nor did those who gave their 4*s.* necessarily do so out of conviction or support for the beauty of holiness. Viscount Scudamore is a rare obvious exception to this rule, so clearly inspired by the ideals of Charles and Laud. At the same time as they were repairing St Paul's he was busy rebuilding the parish church of Dore, and he saw no conflict between the two. By contrast, many replies to the repeated appeals of Charles and Laud stressed the needs of local churches above those of far-away

St Paul's.[120] Much of the propaganda in favour of the collection sought to address localist feeling by emphasising that St Paul's was a church of national importance whose disrepair was a standing disgrace to the whole church of England and an encouragement to popery, but to Scudamore there was no localist case to answer: the repair of all churches was self-evidently a reasonable and rational act. He paid for the rebuilding of Dore church, he gave £100 to the repair of Hereford Cathedral at the Restoration, he supported the restoration of Bristol Cathedral in 1630.[121] But if to the viscount reason proclaimed it self-evident that people should pay for the repair of St Paul's, to most other people it was far less obvious. Here, in the localist case, is the crux of the issue of why the county collections failed. A church was the core of the community, and work on its fabric expressed the unity and solidarity of the parish (even if the repairs often went uncompleted). Since the identity of the parish was bound up with its parish church, any appeal for outside help beyond the parish was a comparatively rare and desperate course, expressing the failure of the community.[122]

To many people throughout England it was inconceivable that a city with the famed riches of London could not afford to repair its own major church. One Essex vicar was censured in court for saying that the city was as able as his parish to maintain St Paul's. Misconceptions such as this led on to two further misunderstandings which circulated widely in the mid 1630s. The first was that the bishop, dean and chapter in London held sufficient land to pay for the repairs themselves. The second was that therefore Charles must want the money for some other purpose, and meant the commissions only to delude his too loving subjects.[123]

I have said that the county collections cannot be read as a simple measure of popular attitudes to Laudianism, but here is a way in which they reflected attitudes to the king. A few men such as Scudamore eagerly furthered the collections as part of their understanding of worship and the church. A few others actively resisted, either, like John Bastwick, out of hatred of Laudianism or, like James Clarke, from a conviction that the collections represented unconstitutional extraparliamentary taxation. The majority, however, whether they paid their few shillings or evaded the commissioners, were concerned by two issues. The first was that what initially appeared to be a one-off appeal, not dissimilar from the other church briefs that marked their Sundays, was being turned by king, archbishop and council into a regular, annual tax. The second was that Charles was using the decay of St Paul's merely as a pretext to 'gett some great summe of money together, and then to turne it to other uses'. Both issues turned on the matter of trust. A king who found it hard to trust others was beginning to find that others did not trust him. There were still many – indeed, the majority in England in the mid 1630s – who like Scudamore trusted the king. In 1628 Scudamore had implored MPs to 'trust him that God has trusted with us'.[124] But there was a small and growing group who were having second thoughts. In the practice of politics and the responsibility of ruling, trust is an essential but fragile commodity which sovereigns disregarded at their peril.

In badgering the king in the autumn of 1625 about Scudamore's loyal and efficient service, the first project that Roger Palmer chose to highlight was the militia. Under Scudamore's leadership, Palmer explained to Charles, the trained bands of Herefordshire were the equal of any in the country. Moreover, such was the 'power and loue' of Scudamore, captain of the county horse, 'that all men weare the more willing and forward to be well accommodated, in his majesties service, for the honor of theyr Captayne'.[125] Once again, Palmer had chosen his words bravely, for a perfect militia was one of the projects closest to Charles's heart. The state of the militia affected England's ability to fight foreign wars and repel foreign invasions. It touched, therefore, on the monarch's honour, and never was a king so jealous of his honour (or so undeserving of it) as Charles I. Furthermore, where James I had been *Rex Pacificus*, his son was, in Michael Young's phrase, *Rex Bellicosus* who 'spent nearly half his reign at war – with Spain, with France, with his own subjects'. 'Never man,' Godfrey Goodman recalled, 'did desire wars more than King Charles.'[126] As the civil wars were later to show, Charles enjoyed soldiering. In September 1628, after the assassination of the duke of Buckingham, Charles announced that he would take on the oversight of the militia personally, and that no longer would a mere outward show of compliance suffice: the king would 'require realities and effects'.[127]

Palmer was not alone in praising Scudamore's efforts for the militia, for Northampton, the lord lieutenant, echoed his words over a year later. He singled Scudamore out from the other Herefordshire deputies, praising him to the privy council for being 'very carefull' in his 'particular and personall action'.[128] The Herefordshire militia papers testify to Scudamore's hard graft, though the loss of the quarter sessions and assize papers inevitably focuses attention on his work as a deputy rather than as a justice.[129] The achievement of Scudamore and the other deputies and captains was in many ways considerable. In 1626 they could claim that the trained foot bands were complete and their arms, all modern, 'soe little defective' that they would be perfect within a month. This was not just idle boasting, for it was based on nearly a decade of hard work by the lieutenancy in modernising weapons, replacing swords and shields with muskets. Northampton testified to his deputies' efforts: he had personally viewed the Herefordshire trained bands and commended their readiness. The foot were trained by veteran soldiers. The deputies boasted that every point of the instructions for a perfect militia had been, or would soon be, implemented, even down to fixing the proper size of the supply carts. Moreover, much of the initiative and energy behind this implementation was Scudamore's.[130]

Moreover, Scudamore had grand ideas of great changes afoot. Nationally the horse were regarded as the most defective arm of the militia, but king and council were so preoccupied with the foot that the horse were almost ignored.[131] Despite Kevin Sharpe's optimistic recent judgement that the privy council functioned 'impressively', it seems rather that the board was capable of concentrating fully on only one issue at a time.[132] As captain of the horse troop the training of the horse was Scudamore's responsibility. Where the privy council provided no horse drill Scudamore sought his own, swopping with Sir Henry Herbert details of Dutch methods for a fine horse from the Holme Lacy stables and obtaining further information about tactics from his younger brother James, who was serving as a soldier in the Low Countries. Among the Scudamore manuscripts there remain many papers detailing military training, such as 'Rules to order a horse Troope' explaining how to 'Diuide your Troopes into two diuisions and scarmach on against another with false powder'. Not all the papers are for horse, there are descriptions and diagrams for exercising muskets and pike, and 'What is to be donn when the army is composid of soudiars vnacustomd to fyght in battayle'.[133] Scudamore's interest did not stop with drill and tactics; the spiritual health of the soldiers mattered too, and he obtained fourteen kinds of prayers for soldiers in various circumstances.[134]

Scudamore's concern ended neither with his horse troop nor with the county trained bands. Following Charles's orders, Scudamore and his fellow deputies enrolled all the able-bodied men, preparatory to forming a reserve militia, and they 'dealt with some of the gentlemen and best able men of this countie for the furnishing of themselves with necessary armes ... to encourage all sortes of people to the exercize of armes'. One of the practical results of this can be seen in Scudamore's household: by May 1627 he had formed twenty-four of his household servants and twenty-one of his retainers into a separate company of his own trained men.[135] We have already seen how Scudamore expounded some of his ideas in a speech to the assembled county gentry, propounding a vision of the well-ordered military commonwealth.[136] Anthony Fletcher has emphasised how the 'ties of household service and landlordism' were reinforced 'by the more formal loyalty that men owed to their militia captain', but the relationship worked the other way too. In Scudamore's county troop of horse most of the officers were Scudamore's clients, servants or retainers. The trumpeter, John Partridge, and John Hooper, corporal, were his retainers, the other corporal, William Cornewall, was one of his household servants, and the cornet, Rowland Scudamore, was his cousin. Furthermore, Francis Berrington, another of his trained retainers, was also a conductor for the Herefordshire levies sent to Plymouth in August 1627.[137] Such ties should have made Scudamore's grip on the militia that much tighter and have enabled him to control it that much more closely.

We have seen how Scudamore projected a military self-image in the 1620s. His duties as a militia captain and deputy lieutenant were important in sustaining the image and in nourishing the king's good opinion of him, but his work with the trained bands had a further effect on the exercise of his rule. Although little evidence has survived, it appears that the trained bands could be very useful in providing the pageantry at set-piece displays of power, loyalty and authority. One description of a muster in July 1665 depicted the cavalry and pikemen in new buff coats, with the musketeers in blue coats and low-crowned hats. Scudamore's return to Herefordshire in 1639 after his embassy to Paris was another carefully stage-managed occasion, described in a commendatory Latin epistle by Robert Tetlow. Scudamore rode to Holme Lacy accompanied by 'a numerous assemblage of fellow nobles', a gathering of his friends and others from far and wide, and flanked, 'as if with a bodyguard', by the trained bands. The whole procession set out in miniature the orders and rankings of local society, with Viscount Scudamore at its apex.[138]

Behind the rhetoric of Scudamore and Palmer lay a distinctly limited and selective success, not 'realities and effects', as the king expected, but mere formalities, particularly with the horse. In 1616 Sir James Scudamore, then the captain of the horse, had described his troop as 'altogether unserviceable'.[139] The situation never really improved. In 1619, under Sir James, nineteen of the ninety-strong troop defaulted at the muster. In 1621 under his son there were sixteen defaulters; in 1622 twenty-four, including the lieutenant, Edward Vaughan, who was consequently replaced by Herbert Westfaling; in 1624 twenty defaulted. In the early years of Charles's reign, to match the privy council's renewed zeal in the face of war, Sir John Scudamore tightened his standards, demanding not only appearance at the muster but suitable arms and horse. In consequence only thirty-one riders were approved as properly armed and mounted. This hardly matched Scudamore's proclaimed vision of the cavalry. Even more serious was the number of persistent offenders. One hundred and five people were recorded as having defaulted at one or more of the ten musters for which partial or complete lists survive between 1619 and 1640; of these twenty-three, or 22 per cent, were persistent offenders, defaulting at three or more musters.[140] By comparison, a study of Lancashire found that only 13 per cent of defaulters were persistent offenders, failing at three or more musters.[141] This was not a case of higher standards being expected in one county than in another. Sir Edward Powell defaulted at five musters, Eustace Whitney at six. Five men from Hereford attended no musters at all. They defaulted by order of the mayor, 'it beinge as he pretendeth an infringinge of theyr liberties to furnish horse with the county'. The city persistently claimed exemption from the jurisdiction of the deputy lieutenants, refusing to repair

St Owen's Gate in the city, where the county magazine gradually decayed for want of repairs to the building, and refusing to allow coat and conduct money to be assessed within the city.[142] Such a situation hardly bears out Palmer's claim that Scudamore's 'power and loue' in Herefordshire were so great that all men were 'willing and forward' to perform his majesty's service 'for the honor of theyr Captayne', especially given that of all the deputies Scudamore had the closest ties with the corporation of Hereford, he being their high steward from 1630.[143] Can a militia service avoided by the city of Hereford and a significant proportion of those rated really deserve Palmer's boast of being better than in any other county? Gervase Markham was horrified by defects which 'hang seaven yeares without any amendment'. In Herefordshire some defects hung twenty years and more without improvement.[144]

Partly these problems were structural. As Derek Hirst has emphasised, the privy council was incapable of following a consistent and coercive policy over the militia, as with so many other issues: it could deal with only one concern at a time. Consequently, offenders escaped without punishment. Northampton appealed for stronger powers to punish defaulters, but the council merely replied that there was no better course than the accustomed one, which meant in practice that the recalcitrant continued in their accustomed defiance.[145] The privy council was also powerless in the face of recalcitrant deputy lieutenants. For in fact behind the rhetoric of Scudamore and the other Herefordshire deputies lay a less glittering reality. Scudamore wanted to impress king and council, but he wanted a militia on his terms, where outward appearance counted for more than true content.

Scudamore's attitude is nicely illustrated by the case of the Herefordshire muster master, whose plight deserves as much recognition as more famous disputes elsewhere, particularly neighbouring Shropshire.[146] Muster masters were disliked across the country; the deputies resented a nominee of the lord lieutenant checking on the standards of their work, while others were disinclined to pay for his salary.[147] In Herefordshire the office of muster master had never been firmly established. There was opposition to the earl of Pembroke's man John Hartgyll, Lord Gerrard's nominee Mr Woodford went unpaid and when Northampton forced the county to accept his secretary Charles Herbert the justices and deputies reacted by setting his wages at the low figure of £40 a year in protest; even that was often unpaid.[148] On Northampton's death in 1630 the deputies refused Herbert's arrears to his brother Edward and declined to pay his successor Hugh Vaughan.[149]

Scudamore, despite his zeal for disciplining and training, despite his rhetoric to the assembled gentry only a few years earlier, despite his efforts to obtain copies of the latest Dutch tactics, was no supporter of the muster master. Northampton's successor as lord lieutenant and lord president, the earl of Bridgewater, had no more success with Scudamore and the other deputies than his predecessors. After Northampton's death, Scudamore openly opposed the muster master, a far cry from the attitude demanded in a paper in his possession detailing the authority of all officers in the army: the muster master, it declared, 'shalbe respected and obeyed in the execucion of his office'; not even a colonel or a captain could deny his orders. Scudamore refused to sign the assessment made for Vaughan's pay in October 1633. When a collection for the muster master's pay was made, most of the hundreds paid in full, but not Scudamore's division, which accounted for almost the entire sum of the arrears: one-third was unpaid in Wormilow, half in Webtree, and nothing at all was paid in Grimsworth. Despite an interview with Bridgewater at Ludlow, he continued his opposition. 'We are nowe out of the way of excuses,' wrote Bridgewater. 'I must expect to haue course taken that his Majesty's pleasure, and comaund ... be obayed, and performed, otherwayes I can not foresee any good euent.'[150] Nonetheless, Scudamore and the other deputies were still resisting the muster master levy in July 1635 when the viscount left on his embassy to Paris. Viscount Scudamore had been central to the opposition to the muster master, and with his departure the resistance of the other deputies crumbled. A muster master rate was levied, but even then Scudamore's servant Henry Sampson had great difficulty in collecting the money. Resistance ran much deeper than the deputy lieutenants.[151]

The hardening of Scudamore's attitude towards the muster master was symptomatic of a shift in his attitude to his duties as a deputy lieutenant after his elevation to the Irish peerage in 1628 and Northampton's death two years later. Where Northampton had been a vigorous and attentive lord lieutenant, Bridgewater was distant and lax, preferring his house in the Barbican to life on the Welsh borders.[152] By 1630 Scudamore's hard work for the militia was over. He continued as captain of horse and deputy until the civil war, but his commitment to his duties disappeared.[153] At the muster of September 1634 only twenty-eight horse turned up satisfactorily, one of the worst attendances of Scudamore's captaincy so far. In the early 1630s he left many of his duties, such as the summoning of defaulters, to his brother-in-law John Scudamore of Ballingham (1600–45).[154] Scudamore's activities as a deputy lieutenant and militia captain illustrate clearly the careful and delicate brokerage required of a local governor, mediating the demands of the crown to the localities, and vice versa, and further mediating within the locale. The Herefordshire deputies, faced with the council's more insistent demands for an exact militia during the wars of the 1620s, considered changing the way the trained bands were paid for, proposing switching the burden from the trained bandsmen and their maintainers to all taxpayers across the county, but in the end left the system unaltered. Perhaps they feared the sort of resistance encountered over coat and conduct money: at least twenty-eight refused to pay in 1628, with one hapless constable assaulted when he issued the demand for payment.[155]

Additionally, the lack of a legislative basis for the militia after the repeal, in 1604, of the Tudor statutes which secured the obligation to muster cannot have encouraged any deputy lieutenants to experiment with new ways of funding the trained bands, for fear of legal dispute or parliamentary scrutiny.[156] The price of the Herefordshire deputies' activity in the 1620s was their refusal to pay for the muster master. Scudamore's proceedings show further the limits of co-operation with the privy council. They show, moreover, the basis on which his activities lay. In return for his efforts, as Palmer implied, he expected not only the support of the king in maintaining his local authority but further preferment. For all his rhetoric, Sir John Scudamore seems to have treated his duties as deputy lieutenant as merely a stepping stone to greater preferment and honour. Once Scudamore had been honoured with an Irish viscountcy in 1628, he abdicated most of his responsibilities over the militia until the civil war. Then his struggle to win them back cost the king and the royalists the city of Hereford.

Scudamore's successes as a local governor can be judged from his ability to mediate between competing claims while preserving his reputation. The comparison with the fate of Sir Robert Phelips in Somerset is instructive. Phelips was accused by his local enemies of seeking 'to gayne a double reputacion to himselfe One aboue by pretendinge good Affeccions to the Seruice, another here by shewinge his dislikes against itt'.[157] Scudamore was not so unwise. He was more careful, balancing refusal or reluctance to carry out some royal or conciliar policies with other instances of their zealous prosecution.

Moreover, his local power and reputation rested not merely on his ability to stand between the centre and the localities; as important was his care in mediating between diverse groups on the local stage, manipulating and fashioning images to suit competing local demands and judging between rival claims within the city of Hereford or between the city and the county.

Scudamore's ability to gain respect and reputation by the juggling of seemingly contradictory demands is clearly shown by the case of the weirs and forges on the river Wye, one of the burning local issues in southern Herefordshire in the sixteenth and seventeenth centuries. The forges were opposed for destroying timber and making firewood prohibitively expensive in Hereford. The weirs were disliked for destroying fish and preventing the passage of boats to Hereford; if only the river were made navigable, it was hoped, cheap coal could be imported and cider exported. The principal advocates of the navigation were the city and corporation of Hereford, its main opponents the weir owners whose property would have to be destroyed to make the river passable for boats.[158] Scudamore had a foot in both camps. He was high steward and a common councilman of the city, and he was also a weir owner with an interest in an iron forge at Carey Mill, downstream from Holme Lacy.[159] He was in a very ambiguous position, sometimes involved in the promotion of schemes for the navigation of the Wye, either personally or through his deputy steward for Hereford, sometimes presented by local juries as one of the hated weir owners or complained against for destroying woods. He was solicited on all sides for his support.[160] Throughout he preserved his reputation and increased his power in Hereford and, despite his ironworks and links with other iron masters, he was praised by John Beale as a notable preserver of timber.[161]

Throughout his career as a local governor Scudamore was often depicted as pursuing the public good or the interest of the commonwealth above his own private interest. It was an image that he fashioned for himself. When a prisoner of the parliament in 1643 he excused his royalism in terms of his 'conscientiousnes of duty' and denied that he had been moved by any private concerns. In 1660 and 1661, in two speeches before the county election to the Commons, he advanced candidates in terms of their love of their country and service of king and county. Despite proposing his son he denied any private or family interest and recommended voters to choose 'true Louers of their Country wherin they liue'.[162] A number of sources suggest Scudamore's success in the use of this discourse and show that others accepted and promoted the image. Mary Fage's anagram on Scudamore's name, 'more hony caus'd', evoked comparisons of honey and the public good. The accompanying verse made the comparison plain. Scudamore was the 'industrious Bee' seeking the 'Countries good' and by his labour bringing 'more honey to the Hive'. Fage's work was derivative and general, but it did seek to express the true nature of each of its 396 subjects in anagrams and acrostics. Those closer to Scudamore and with a more personal knowledge of him spoke with the same voice. John Tombes, for example, praised his eminent prudence and integrity as applied to the government of Herefordshire, while Martin Johnson recounted how Scudamore's wisdom was put to practical use, in cultivating cider and in government, so that 'Herefordshire, Elijah-like, from thence / Deriv'd her Counsells, and Benevolence'. Scudamore came first in John Beale's list of 'admirable Contrivers for the publick good'.[163] Despite Scudamore's enforcement of unparliamentary levies like the forced loan and knighthood fines he earned for himself, and preserved, the reputation of an honest patriot, a fame historians and contemporaries generally restricted to critics of the court and opponents of the loan. The final judgement on Scudamore as a local governor belongs to the rector of Ross, who remembered the first viscount as an 'Honourable and much lamented Patriot of our Country' and an Elijah, 'the Glory of our Countrey'.[164]

NOTES

1 PRO, C115/N5/8632, datable by the court's presence at Salisbury and other internal evidence: J. F. Larkin and P. L. Hughes, eds, *Stuart Royal Proclamations* (2 vols, Oxford, 1973–83), I, no. 29, pp. 64–5. For Palmer's relationship with Scudamore see below, pp. 139–40.

2 J. P. Sommerville, *Politics and Ideology in England, 1603–40* (Harlow, 1986), pp. 236–7.

3 M. J. Braddick, *Parliamentary Taxation in Seventeenth-Century England* (Woodbridge, 1994), p. 114; Matthew 12:31–2; Mark 3:29; Luke 12:10.

4 BL, Harl. MS 188, fol. 6v; Braddick, *Parliamentary Taxation*, p. 111.

5 Somerset RO, DD/PH/222/19.

6 Braddick, *Parliamentary Taxation*, pp. 106–9; R. P. Cust, *The Forced Loan and English Politics 1626–1628* (Oxford, 1987), pp. 33, 48–9, 336.

7 PRO, C231/4, fols 135r, 138v.

8 PRO, E372/468–73; Surrey (Guildford) RO, LM 1758; HRO, Q/SO/1; Atherton, thesis, p. 135; F. C. Morgan, ed., 'The Steward's Accounts of John, First Viscount Scudamore of Sligo (1601–1671) for the Year 1632', *Transactions of the Woolhope Naturalists' Field Club*, 33 (1949–51), p. 167.

9 Surrey (Guildford) RO, LM 1758.

10 F. Godwin, *Annales of England*, trs. M. Godwin (London, 1630); BL, Add. MS 11055, fols 108–9.

11 Worcester (St Helen's) RO, MS 705:423 BA 3164/7; PRO, C115/A3/86, C115/B1/529, PROB11/175/159, fol. 314r. Bridges was godfather to Scudamore's son James, born in 1624.

12 PRO, C115/E12/2352–3, C115/D24/2079, C115/I1/5569.

13 BL, Add. MSS 11042, fols 85–6, 11055, fols 121–2; PRO, PROB11/133/50, fols 401v–3v, C115/A7/211–12, C115/A8/236–8, C115/A8/265, C115/E12/2356, C115/E12/2358, C115/F9/2985; HCA, R820, R1042.

14 Birmingham City Archives, Coventry MS 603503, no. 221; PRO, C231/5, p. 77, C115/I1/5587, C115/M14/7286, C115/R1, 11 July 1644.

15 Atherton, thesis, p. 134.

16 PRO, C231/5, p. 15, E372/476–9, C115/I1/5596; BL, Add. MS 11044, fol. 191r; HCA, R820; Birmingham City Archives, Coventry MS 603503, no. 2.

17 W. S. Powell, *John Pory, 1572–1636* (Chapel Hill, 1977), microfiche, pp. 279, 339; PRO, C115/A2/28–9, C115/A8/237, C115/A8/241, C115/D19/1910; BL, Add. MS 11052, fols 17–19, 28–9, 31–4.

18 I. J. Atherton, 'An Account of Herefordshire in the First Civil War', *Midland History*, 21 (1996), pp. 142, 146; HCA, 6417, fol. 19r; HCL, MS L.C. 647.1 'Scudamore MSS: Accounts 1641–42', fol. 23r; PRO, C115/H25/5457.

19 The earliest surviving of the Herefordshire quarter sessions papers is an order book, 1665–73, HRO, Q/SO/1. Apart from one sole recognisance the assize papers for Herefordshire begin in 1660: PRO, ASSI5/1/3, ASSI5/1/10.

20 PRO, C115/N5/8632.

21 E. Hyde, earl of Clarendon, *The History of the Rebellion and Civil Wars in England*, ed. W. D. Macray (6 vols. Oxford, 1888), I, p. 4; F. C. Dietz, *English Public Finance 1558–1641* (2nd edition, London, 1964), pp. 220–3; T. Cogswell, *The Blessed Revolution: English Politics and the Coming of War, 1621–1624* (Cambridge, 1989), pp. 242, 244; B. Coward, *The Stuart Age: England, 1603–1714* (2nd edition, London, 1994), p. 160.

22 Braddick, *Parliamentary Taxation*, pp. 71–2.

23 PRO, E179/119/440, E179/119/481, E179/283; BL, Add. MS 11051, fols 19, 22, 24, 26, 141–2; Braddick, *Parliamentary Taxation*, pp. 66, 75; H. Best, *Farming and Memorandum Books* (London, 1984), pp. 91–2, 94.

24 Braddick, *Parliamentary Taxation*, p. 114; W. B. Willcox, *Gloucestershire: A Study in Local Government 1590–1640* (New Haven and London, 1940), p. 116 n. 37.

25 R. S. Schofield, 'Taxation and the Political Limits of the Tudor State', in C. Cross, D. Loades and J. J. Scarisbrick, eds, *Law and Government under the Tudors* (Cambridge, 1988), pp. 232, 239–41; Braddick, *Parliamentary Taxation*, pp. 79–84.

26 Schofield, 'Taxation and the Political Limits of the Tudor State', pp. 253–4.

27 PRO, E179/118/393, E179/118/432.

28 PRO, C115/M24/7768, in H. R. Trevor-Roper, *Archbishop Laud 1573–1645* (London, 1940), p. 440.

29 PRO, E179/118/426, E179/119/481, E179/118/432, E179/119/462–3.

30 Braddick, *Parliamentary Taxation*, p. 108.

31 PRO, E179/119/462, E179/118/426, E179/119/481; 35 Eliz. I c. 13, *The Statutes of the Realm* (new edition, 11 vols in 12, London, 1963), IV, part ii, p. 867; *APC 1621–23*, p. 24; *APC 1625–26*, pp. 364–5.

32 Braddick, *Parliamentary Taxation*, pp. 29, 74 n. 52, 93; A. J. Fletcher, *A County Community in Peace and War: Sussex 1600–1660* (London, 1975), pp. 203–4.

33 PRO, E179/119/440, E179/119/462, E179/119/481, E179/283; BL, Add. MS 11051, fols 17–19, 22–7, 141–2.

34 Braddick, *Parliamentary Taxation*, pp. 65–6, 72–3, 77–8; A. J. Fletcher, 'Honour, Reputation and Local Officeholding in Elizabethan and Stuart England', in A. J. Fletcher and J. Stevenson, eds, *Order and Disorder in Early Modern England* (Cambridge, 1985), p. 105.

35 PRO, E359/65, C115/A2/29, C115/D20/1931, C115/H26/5502, C115/I2/5607, C115/I13/6056, C115/I13/6058, C115/M5/6905, C115/M6/6919, C2/CHASI/M3/11, PROB11/159/21, fol. 161v, WARD9/538, p. 173; BL, Add. MS 11042, fols 85–6.

36 PRO, E179/283, E359/65–6, E401/1906–7, C115/E1/2151; BL, Add. MSS 11044, fols 172–9, 11053, fol. 95; FSL, Vb 3(2); W. Skidmore, *Thirty Generations of the Scudamore/Skidmore Family in England and America* (Akron, 1991), p. 62. The names of fifty-two high collectors for these seven hundreds are known. It is possible that I have confused two people of the same name, but there may be other instances where I have missed a connection between Scudamore and a high collector.

37 BL, Add. MS 11044, fol. 11v; PRO, C115/N5/8631; C. Russell, *Parliaments and English Politics 1621–1629* (Oxford, 1979), pp. 375–6.

38 J. P. Cooper, ed., *Wentworth Papers* (Camden, 4th series, 12, 1973), pp. 152–7; *APC 1625–26*, p. 364.

39 BL, Harl. MS 188, fol. 17r; Braddick, *Parliamentary Taxation*, pp. 72–3.

40 Schofield, 'Taxation and the Political Limits of the Tudor State', p. 227; PRO, C115/N5/8632.

41 Somerset RO, DD/PH/229/112, DD/PH/229/114.

42 Schofield, 'Taxation and the Political Limits of the Tudor State', p. 255.

43 Braddick, *Parliamentary Taxation*, pp. 77–8, 124.

44 Schofield, 'Taxation and the Political Limits of the Tudor State', p. 255; Braddick, *Parliamentary Taxation*, p. 99. Braddick (p. 71) says that it is 'beyond the scope' of his study 'to assess whether loyal service in the subsidy collection led to rewards'; it is this issue that I have tried to pursue.

45 R. P. Cust, 'Charles I and a Draft Declaration for the 1628 Parliament', *Historical Research*, 63:151 (June 1990), pp. 153, 157.

46 A. Hughes, *Politics, Society and Civil War in Warwickshire, 1620–1660* (Cambridge, 1987), p. 94; BL, Add. MS 11051, fols 22–7, 30–1, 130; PRO, C115/N2/8523, E401/1912.

47 Hughes, *Warwickshire*, p. 94; BL, Add. MSS 11051, fol. 21, 11053, fols 98–9.

48 PRO, SP16/18/72i, fol. 98, with draft in Sir Robert Harley's hand at BL, Add. MS 70001, fol. 197; PRO, SP16/18/33, fols 47–8, SP16/18/72, fol. 97r; BL, Add. MS 11044, fols 5r, 7r. Northampton's gentle chiding of the Herefordshire deputies and his eventual return to the privy council compare with his apparent inactivity in Warwickshire, where he was also lord lieutenant, and suggest his greater power and knowledge of local affairs in Herefordshire, no doubt a product of his lord presidency and frequent presence in Ludlow. Hughes, *Warwickshire*, pp. 60, 94.

49 PRO, SP14/132/40, fol. 59; J. Eales, *Puritans and Roundheads: The Harleys of Brampton Bryan and the Outbreak of the English Civil War* (Cambridge, 1990), p. 85.

50 Fletcher, *Sussex*, p. 211; Hughes, *Warwickshire*, p. 94; Cust, *Forced Loan*, p. 37; *APC 1625–26*, pp. 170–1, 419; PRO, E401/1913, 16 May, 3 June 1626, E401/2323, privy seal loan, 9 May 1627. The council's new punitive scheme of August 1626 (Cust, *Forced Loan*, pp. 37–9), was cancelled before it reached Herefordshire, and none of those assessed came from the county: PRO, E401/2586, pp. 459–77.

51 PRO, C115/N4/8576, C115/N3/8539, C115/M24/7758. For Scudamore and Herbert see below, p. 139.

52 PRO, C115/N1/8493–5, 8497–503; Atherton, thesis, p. 442.

53 BL, Add. MS 11051, fols 32–3; PRO, SP16/54/2 and 2i, fols 3–4, C115/I26/6508.

54 PRO, SP16/54/28, fols 51–2, SP16/79/81, fol. 126; *APC 1627*, pp. 89–90.

55 Cust, *Forced Loan*, pp. 60, 301; R. P. Cust, 'The Forced Loan and English Politics, 1626–28' (London University Ph.D. thesis, 1983), pp. 79, 350; *APC 1627*, p. 129; T. Birch and R. F. Williams, eds, *The Court and Times of Charles the First* (2 vols, London, 1848), I, p. 212; PRO, SP16/71/46 and 78, fols 66r, 122r; I. M. Calder, *Activities of the Puritan Faction of the Church of England* (London, 1957), pp. xix, 40, 55, 80–1, 89, 100.

56 *APC 1627*, pp. 387–8, 492–5; BL, Add. MS 11051, fol. 34; PRO, SP16/73/17, fol. 23.

57 Cust, *Forced Loan*, p. 92.

58 PRO, SP16/80/31, fol. 123r, SP16/80/18–18ii, fols 98–100, E401/2322–4. £2,648 9s. 4d. was returned to the exchequer, and £55 6s. 8d. allowed for the conduct of 100 soldiers for the expedition to Cadiz in 1625: BL, Add. MS 11051, fols 35–8; Atherton, thesis, pp. 115–16.

59 PRO, SP16/80/18–18ii, fols 98–100 (Sixty-two subsidy payers in Broxash and Radlow certified as too poor to contribute); Cust, *Forced Loan*, p. 254; K. Sharpe, *The Personal Rule of Charles I* (New Haven and London, 1992), p. 16.

60 Cust, *Forced Loan*, p. 310; Cust, 'Forced Loan', pp. 394–404; PRO, SP16/54/2i, fol. 4r, SP16/80/31, fol. 123. Sir Walter Pye, the senior knight of the shire, was mainly resident in London and uninvolved in the collection of the loan, but he was not a refuser: Atherton, thesis, p. 116 n. 115. John Hoskins, MP for Hereford, paid the loan in London, a typical response of those who wanted to lie low over the loan: PRO, E401/2322.

61 H. H. Leonard, 'Distraint of Knighthood: The Last Phase 1625–41', *History*, 63 (1978), pp. 26, 33; Sharpe, *Personal Rule*, pp. 113–14.

62 BL, Add. MS 11051, fol. 132r; PRO, SO1/2, fol. 26r. The other Herefordshire commissioners were Sir Giles Bridges, Sir Walter Pye, Ambrose Elton and William Scudamore of Ballingham. Fitzwilliam Coningsby was added when the commission was renewed on 12 February 1631, but replaced by John Rudhall in the third commission of 29 June 1631: PRO, E178/5333. Only the council's covering letter of 29 February 1632, some working papers and a copy of the return survive of the fourth and final Herefordshire commission: PRO, C115/M23/7671, 7722, 7737–8, 7740.

63 Sharpe, *Personal Rule*, p. 114; Clarendon, *Rebellion*, I, p. 85.

64 BL, Add. MS 11051, fols 134–7; PRO, C115/M23/7723, E407/35, fol. 85; Leonard, 'Distraint of Knighthood', p. 29.

65 PRO, E407/35, fols 85–6r, C115/M23/7671, 7718. In Norfolk knighthood compositions raised the equivalent of one subsidy, in Sussex, slightly more than a subsidy. For these calculations, and for the difficulty of ascertaining precisely how much knighthood fines raised nationally, see Atherton, thesis, pp. 139–40.

66 Rudhall's is the only signature that does not appear on any of the surviving papers of the commissioners. Rudhall is difficult to fathom: after being so zealous for the privy seal loan of 1625–26 he seems neither to have paid the forced loan nor to have acted as a knighthood commissioner.

67 Leonard, 'Distraint of Knighthood', p. 27; HMC, *Report on the Manuscripts of the Duke of Buccleuch and Queensbury* (3 vols, London, 1899–1926), III, pp. 351, 353; E. S. Cope, *The Life of a Public Man: Edward, First Baron Montagu of Boughton, 1562–1644* (Memoirs of the American Philosophical Society, 142, 1981), p. 135.

68 Fletcher, *Sussex*, p. 212. Fletcher found little overlap between the lists of those assessed for privy seal loans in 1625, supposedly the richest in the county, many of whom should therefore have compounded for knighthood, and those actually summoned for knighthood fines. The Herefordshire lists show a much better correlation: seventy-five were assessed for privy seal loans; approximately thirty-eight of these compounded for knighthood or were returned into the exchequer as refusers (PRO, E401/2586, pp. 277–81). Given the intervening years, the difficulty of identifying those with common names, and that the same people were not always liable in 1625 and the 1630s, this seems to be a reasonable correlation.

69 PRO, C115/M23/7698–714 (warrants and schedules for three of the twelve hundreds are missing, so the actual totals of those excused would have been greater), E178/5333. Unfortunately it is not known precisely on what grounds these persons were excused.

70 PRO, C115/M23/7673, C115/M23/7687, C115/M23/7740.

71 Compositions were to be two and a half times the subsidy assessment; in the second and subsequent commissions this was raised to three and a half times. Minimum fines were £25 for JPs and £10 for everyone else: Leonard, 'Distraint of Knighthood', pp. 25, 31.

72 PRO, E179/119/456, E407/35, fol. 85, C115/A3/86; HCL, L.C. 647.1, 'Scudamore MSS; Accounts 1635–37[8]', fol. 104. There were many other examples of underassessment.

73 PRO, E401/1918, 14 November 1631; BL, Add. MS 11051, fol. 138v.

74 PRO, C115/M23/7671.

75 H. M. Colvin, ed., *The History of the King's Works* (6 vols, London, 1963–82), III, pp. 63–6, 148; G. Parry, *The Golden Age Restor'd: The Culture of the Stuart Court, 1603–42* (Manchester, 1981), pp. 247–8, J. King, *A Sermon at Paules Crosse* (London, 1620); H. Farley, *The Complaint of Pavles* ([London], 1616); H. Farley, *St. Pavles-Chvrch her Bill* ([London], 1621]); H. Farley, *Portland-stone in Paules-Church-Yard* (London, 1622).

76 Hampshire RO, 21M65/A1/31, fol. 13v.

77 Quoted in T. G. Barnes, *Somerset 1625–1640: A County's Government during the 'Personal Rule'* (London, 1961), p. 172.

78 Parry, *Golden Age Restor'd*, pp. 249, 261, 262 n. 33. E. Waller, *Poems*, ed. G. T. Drury (London, 1893), p. 17; PRO, SP16/391/47, fol. 71; compare SP16/195/32, fol. 94v.

79 PRO, SP16/188/37, SP16/188/28 and 28i–iii, SP16/213, fols 11v, 23v, 28v, PC2/41, p. 234/fol. 117v, PC2/42, p. 30/fol. 10v, pp. 251–4/fols 116–17, C231/5, p. 92.

80 PRO, C115/M35/8402; Powell, *Pory* microfiche, pp. 257–8.

81 BL, Add. MS 11044, fols 247–9.

82 II Samuel 7:2–13; I Chronicles 17:1–12.

83 Hampshire RO, 21M65/A1/31, fol. 14r. Curle was echoing Laud's words to him: F. R. Goodman, ed., *The Diary of John Young* (London, 1928), p. 98 n. 4.

84 W. S. Simpson, ed., *Documents Illustrating the History of S. Paul's Cathedral* (Camden Society, 2nd series, 26, 1880), p. 136. For copies of Corbet's speech see: PRO, SP16/266/58; BL, Harl. MS 750, fols 172v–3v, Burney MS 368, fol. 141.

85 A. Milton, *Catholic and Reformed: The Roman and Protestant Churches in English Protestant Thought, 1600–1640* (Cambridge, 1995), pp. 71, 78, 314–16.

86 BL, Add. MS 11051, fol. 198v.

87 For example PRO, SP16/257/114, fols 186r–7r.

88 Parry, *Golden Age Restor'd*, pp. 242, 247–8; J. Davies, *The Caroline Captivity of the Church: Charles I and the Remoulding of Anglicanism* (Oxford, 1992), p. 22.

89 Hampshire RO, 21M65/A1/31, fol. 13v.

90 Parry, *Golden Age Restor'd*, pp. 248, 261 n. 31; Sharpe, *Personal Rule*, pp. 209–35.

91 BL, Add. MS 11051, fols 198v, 200, Cotton Charter i 14; Hampshire RO, 44M69/G3/

199/15, 21M65/A1/31, fols 13v–14r; G. Fleming, *Magnificence Exemplified: and, The Repaire of Saint Pauls exhorted unto* (London, 1634), p. 47.

92 Davies, *Caroline Captivity*, p. 79.

93 PRO, SP16/257/114, fol. 186r, SP16/195/32, fol. 94v, SP16/213. fol. 7v; Hampshire RO, 21M65/A1/31, fol. 14r; King, *Sermon*, pp. 46–7; Fleming, *Magnificence Exemplified*, p. 48; Bodleian, MS Bankes 43/63; BL, Sloane MS 2596, fols 112v–3r; L. G. W. Legg, ed., 'A Relation of a Short Survey of the Western Counties made by a Lieutenant of the Military Company in Norwich in 1635', *Camden Miscellany XVI* (Camden, 3rd series, 52, 1936), p. 72.

94 BL, Add. MS 11044, fol. 249r; Guildhall Library, London, 25475/1, fol. 2r.

95 Guildhall Library, 25478, fols 18v, 22r, 32v. The papers for the four northern hundreds under Brabazon have disappeared.

96 B.L., Add. MS 11051, fols 184–200, 204–8, 223–4; PRO, C115/I28/6668–72.

97 PRO, C66/2623 (commission of the peace, 1633).

98 PRO, SP16/311/97, fol. 251r, SP16/368/68, fol. 128, SP16/372/112, fol. 228; Huntington Library, EL 7410–13, 7415, 7418.

99 PRO, C115/I28/6671–2, E179/283; Guildhall Library, 25474/1–6, 25475/1–2.

100 Staffordshire RO, Q/SR/214, no. 4; Hampshire RO, 44M69/G3/199/1, 44M69/G3/199/7; Sharpe, *Personal Rule*, pp. 324, 634.

101 M. D. Gordon, 'The Collection of Ship-Money in the Reign of Charles I', *TRHS*, 3rd series, 4 (1910), pp. 156–62; Guildhall Library, 25474/1–6, 25475/1. The 1635 ship money figures are for the sums originally demanded, before any abatements. The City of London is excluded from both sets of figures.

102 PRO, SP16/213, fol. 45v, SP16/368/46, fol. 77.

103 BL, Add. MS 11051, fols 203–4; PRO, C115/I28/6672, C66/2598, C66/2623, C231/5; Birmingham City Archives, 603503.

104 Guildhall Library, 25475/2, fols 16v, 23–52; *A Brief Declaration of the State of the Accompt of … the Reparation of the Cathedral Church of St. Paul* ([London, 1685]); Colvin, *King's Works*, III, pp. 150–2; Sharpe, *Personal Rule*, pp. 325 pl. 35, 328. The cathedral was, of course, destroyed in the Great Fire of London in 1666.

105 PRO, SP16/361/23, fol. 53r; Bodleian, MS Bankes 43/63; *DNB* (Pindar).

106 Sharpe, *Personal Rule*, p. 324.

107 Essex RO, D/DBa 01.

108 J. T. Evans, *Seventeenth-Century Norwich* (Oxford, 1979), p. 88, V. Pearl, *London and the Outbreak of the Puritan Revolution* (Oxford, 1961), pp. 79, 84, R. Ashton, *The City and the Court 1603–1643* (Cambridge, 1979), pp. 197–8, E. S. Cope, *Politics without Parliaments* (London, 1987), p. 56, all try to do this but come up with confused and conflicting answers.

109 BL, Add MS 11051, fol. 197r; Gloucestershire RO, GBR/F1/11; PRO, PC2/42, p. 374/fol. 175v, SP16/259/69, fol. 150r.

110 BL, Cotton Charter i 14, fol. 4r, Add. MS 11051, fol. 199r; PRO, SP16/391/47, fol. 71r, SP16/257/114, fol. 188r.

111 PRO, SP16/378/73, fol. 184r, SP16/298/38, fol. 74r, SP16/236/36, fols 47–8.

112 PRO, SP16/257/114, fol. 188r; Dorset RO, D53/1, p. 24.

113 BL, Add. MSS 11816, fol. 44, 11044, fol. 15.

114 PRO, SP16/250/1, fol. 1. For the connection between *praemunire* and the petition of right see C. Russell, *The Causes of the English Civil War* (Oxford, 1990), p. 138.

115 PRO, SP16/78/46i, fol. 93r, E178/5333, C115/M23/7671; BL, Add. MS 11051, fols 137v, 224r; W. R. Williams, *The Parliamentary History of the County of Hereford* (Brecknock, 1896), p. 89.

116 BL, Add. MS 11051, fol. 224r. After stalling for a year, Clarke paid 10s. of his 12s. assessment for St Paul's: PRO, C115/I28/6671–2.

117 J. P. Kenyon, ed., *The Stuart Constitution 1603–1688: Documents and Commentary* (Cambridge, 1966), p. 84.

118 Guildhall Library, 25474/1–6; Hampshire RO, 44M69/G3/199/8–14; Sharpe, *Personal Rule*, p. 327.

119 PRO, SP16/311/97, fol. 215r.

120 PRO, SP16/371/14, fol. 24r, SP16/288/103, fol. 240r, SP16/304/35, fol. 67.

121 BL, Add. MS 11044, fols 293–4; HCA, 2382; Bristol RO, DC/F/1/1.

122 N. Alldridge, 'Loyalty and Identity in Chester Parishes', in S. J. Wright, ed., *Parish, Church and People* (London, 1988), p. 91.

123 PRO, SP16/213, fol. 7v, SP16/257/114, fol. 188, SP16/266/21, fol. 38r; Davies, *Caroline Captivity*, p. 78 n. 178.

124 PRO, SP16/266/21, fol. 38; R. C. Johnson et al., eds, *Proceedings in Parliament 1628* (6 vols, New York and London, 1977–83), III, p. 202.

125 PRO, C115/N5/8632.

126 M. B. Young, *Charles I* (Basingstoke, 1997), p. 17; Cogswell, *Blessed Revolution*, p. 63.

127 Sharpe, *Personal Rule*, pp. 27 n. 150, 32.

128 PRO, SP16/41, fol. 44r.

129 BL, Add. MS 11050.

130 PRO, SP16/41, fol. 44r, SP16/33/51, fol. 75; BL, Add. MS 11050, fols 99r, 100v, 117–24, 150–60r, 195r; HRO, AL19/16, pp. 129–35, 237–42; *APC 1625–26*, pp. 321–5, 496–7; *APC 1626*, pp. 26–8; *LBH*, p. 2.

131 PRO, SP16/33/51, fols 75–6; *APC 1625–26*, pp. 496–7; L. O. J. Boynton, *The Elizabethan Militia* (London, 1967), pp. 227–31.

132 Sharpe, *Personal Rule*, pp. 272–3; D. Hirst, 'The Privy Council and the Problems of Enforcement in the 1620s', *Journal of British Studies*, 18 (1978), pp. 46–66.

133 Barnes, *Somerset*, p. 252; PRO, C115/N3/8537–8, C115/M13/7271; BL, Add. MS 11050, fols 176–7, 217r–38r.

134 HMC, *Seventh Report* (London, 1879), p. 692.

135 *APC 1626*, pp. 73–4; PRO, SP16/33/51, fol. 75r; FSL, Vb 3(2).

136 Above, pp. 36–41.

137 A. J. Fletcher, *Reform in the Provinces* (New Haven, 1986), pp. 298–9; FSL, Vb 3(2); BL, Add. MS 11050, fol. 126r; PRO, SP16/75/78, fol. 142.

138 N. E. Key, 'Politics beyond Parliament: Unity and Party in the Herefordshire Region during the Restoration Period' (Cornell University Ph.D., 1989), p. 277; BL, Add. MS 11044, fol. 89r.

139 BL, Add. MS 11050, fol. 87r.

140 BL, Add. MSS 70086, no. 6, muster list, 1619, 11050, fols 71, 75r, 78r, 96v–7r, 103r, 105r, 125–6, 198–9, 211–12.

141 D. P. Carter, 'The "Exact Militia" in Lancashire, 1625–1640', *Northern History*, 11 (1976 for 1975), p. 91.

142 BL, Add. MS 11050, fol. 190r; PRO, C115/M21/7638.

143 PRO, C115/N5/8632.

144 G. Markham, 'The Muster-Master', ed. C. L. Hamilton, in *Camden Miscellany XXVI* (Camden, 4th series, 14, 1975), p. 62.

145 Hirst, 'Privy Council'; PRO, SP16/41, fol. 44v; *APC 1627*, p. 131–3. A search of the printed indexes of the *APC* produced no recorded examples of Herefordshire refusers being hauled before the board.

146 E. S. Cope, 'The Dispute about Muster Masters' Fees in Shropshire in the 1630s', *Huntington Library Quarterly*, 45 (1982), pp. 271–84; Sharpe, *Personal Rule*, pp. 494–7.

147 Boynton, *Elizabethan Militia*, pp. 288-90; Fletcher, *Reform*, p. 315; *Commons' Journals*, I, p. 768.

148 *APC 1600–01*, pp. 399, 475–6; BL, Add. MS 11050, fol. 193r; PRO, SP16/247/15i, fol. 23r, SP16/41, fol. 45r; Markham, 'Muster-Master', p. 56 and n. 2; *APC 1627–28*, p. 216.

149 PRO, SP16/181/18, fol. 46r, SP16/251/63, fol. 124r.

150 PRO, SP16/247/15, fol. 22r; BL, Add. MSS 11050, fols 200r, 213r, 231r, 11052, fols 39v–40r.

151 Cope, 'Muster Masters' Fees', p. 282 n. 23; PRO, SP16/362/95, fol. 193r.

152 Davies, *Military Directions*, sig. A2r; Boynton, *Elizabethan Militia*, p. 250; Fletcher, *Reform*, pp. 294–5; Shropshire RO, 212/364; Huntington Library, EL 7350, 7352, 7355, 7364–6.

153 PRO, C115/I9/5839, C115/I26/6509, C115/M21/7638; Huntington Library, EL 7443.

154 BL, Add. MS 11050, fols 198–9, 211–12.

155 PRO, SP16/33/51, fol. 76r, SP16/126/15, fol. 41; Huntington Library, EL 7674.

156 Sharpe, *Personal Rule*, pp. 28–9.

157 Somerset RO, DD/PH/222/19.

158 HMC, *Thirteenth Report, Part IV. MSS of Rye and Hereford Corporations* (London, 1892), pp. 322–3; R. Vaughan, *Most Approved, and Long-experienced Water-works* (London, 1610), sigs. G2v–Hv; HRO, W15/2, Vaughan to Coningsby, 14 November 1621, Hereford City Records, vol. V, fol. 5r, law day papers, 1655–71, file for 1662, quarter sessions papers, 1661–63, file for 9 January 1662; BL, Add. MSS 11053, fols 71–130, 6693, fol. 305; Nottingham University Library, Pw 2 Hy 58; Nottingham RO, DD4P/73/2; Atherton, thesis, pp. 385–7.

159 HRO, Q/SO/2, fol. 115r; BL, Add. MSS 21567, fol. 5r, 11052, fols 52r, 71r, 73r, 75–6, 86, 97, 107, 109, 117v–18r, 122–3; Nottingham RO, DD4P/73/3; E. Taylor, 'The Seventeenth-century Iron Forge at Carey Mill', *Transactions of the Woolhope Naturalists' Field Club*, 45 (1985–87), pp. 450–68.

160 PRO, C115/M21/7636, C115/M13/7266; BL, Add. MSS 11047, fol. 104r, 11049, fols 12-13, 11052, fols 52r, 73–4, 87–8, 97, 127–36, 70086, no. 2, Herefordshire JPs to Scudamore and Harley, 7 April 1624.

161 PRO, C2/CHASI/K17/58, C115/D24/2079; BL, Add. MS 11052, fols 117v–18r; J. Beale, *Herefordshire Orchards, a Pattern for All England* (London, 1724), p. 22.

162 FSL, Vb 2(2), Vb 2(6); BL, Add. MS 11044, fols 250–1, 253–4.

163 M. Fage, *Fames Rovle* (London, 1637), pp. 224–5; J. Tombes, *Christs Commination against Scandalizers* (London, 1641), sig. *4r; FSL, Va 147, fol. 38r; Beale, *Herefordshire Orchards*, p. 22.

164 Cust, *Forced Loan*, pp. 225–6; Cogswell, *Blessed Revolution*, pp. 84–5; J. Newton, *The Compleat Arithmetician* (London, 1691), sig. [A5].

Chapter 5

The search for preferment

When Roger Palmer interrupted the king's dinner in October 1625 with a prolonged encomium on Scudamore, he had but one aim: to seek his friend's advancement. He told Charles that Scudamore was 'worthy of his favour and gratious opinion for many noble parts of knowledge and merite'. Charles's reaction may have seemed somewhat disappointing, merely thanking Scudamore for his care, especially of the county horse, while reminding Palmer that the horse 'wear defectiue all England ouer', but Palmer, for the sake of his friend, put the best spin on the king's reply that he could: 'his majestie asmuch with gestures as of otherwise gaue me that am read in his disposition (if I flatter not myselfe) apparent new confirmation of his especiall good opinion of you'.[1] The exchange between king and courtier, and Palmer's recounting of it to a friend in the country, remind us that courtiers had to be adept not only at deciphering the sometimes delphic utterances of a taciturn monarch such as Charles I, but also at decoding his body language where words failed. Moreover, in a monarchy such as early Stuart England, the episode is testimony both to the almost desperate dependence of local magnates on the royal will and the royal whim, with local governors ever casting one eye on the sovereign for reassuring signs of royal favour, and to the networks of patronage and court friends and brokers that mediated so much contact between king and kingdom.

Advice books for aspiring gentry stressed the importance of having friends at court: 'to have some Dependance ... upon some Person of Honour and Power, who may give you Countenance' at court, advised Sir Christopher Wandesford, 'will be needfull'. Such people could protect their client's reputation in the competitive, backbiting world of the court; they could oil the wheels of government to make sure that they turned in the right direction at the right time; they could seek their client's inclusion on favourable commissions and exclusion from burdensome ones; they could forewarn of impending elections, changes of policy, and anything else that might affect their client's power and status in the locality; they could intercede with the great and with the king for favours. They were rather like saints interceding with God at the court of heaven, and such quasi-religious language was sometimes used to describe their role.[2]

Scudamore had a range of contacts at court, but with many the precise nature of the relationship is shrouded in mystery, and it is not always clear who was doing what for him and when. It is not known who, for example, ensured that he was not pricked as sheriff in 1625, when he was shortlisted.[3] He thanked Sir John Coke, secretary of state but also his Herefordshire neighbour, in December 1626 for the real and noble favours he had done, but what they were is unknown.[4] Patronage networks were a form of exchange, firmly embedded in a gift-giving culture, with both client and patron receiving rewards and benefits, some tangible, such as offices and money, others less so, such as honour, reputation, power. Scudamore tried to woo courtiers with the 'many yet small gifts' that were commonplace from aspiring and established clients.[5] Towards the end of 1627, for example, Scudamore sent two gold pots to Lord Keeper Coventry and 'rondlettes of syder', a speciality of the Holme Lacy estate, to Sir Thomas Edmondes the treasurer of the household, the duke of Buckingham, the earl of Worcester, Sir Roger Palmer and William Laud.[6] These were the sort of people he felt it necessary to sweeten. Additionally, in the 1620s he could perhaps rely on the support of his wife's uncle Henry, Lord Danvers, after 1625 the earl of Danby. All these men, bar Palmer, were privy councillors.[7] The Somerset family, earls of Worcester, was also the richest in southern Wales and the marches, with a correspondingly broad influence. Sweetening such figures for support at court and in the localities shows the compenetration and interdependence of centre and locality and was part and parcel of the duties of a local politician such as Scudamore.

It is possible to study the links between Scudamore and three men in more detail: William Laud, Sir Henry Herbert and Sir Roger Palmer were long-term, important court contacts. Scudamore's friendship with Laud was well established by February 1622, the date of the earliest surviving letter from Laud to him, and a deep and abiding mutual friendship developed. It is not necessary for them to have met in Buckingham's service, as Hugh Trevor-Roper thinks; they could have met during the 1621 parliament, or even earlier, when Laud was dean of Gloucester: Laud also knew Scudamore's grandfather, wife and mother-in-law.[8] Laud fulfilled many roles. He was Scudamore's divinity tutor, advising him on points of theology such as the variations between different translations of the Bible but warning him to 'Booke it not to much'; his spiritual friend, consoling him on the deaths of his children; his pastor, guiding him on cases of conscience. He fussed over Scudamore's health, and that of the viscountess, like an over-anxious parent, advising his charge to beware of the January cold and make sure he got enough sleep, worrying about Elizabeth's persistent depression. Indeed, the difference in age between the two men (twenty-eight years), the separation of Scudamore's parents in 1609, and the early death of his father in 1619, may well suggest a proxy father–son relationship between the unmarried prelate and the young, insecure, pious baronet. Laud even acted as a kind of benevolent uncle to whom the whole family turned: Scudamore's brother Barnabas consulted Laud for advice about Oxford colleges, his sister sought Laud's help in the preferment of her husband. The two men met at Holme Lacy as Laud travelled between London and diocesan responsibilities (Laud preached at Holme Lacy on Sunday 20 November 1625, for example), and in London when Scudamore's affairs brought him there. From Laud Scudamore sought news of parliament and the court, influence in his affairs, and help for his friends.[9]

Politically speaking, Laud was Scudamore's key friend and patron. He was an important source of information about impending royal initiatives, and was one of the few people close to Charles, though not to James. While the duke of Buckingham lived, however, Laud had little influence over secular patronage. This all the Scudamores were slow to realise. In 1626 Scudamore's sister Elizabeth importuned Laud to move Buckingham to procure her impoverished husband William Meek a place in the Inner Temple, or in the queen's household. Laud failed in the first, and dared not meddle in the second, for 'that was a business too big for me'. William Meek ended up in prison, a debtor. Laud's relations with Henrietta Maria, as with all women, were uneasy.[10] Scudamore too was disappointed by the prelate's attempts to act as a patronage broker: for a decade Laud tried and failed to find a place for Scudamore's servant William Staple.[11]

Laud's friendship proved more important in the 1630s when he himself was in a much more powerful position and when patronage was more fluid than it had been in the early years of Charles's reign when Buckingham held sway. It was undoubtedly Laud who procured Scudamore's appointment in 1635 as ambassador to France. Moreover, throughout his three and a half years in Paris, the viscount relied heavily on Laud for the continuance of his mission. Even in the 1630s, however, Laud was unable to provide solid foundations for the furtherance of his client's career. Though Scudamore's appointment as ambassador was Laud's work, this achievement was testimony not to his political power and cunning as much as to a chance conjunction of affairs at the end of 1634. Since the assassination of Buckingham Charles's most powerful minister had been the earl of Portland, but from the spring of 1634 his health rapidly declined and with it his sway over affairs; he died in March 1635.[12] In two areas, finance and foreign policy, Laud was able to increase his power as Portland's fell, but only by effecting a temporary rapprochement with Henrietta Maria. Laud's power was rising. The queen's was rising faster, but from a much lower point, the disastrous reverse her political fortunes had suffered with the collapse of Châteuneuf's conspiracy against Richelieu, in which she had been closely involved. At the end of August 1634 Laud recorded in his dairy that 'The Queen sent for me, and gave me thanks for a business with which she trusted me; her promise then, that she would be my friend'.[13] Less than five months later Scudamore was appointed ambassador to France. For the next two years Laud had a considerable, but ever declining, influence over foreign affairs. It was a power which has been largely ignored by historians: Dr Sharpe, for example, in one of the most recent accounts, thinks that the archbishop 'exercised little sway in foreign policy'. Yet Laud was added to the foreign committee in March 1635, while in the summer of 1636 the marquis of Hamilton recognised his power over the appointment of ambassadors.[14] Two appointments in 1636, however, symbolised the waning of Laud's influence in secular affairs: Bishop William Juxon as lord treasurer in March, and the earl of Leicester as extraordinary ambassador to France in April. Juxon, it has lately been suggested, was Laud's rival for the lord treasurership, not his creature, and Juxon's appointment marks not his power as a patron, but his unwilling-ness to oil the wheels of patronage for anyone but himself. Leicester's appoint-ment, meanwhile, was engineered by the queen and her faction at the expense of Scudamore and Laud, and marked her resurgence in political affairs.[15]

The one triumph of Scudamore's appointment as ambassador apart, Laud was not suited to the promotion of a client's political ambitions. Outside the church Laud never created a party for himself. He was not an adept politician and his position rested on his friendship with Charles and their shared views, not on the control of any large clientage group, nor on being able to influence others at court, where he was never well liked. He seems genuinely to have disliked being surrounded by importuning suitors (as Scudamore's relatives found to their disappointment), the mainstay of the reputation of any politician or courtier, and put them off as much as he could. Laud was fond of telling suitors that Charles 'is not pleased I should trouble him with any thing but Church business', a patent lie which we should perhaps interpret as meaning that Laud was often happy to press religious suits and none other.[16] Perhaps what he saw as the apostasy of Windebank, crossing him in policy after he had supported Windebank's candidature for the secretaryship, further dissuaded Laud from creating his own faction. The few he did promote to position showed no single political outlook; they were merely his friends. Laud could call on no one else to second his pleas to the king to promote his friends. Consequently, as Scudamore discovered, it was not enough to base one's career on the archbishop alone.

Two other courtiers with whom Scudamore enjoyed close, personal friend-ships which have left sufficient traces in the written record for them to be studied were Sir Henry Herbert and Sir Roger Palmer. Neither had the power and standing of a great courtier or minister, but both were important contacts at court who could effect introductions with the great, and both, but especially Palmer, had that most precious of all courtly favours, access to the royal ear.

Sir Henry Herbert, master of the revels from 1623 to his death in 1674, was one of Scudamore's lifelong friends. Their extant correspondence stretches from 1624 to 1670. His brothers were George Herbert the poet and Edward, Lord Herbert of Cherbury. Scudamore and Herbert were very distantly related through the Danvers family: Scudamore's mother-in-law was a Danvers, while George, Edward and Henry's widowed mother Magdalen married Sir John Danvers (who was friendly with Scudamore) in about 1609. Both Scudamore and Sir Henry nourished a lively personal piety.[17] Sir Henry was politically useful to Scudamore in three ways. First, as a gentleman of the privy chamber from March 1622, he had a measure of access to the royal ear.[18] Second, Sir Henry was acknowledged as a wily and cunning political operator. His brother Edward described him as 'dextrous in the ways of the court, as having gotten much by it', while Richard Baxter was advised that Sir Henry Herbert was the man at court to set him 'in a rising way'.[19] Sir Henry's letters show that he was concerned to see Scudamore set in a rising way also. He was an important source of often weekly information and London gossip. Third, Sir Henry was a possible channel of communication to his more powerful kinsman William Herbert, third earl of Pembroke (1580–1630), a man important locally in south Wales and the marches (he was steward of Hereford in the 1620s) as well as being one of the most powerful privy councillors. Pembroke, and his brother Philip, earl of Montgomery, stood godfathers to Sir Henry's son William in 1626, and it was Pembroke who procured both Sir Henry's knighthood and his office at the revels, in 1623.[20]

Sir Roger Palmer, and his brother James, were others of Scudamore's court relatives with connections to Pembroke and Montgomery. Roger was uncle of Scudamore's wife Elizabeth and an overseer of her father's will. Both Palmer brothers had a long career in the household. Roger was cupbearer to Henry, prince of Wales, and then to Charles as prince and king. He was knighted in 1626. By February 1627 he was master, and in 1632 cofferer, of the household. James became groom of the bedchamber in 1622 and was later gentleman of the privy chamber.[21] Roger and James were both close to Montgomery, who secured their election to Kentish boroughs in his patronage in the parliaments of the 1620s.[22] Though the Palmers were connected with the Herberts, their careers show that historians err when they see patronage groups or factions as monolithic and self-exclusive. James had been placed in the bedchamber by Buckingham, while Roger wrote to Scudamore of Buckingham and Pembroke that 'I honor both these Grandees with much affection'.[23] Many historians have considered that, under Charles, Buckingham wholly monopolised patronage, but Charles's bedchamber was never controlled by the duke. There was, thus, maintained a route to the king's ear through men like the Palmers which perhaps bypassed the duke. Buckingham did wield enormous patronage and was, especially after 1626, usually able to ensure that his enemies were denied important office, but it is not true to say that all patronage was concentrated solely through the duke.[24] It was the gentlemen of the bedchamber and the officials who waited on the royal table, such as the cupbearers, who had the greatest personal contact with the king, and we have already seen Roger's use of his court duties on behalf of Scudamore.

Viscount Scudamore's court friends were essential to the pursuit of his political ambitions in the 1620s and 1630s. Nevertheless, his initial political position was carefully built up for him by his grandfather, old Sir John Scudamore. We have already see how he stepped into his father's position as captain of the county horse within months of Sir James's death. Over the following four years his grandfather adroitly ensured young John's smooth inheritance of family's offices, power and prestige. Four steps nimbly secured his grandson's pre-eminence in the county. First in order of importance, he bought a baronetcy for young John; the title was granted on 1 June 1620. As the first person in Herefordshire to be so elevated, and since there was no resident peer in the county, at a stroke young John gained precedence in the county on all commissions and at all meetings of quarter sessions.[25] Such symbolic pre-eminence was a matter of great prestige. Second, in February 1622, as soon as he was twenty-one, Sir John the younger was placed in the commission of the peace, and only eleven weeks later old Sir John surrendered his office of *custos rotulorum* to his grandson. (He had previously surrendered the office to his son in 1616, only to resume it on Sir James's death in 1619; there could be no clearer indication that the Scudamores regarded the *custos*-ship as their own family office, essential to maintaining their position in the county.)[26] The *custos* had not only considerable local power, as chairman of the sessions with the right of appointing the clerk of the peace, he was held to be, in the words of William Lambarde, 'a man picked out either for wisdom, countenance, or credit'. Third, by May 1622 Scudamore was made a deputy lieutenant.[27]

The baronetcy, *custos*-ship and deputy lieutenancy all depended on old Sir John's connections with courtiers and officials, and in particular with two men: the earl of Northampton, whose importance we have already seen in young John's appointment as captain of the county horse, and his Herefordshire neighbour Sir Walter Pye the elder (1571–1635). Pye was known as an unscrupulous, covetous and crafty lawyer who, when he died in December 1635, was mocked as 'the divells Christmas Pye', but he was willing to place these skills in the service of old Sir John Scudamore and his son Sir

James, who often used him as their legal counsel.[28] In his will Sir James asked Pye, 'my lovinge Cosen', to be 'lovinge and kinde vnto my children, as he hath alwaise bene to me'.[29] Pye was particularly useful for his contacts. Until 1621 he was close to the lord chancellor, Sir Francis Bacon; the importance of courting the lord chancellor was widely recognised, for he had control of all commissions and could make or put out justices.[30] At the beginning of 1621, as part of the manoeuvring that brought Bacon's downfall, Pye switched allegiance to Buckingham and was rewarded with a knighthood and the attorneyship of the court of wards. Sir Walter Pye was now a conduit to the rising power in the kingdom.[31]

Old Sir John Scudamore had to persuade not only the lord president and the chancery of his grandson's worth, he had also to induce his neighbours to acknowledge young John's virtue and reputation. Parliamentary selection was one of the key public confirmations of honour on the wider political stage of early modern England, and old Sir John set out to secure his grandson's election to the 1621 parliament. His task was eased by an agreement in Herefordshire which restricted pre-election canvassing and delivered the effective voice in elections to an inner circle of the greater gentry.

On the rumour of a parliament late in 1620 Sir Robert Harley entreated the leading county families, including the Scudamores, to reserve their voices until they could all meet together 'to consult of the fittest men for that service that affection possesse not the place of discretion in our election'. The initiative spawned an agreement as an attempt to curb the 'dissention, faction and charge as followed upon former Elections'. On 12 December 1620 twenty justices and others, including Sir John Scudamore the elder, Sir Robert Harley and Fitzwilliam Coningsby, agreed that whenever an election was ordered for the county they would meet together to decide upon two knights of the shire to be proposed to the freeholders for election, 'and to bend our whole endeauores with one consente to aide and assiste those whoe by them and vs shalbe soe thought fitt'. On this occasion young Sir John Scudamore was thought fit and elected as senior knight for Herefordshire (with Fitzwilliam Coningsby as his junior colleague); what one Herefordshire gentleman called 'the greate servise of our country'. This was the fourth of his grandfather's steps.[32]

By the time that old Sir John Scudamore died on Easter Monday, 14 April 1623, a smooth transition of power and position had been effected from grandfather to grandson. With his grandfather's death, Scudamore assumed the last of the family's offices, the (honorific) stewardship of Kidwelly Castle, Carmarthenshire, which had been held in the family of the duchy of Lancaster since at least 1557.[33] The baronet's appointment to the council of Wales, in place of his grandfather, was recognition that he had succeeded to his family's place at the head of the county's administration and ranks of honour.[34] Scudamore could not rest content, however. First, as we have seen, the honour culture was intensely competitive: there could be no standing still, only striving for further honour. Second, as we shall see, Scudamore was ambitious not merely to maintain his power and position, but to extend it. Third and finally, the rise of Buckingham had serious repercussions for the Hereford-shire gentry in the early 1620s. Buckingham gained a direct influence in the area by buying the manor of Leominster from the crown in 1620; with it came influence over the borough's two parliamentary seats. The Coningsbys, who had previously exercised sway over the town, thereafter lost the electoral patronage to Buckingham. Fitzwilliam Coningsby did not to regain the local power which his father Sir Thomas had wielded until the 1640s.[35] Moreover, two Herefordshire gentry attached themselves to Buckingham in the early 1620s and rose to prominence on his shirt-tail: Sir Robert Harley (1579–1656) and Sir Walter Pye the elder. Harley came from an old Herefordshire family, but his local career did not really take off until the 1620s. In 1623 he married as his third wife Brilliana, daughter of Sir Edward Conway. Conway was close to Buckingham, and introduced his new son-in-law to the favourite's circle. The fruit of this was Harley's election as junior knight of the shire in 1624. (Scudamore again took the senior knight's place.) Two years later Harley was rewarded by the duke with the mastership of the Mint.[36] The Pyes too were an old Herefordshire family, but they remained only minor gentry until they hitched themselves to the new favourite. The rise of such men created problems for Scudamore, as for others. The pattern of Herefordshire politics over the previous five decades – of a tussle for pre-eminence between the Crofts and their allies the Scudamores on the one side, and the Coningsbys on the other – was finally broken. Where Walter Pye had been an invaluable client and servant of Sir John Scudamore the elder, to the younger Sir John Scudamore Sir Walter was an equal, not a servant. Symbolic of the new importance of Pye and Harley came in the crown's forced-loan commission for Hereford city in late 1626 or early 1627: three county gentry were included, Scudamore, Pye and Harley.[37]

Within two years of his grandfather's death, Scudamore faced a series of crises – personal, political and economic. His handling of them, and his recovery from them, were to shape his future political and spiritual life.

The elections of 1625 and 1626 were symptomatic of these crises and of the shifts of power in Herefordshire. In 1625, for the only the third time since 1572, no Scudamore represented the county. Unable to win the backing of Pye for his own candidature, Scudamore was advised to forgo standing

> for the quiet of the country and reconsilement of other competiters (which will be a good work) to avoyd hart burning, wherof inconveniences will grow amongst your selves and hurt to the cuntrey, perhappes for many yeres, as it hath don in former times.

Scudamore was forced to withdraw from the county election, and instead sought election, successfully, as MP for Hereford.[38]

The 1626 election was a further mark of the decline of Scudamore's power. Once again he did not stand for the county, nor did he stand for any other seat, surprising his London friends, who had expected to see him as usual in Westminster.[39] Pye and Harley stood together for the shire, a virtually unstoppable combination, given their connections with Buckingham. As the price of his support, however, Scudamore intended that Pye should be elected as the senior knight, Harley as the junior. Harley took this as a grave affront, believing he, as a knight of the Bath, should have precedence over Pye, a mere knight bachelor. Pye had precedence in the commission of the peace, but in the end Pye conceded the senior place to Harley, not, he said, out of right, but for the love he bore him.[40] Scudamore had tried to assert his authority and failed. Soon after, Harley and he were involved in a dispute; the details are lost, and it is unclear whether Scudamore's impugning of Harley's honour during the election contest was symptom or cause. They chose judges to adjudicate: Harley picked the earl of Danby, Scudamore's uncle, and Scudamore chose Lord Conway, Harley's father-in-law. They patched up the quarrel, and the following year Scudamore acted as a trustee for Harley's purchase of a local manor.[41] Nonetheless, Scudamore had received and the world had seen a visible reminder that he could not rule Herefordshire as his family had once done.

Troubles travel in threes: on top of Scudamore's political crisis came economic and personal ones. Between May 1625 and February 1627 four of his sisters married; at the same time he had to pay the debts of his uncle and, in an attempt to patch up the family quarrel between the Scudamores and his mother, pay her debts and find her an annuity.[42] The strain of providing large sums proved too great for Scudamore's finances.[43] He had to borrow heavily and considered selling land, a drastic step, given the stress in gentry culture on keeping one's patrimony intact and the links made between debts and land sales on the one hand and moral failure and dishonour on the other. He wrote to Laud for advice whether he could raise money by selling former abbey lands, or whether the profits of such a sale properly belonged to the church. His fears about his possession of former ecclesiastical property were to haunt him for the rest of his life. Laud's answer set the impressionable young Scudamore on the quest to avoid sacrilege that came to dominate much of his life.[44] His economic crisis had become a personal and spiritual one. Historians are familiar with the topos of an economic crisis producing a classic Calvinist or puritan conversion, as in the case of Oliver Cromwell, but a political and financial crisis leading to a moment of Laudian conversion is less common.[45] Convinced that the profits from the sale of church lands belonged to the church, to solve his own financial problems he was forced to dispose of his outlying estates instead, and he sold five Worcestershire manors, along with other property in Droitwich, including a salt works.[46]

By the beginning of 1628 Scudamore's finances were on a sounder footing. His skills in accounting and housekeeping were later praised by William Higford, who proclaimed that Holme Lacy House was so perfectly run that it illustrated the maxim that 'Thrift is the jewell of Magnificence'.[47] The crisis had, however, been real enough.

Scudamore's waning political power was harder to right. The root problem was the rise of others, particularly Pye and Harley, to local prominence and court office through association with the duke of Buckingham. From Scudamore's first biographer onwards historians have been fooled by later events into believing that Scudamore had long been a client of the duke. Hugh Trevor-Roper, for example, wrote that Scudamore lost no time worshipping the rising sun, and was in the favourite's service by 1621.[48] Such claims are unfounded. Rather, the evidence suggests that it was not until the end of 1625 that Scudamore took a conscious decision to seek Buckingham's favour, probably through the mediation of Laud, and only after an appeal for Charles's favour through Roger Palmer's agency, effectively bypassing Buckingham, had proved fruitless. By March 1626 Laud, in a letter to Scudamore, could describe the duke as 'our honorable frend' and lament the parliamentary proceedings against him.[49]

Thereafter, Scudamore rapidly became an admirer of the favourite. In a letter of June 1626 to his great-uncle he greeted the news of the dissolution of parliament with dismay for the damage done to Buckingham's reputation: 'It sharpneth hatred against the Duke,' he bemoaned, 'who being twice Parliament blasted will bee hardly acceptable to a third.' When, in the following spring, Buckingham was 'raising a troop of horse amongst his own frends and followeres' for the impending expedition to assist the beleaguered French Protestants of La Rochelle, Scudamore sent horses which the favourite valued all the more as 'euident testimonie' of Scudamore's love and affection to him. However, the often repeated story that Scudamore accompanied Buckingham on the Rhé expedition is false: Scudamore remained behind in England. Later the same year the duke was one of the recipients of a gift of cider from Scudamore.[50]

Scudamore had all the zeal of a new convert to Buckingham's cause. There is no evidence from Scudamore's first three parliaments, 1621, 1624 and 1625, to support Palmer's claim that Scudamore 'by all dutifull meanes' procured friends for the king (his only impact on the records of the Commons in 1621 was to miss the beginning of the parliament through illness), although any work of private lobbying will have gone unrecorded in the sources, but the 1628 parliament, when he was again elected for Hereford, was a different story.[51] He prepared himself carefully for the impending debates. As soon as a parliament was called Ralph Starkey wrote to Scudamore, suggesting that the first business to be discussed would be 'for the subiectes libertye and a playne exposicion of Magna Charta and other lawes to this purpose' and an examination of the five knights' case. Starkey claimed to have the best copy of proceedings relevant to these and promised to prepare a transcript against Scudamore's arrival in London.[52]

Throughout the first session Scudamore proved a vigorous but ineffectual supporter of Charles and Buckingham. He attacked the petition of right as both futile and unnecessary. Any king who would break his word would not be bound by a petition of right, but Charles was not such a sovereign; Charles was trustworthy and would keep his word. He urged MPs to 'trust him that God has trusted with us'.[53] Several times he tried to bring the house round to a consideration of supply, both as a means of distracting it from attacking the duke and from a conviction that voting supply was the best means to 'Make the king in love with parliaments: [and] take away misunderstandings'. 'The King is tied to ease the subject, and the subject to relieve the King. Let the subject begin first,' he proposed vainly.[54] Finally, Scudamore was one of the few members to stand up and defend the duke. Toeing the official line that the favourite was the first mover of the parliament (rather than the reality that the duke opposed its calling and that the decision to send out the writs was made in the duke's absence by a secret all-night meeting of the privy council), Scudamore described Buckingham as the cause of the calling of the parliament. Buckingham 'has done many good offices. As for his power, he uses it for our good.' It was a picture of the duke few would have recognised by 1628.[55] Already a member of the seventeenth century's most select band, the lay Laudians, Scudamore had joined its second smallest, the supporters of the duke, earning himself a public lampooning in the process.[56] In the summer of 1628 Scudamore prepared to accompany Buckingham on the second expedition to La Rochelle; the earl of Clare reported on 2 July that the duke's 'followers ar commanded to prepare themselves'.[57]

Scudamore's conversion may have been late, and timed just as many of the duke's earlier supporters were turning against the favourite, but there was no doubting the depth of his feelings or the extent to which he had penetrated Buckingham's circle. Two letters, both written more than a year after the duke's death, bear this out. One shows him still in the social circle of the duke's friends, socialising with men such as Viscount Lumley and the duke's kinsman John Ashburnham. In the other, Scudamore wrote to Edward Nicholas, who had been the duke's secretary, to say that he held Nicholas in high regard not only for his own worth, nor just for Nicholas's regard for Scudamore's friend Ashburnham, but 'aboue all, I will ever love you for your unfeined fidelitie to the memorie of my dearest Lord your master', the late duke. Indeed, Scudamore retained his links with the Villierses in the 1630s, visiting the duchess of Buckingham in 1632.[58] In the debate in the Commons on 5 June 1628 the duke was defended by Scudamore and four others: Ashburnham, Nicholas, Sir William Beecher and William Murray. Only in the case of Murray is there no evidence of a friendship with Scudamore.[59] The paradox of the favourite was that he could arouse strong emotions from all those who knew him, violent hatred from his enemies and great devotion from his friends.

Scudamore's reward for his devotion and public defence of the duke came in July 1628, when he was elevated to the Irish peerage as baron of Dromore and Viscount Scudamore of Sligo.[60] March 1628 had seen a quickening of the grants of Irish peerages to Englishmen with neither estates nor connection in Ireland: by the end of 1628 twelve such titles had been created. Charles and Buckingham were using Irish titles as a means of rewarding loyal supporters and as a fund of titles to be sold for money: by the end of 1629 James and Charles had created seventy-eight new Irish peers.[61] Contemporaries emphasised that the current group of creations came through the favourite, mostly for money. Sir Richard Hutton noted in his diary that 'all is procured by the duke of Buckingham ... and all for his private profit and gain'.[62] Although the going rate for an Irish viscountcy was £1,500, not all the titles were sold, and Scudamore's was probably a reward for outspoken loyalty rather than a cash transaction.[63]

Scudamore was aiming higher than merely an Irish title, however; he was looking for further office, in particular the chancellorship of the exchequer, vacated by the appointment of Sir Richard Weston as lord treasurer. Throughout July uncertain rumours filtered out from the court, some that Edward, Lord Barrett of Newburgh, or Sir Edward Sawyer was to receive the post, others that the chancellorship was 'not yet determined'.[64] In the end Barrett triumphed; he was sworn a privy councillor on 20 July and received the patent of the chancellorship on 15 August, taking the oaths five days later. As late as 1 August Sir Henry Herbert, writing from his Worcestershire seat and so a few days behind with the latest news, wrote to Scudamore that

> The Lord Barrets plase I did and doe wishe your Lordship hereafter, which may easilier happen in apparance; for no man seemd vnlikelier for itt then himselfe, nor, was he so much as named when I came from London.[65]

Barrett had several advantages as a candidate over Scudamore. He was distantly related to Buckingham and had been a suitor to him for employment as early as 1623. In 1625 he had been appointed ambassador to France but had never left England, his appointment overtaken by the duke and the twists of Anglo-French relations. The deciding factor in his appointment seems to have been that for the duke's support he promised a large sum of money, rumoured to be the reversion after his own death of land worth £1,200 a year to Buckingham's younger brother, Christopher, earl of Anglesey.[66]

Faced with one disappointment, Scudamore was soon to face another, far more grave: Buckingham's assassination on 23 August. He seems to have been attending the duke at Portsmouth: he was the first to send Laud an accurate report of the assassination, 'the saddest Newes that euer I heard in mye life ... I knowe your pen writt those Leters from a hart full of sorrowe for that great loss,' recounted the bishop in his reply to Scudamore. There was even a family tradition told to Matthew Gibson in the early eighteenth century that Scudamore attended the duke to the grave.[67]

Buckingham's assassination effectively ended the period of English politics that had begun over four years earlier with the return of duke and prince from Madrid. By the time of his death the duke had so concentrated power and position in his hands that change at court was inevitable. Within a week of the assassination the earl of Clare was forecasting 'a great alteration' at court, and only a fortnight later Laud was bemoaning to Scudamore, 'Nowe the Court seems Newe to me, and I meane to turne a Newe leafe in it, for all those things which ar changable. For the rest, I must be the same I was, and patientlye both expect and abyde what God shall be pleased to laye vpon me.' Such fatalism was unsuited to the times, and a modest scramble for office ensued – 'this change of persons', in the words of Viscount Dorchester. Many court gossips expected a change of direction from the king, and it was rumoured that Charles minded 'nothing so much for the present as the advancement' of Buckingham's 'friends and followers'. It was soon clear that Charles was going to keep a much tighter rein on patronage than while his favourite had lived, that he was going to live out the theory of honour that held him to be 'the absolute dispenser and disposer of honours, titles, and places'.[68] Viscount Scudamore, and the rest of the English, Scottish and Irish peers, were soon to have a clear indication of Charles's absolute dispensation of honours.

The conjunction of the Stuarts' rule in three kingdoms – England, Scotland and Ireland – and the penchant of James and Charles for creating new honours and titles on a large scale, caused friction within the honour community. How the precedence between the nobility of the three kingdoms was to be organised and ranked was a persistent problem, exacerbated by the traditional prickliness of nobles about their personal honour and precedence. Many disputes arose. To this unstable cocktail were added the new creations of the early Stuarts. They were not merely so great in number, they were traded and sold for money so openly ('temporall simony', protested the traditionalists). Furthermore, James invented the order of baronets, intruded between peers and knights, in 1611. James and Charles seemed bent on recreating the whole frame of commonwealth and honour. There were complaints in the Commons in 1614 against baronets and in the Lords in 1621 and in the council of war in 1624 against Irish peers. Theories of honour were usually able to hold in creative tension the divergent views that honour was fixed, dependent on time and lineage, and that titles were mutable, the gift of the crown, but the actions of James and Charles risked straining the bonds beyond breaking point. Since the new creations of the 1620s were so closely linked with the duke, with many openly sold by him or going to his partisans, there was also an element of anti-Buckingham prejudice in the complaints about the Irish viscounts and their precedence over English barons.[69]

Scudamore's two titles, his baronetcy in 1620 and his Irish viscountcy eight years later, did not strain the bonds of the honour community in Herefordshire, a county with no resident English peer, because they reconfirmed, rather than reinvented, the traditional hierarchy: the Holme Lacy Scudamores were the wealthiest family in the county and for eighty years they had been at the peak of local society, socially and politically. Elsewhere, however, new creations threatened to unbalance the commonwealth. A number of English counties such as Cheshire and Shropshire saw precedence disputes over baronetcies and Irish peerages threaten to destabilise the running of local government in the 1620s.[70]

The most serious dispute erupted in the Lords during the 1629 session of parliament. An English peer, Lord Fauconberg, introduced a motion on behalf of his relative Thomas, Lord Fairfax of Cameron, a Yorkshireman and a Scottish baron, which threw the Lords into uproar, and a vote was quickly passed that 'no foreign nobility hath any right of precedence in this Realm of England before any peer of this Kingdom'. By custom foreign peers, however poor and base, were in England accorded the same precedence as English peers; it rankled with many English peers that, in Sir Edward Walker's phrase, 'their inferiors and equals in all Assemblies to have place before them; according to their Degrees every Irish Earl or Viscount, though but of yesterdays Gentry and Creation preceding the old Baronage and ancient Families of England'. So many Irish titles had been created, Walker continued, 'so as there is hardly a Town of note, much less a County, but hath some Earl, Viscount or Baron of it'.[71] Walker's complaint, and the accusations that the recently ennobled English gentry had no connection with the countries from whence they took their titles, had some justification. When in 1628 Sir William Pope was offered the Irish towns of Lucan and Granard for his title his son was sent scurrying to the atlas to see whether such places did indeed exist, but his map was to such a scale that it showed only counties, not towns. I am certain, the son informed the father,

> that their is such townes as Lucan and Granard but cannot find it in the mape but diuers teles me for scertane there is such plases, for I entertained isterday an Irishman whoe is of the kinges scounsel for all his bisnes in Ierland, whoe hath

asshured me their is such a plases and both market townes ... but sence I cane not find that towne in the mape if it is posible we will changes Granard for a hole countie ... my care has bin as grate as possible I can but in this case a man can not tel hoe to trust.

Still not sure whether he was being duped for his money, but too embarrassed to ask anyone openly for fear of looking a fool, in October Pope took the alternative, and more certain, title of baron of Bealtirbit and earl of Downe.[72]

Viscount Chaworth of Armagh, still smarting under the imagined injustice of believing that he had paid double the going rate for his title, and convinced that he should have been made an English peer rather than an Irish one, took it upon himself to organise the resistance of the foreign peers. He told Viscount Scudamore that the vote of the Lords amounted to the 'putting Vs out of our owne place to giue Vs none'.[73] Twice he wrote to Scudamore to stir him to action, claiming that 'I dare trust the manaugement of this Cause in no mans handes but your Lordships for we are weaker then you imagen'. Chaworth probably already knew Scudamore through Sir Giles Bridges, Scudamore's brother-in-law, who had accompanied Chaworth on his embassy to Brussels in 1621. Nevertheless his trust in Scudamore, unless it was meant merely to flatter, is rather mysterious; perhaps he trusted in Scudamore's friends at court and particularly Laud, who, the previous year, had framed a proposed royal pronouncement defending the king's creations as 'rewards of desert and pains ... as the preferments ... [are] ours so we will be the judge of the desert Our self and not be taught by a remonstrance'.[74] Scudamore's inaction suggests that any faith in him was misplaced. Chaworth pleaded with him to come down to London, the cause needing 'all our Vttermosts', yet the cautious, not to say timid, Scudamore refused, dithering in his reply. His draft reply to Chaworth played upon notions of honour, courage and manliness in a similar way to his earlier speech on the militia: 'Hee that is not sensible in a case of this quality, degenerateth from the spiritt of a man: And for my part, I should bee ashamed to bee wanting either to so good a cause, or to the dignity of so many braue gentlemen as beare these titles.' Yet with each revision of the draft Scudamore toned down his support. Having only at the last minute decided not to attend the 1629 session of the Commons, his resolution could not be broken. He feared being isolated against strong adversaries if he openly declared himself and wanted to know who else supported Chaworth's stand. He had uncharacteristically declared a bold hand in publicly defending Buckingham a year earlier, but then he had been assured of the support of the king and those closest to him. On this matter he could be less certain of Charles's stand. 'Those that petition against vs are potent and neere to his Majesties person,' he warned, and he asked Chaworth 'whether from his Majesties inclination probability may bee gathered concerning the effecting of our wishes, that wee may not seeme to attempt things which are not possible by us to bee gained'.[75]

Since Scudamore refused to commit himself openly, the main protagonists of the foreign peers' cause became, after Chaworth, the bolder lords Lumley, Savile and Monson. According to a note Chaworth sent to Scudamore, a further seven supported the case: the earl of Downe, and Lords Somerset, Castleton, Cholmondeley, Strangford, Wenman and Fairfax. Scudamore meanwhile remained in Herefordshire, sending only money and moral support.[76]

After petition and counter-petition in an acrimonious dispute,[77] Charles came up with a compromise in June owing its inspiration neither to the vituperation of the English peers nor to Chaworth's careful attempts to manipulate royal attitudes, but rather to Charles's twin obsessions, order and hatred of open disputation. The king refused to alter the traditional forms of precedence, leaving Irish and Scottish viscounts above English barons, but hoped to remove a cause of open dispute, and to encourage the English peerage 'with all alacritie to go on, in the management of the affaires of the Common wealth' by ordering that no Scottish or Irish viscounts without land in those kingdoms 'be nominated, or inserted, or conteyned, as commissioners without speciall direction from his Majestie, or vntill his Majestie shalbe pleased otherwise to determine'.[78] Charles was not a king suited to compromise, and this move pleased neither side. The English peers' resentment remained, and there were rumours in 1640 of a further attempt to deny the customary precedence to foreign peers.[79] To the English holders of Irish and Scottish titles this was a very grave affront. Removal from the commission of the peace was a weapon of royal disapproval, most recently used in 1626 against Buckingham's opponents. It was, the last petition from the foreign peers recounted, a 'badge of your Highnes displeasure alwaies reserved for and laied on those onely who were publique offendors against Lawe or against your Majestie'. The king's declaration implied, they continued, that they were 'made guiltie of great Crimes' by receiving honours from the royal hand.[80]

The plight of the Irish and Scottish peers cut to the heart of the essence of honour and nobility and their role in society. The *raison d'être* of the nobility was to serve the king; now they found that their service was not required. The English peers had argued that foreign titles were 'very disserviceable to his Majesty' and 'derogatorie to the very foundacion of nobillitie it selfe' and bred 'ill effects to the seruice of your Majestie and the publique'. Put out of all commissions like a recusant after twenty-four years' service to the crown, Chaworth complained that Charles had deserted the Irish peers.[81] Moreover, service to the crown, for example as a justice, was not merely essential to the code of honour, it was a way of enforcing and maintaining one's awe and the mystique of power in the face of the common people. As Sir John Oglander told his grandchildren, 'If thou has not some command in the country, thou wilt not be esteemed of the common sort of people who have more of fear than love in them.'[82]

The Irish viscounts had discovered that they had neither role nor voice in England; the next decade would demonstrate that the same was true in Ireland. Though by rights they had seats in the Irish House of Lords, they were forced to surrender them to others. Wentworth privately admitted that he would 'rather have their proxies than their company'.[83] For the Irish parliaments of 1634 and 1640 Scudamore received the writ of summons to the House of Lords together with a royal warrant not so much allowing him as instructing him to be absent. Nor did he and his fellows have a say in the appointment of their proxies. They were sent a proxy form and instructions to sign and leave it blank for the name of the proxy 'to be inserted as shalbe thought fittest' – in other words, by the lord deputy.[84]

In addition, despite Chaworth's guess that Scudamore would 'as Vnwillingly yeeld to be troden on as I or any', he had no choice but to be a victim of the Irish parliament, which in 1634 voted to render peers like him with no land in Ireland liable to subsidies nonetheless; there was even a plan to make all Irish viscounts purchase estates in Ireland. There is a certain justice that Scudamore, having been eager to show in the 1628 English parliament how zealous he was for the raising of English subsidies for Charles, was made to pay in Ireland also.[85] The Irish peers discovered that their titles had become an expensive bane, neither a reward nor much of an honour. David Smith and John Adamson have recently argued that the personal rule 'dramatically highlighted the surviving feudal aspects of English government' and re-emphasised the natural role of the peerage in society, but this was not the case for the English holders of Scottish or Irish titles.[86] Their predicament may not seem among the most pressing of Charles's problems of the three kingdoms, though the Irish viscounts argued that foreign titles could help to unite kingdoms, but 28 June 1629 was a black day for the Irish peers, put out of all commissions.[87]

A black day for all, that is, except Scudamore. All the others were dismissed from the bench – Cholmondeley from Cheshire, Lumley from Durham, Chaworth from Nottinghamshire, Kilmorey from Shropshire, and so on.[88] For Scudamore the king's declaration meant that he was put out of *oyer* and *terminer* commissions for both the Oxford circuit (which included Herefordshire) and Wales, and put out of the local commissions for sewers and swans, and that he was not included in any new commissions for charitable uses.[89] What the king's declaration did not mean, however, was dismissal from the commission of the peace: he appears to have been the only Irish peer retained on a county bench, a unique sign of royal favour.[90] While his exclusion from commissions of *oyer* and *terminer* (by which cases were tried at assizes and an important mark of status) was theoretically a severe limitation of his powers, his continuance on the commission of the peace, and his inclusion in the 1630s on commissions for knighthood and the repair of St Paul's, were signal marks of his power and standing in the eyes of the crown.[91] In the matter of the Scottish and Irish peerage, Viscount Chaworth had played the champion of the foreign nobility and thereby incurred the king's anger for seeming to stir up trouble, and had lost. Bitter and isolated, his political career in ruins, he spent the remaining ten years of his life complaining of his treatment and comparing the waters at the spas of Europe.[92] Scudamore, by contrast, had kept his head down and from his sheltered position observed the disposition of the king. Playing the game of politics cautiously but wisely, he won, and by 1630 had emerged stronger than ever.

A sign of Scudamore's honour and reputation was his election as high steward of the city of Hereford, following the death of the earl of Pembroke, the previous high steward, in 1630. The Holme Lacy Scudamores had a long and often close, but not always entirely happy, relationship with the city of Hereford. The corporation attempted to be fiercely independent, and though it retained control over its own parliamentary seats, during the reigns of Elizabeth and James it had become a pawn in rivalries between county families, especially in the feuding between Croft and Coningsby. The viscount's great-great-grandfather John Scudamore had been steward in the 1560s, while his grandfather Sir John Scudamore had twice been elected steward, in 1590 and 1602, and twice deposed in favour of others by the faction-ridden city corporation.[93] Viscount Scudamore's election proved more permanent: he was not removed until 1646, when the newly installed parliamentary regime elected Sir Robert Harley in his stead, but he was restored in 1660 and succeeded on his death by John, second Viscount Scudamore.[94] Holme Lacy was a mere five miles from Hereford, and Scudamore owed his power in the borough to a network of clients and friends on the city corporation, especially Philip Trehearne (mayor in 1622–23 and 1643–44) and James Barroll (mayor 1639–40).[95] Scudamore did face opposition from within the city, but this he was always able to overcome.[96]

As high steward Scudamore had two principal duties: to uphold the rights, liberties and privileges of the city against all encroachers, and to act as the arbiter of local disputes. The first power that Scudamore had by virtue of the office was, thus, that of arbitration. His position, within and without the corporation, as a link between it and the wider world, and especially the central government, brought with it the powers and responsibilities of representing the city to others and outside interests within the city. Such duties allowed considerable leeway for Scudamore's individual judgement and mediation. In April 1631, for example, the privy council asked him to adjudicate a dispute within Hereford which had arisen out of the billeting of soldiers three years earlier. In 1641, when Scudamore's deputy as high steward, Richard Seaborne, one of the city's MPs, introduced a bill into the Commons on behalf of the city for the navigation of the river Wye, supporters and opponents of the bill alike appealed to Scudamore to bring his influence to bear on the issue. In 1667 Scudamore helped to compose a dispute about the hearth tax which had caused a riot in the city, thereby balancing crown and local interests.[97]

The second power that the high stewardship conferred was electoral influence. Scudamore had been elected MP for the city in 1625 and 1628 and was able to control further electoral patronage as high steward. His deputy steward, Richard Seaborne, was elected to the Short and Long Parliaments, while his son James was returned at a bye-election in July 1642. In 1644 the viscount's brother Barnabas was appointed governor of the royalist garrison of Hereford through the mediation of the viscount's friends in the city, especially Trehearne and William Cater, and in recognition of the viscount's honour and reputation.[98]

In the early 1630s Scudamore was still actively seeking preferment. The changed situation after the assassination of Buckingham altered the way he carried on business, but not his aims. He managed the different politics after the duke's death more adroitly than his rivals Harley and Pye. Harley was cut off from the court after the death of his patron Viscount Conway in 1631, while his puritanism increasingly isolated him from the political mainstream in the 1630s; he lost his place at the Mint in 1635 and was forced, as he put it, to play the 'country gentleman'. Hatred against Pye, seen as a rapacious money-grabber, grew, and only his death in 1635 saved him from being dismissed from the court of wards.[99]

Scudamore's virtually insatiable appetite for news in the 1620s and 1630s can be studied in the context of his continuing search for preferment. Seventeenth-century English folk of all degrees were eager for news reports – oral, printed and manuscript – and news hunger became a feature of the culture of Stuart England. The usual greeting of the common folk was 'What news?', that of the more learned 'Quelles nouvelles?' or 'Quid novi?'. Even in a century when the 'itch of news' grew to epidemic proportions, Scudamore was more deeply infected than most with the love of news.[100] Barely a friend or a relative was allowed to leave Herefordshire without first promising to write back regularly with whatever news and gossip came to hand. Among his surviving papers are over 1,000 newsletters or letters conveying lines of news. Many more have been lost, such as those with Italian news procured through Amerigo Salvetti, or those of Mr Tucker. John Pory advised Scudamore to commit his newsletters 'to the safest secretary in the world, the fire'; we must be thankful that Scudamore did not always follow such advice.[101]

Scudamore's relationships with his correspondents and newsfactors are better described in the language of patronage and clientage than in commercial terms, but there were significant monetary costs involved in the collection of news. One of the rationales behind the lighter controls applied by the government to the circulation of manuscript news (letters and separates) compared with the heavy censorship attracted by its printed cousin was that manuscript news was expensive and so could circulate only among the well educated and politically more stable gentry, less likely to be swayed by news and rumour than the ill-tempered and easily led masses. Scudamore paid John Pory £20 to subscribe to a year's worth of weekly newsletters in 1632. We do not know what he paid his other correspondents, but in the same year he was receiving another weekly newsletter from John Flower (for which he paid £11 for an unspecified period) and occasional news from Sir Henry Herbert. Ralph Starkey, who specialised in providing separates, had a sliding scale of charges ranging from 20s. a quire for parliamentary proceedings to £7 for a copy of the Black Book of the Royal Household (five quires) and £10 each for a volume of the office of earl marshal and high constable and a copy of the Black Book of the Order of the Garter (eight quires each). Even for a viscount whose annual income was around £2,500 his expenditure on newsletters, quite apart from separates or corantos, was a not insignificant sum. In 1632, for example, Scudamore spent £76 on apparel and £57 journeying to London. He lost £3 11s. 6d. at cards and spent £6 15s. on his bowling green, £5 19s. 3d. on pitching and 6s. 8d. at shuffleboard. Scudamore was clearly a man of moderate tastes, but the money and energy he expended on news were so much more than on other pastimes as to suggest that the collecting and reading of newsletters was no mere diversion or simple entertainment.[102]

There were many reasons for reading the news – entertainment, instruction, the quest for the hidden hand of providence behind the unfolding of affairs – but particularly relevant here to Scudamore's quest for preferment were the uses of the news in supporting and furthering one's political career. News-factors such as Pory and Flower did far more than simply convey the news. Each week they sent Scudamore and their other clients a package (all of which have long been broken up), the full contents of which are only sometimes incidentally mentioned. Among Scudamore's papers is a bill from one such newsfactor for some of the additional items sent, including twenty-nine corantos, twenty-three London bills of mortality, three proclamations, two copies of letters, one abstract of a letter, one copy of a dialogue and some verses. Flower sent Scudamore newsletters, separates about foreign news, recently published books, including Christopher Potter's *Want of Charity*, 'because it is much commended', a book which had been banned, a printed relation of Wallenstein's death, masque books, bills of mortality and the French gazette.[103] Pory was most insistent that Scudamore should read the printed corantos (precursors of the newspaper and limited, by royal edict, to foreign news only), even though they were recognised to be notoriously unreliable.

> The reason why I would have your lordship read all Corantos are, First because it is a shame for a man of quality to be ignorant of that which the vulgar knowe.

Secondly a man that reads those toyes every week as they come forth is like one that stands in a fielde of Archers, where though hee sees not the marke, but observing how the arrowes fall, some short, some gone, some on the right and some on the lefte hand, he hath a near guesse where about the marke is; so that hee that reads those bable for a year or however will be able very handsomely to conjecture at the general state of Christendome.[104]

Reading the news enabled the gentry to set events in a wider context, the local in the national and the national in the international. For this reason reading the news was essential for every politician and political aspirant. Starkey provided Scudamore with separates relating to the hottest issues of the day, predicting what would be the first business debated in the 1628 parliament and offering the best transcripts of the five knights' case, for example. Herbert's newsletter to Scudamore justified the forced loan on the grounds that there would then be sufficient money to send 10,000 men to Christian IV of Denmark. In 1621 Scudamore himself was concerned that the Herefordshire deputy lieutenants should impose no militia rates until they had received news of what was done elsewhere.[105] Newsletters were important in giving information on how royal initiatives were received elsewhere and how the reaction of those localities was judged by king and council. Over difficult and contentious issues such as the forced loan such information was invaluable in enabling people like Scudamore to make informed decisions in a national context and avoid exposing themselves by their actions.

Although newsletters often contained inaccurate rumour, the regular despatch of a weekly newsletter ensured that if a letter was lost in the post its absence would be quickly noted. The delivery of newsletters was, therefore, probably more reliable than that of privy council letters, which could take weeks to arrive, especially if they were sent first to the lord president in Ludlow and only then forwarded to a deputy lieutenant or justice; others would have to wait their turn for the letter, or might hear nothing until a meeting of all the deputies or justices was called.[106] Newsletters, therefore, could give the first warning of impending royal business. Pory warned Scudamore in May 1632 of the forthcoming commission for the repair of St Paul's, but the commissions themselves were not issued until September. One of Herbert's 1634 newsletters advised Scudamore that an Irish parliament had been called and suggested that he entreat Laud about making his excuses in time.[107]

As the last example suggests, one of the great problems for any politician was how to manage absence from court, for away from the presence of the king, privy councillors and other courtiers, politicians could not be sure of how their credit and reputation stood, or that of their rivals, nor could they know the latest rumours or be certain of what king or council might do next. For such politicians regular news provided the next best thing to attendance at court. Some of the earliest newsletter services had developed for ambassadors for just these reasons, with their agent or newsfactor reporting regularly on each turn of faction or personality at court, and how they stood in the rank of favour. When Scudamore was in London he did not bother receiving newsletters, for he could visit the Exchange or St Paul's Walk in person, and his newsmongers were careful to avoid relating what they thought he would already know.[108]

While the newsletters were important for the information they contained, good newswriters were useful for the networks of contacts they built up in the pursuit of their trade. Over his career, Pory had contact with various lord mayors of London and with, among others, Archbishop George Abbot, Dudley Carleton, Sir Paul Pindar and Sir Ralph Winwood. The cultivation of such writers and their contacts was as important to men like Scudamore as the reading of their letters. Georg Weckherlin's newsletters were important to Scudamore in that they opened a channel of communication, or reinforced an existing one, with Secretary Coke. For the same reason Scudamore asked Windebank's secretary, Robert Reade, to send news to him.[109] This, no doubt, was one of the reasons why Scudamore, along with many of the political elite of the nation, subscribed to Sir Joseph Williamson's newsletter service after the Restoration, receiving letters once or twice a week for only £5 a year and keeping open a channel to the heart of the Restoration government. The government thereby ensured that its governors in the localities were kept informed of what they needed to know; the recipients thereby were assured that they were getting some of the most reliable news; the government could hope that the provision of news to those who needed to know might sweeten them and keep them happy; both sides kept open a means of communication between the centre and the localities.[110]

The final use of the news to an ambitious man like Scudamore was its concentration on the king – what he was doing, where he was going, his speeches and his disposition. Such information was vital, particularly after 1628, when Charles took upon himself many more of the burdens of government and, in particular, the distribution of royal favours. In the absence of a favourite all eyes were turned upon the king. It was also true that Charles's eyes were fixed upon everyone else; the English polity was a case of the subjects watching the king watching them. Charles repeatedly emphasised that he observed the actions of justices keenly, ever vigilant for signs of disloyalty or, in his eyes the obverse of the same coin, popularity. In the matter of preferment, Clarendon stressed that Charles 'saw and observed men long before he received any about his person, and did not love strangers'. For just this reason Herbert advised Scudamore to join the royal progress to Scotland in the summer of 1633 to make further contacts at court and to be better known to the king. Scudamore did not take his friend's advice and remained at Craddock (now Caradoc Court) in Sellack, the house which he had inherited two years earlier on the death of his great-uncle Rowland Scudamore.[111] The summer of 1633, nonetheless, brought Scudamore a double comfort in the shape of the promotion of Windebank to the secretaryship. First, as Herbert advised,

> thogh it cannot bee beleiud that he lookt not for it, yet, few men lookt he should haue it; By which rule your Lordship is nearer preferment at Cradocke, then Courtiers at Courte, espetially when the Kinge is pleasd to reache men by his choyse wheresoeuer they are, and rather to fitt men for places, then places for men.

Second, the man behind Windebank's knighthood and preferment was Laud.[112] Perhaps Scudamore was not as far from advancement as he may have feared.

Despite Herbert's comment in 1633, on his return from his French embassy early in 1639 Scudamore chose to live mainly in London. Before he quit Paris his wife, Sir John Finet, Sir Roger Palmer and others had been looking for a London house for him. At first he found one in St Martin's Lane, but by September 1640 he had moved to a house in Petty France, Westminster.[113] He let Craddock to tenants; Petty France was to be his London address for the rest of his life and his main residence until the summer of 1642. It was convenient for the parliament (though he never again sat in parliament), and it was convenient for the court and for mixing with other courtiers, many of whom also had houses in the parish, such as his friends Sir Henry Herbert, Sir Roger Palmer and Sir Robert Pye.[114]

Few of the viscount's papers survive for the period 1639–42 (they were probably lost when his goods in Petty France were seized by the parliament in 1643), but it is clear that Scudamore's move to London marked a definite change in self-presentation and strategy.[115] Before 1635 he had been a country gentleman, visiting London but based firmly in the southern marches. After 1639 he turned courtier – a term which could still be used without pejorative overtones of ambition, degeneracy or moral laxity.[116] Before his embassy Scudamore had contrived to use his position in Herefordshire as a stepping stone to preferment, seeking to pose as trustworthy and efficient local magnate and crown servant while not alienating the subsidy payers of the county. After his embassy Scudamore sought preferment through the court. In part, no doubt, during his time in Paris he had grown accustomed to the sophistication of courtly life, but it was also the case that returning ambassadors could expect preferment at court. For example, Sir Thomas Parry, ambassador to France 1602–06, was made chancellor of the duchy of Lancaster in 1607, while Sir Thomas Edmondes was sworn treasurer of the household within three months of his return from Paris in 1617. All early Stuart ambassadors to France eventually received further political advancement, with only three exceptions: Sir Isaac Wake, who died in office; Jerome Weston, who had only a minor mission in 1632, and Viscount Scudamore.[117]

For nearly three years after his return rumour persistently named Scudamore as the next secretary, or failing that, the earl of Bridgewater's replacement as lord president of the council of Wales. So unusual was it for a returning ambassador not to be preferred that the gossips cast around for any suitable post he could be named to. Even before he left Paris he was suggested as Coke's replacement in the secretaryship, but rumour was always eager in pensioning Coke off. The old secretary was, in fact, negotiating to sell his place to Scudamore's rival and co-ambassador in Paris, the earl of Leicester, the bane of Scudamore's life for the past three years.[118] Leicester too was frustrated in his search for a secretaryship; the queen favoured him, but Laud was opposed to his promotion, not least for his ill treatment of Scudamore. Nonetheless, when Leicester returned to England less than a month after Scudamore and for only a temporary sojourn he was sworn a privy councillor.[119] This was rubbing salt in Scudamore's wound.

Disappointed in his hopes of preferment, Scudamore retained some credit at court. Despite the shortage of money as the government prepared to fight the Scots, Scudamore had his outstanding ambassadorial expenses paid quickly when the norm was for years to pass before ambassadors' were fully reimbursed.[120] On his return Scudamore was received in generous fashion by Marie de Medici, the queen mother, then in London. Nearly a year later Montreuil, the French ambassador in London, reported that Scudamore 'has been looked upon favourably by the king and queen'.[121] He retained a role in foreign affairs, though its exact nature is indefinable. He was summoned to court in January 1640, probably to advise about the return of the French ambassador Bellièvre or the negotiations to secure the release of the Elector Palatine. Montreuil and Bellièvre kept up a correspondence with Scudamore and exchanged gifts with him: Bellièvre had two horses from Holme Lacy. Thomas Chambers, when he came over to England, was eager to meet Scudamore in secret.[122] Former ambassadors were one of those groups at court that diplomats were usually urged to seek out and cultivate.[123] Scudamore maintained a secret correspondence with friends at the French court, including keeping a channel open to the French queen.[124] Hugo Grotius, the Swedish ambassador in Paris, continued writing to Scudamore, discussing foreign relations, believing that he was an effective channel to Charles and Laud. Grotius proposed swopping weekly intelligence with Scudamore, a suggestion the viscount declined as unfitting, perhaps fearing that sending weekly newsletters to the agent of a foreign state might be interpreted as impugning his loyalty to Charles.[125] Indeed, Scudamore went to great pains to prove his loyalty to Charles. He sent £200 to purge his personal attendance on the king at York when Charles went north against the Scots even though, as an Irish peer, he was probably not liable to the summons at York, and he forwarded to Windebank a copy of a seditious covenanter tract.[126]

On his return from Paris Scudamore sought further preferment, retained favour with the king and was a useful channel for various people between the English and French courts. Channels, however, are rarely important in themselves, and Scudamore remained unpreferred. Four factors counted against his further advancement. First, Charles and the whole English government were preoccupied with Scottish affairs: less than a month after Scudamore returned to England Charles left for York.[127] Second, although major offices were at the disposition of the king they also had a purchase price attached to them: the secretaryship was rumoured to be priced at £4,000, and it is by no means clear that Scudamore could afford so much at a time when his embassy had left him at least £6,000 in debt.[128] Third, Scudamore had no major court patron but Laud. Although the archbishop was reported to be at the height of his powers in 1639, one of the very small band of English councillors allowed to discuss Scottish affairs, he was ineffective as a patron and never built up a client network that could act as a lever on the king.[129] The fourth and final factor standing in Scudamore's way was his own record as ambassador. Whatever the praises heaped upon him in Herefordshire and by later generations, his embassy had been no sparkling success. It had won him no new friends, merely a crop of new enemies. The powerful Percy connection, which had procured Leicester's seat on the privy council, was now against him, as was Windebank, but Scudamore had shown no sign of realising that the secretary, his former ally, had deserted him. Scudamore lacked courtly skills and political acumen. Northumberland perceived more than the gossips: Laud had 'a particular Kindnesse and Care' of Scudamore, 'yet do I not think him neere any present Preferment'.[130]

In some respects the viscount's three and a half years in Paris had got him nowhere: he returned as he left, a county magnate looking for preferment. The civil war dealt the final, crushing blow. Siding with the royalists, Scudamore was captured at Hereford in April 1643 by the parliamentarians, taken to London and placed under house arrest; he was not released until March 1647. He spent the next thirteen years living peaceably in Westminster and Herefordshire, collecting certificates and testimonials of his good behaviour, contemplating divinity, apple trees and cattle, and relieving distressed Anglican clergy, while others, generally lesser gentry, assumed the government of the county. Like many of his generation (he was forty-one when the civil war broke out and fifty-nine when Charles II was restored), the civil wars and Interregnum spelt the end of his political ambitions.[131]

The Restoration saw Lord Scudamore returned to almost all his old local offices; the English holders of foreign titles were no longer barred from commissions. He was restored to the Herefordshire commission of the peace as *custos rotulorum* on 11 July 1660; he was reappointed steward of the dean and chapter of Hereford on 30 August; the corporation of Hereford agreed to 'Elect (or rather Restore)' him as their high steward on 1 October.[132] No longer, however, was he seeking further preferment for himself; instead he sought it for his son James, aged thirty-six in 1660. The only offices to which Viscount Scudamore did not return were in the militia; instead James assumed his father's old position as deputy lieutenant and captain of a horse troop.[133] The viscount was endeavouring to obtain the continuity of Scudamore power and influence in the southern marches, carefully managing the introduction of his son, just as his own grandfather had arranged for a smooth transfer of the family's position to him in the early 1620s.

Overseeing his son's introduction to power and authority was a delicate business. First, he had to rebuild his own power and preserve his reputation for the care of the country without it seeming as if he were abandoning responsibility for it. When, in March 1661, he was asked by the mayor and corporation of Hereford to stand for parliament for their borough he declined, but couched his refusal in terms of his care for the city, its peace and well government. He stressed that he wished to avoid a contested election: three people had already put themselves forward, and a fourth could only 'encrease the flame' which would be 'very contrary to the love I have towards the Citty and the quietnesse therof'. That year he also oversaw his son's election as senior knight of the shire.[134]

James Scudamore could, to a great extent, ride on the back of his father's and his family's status and reputation. It was mooted that James should be created a knight of the Bath at the coronation in April 1661 but he declined. In part he could not afford the expense; in part such a move was unnecessary, for, as the eldest son of a viscount, he took precedence on the Herefordshire bench after his appointment in August 1661 before all baronets, knights of the Bath and ordinary knights.[135] The second problem standing in the way of Scuda-more's hopes for his son was James's own waywardness. In the early 1650s he had gambled his way into serious financial difficulties. He described himself as being 'enslaued, by my imprudent easiness ... to wicked gaming'. In one evening in October 1655, for example, when he was 'farr gone in drinke', he had lost £1,300 to two notorious gamesters and tricksters. To escape his creditors he had fled abroad. Despite taking 'an vnalterable vowed resolution' never again to gamble 'whilst I breath', he continued in his old ways and left a trail of further creditors across France as he wagered and diced his way from town to town, changing his name in each new place in a not always successful bid to evade arrest, pursued by those not fooled by his disguises or too ashamed to admit that they had been duped by such a charlatan. He was described as living like a madman, a 'monster' whom 'the suburbs of hell can scarse yield the like', and it was said that he owed money 'from the President to the Cobler' but, being 'ruined at home and abroad', could pay none of them.[136] To escape his pursuers in France James fled further east, first to Padua and Venice, then round the eastern Mediterranean to Egypt (where he saw the pyramids) and Tripoli. His ship nearly foundered in a storm, and was attacked by pirates, Spaniards and Neapolitans; James was captured and freed. At Candy (Iráklion) on Crete he fought the Turks; on Zante (Zákinthos) in the Ionian Sea he nearly died in the pest house. He did not return to England and 'those vnhappy bryars I myselfe planted' until 1661, after more than five years' wanderings. It was left to the father to try to piece together the ruins of his son's estate, a process that continued to the end of the viscount's life.[137] Lord Scudamore succeeded in introducing his son to county government at the Restoration: James was added to the commission of the peace for Hereford-shire in August 1661, and was made a deputy lieutenant and given command of a county troop of horse.[138] Nevertheless, he could not entirely shake off the blemish that James's gambling had left on his character: there was always concern that anyone who showed such a lack of mastery and government over himself would be unfit to be master and in government over others. In 1661, for example, James Lawrence of Hereford reacted angrily to rumours that James would be elected MP for Hereford: 'I should be looth that man should sit at the helm of Government, I must expect little good from him, that hath so great a neglect of himself.'[139]

Lord Scudamore's plans were finally thwarted by the death of James on 18 June 1668. The heir to the Holme Lacy estates was now Jack Scudamore, not yet nineteen.[140] The impression gained is that this is was a blow from which the first viscount never recovered: in 1668 he retired from active involvement in local affairs, three years before his death at his house in Petty France on 19 May 1671.[141]

Three factors kept the greater gentry on what John Morrill calls the 'treadmill of endeavour', that ceaseless round of ruling as commissioner, justice and deputy lieutenant:[142] the duty of service to the commonwealth imposed by the early modern code of honour; the power gained through the exercise of such offices; and the hopes of further preferment. Scudamore himself wrote of the 'sweetnes of gouerning and commanding' as both a 'pleasure' and 'that delicious bitt', suggesting at one and the same time the sweet taste of rule, the restrictions of the bridle and the chafing of the bit.[143] The code of honour stipulated that a gentleman was born not for himself but to serve others, and that a gentleman must protect and defend the honour which he held in trust for his family and future generations as their greatest inheritance. Happily, such dictates coincided in providing, in service to the crown and commonwealth, one of the best arenas for seeking further preferment. Charles I's near paranoia about loyalty, and his pronouncements that responses to royal policies were closely observed as a register of loyalty to him, meant that the task of local governors in mediating royal policies to the locale and representing the locality to the centre was made more difficult. But in also assuring local politicians that the crown took note of what they did they held out the hope that loyal or effective service might be rewarded. Scudamore seized on such an opportunity. Loyal or effective – the distinction was important. In Charles's mind there may have been no difference, but to local governors, those charged with enforcing the king's will, the untrammelled, unthinking and unmediated imposition of royal policies could have spelled personal political disaster; nor would it have secured the effective execution of royal policy. Scudamore exploited the distinction. To the king he posed as the loyal instrument of the royal will; in the shire he might mould policies to suit local needs and his own ends. If the final result was that initiatives were not always enacted as the king and council intended (the militia or the subsidy), it did mean that resentment was contained (the forced loan), the council satisfied and Scudamore's prestige, locally and at court, enhanced.

Creating an image of loyal and effective service, nourishing the 'good opinion' that the king had of a gentleman, was a necessary but not a sufficient route to preferment. As essential – perhaps more so – was a network of powerful friends and patrons at court. Greater honours first came to Scudamore when he hitched himself to the duke. After Buckingham's death Charles's greater, personal control of patronage meant that the ambitious, like Scudamore, needed to exercise greater patience, for the king expected to study suitors and know them personally, and he demanded stricter standards of loyalty. Scudamore's career, however, shows how there was still some room for manoeuvre in the execution of policy (as in the case of the muster master), space in which to fashion a public image. It was, perhaps, fortunate for the viscount that he was not in England for most of the time that ship money was levied, and so he avoided being sucked into the disputes over rating which racked Herefordshire, as elsewhere.[44] Scudamore's career showed also, however, the continued importance of faction and influential friends at court in the 1630s, and the shortcomings of his reliance on Laud. At no point in his career were the archbishop's limitations more apparent than during his embassy to France, to which we now turn.

NOTES

1 PRO, C115/N5/8632.

2 C. Wandesford, *A Book of Instructions* (Cambridge, 1777), p. 61; L. L. Peck, *Court Patronage and Corruption in Early Stuart England* (London, 1993), p. 17; R. Lockyer, *Buckingham: The Life and Political Career of George Villiers, First Duke of Buckingham 1592–1628* (London, 1984), p. 113.

3 PRO, SP16/9/43, fol. 63v.

4 HMC, *Twelfth Report, Appendix, Parts I–III. The Manuscripts of the Earl Cowper* (3 vols, London, 1888–89), I, p. 289; M. B. Young, *Servility and Service: The Life and Work of Sir John Coke* (Woodbridge, 1986), pp. 35, 225.

5 Peck, *Court Patronage*, pp. 18–19; L. L. Peck, '"For a King not to be Bountiful were a Fault": Perspectives on Court Patronage in Early Stuart England', *Journal of British Studies*, 25 (1986), p. 43.

6 PRO, C115/G3/3400, C115/E12/2385, C115/E12/2389.

7 F. N. Macnamara, *Memorials of the Danvers Family* (London, 1895), pp. 285–93; BL, Add. MSS 11042, fols 71–3, 11044, fols 5–7; PRO, C115/M24/7772; *APC 1627*, p. 312; *APC 1627–28*, pp. 330–1.

8 PRO, C115/M24/7766–7; H. R. Trevor-Roper, *Archbishop Laud 1573–1645* (London, 1940), pp. 63, 438. On one of Laud's letters to Scudamore (PRO, C115/M24/7765) is the date '1618' but, as Trevor-Roper has shown (pp. 443–4), this is a mistake for 1625/26. Those who have accepted the earlier date, such as Matthew Gibson, thereby distort and misdate Scudamore's relationship with his mentor.

9 PRO, C115/M24/7758–76, printed in Trevor-Roper, *Laud*, pp. 437–56; W. Laud, *Works*, ed. W. Scott and J. Bliss (7 vols, Oxford, 1847–60), III, p. 175, VI, pp. 366–8. For the viscount's parents see Atherton, thesis, pp. 41–67.

10 PRO, C115/M24/7759, C2/CHASI/M3/11.

11 PRO, C115/M24/7771; Laud, *Works*, VI, pp. 366–8.

12 M. A. van C. Alexander, *Charles I's Lord Treasurer: Sir Richard Weston, Earl of Portland (1577–1635)* (London, 1975), pp. 190–201, 218.

13 R. M. Smuts, 'The Puritan Followers of Henrietta Maria in the 1630s', *English Historical Review*, 93 (1978), pp. 34–5; Laud, *Works*, III, p. 222.

14 K. Sharpe, *The Personal Rule of Charles I* (New Haven and London, 1992), pp. 537, 837; Laud, *Works*, III, p. 223; Warwickshire RO, CR2017/C5/61.

15 B. Quintrell, 'The Church Triumphant? The Emergence of a Spiritual Lord Treasurer, 1635–1636', in J. F. Merritt, ed., *The Political World of Thomas Wentworth, Earl of Strafford, 1621–1641* (Cambridge, 1996), pp. 81–108; Atherton, thesis, ch. 5.

16 J. Davies, *The Caroline Captivity of the Church: Charles I and the Remoulding of Anglicanism* (Oxford, 1992), p. 44; PRO, SP16/363/103, fol. 203; Sharpe, *Personal Rule*, p. 144; P. Warwick, *Memoires of the Reigne of King Charles I* (London, 1701), p. 78.

17 PRO, C115/N3/8536–74, C115/N9/8882, C115/N9/8844–5; BL, Add. MS 11043, fols 80, 93–6; Atherton, thesis, pp. 429–30; A. M. Charles, 'Sir Henry Herbert: The Master of the Revels as a Man of Letters', *Modern Philology*, 80 (1982–83), pp. 1–12. There is no evidence of any contact between Scudamore and George or Edward.

18 N. Carlisle, *An Inquiry into the Place and Quality of the Gentlemen of his Majesty's most honourable Privy Chamber* (London, 1829), pp. 132–3; Atherton, thesis, p. 88 n. 57.

19 Edward, Lord Herbert of Cherbury, *Autobiography*, ed. S. Lee (2nd edition, London, 1907), p. 12; R. Baxter, *Autobiography*, ed. N. H. Keeble (London, 1974), p. 12.

20 R. Warner, *Epistolary Curiosities; Series the First* (Bath, 1818), p. 3; H. Herbert, *Dramatic Records*, ed. J. Q. Adams (New Haven and London, 1917), p. 8.

21 PRO, C115/E13/2415; Atherton, thesis, pp. 88, 431.

22 C. E. Woodruff, 'Notes on the Municipal Records of Queenborough', *Archaeologia Cantiana*, 22 (1897), p. 183; J. K. Gruenfelder, *Influence in Early Stuart Elections* (Columbus, 1981), pp. 130–1, 172 n. 15, 193.

23 K. Sharpe, 'The Image of Virtue: The Court and Household of Charles I, 1625–1642', in D. Starkey *et al.*, eds, *The English Court* (Harlow, 1987), p. 190 and n. 43; PRO, C115/N5/8632.

24 Sharpe, 'Image of Virtue', pp. 232–4; K. Sharpe, 'Crown, Parliament and Locality: Government and Communication in Early Stuart England', *English Historical Review*, 101 (1986), pp. 321–50.

25 PRO, SO3/7, May 1620, C231/4, fol. 106v, C181/3, fol. 33r, IND1/6746, May 1620.

26 PRO, C231/4, fols 30, 83r, 135r, 138r, C66/2259, C66/2285, C193/13/1, fol. 44r.

27 R. Xiang, 'The Staffordshire Justices and their Sessions 1603–42' (University of Birmingham Ph.D. thesis, 1996), p. 32; Atherton, thesis, pp. 71–2.

28 Bodleian, MS Tanner 465, fol. 62r; Cambridge University Library, Add. MS 6863, fol. 81r; BL, Add. MS 11042, fols 11–12; PRO, C115/H26/5482, REQ2/307/12, C2/JAMESI/S26/16, C3/300/20, STAC8/181/13.

29 PRO, PROB11/133/50, fol. 403r.

30 PRO, C115/M18/7527; Wandesford, *Booke of Instructions*, p. 61; Xiang, 'Staffordshire Justices', p. 60.

31 Sheffield Archives, EM 1331, fol. 7r; BL, Harl. MS 1581, fol. 118r; G. E. Aylmer, *The King's Servants* (London, 1961), pp. 308–10.

32 BL, Add. MS 61989, draft letters to the Scudamores, Sir Thomas Coningsby, Sir Richard Hopton and James Tomkins, towards the rear of the volume, printed in *LBH*, pp. xlii–xliv; FSL, Vb 2(21); HRO, W15/2, John Wigmore to Fitzwilliam Coningsby, 22 December [1620].

33 PRO, SO3/5, January 1612, C115/G8/3606, C115/H26/5494, C115/M14/7283, fol. 4r, C115/M17/7424.

34 HRO, AL17/1; PRO, C142/404/114, WARD7/68/122; BL, Egerton MS 2882, fols 131r, 20r, 28r, 39v.

35 C. J. Robinson, *A History of the Manors and Mansions of Herefordshire* (London and Hereford, 1873), p. 174; Atherton, thesis, p. 77.

36 J. Eales, *Puritans and Roundheads: The Harleys of Brampton Bryan and the Outbreak of the English Civil War* (Cambridge, 1990), pp. 6, 21, 29–33, 73–5; R. E. Ruigh, *The Parliament of 1624* (Cambridge, Mass., 1971), pp. 85–6 n. 74; Gruenfelder, *Influence*, pp. 149, 232.

37 PRO, C193/12/2, fol. 83.

38 HCL, L.C. 929.2, 'Webb MSS: Pengelly and Scudamore Papers', p. 109.

39 PRO, C115/N1/8490, C115/N4/8575; BL, Cotton MS Julius CIII, fol. 336r.

40 Harley to Pye, 6 and 12 January 1626, drafts, with Pye's replies, 9 and 14 January, BL, Add. MS 70108, misc. 39(i), (also Add. MS 70001, fols 195–6); PRO, C66/2367. Compare A. J. Fletcher, 'Honour, Reputation and Local Officeholding in Elizabethan and Stuart England', in A. J. Fletcher and J. Stevenson, eds, *Order and Disorder in Early Modern England* (Cambridge, 1985), pp. 98–9.

41 BL, Add. MS 11044, fols 5–7; J. S. Levy, 'Perceptions and Beliefs: The Harleys of Brampton Bryan' (University of London Ph.D. thesis, 1983), p. 95; PRO, C115/I3/5679, C115/C12/1219.

42 W. Skidmore, *Thirty Generations of the Scudamore/Skidmore Family in England and America* (2nd edition, Akron, 1991), p. 54; PRO, C115/I1/5537–8; Berkshire RO, D/A1/119/18a.

43 PRO, C115/E12/2348–54, C115/E12/2356, C115/E12/2358–65, C115/E12/2371, C115/I1/5535.

44 F. Heal and C. Holmes, *The Gentry in England and Wales 1500–1700* (Basingstoke, 1994), pp. 98–9; PRO, C115/M24/7758; above, chapter 3.

45 J. S. Morrill, 'The Making of Oliver Cromwell', in J. S. Morrill, ed., *Oliver Cromwell and the English Revolution* (Harlow, 1990), pp. 21–36.

46 W. Page and J. W. Bund, *The Victoria History of the County of Worcester* (vols 2–4, London, 1906–24), III, pp. 46, 191, 262, 355, IV, p. 234; T. Habington, *Survey of Worcestershire* (2 vols, Worcestershire History Society, 1893–9), I, pp. 57, 325; BL, Add. Ch. 1926.

47 PRO, C115/E12/2383, C115/E12/2393; W. Higford, *The Institution of a Gentleman* (London, 1660), p. 83.

48 M. Gibson *A View of the Ancient and Present State of the Churches of Door, Home Lacy, and Hempsted* (London, 1727), pp. 67–70; Trevor-Roper, *Laud*, p. 63; Ruigh, *Parliament of 1624*, p. 37.

49 PRO, C115/N5/8632, C115/M24/7765.

50 BL, Add. MSS 11044, fols 11–12, 11049, fols 16–17; PRO, SP16/63/33, fol. 43r, C115/E12/2385; Atherton, thesis, p. 85.

51 PRO, C115/N5/8632; HRO, Hereford City Records, vol. IV, fols 56–7.

52 PRO, C115/N4/8579.

53 R. C. Johnson *et al.*, eds, *Proceedings in Parliament 1628* (6 vols, New Haven and London, 1977–83), III, pp. 194, 200, 202, 204, VI, p. 82.

54 Johnson, *Proceedings in Parliament 1628*, III, pp. 191, 193–4, IV, pp. 17, 116, 120, 126, VI, p. 62.

55 Johnson, *Proceedings in Parliament 1628*, IV, pp. 116, 120, 126, 249, 266, 277; R. P. Cust, *The Forced Loan and English Politics 1626–1628* (Oxford, 1987), pp. 77–8 and n. 15, p. 83; R. P. Cust, 'News and Politics in Early Seventeenth-Century England', *Past and Present*, 112 (August 1986), p. 72.

56 F. W. Fairholt, ed., *Poems and Songs relating to George Villiers* (Percy Society, 1850), p. 27.

57 Gibson, *View*, p. 67; P. R. Seddon, ed., *Letters of John Holles* (3 vols, Thoroton Society, record series, 31, 35–6, 1975–86), III, p. 383.

58 BL, Add. MS 11044, fols 13–14; PRO, SP16/149/10, fol. 12r, C115/N3/8544; HCA, 6417, fols 26r, 27r; HCL, L.C. 647.1 'Scudamore MSS: Accounts 1635–37[8]', fols 81r, 98r.

59 Johnson, *Proceedings in Parliament 1628*, IV, pp. 116–17; PRO, C115/M35/8383, C115/M35/8398.

60 PRO, C231/4, fol. 248r, IND1/6747, June 1628, SO3/9, June 1628.

61 G. E. Cokayne, *The Complete Peerage*, ed. V. Gibbs *et al.* (2nd edition, 13 vols in 14,

London, 1910–40), III, appendix H, and Deputy Keeper of the Public Records, *Forty-seventh Annual Report* (London, 1886), appendix 6, pp. 78–138; C. R. Mayes, 'The Early Stuarts and the Irish Peerage', *English Historical Review*, 73 (1958), p. 233.

62 C. R. Mayes, 'The Sale of Peerages in Early Stuart England', *Journal of Modern History*, 29 (1957), pp. 21–37; Mayes, 'Early Stuarts and the Irish Peerage', pp. 238–9; HMC, *Eleventh Report, Appendix, Part I. The Manuscripts of Henry Duncan Skrine, esq. Salvetti Correspondence* (London, 1887) p. 142; Cambridge University Library, Add. MS 6863, fol. 43r.

63 A. J. Kempe, ed., *The Loseley Manuscripts* (London, 1836), p. 485; Mayes, 'Early Stuarts and the Irish Peerage', p. 238; Atherton, thesis, p. 120.

64 Seddon, *Holles Letters*, III, pp. 383–6; T. Birch and R. F. Williams, eds, *The Court and Times of Charles the First* (2 vols, London, 1848), I, pp. 375–9, 382; HMC, *Cowper*, I, p. 359.

65 *APC 1628–29*, p. 42 no. 140; BL, Harl. MS 1579, fol. 164; HMC, *Cowper*, I, p. 360; PRO, C115/N3/8543.

66 BL, Harl. MS 1581, fol. 254; T. B. Lennard, *An Account of the Families of Lennard and Barrett* (privately printed, 1908), pp. 372–3, 377–9, 396–7; W. S. Powell, *John Pory, 1572–1636* (Chapel Hill, 1977), microfiche, p. 142; Birch and Williams, *Charles the First*, I, p. 452.

67 PRO, C115/M24/7763; Gibson, *View*, p. 70.

68 PRO, C115/M24/7763; Birch and Williams, *Charles the First*, I, pp. 388, 396; Sharpe, *Personal Rule*, pp. 49–50; Birmingham City Archives, Coventry MS 602427, no. 2, Heath to Coventry, 25 August 1626.

69 C. Herrupp, '"To Pluck Bright Honour from the Pale-faced Moon": Gender and Honour in the Castlehaven Story', *TRHS*, 6th series, 6 (1996), p. 148; BL, Add. MS 11690, fols 30–4; Peck, *Court Patronage*, p. 286 n. 10; R. C. McCoy, 'Old English Honour in an Evil Time: Aristocratic Principle in the 1620s', in R. M. Smuts, ed., *The Stuart Court and Europe* (Cambridge, 1996), pp. 140–2; L. Stone, *The Crisis of the Aristocracy 1558–1641* (Oxford, 1966), pp. 82–97, 104–5; J. Selden, *Titles of Honor* (2nd edition, London, 1631), pp. 906–11.

70 M. D. G. Wanklyn, 'Landed Society and Allegiance in Cheshire and Shropshire in the First Civil War' (Manchester University Ph.D. thesis, 1976), pp. 84–5; J. S. Morrill, *The Nature of the English Revolution* (Harlow, 1993), p. 198 n. 21.

71 HMC, *Report on the Manuscripts of the Duke of Buccleuch and Queensbury* (3 vols, London, 1899–1926), III, pp. 334–6; Cokayne, *Complete Peerage*, V, pp. 264, 229; G. E. Cokayne, *Complete Baronetage* (5 vols, Exeter, 1900–9), I, p. 43; E. Walker, *Historical Discourses* (London, 1705), p. 307.

72 Bodleian, MS North c.7, fol. 114; Cokayne, *Complete Peerage*, IV, pp. 449–50.

73 Surrey (Guildford) RO, LM 1327/9, fols 47v, 48v–9v, 54r–62r, [66r]; Kempe, *Loseley Manuscripts*, pp. 483–7; PRO, C115/M13/7238.

74 PRO, C115/M13/7238–9; Surrey (Guildford) RO, LM 1327/9, fols 3v, 6r; Peck, *Court Patronage*, pp. 98, 253 n. 111.

75 PRO, C115/M13/7240; BL, Cotton MS Julius CIII, fol. 337r.

76 PRO, C115/M13/7241–2, C115/M13/7250.

77 PRO, C115/M13/7238–50; Bodleian, MSS North b.1, fols 53–6, 60–83, 175–6, North c.7, fols 111–13.

78 College of Arms, London, MS I.25, fol. 61; copies: BL, Add. MS 64898, fols 41–2; HMC, *Cowper*, I, pp. 373–4; Bodleian, MSS Ashmole 857, fols 102v–3r, North b.1, fols 79–80.

79 BL, Add. MS 11045, fol. 147v.

80 Fletcher, 'Honour', pp. 95–7, R. P. Cust, 'The Forced Loan and English Politics' (London University Ph.D. thesis, 1983), pp. 294–6; Surrey (Guildford) RO, LM 1327/9, fols [65v–6v]; Bodleian, MSS North c.7, fol. 111, North b.1, fol. 83r.

81 HMC, *Buccleuch and Queensbury*, III, p. 336; PRO, C115/M13/7244; Surrey (Guildford) RO, LM 1327/9, fols [65v–6v].

82 A. J. Fletcher, *Reform in the Provinces: The Government of Stuart England* (New Haven, 1986), p. 31.

83 PRO, SP63/274/29, fol. 57v; H. F. Kearney, *Strafford in Ireland 1633-41* (Manchester, 1959), p. 51 and n. 1.

84 BL, Add. MS 11044, fols 18–27, 35–42; PRO, SO1/2, fol. 181v.

85 PRO, C115/M13/7237; H. R. Morres, *The History of the Principal Transactions of the Irish Parliament* (2 vols, Shannon, 1971), I, pp. 318–19, 322–3, II, p. 15; Kearney, *Strafford in Ireland*, pp. 50–1; BL, Add. MS 11044, fols 29, 34, 43–51; PRO, C115/I9/5852, SP63/260/8, fols 90–1; Johnson, *Proceedings in Parliament 1628*, IV, pp. 17, 120.

86 D. L. Smith, 'The Fourth Earl of Dorset and the Personal Rule of Charles I', *Journal of British Studies*, 30 (July 1991), p. 286; J. S. A. Adamson, 'The Baronial Context of the English Civil War', *TRHS*, 5th series, 40 (1990), pp. 93–4.

87 PRO, C115/M13/7246.

88 Atherton, thesis, p. 132.

89 PRO, C181/3, fols 33r, 137, 154, 178v–9, 191–2, 207, 226–8, 260, 267–72, C181/4, fols 12–13, 43–4, 50–1, 71, 96–7, 112, 117, 143–4, 168, 185–6, 194–5, C181/5, fols 6–219, C192/1. Scudamore was restored to many commissions at the Restoration: PRO, C181/7; BL, Add. MS 11052, fol. 130.

90 PRO, C66/2527, C66/2536, C66/2577, C66/2598, C66/2623, C66/2654, C66/2725, C66/2761, C66/2858, C66/2859, SP16/212, C193/13/2, SP16/405, C115/F16/3175, C115/F14/3138.

91 J. S. Cockburn, *Calendar of Assize Records, Home Circuit Indictments, Elizabeth I and James I. Introduction* (London, 1985), pp. 18–19.

92 HMC, *Cowper*, I, pp. 409, 415, II, pp. 57–8, 81; PRO, C115/M13/7237, C115/M13/7243, C115/M13/7251; Surrey (Guildford) RO, LM 1327/9, fols [66–7r].

93 R. Johnson, *The Ancient Customs of the City of Hereford* (Hereford and London, 1868), p. 165; HRO, Hereford City Records, vol. VI, fols 54, 60–1, 72v, 84–5; W. J. Tighe, 'Courtiers and Politics in Elizabethan Herefordshire: Sir James Croft, his Friends and Foes', *Historical Journal*, 32 (1989), pp. 274–7; Atherton, thesis, pp. 126–7.

94 BL, Add. MS 70005, fols 83 (third series), 34–5 (fourth series), mayor to Harley and reply, 2 December 1646, 3 March 1647; PRO, C115/M21/7640, C115/M21/7642.

95 Johnson, *Ancient Customs*, p. 172; FSL, Vb 3(2); PRO, C115/H25/5457; BL, Add. MS 11052, fol. 17.

96 BL, Add. MS 11052, fols 52r, 73–4; HRO, Hereford City Records, vol. IV, fol. 81v.

97 C. F. Patterson, 'Leicester and Lord Huntingdon: Urban Patronage in Early Modern England', *Midland History*, 16 (1991), pp. 45–62; *APC 1630–31*, p. 290; BL, Add. MS 11052, fol. 87–8; PRO, C115/M13/7266; HRO, Hereford City Records, quarter sessions papers 1665–68, 8 January 1667; N. E. Key, 'Politics beyond Parliament: Unity and Party in the Herefordshire Region during the Restoration Period' (Cornell University Ph.D. thesis, 1989), pp. 281–7.

98 W. R. Williams, *The Parliamentary History of the County of Hereford* (Brecknock, 1896), pp. 89–90; I. J. Atherton, ed., 'An Account of Herefordshire in the First Civil War', *Midland History*, 21 (1996), p. 146.

99 Eales, *Puritans*, pp. 6, 63–4, 84; Cambridge University Library, Add. MS 6863, fol. 81r; Bodleian, MS Tanner 465, fol. 62r.

100 M. A. E. Green, ed., *The Diary of John Rous* (Camden Society, 1st series, 66, 1856), p. 44; T. Cogswell, *The Blessed Revolution: English Politics and the Coming of War, 1621–1624* (Cambridge, 1989), p. 22; Bodleian, MS Eng. hist. e. 28, p. 481; S. C. A. Pincus, *Protestantism and Patriotism: Ideologies and the Making of English Foreign Policy, 1650–1668* (Cambridge, 1996), p. 276; J. Sutherland, *The Restoration Newspaper and its Development* (Cambridge, 1986), p. 23. For the circulation of news see also I. J. Atherton, 'The Itch Grown a Disease: Manuscript Transmission of News in the Seventeenth Century', in J. Raymond, ed., *News, Newspapers, and Society in Early Modern Britain* (London, 1999).

101 PRO, C115/N1/8487, C115/N1/8496, C115/M35/8388.

102 Atherton, thesis, appendix II; Powell, *Pory*, p. 55; PRO, C115/N4/8575; HCA, 6417, fol. 47r.

103 PRO, C115/M30/8104, C115/M30/8113, C115/M31/8132, C115/M31/8153, C115/M31/8185, C115/M31/8194, C115/M32/8211, C115/M32/8213.

104 PRO, C115/M35/8396.

105 PRO, C115/N3/8539, C115/N4/8579, C115/M12/7218.

106 BL, Add. MSS 11044, fol. 7r, 11050, fols 104v, 139–44, 154–7, 174r: PRO, SP16/73/17, fol. 23. The council's instructions for the disarming of recusants, sent to the lord president of the council in Wales on 2 October 1625, did not reach Scudamore until 30 October: BL, Add. MS 11055, fols 232–3.

107 PRO, C115/M35/8402, C115/N3/8554, SP16/213, fols 23v, 28v, PC2/42, pp. 251–4/fols 116–17.

108 S. Brigden, ed., 'The Letters of Richard Scudamore to Sir Philip Hoby, September 1549–March 1555', *Camden Miscellany XXX* (Camden, 4th series, 39, 1990), pp. 67–148; PRO, C115/M35/8385.

109 Powell, *Pory*, pp. 56–7; PRO, C115/M37/8455–76, C115/N9/8855–6.

110 PRO, SP29/161/137, SP29/242/193, SP29/249/78, SP29/231; P. Fraser, *The Intelligence of the Secretaries of State* (Cambridge, 1956), pp. 28–34, 143.

111 PRO, C115/N3/8550; E. Hyde, earl of Clarendon, *The History of the Rebellion and Civil Wars in England*, ed. W. D. Macray (6 vols, Oxford, 1888), IV, p. 490; HRO, BE7/1, fols 1v, 27r, 35r; HCA, 4681 (III–V); PRO, C115/A3/86, C115/B1/529.

112 PRO, C115/N3/8549; Laud, *Works*, III, pp. 215–16.

113   PRO, C115/N8/8827, C115/M13/7267; Arundel Castle Archives, 'Howard Letters and Papers 1636–1822, II Various', Scudamore to Dupont and Turner, 23 November/3 December 1639.

114   HRO, MS D71/5; PRO, C115/M13/7265; Westminster City Archives, E23, 1641 pew rents, E154–84, E2413, E2568A; PRO, E115/363/23, E115/361/99; BL, Add. MS 11044, fol. 49.

115   BL, Add. MS 11044, fols 193–6; FSL, Vb 2(22).

116   Compare Eales, *Puritans*, p. 84; J. H. Bettey, *Calendar of the Correspondence of the Smyth Family of Ashton Court 1548–1642* (Bristol Record Society, 35, 1982), pp. 67, 72–3.

117   G. Goodman, *The Court of King James*, ed. J. S. Brewer (2 vols, London, 1839), I, p. 186; Herbert of Cherbury, *Autobiography*, p. 139; C. H. Firth and S. C. Lomas, *Notes on the Diplomatic Relations of England and France* (Oxford, 1906).

118   HMC, *Report on the Manuscripts of Lord De L'Isle and Dudley* (6 vols, London, 1925–66), VI, pp. 158, 226, 228–9; PRO, SP16/486, fols 55–6; A. Collins, ed., *Letters and Memorials of State* (2 vols, London, 1746), II, pp. 514, 591–2.

119   PRO, SP78/107, fol. 114r; HMC, *De L'Isle*, VI, pp. 164, 171; BL, microfilm M285, vol. XIV, fol. 241v, M772(52), MS 1110B, entry for 1639; Collins, *Letters*, II, p. 629.

120   HMC, *De L'Isle*, VI, p. 152; PRO, E403/1753, 12, 13 and 17 July 1639, SP16/423/26, fol. 52r, SP16/412/77, fols 159–60; HMC, *Cowper*, II, p. 232.

121   PRO, PRO31/3/72, fol. 18r; A. J. Loomie, ed., *Ceremonies of Charles I: The Note Books of John Finet 1628–1641* (New York, 1987), p. 258.

122   HMC, *De L'Isle*, VI, p. 229; *CSPV 1636–39*, pp. 596, 598, 601; *CSPV 1640–42*, pp. 1, 4–5, 7, 11; PRO, PRO31/3/72, fols 18r, 100r, 107r, 116r, 179r, 223r; Bibliothèque Nationale, Paris, MS Fonds Français 15916, fol. 294; BL, Add. MS 11044, fol. 85v. For Chambers see below, p. 205.

123   BL, Harl. MS 1579, fol. 56r.

124   Arundel Castle Archives, 'Howard Letters and Papers 1636–1822 II Various', Scudamore to Dupont, 5/15 September 1639, and to Dupont and Turner, 23 November/3 December 1639; PRO, C115/M24/7780, C115/N9/8873.

125   BL, Add. MS 11044, fols 100–5; H. Grotius, *Epistolae* (Amsterdam, 1687), p. 626; Gibson, *View*, pp. 103–5; PRO, C115/M24/7780.

126   PRO, SP16/538/84, fol. 150v, SP16/427/81, fol. 188; Atherton, thesis, p. 253.

127   Loomie, *Ceremonies*, p. 258; Laud, *Works*, III, p. 232, VII, p. 549.

128   HMC, *De L'Isle*, VI, p. 18; FSL, Vb 2(18).

129   HMC, *De L'Isle*, VI, p. 158; C. Russell, *The Fall of the British Monarchies* (Oxford, 1991), pp. 90–1; BL, microfilm M285, vol. XIV, fols 238–9; BL, Add. MS 15552, fol. 12r. Compare C. Carlton, *Archbishop William Laud* (London and New York, 1987), pp. 170–83, 228, for a different assessment of Laud's power.

130   BL, Add. MS 11044, fol. 89r; A. Collins, *The Baronetage of England* (2 vols, London, 1720), II, p. 175; Balliol College, Oxford, MS 333, fols 18r, 23r; Collins, *Letters*, II, pp. 629, 637; below, pp. 199–200, 206.

131   FSL, Vb 2(6), Vb 2(20), Vb 2(27); PRO, SP23/198, p. 775, C115/M14/7294; Atherton, thesis, pp. 380–1; G. E. McParlin, 'The Herefordshire Gentry in County Government, 1625–1661' (University College of Wales, Aberystwyth, Ph.D. thesis, 1981), pp. 105–213.

132 PRO, C181/7, pp. 10–12, C231/7, p. 12, C115/14/5690, C115/M21/7636.

133 HRO, R93/8354; M. A. Faraday, ed., *Herefordshire Militia Assessments of 1663* (Camden, 4th series, 10, 1972), p. 6. The jurisdiction of the council of Wales over the four shires had been effectively abolished, so there was no need for Scudamore to be reappointed to it.

134 BL, Add. MS 11044, fols 240–1, 253–4; B. D. Henning, ed., *The House of Commons 1660–1690* (3 vols, London, 1983), I, p. 262.

135 BL, Add. MS 15858, fol. 139r; Henning, *House of Commons*, III, p. 407; PRO, C231/7, p. 127, C66/3022, C193/12/3, fols 42v–4v.

136 PRO, KB27/1771, m. 584, KB27/1780, m. 760, SP18/130/130, fols 204–5, SP18/153, fols 18–19, 153–4, 277–8, C6/179/45, C9/410/261, C22/171/31; Essex RO, D/DGd F88, James Scudamore to Richard Bennet, 10 April 1654; House of Lords RO, Box 181/23; BL, Add. MS 15858, fols 135–8.

137 Arundel Castle Archives, 'Howard Letters and Papers 1636–1822 II Various', letters between James Scudamore and Lord Scudamore of 19/29 January 1657, 26 January/5 February 1657, 9/19 July 1658, 28 October/7 November 1659, 4/14 November 1659; House of Lords RO, Box 181/23; *Commons' Journals*, VIII, pp. 305–7, 373, 378; *Lords' Journals*, XI, pp. 399, 401; PRO, C5/56/38.

138 PRO, C231/7, p. 127; HRO, R93/8354; Faraday, *Herefordshire Militia Assessments*, p. 6.

139 *An Answer of Truth to a Scandalous and False Pamphlet* (London, 1661); there is a copy at HCL, 324.242.

140 HRO, BE7/1, fol. 35r, AL17/1.

141 Atherton, thesis, p. 383; H. G., 'Sepulchral Memorials of the Scudamore Family at Home-Lacy', *Collectanea Topographica et Genealogica*, 4 (1837), p. 257.

142 Morrill, *Nature of the English Revolution*, p. 187.

143 BL, Add. MS 11044, fol. 251r.

144 M. A. Faraday, 'Ship Money in Herefordshire', *Transactions of the Woolhope Naturalists' Field Club*, 41 (1974), pp. 219–29; Eales, *Puritans*, pp. 87–8.

Chapter 6

Scudamore as ambassador, 1635–39

In January 1635 Scudamore was appointed Charles's ambassador in ordinary to Louis XIII of France. It was the summit of his political career so far, the fulfilment of his political ambitions. George Wall, preaching on the text 'a faithful ambassador is health' (Proverbs 13:17) shortly before Scudamore's departure to France and in a sermon subsequently dedicated to the viscount, noted that, as Scudamore honoured God, so Charles honoured him.[1] Scudamore's management of local affairs in Herefordshire, and his service as an MP in the 1620s, had been rewarded. His carefully crafted image of loyal service to Charles had paid off. Scudamore's service as an ambassador, however, would demand new skills of negotiation and intrigue. It required a remodelled self-fashioning, a different self-presentation, from that which had served him so far. It threw him on to a far larger stage, peopled with politicians of greater skill than he had encountered hitherto, an arena where his family's reputation and traditions were far less useful. Events were to show that Scudamore was not up to the task.

Self-fashioning as an ambassador was a less creative and a more prescriptive process than self-fashioning as a gentleman or local politician. Presenting oneself as an ambassador meant conformity to two norms: consonance with notions of the 'perfect ambassador' and congruity with the royal will. In the first the diplomat had to represent in himself those virtues thought most meet in an ambassador; in the second he had to represent the views and person of the king.

As we have seen, the code of honour spoke with many voices about the virtues of a gentleman, allowing considerable scope in fashioning a variety of self-images to suit the occasion or the stage, and creating the possibility of self-promotion in that kaleidoscope of rhetorics and presentations. By contrast, the code of honour spoke with only one voice concerning the virtues of the perfect ambassador, leaving much less space for the ambitious diplomat to turn events to his own advantage. The fortunate and skilful ambassador might be able to promote himself and fashion his own image in the gaps between the dictates of the diplomatic code and the desires of his royal master. By contrast, the hapless ambassador who was unlucky, unpractised, unskilful or uncertain in the ways of diplomacy (and Scudamore was, as we shall see, all four) might find himself crushed between two millstones: the representative image forced upon him by the code of honour and his master's will; and the necessity of success in his negotiations for the furtherance of his image, reputation and career.

Writing on the 'perfect ambassador' was a popular European genre in the sixteenth and seventeenth centuries, with at least 176 works devoted to the subject published between 1626 and 1700. So uniform were these in their conclusions, and so heavily plagiarised, one from another, that a recent commentator has dismissed them as a 'dreary' and 'uninspiring and repetitive body of writing', but this is seriously to undervalue both their importance and their appeal to an early modern audience. Scudamore, for example, was charged by his instructions to 'informe yourself in the ceremonies and offices belonging to Ambassadors'.[2] Throughout the literature, there was unanimity on what constituted the correct attributes of an ambassador: he should be wealthy (sufficient to keep up the proper state and expense of an embassy), well born, virtuous, prudent, discreet, brave, loyal and learned. Only on the issue of his honesty was there disagreement. Under what circumstances (if any) should an ambassador transgress moral laws or impugn his own honour in the pursuit of his master's business, for example in spying? Overall it was a high ideal: Francis Thynne, writing in 1578, concluded that the perfect ambassador would be 'adorned with all virtues required, and commendable, in a good man, and unfurnished of any vice to blemish his credit, or that may win him the Surname of a wicked man'.[3]

While such a list of virtues was similar to that demanded of any gentleman, there were particular emphases that distinguished the perfect ambassador from the perfect gentleman. An ambassador drew authority from speaking. The power of the word was his main weapon and one of his main preoccupations (hence, as we shall see, the long arguments about the use of particular words and titles). The term 'orator' was a common early modern synonym for ambassador.[4] Depictions of the ideal ambassador focused on the importance of elocution and 'well-speaking'; without them, thought Jean Hotman, 'he shall do no great good in his Ambassage' and 'he shalbe oftentimes the iest of Courtiers'.[5] Allied to this issue was a consideration of the language in which an ambassador should conduct his negotiations. It was generally held both a tactical advantage and an honour to one's master for an ambassador to be able to speak his native tongue, but, failing that, Latin was often accepted as a common diplomatic language.[6] Diplomats' words were like those of kings, imbued with their own vivifying, constructive force. In this sense they were like the divine logos, words with a constructive power of their own. Indeed, many parallels were drawn between ambassadors and clergymen in seventeenth-century discourse. Clergy were frequently described as 'God's ambassadors'. Like ambassadors, they drew identity from speaking. They were God's messengers as ambassadors delivered messages between kings. They were His observers in local communities while ambassadors watched and reported on the state of international affairs. Ambassadors possessed certain legal immunities, their persons were 'sacred and inviolable,' thought George Wall, just as clergy should be respected and revered. Clergy were Christ's representatives on earth, ambassadors were princes' representatives to other princes.[7] Just as the code of honour for clergy was narrower than that for gentlemen, with fewer routes to honour and fewer avenues of action, so the ways of acting for ambassadors were more limited.

The representative function of an ambassador laid upon him a number of further requirements and patterns of behaviour. An ambassador was to be magnificent and munificent, as a due representation and assertion of his master's greatness. It was a commonplace that, as one anonymous seventeenth-century French commentator remarked, 'an ambassador must represent the grandeur of his master'. In the words of Martin Johnson's 'Elegie' on Lord Scudamore himself, 'Our Envoys are Kings Images, when sent, / Their Masters Witt, and Greatness represent.'[8]

Ambassadors were the personal representatives of the sovereigns who sent them. Three factors reinforced the symbolism inherent in such a personal representation. Firstly, early modern English political theory was particularly corporeal, dwelling on the prince's two bodies and stressing how the royal body, the 'lively image', was 'the master symbol of the office' and 'an essential instrument of political management', to use David Starkey's phrase. Secondly, the language of early modern diplomacy was personal, familial and bodily, subsuming kingdoms into kings. Relations between countries were expressed in, and by implication turned on, personal relations between monarchs. Diplomatic discourse expressed an identity between the health of kings and the health of kingdoms. The very first thing that Charles charged Scudamore with saying was to 'tell Our good brother how glad Wee are to heare of his good health ... And wish the continuance of his health and prosperitie in all his vndertakings, tending (as Wee hope) to a much desired common peace.' Scudamore's instructions of June and November 1635 were shot through with the language of fraternal and familial relations between Charles I and Louis XIII, expressing Charles's desire for 'Our nearer personal alliance with that King Our brother'. An ambassador, therefore, was a representative of and a substitute for personal relations between kings; he was, in the words of Scudamore's instructions, 'a pledge and continual remembrancer of Our sincere intentions towards him ... to settle and encrease brotherlie loue and correspondence for the good of both Crownes'. Thirdly, it followed that an ambassador stood in place of his master, a symbol of the fact that, had circumstances been different, a king would have come in person. Royal 'summits' or face-to-face meetings had their heyday in the late fifteenth and early sixteenth centuries; nevertheless, faced with a particularly intractable negotiation (the Spanish match) Prince Charles rushed to Madrid in 1623 in the belief that he could pull off what the ambassadors, his father's pledges and remembrancers, had failed to accomplish. In sum, early modern ambassadors were personal representatives of their masters and symbols of their prince's greatness first, and negotiators capable of independent action only second.[9]

The image and reputation of an ambassador were the image and reputation of his master. The ideal ambassador, it was said, should be physically handsome, not merely on the Aristotelian principle that beauty was the best letter of introduction, but because he had to be 'a comely and graceful Person being to represent the person of his Prince'.[10] An ambassador had to be treated as if he were the prince in whose stead he had come. Thomas Bilson had explained the doctrine in the mid sixteenth century:

> The reverence given to the officers, arms, or images, which Princes send to be set up, unto themselves, is accepted as rendered to their own persons when they cannot otherwise be present in the place to receive it but by a substitute or sign that shall represent their state.

Godfrey Goodman stated the case more succinctly: ambassadors 'bear their prince's person, and therefore are to have honour, place, and precedency which belongs to their masters'.[11] Thus it was that no ambassador could allow himself to be treated in a way that the king his master would not find acceptable. A tension was immediately set up, however, because ambassadors were not kings; they could not claim the equality with their host sovereign that their representative symbolism implied, but neither could they assume too subordinate a role in the face of the claims of the monarchy to which they were sent. An ambassador, however, represented his prince not merely to the prince to whom he was sent. He was also a lively image of his prince to all the other ambassadors whom he met; in their company he was among peers and could press his master's claims unambiguously and to the full. Thus it was that whenever two or three ambassadors gathered together, conflict followed as sure as night followed day.

Ambassadors, wrote Hotman, must 'be iealous of the degree and place which is due vnto his Maister, without yeelding any iote thereof vnto an other'. On this point all writers were in agreement. 'An ambassador must not permit or allow anyone to challenge or in any other way offend the honour of his Prince on any subject at all'. Scudamore's instructions reinforced the point: he was never to forget his 'first and chief rule and dutie, which is, neither to doe nor suffer anie thing in the course of your imployements, that may derogate from Our honour, or may lett faile or prejudice the dignitie and praerogatives of Our Imperial Crowne in the least degree'.[12]

Much of Scudamore's time and energy as ambassador was taken up with the details of the process of negotiating, rather than the substance: whether his wife was allowed to sit in the presence of the French queen; who was allowed to sit next to whom in a coach; whether the *conducteur des ambass-adeurs* should meet him at the top or the bottom of a flight of stairs; who should give the hand to whom, and so on. These were not trivialities, they were part of the essence of an ambassador's function. It has been remarked that the way that negotiations are carried out is almost as important as what is negotiated.[13] Every instance of diplomatic ceremony, every tittle of protocol, mattered intensely, and each instance was recorded, pored over, discussed, kept for future referral, sometimes even published.[14] Disputes between ambassadors and others over precedence were the norm, turning the formal entries of ambassadors into chariot races as coaches jostled and scuffled their way through the Parisian streets. When the Dutch ambassador entered Paris in 1637 the coach of the Swedish ambassador (Hugo Grotius) tried first to force its way ahead of the coach of the English extraordinary ambassador (the earl of Leicester), but yielded when Leicester's servants gave the Swedes a bloody nose; the Swedes then raced ahead of Scudamore's coach. Twice the procession had to be halted when swords were drawn, before the Swedes eventually retired, disgraced. The incident was later remembered as redounding to the glory of the English crown.[15] Every incident touched upon the honour not just of the ambassador involved but of the monarch he represented. Even the question of whether the French made the English agent Henry de Vic stand while he was interpreting, or whether Scudamore insisted that he should be allowed to sit down, was held to reflect on Charles's honour.[16]

The image projected of protocol and upholding the king's honour was of a fixed and unchanging system. In reality there was flexibility in the system, but it was to be used for the benefit of princes and not for the advancement of ambassadors. Ceremony could be a weapon used to bring pressure to bear on princes, in which case ambassadors were the anvil on which the blow was struck, or protocol could be a language to convey nuanced messages between princes, with ambassadors merely as the messengers. When in December 1636 the French wanted to bring further pressure to bear on Charles to conclude a treaty, they reinforced the message in two non-verbal ways. First, they stopped sending the *conducteur des ambassadeurs* to the English embassy, sending only the *sous-conducteur* instead. Second, they refused to give Scudamore and Leicester the customary dinner after their audience, forcing them to eat bread and cheese at a local tavern.[17]

Performing as an ambassador was a more restrictive role than performing as a gentleman. Representing the king did not allow much room for manoeuvre; the negotiation between prince and prince was quite different from the negotiation between prince and locality inherent in the role of a county magnate, for example. An ambassador spoke with the power of the word, and the words were his master's, not his own. An ambassador acted as the representative of his prince, and the actions were those of his prince, not his own. When, for example, the coaches of Grotius and Scudamore contested precedence in the streets of Paris, both sides recognised that Grotius was acting out his duty on behalf of the Swedish crown, and not out of any personal vainglory, and there was said to be no personal animosity between him and Leicester or Scudamore; indeed, Grotius and Scudamore remained good friends.[18]

If conformity to the notions of a perfect ambassador and representation of the royal person left little scope for independent action or self-fashioning, the final part of an ambassador's role, congruity with the royal will, usually allowed no more individuality or creativity. Once again it was a case of representing and acting out the sovereign's wishes, but here ambassadors faced an immediate problem: discerning what was the true royal will. The king rarely wrote directly to ambassadors; rather, royal instructions and their inter-pretation were in the hands of the secretaries of state. The rivalry between the two English secretaries, Sir John Coke and Sir Francis Windebank, compli-cated matters for ambassadors, for the secretaries interpreted the royal will themselves to suit their own ambitions and political preconceptions, putting their own gloss on Charles's intentions: Windebank was much more inclined to follow a Spanish alliance than was Coke. Moreover, Charles himself did not deal openly with his secretaries, keeping Coke in the dark about his negotiations with the Habsburgs. So, while there was a formal division of labour between the two secretaries, Coke being responsible for correspondence with northern Europe (including France) and Windebank for that with southern Europe, it was necessary for ambassadors to deal with both secretaries in order to understand the full picture.[19] Scudamore's informal correspondence with Windebank was often more instructive (and more detailed) than his formal correspondence with Coke, for example.

Parallel to the problem of the filter which the secretaries placed between king and ambassador was the complication that there was, in the mid 1630s, not one royal will but two. The re-emergence of Henrietta Maria as a political force in 1635, with foreign policy objectives of her own – war with Spain – fostered by her puritan courtiers such as the earl of Holland and furthered by her own diplomatic agent – Wat Montagu – further muddied the water for English ambassadors. Although they were sent to represent the king, they could not afford to ignore the influence of the queen: 'God keepe vs from the necessity of hauinge such men to negociate,' was de Vic's judgement on Montagu.[20] It is no surprise, then, to find ambassadors complaining of the difficulty of discerning the royal will which they were meant to embody. Walter Lord Aston, ambassador in Spain, moaned that 'I never have clearly understood what his Majesty for the present would be contented to accept of for satisfaction from Spain, nor what content to return them'. The countess of Leicester warned her husband to follow the king's mind, 'wich it seemes you must understand, though it be not expressed ... for it is a miserable thing not to know what will please best'.[21] For men like Scudamore, cast into the lions' den of diplomacy from the very different world of local politics, the contrast was very marked. As a justice, commissioner and deputy lieutenant, the royal will was clearly expressed in letters signed by the whole privy council, and the skill lay in transmuting what the council demanded into what the locality would bear in ways that enhanced one's own status in the eyes of both. As an ambassador the first skill was to translate the often conflicting signals from the court into a clear expression of the royal will, which had to be interpreted in such a way as to glorify one's master and achieve enough success in the negotiations for some of the honour to reflect back on oneself.

A number of historians have found that they are no more able to understand Charles's foreign policy than either Aston or the countess of Leicester were at the time, and, of those who do claim to have discerned the king's wishes, most have dismissed them as dishonouring the name of a foreign *policy*. Most famously of all, Samuel Gardiner described Charles's negotiations in the 1630s as serving only 'to make the brain dizzy'; rather than persist with an interminable headache, Gardiner decided that Charles 'had no European policy at all'.[22] Here, alas, is not the place for an extended discussion of Charles's foreign policy objectives in the 1630s.[23] Nevertheless, the options before Charles were clear and, although he cannot be made an insightful and clear-thinking strategist, he did pursue a fixed aim in the mid 1630s: the restoration of his nephew Charles-Louis to the Upper and Lower Palatinates and to the electoral title, all of which had been lost by Charles-Louis's father, Frederick V, whose wife was Charles's sister Elizabeth, usually known in England as the queen of Bohemia. For Charles this was neither a strategic nor a religious calculation, but a point of personal and family honour, and a matter of keen importance to the reputation of his imperial crown. It was this, above all else, that Scuda-more was sent to Paris to maintain. The fate of Charles's nephew reflected on the Stuarts' dynastic reputation, crying out for, demanding, Charles-Louis's restoration. As Scudamore never tired of reminding the French, the restitution of the Palatinate concerned them far more than it did Charles in strategic terms 'for vicinitie, or diversion, or leavies of men, or other advantages'; for Charles it was simply a case of 'the neere interest of his affection and blood;

'Wherin the world can witness, how hee hath acquitted himself not only by negociation, and by frends, but by vast expences vpon all occasions.'[24]

Uncertainty entered into English policy in two areas. Firstly, how best to achieve Charles-Louis's restoration? The Lower Palatinate was divided in a kaleidoscope of combinations between French, Spanish, Swedish and imperial troops, depending on the vicissitudes of the current campaigning season, while the Upper Palatinate and the electoral title were held by Duke Maximilian of Bavaria. Charles calculated that the two key players were the French and the Spanish, and that either had the power to restore the Palatinate. (Charles, like many others at the time, perhaps too readily conflated the Spanish and Austrian branches of the Habsburg family, and thought that pressure on Spain could achieve results in Austria.) Charles's navy was, he hoped, the means to make either Louis or Philip dance to an English tune. Many others, including the Spanish chief minister Olivares, thought that the English navy had a potentially vital role to play in either convoying Spanish men and money to Flanders, or cutting off that supply: since the French seizure of Lorraine (1631–34) the English Channel was the only effective route between Iberia and the Spanish Netherlands.[25] The navy-as-carrot strategy had two big advantages to Charles. First, since the navy was funded by ship money, there was no need to call a parliament for war finance. Second, if Charles could involve himself in a cheap, limited naval war in league with either Spain or France, he would earn a seat at the negotiations for a general European peace which were expected to begin almost daily in the 1630s, and use the peace negotiations to secure the restoration of the Palatinate.[26] The question before Charles, then, was not war or neutrality (as it is so often put by historians),[27] but France or Spain. The strategy of holding the balance between the two great powers was one that many in England advocated (or, as Michael Young has recently rephrased the issue, of weighing who was the more powerful, and then courting that king), provided that Charles could judge the moment to play his hand.[28] No one was certain which way Charles would jump, although the safe money was usually on Spain. That Charles kept England out of the Thirty Years' War in the 1630s was a measure not of his success at managing English neutrality but of his failure to involve England in the conflict.

The second uncertainty in English foreign policy arose because it was not good negotiating practice to send one's rivals too clear a message. Charles was, temperamentally, a poor negotiator, although with other kings – his peers – he showed greater skill and flexibility than with his own subjects, from whom he expected simple obedience. At times it was necessary to send out conflicting messages to confuse the courts of Europe, or even (as we shall see) factions at the English court. Sometimes it was also necessary not to let ambassadors into the whole picture. There seems little point in following Gardiner and other historians in criticising these tactics as confused, for they were adopted by all countries at the time. As Scudamore's instructions remarked, it was 'now vsuall to treate on all sides and make warre at once', a maxim enjoined by Cardinal Richelieu.[29] The practice may have made for good statecraft, but it did not make the task of an ambassador, sent to embody his prince's wishes to another court, any easier.

When Scudamore was appointed to Paris in 1635 he was the first ordinary English ambassador to Louis in three years; since 1632 representation had been carried out by two joint agents, Guernsey-born Henry de Vic and the French Huguenot Réné Augier. Scudamore's mission was timed to parallel Aston's embassy to Spain, announced at the same time, and to meet rising French diplomatic pressure at the end of 1634 and beginning of 1635 as Louis prepared for war against Spain with a network of anti-Habsburg alliances.[30] Scudamore's role, however, was to be a mere sop to the French, a delaying tactic while Aston was to conclude secret negotiations for an alliance with Spain (begun in 1632) and a joint Anglo-Spanish maritime treaty to sweep the Channel of Dutch ships.[31] Early in 1635 full powers to treat and conclude an alliance were sent to Sir Arthur Hopton, English agent in Spain. No such powers were given to Scudamore; he did not even leave for France until August.[32]

So it was that when Scudamore landed in Calais on 11/21 August 1635 he came, in the words of Grotius, 'laden with complaints'. Scudamore was accompanied by a train of thirty-seven or so, including his wife Elizabeth, three chaplains (Matthew Turner of Dore, Thomas Manfeild of Holme Lacy and the Oxford classicist and future Bodley librarian Thomas Lockey, who had been recommended by Laud) and Windebank's son Thomas.[33] Scudamore had his first, introductory, audience with Louis XIII at Meaux on Sunday 23 August/2 September; three days later he made his entry into Paris. He was well satisfied by his reception, telling the two secretaries, Coke and Windebank, that 'hitherto I haue receiued nothinge butt faire respect'.[34] Arguably, it was to be the high point of his embassy.

Kevin Sharpe has recently argued that the Peace of Prague of May 1635, by which the leading German Protestant prince, the Lutheran John George, elector of Saxony, made peace with Emperor Ferdinand (and in which the Palatinate was ignored), helped to produce a reorientation of English foreign policy in 1635. According to Dr Sharpe the peace laid bare to Charles the duplicity of the Habsburgs and the hollowness of their previous offers of help for his nephew; the king, therefore, 'reoriented his diplomacy' and turned 'sharply towards France'.[35] Neither the instructions given to Scudamore by Charles, nor the ambassador's behaviour in his first few months, suggest that in the summer and autumn of 1635 Charles was serious about a French alliance. The revolution in English policy did not occur until the end of 1636. Scudamore's general instructions of June 1635 outlined his duties as ambassador such as protecting British merchants, keeping a watchful eye on French military preparations and reassuring Louis of Charles's 'readines to proceede to a firme and good accomodation' and his 'constant intentions for the peace of Christendome'. The sting was in his supplementary instructions, delivered by Coke, no lover of Spain, just before he left England. These stated that he was to explain that no treaty with France could be entertained until three points were cleared up: Louis must publicly give Charles-Louis the title of elector (thereby ratifying France's break with Bavaria); the secret articles of the Franco-Dutch treaty were to be divulged; and the French must drop their opposition to 'our ancient and never yet controuerted dominion of the seas'.[36] These were not answers to mollify the French, and contrast strongly with the offers of leagues in the secret instructions sent to the English diplomats in Spain and Vienna only two weeks later.[37]

Scudamore's actions on his arrival struck the same note. As soon as he had landed in France he presented the deputy governor of Calais with a long list of complaints, alleging French abuses against British shipping. An even longer paper was presented to the French secretary of state Claude le Bouthillier at Scudamore's first meeting. Fourteen points complained of such things as the confiscation of English cloth in Rouen and French interference with British trade in Canada.[38] Scudamore refused to use any language but English, would not visit Cardinal Richelieu, declined to accord the title 'Highness' (*Altesse*) to Mademoiselle (Anne Marie, the infant daughter of Gaston d'Orléans, the king's brother) or the princes and princesses of the blood, and would not attend the services of the (Calvinist) reformed church of Paris at Charenton, frequenting services instead in his own chapel, which he had adorned according to full 'Laudian' practice.[39] The French ambassadors in England, the marquis de Pougny and the marquis de Senneterre, condemned Scudamore's conduct strongly. Some English courtiers agreed, others laid the blame on the viscount's alleged natural haughtiness.[40] He was, in fact, merely being true to his instructions and the wishes of his king and his archbishop.

When the earl of Leicester later quizzed Laud about Scudamore's refusal to go to Charenton, the archbishop replied cryptically, 'he is the wiser'; the king's verdict on Scudamore's chapel – 'In this I cannot fynd falt with my ambassador' – was, by contrast, unequivocal.[41] Scudamore's action was, moreover, part of a wider policy of extending the claims of the church of England abroad. In 1633 the privy council had ordered all English churches and regiments in the United Provinces to observe the liturgy, rites and ceremonies of the church of England; Peter Heylyn later alleged that 'The like [was] done also for regulating the Divine Service in the Families of all Ambassadours ... It was now hoped that there would be a Church of England in all courts of Christendom ... by which it might be rendred as diffused and Catholick as the Church of Rome'.[42]

Scudamore had royal warrant for his other actions. His refusal to treat with Richelieu in person rested entirely on his instructions, which commanded him 'to haue no publique or personnal entercourse' with cardinals and nuncios, 'Their pretences not comporting with the dignities of Our person which you represent' (in particular Richelieu's claim to the right hand of the ambassador within his own house). The privy council debated the point but Charles was adamant, despite the opinion of many that he was effectively cutting off his nose to spite his face, since all negotiations had to go through the cardinal. The diplomat Abraham de Wicquefort later dwelt on what he saw as the folly of this policy, which, in his opinion, in no way advanced English interests: 'There is nothing that perplexes more an Embassador, than the Orders he receives not to negotiate with the first Minister'; he even saw in it 'one of the chief Causes' of the civil wars.[43] Nonetheless, Scudamore kept communication open with the cardinal through various juniors: his teenage son James, the two agents and Richard Browne, a secretary at the embassy in 1635 whom Scudamore took over as his own.[44] For the refusal of the title *Altesse* Scudamore again had royal warrant, and consequently he did not visit Mademoiselle or the princes and princesses of the blood until October 1637. The title was a novelty, only recently introduced by Louis's brother from the Spanish Netherlands, and the question of whether to use it or not divided the diplomatic community in Paris.[45] Finally, Scudamore justified his treating only in English on the grounds that the king had charged him to negotiate clearly, which he could do best if he stuck to English. He was in fact following normal diplomatic practice, but it did nothing to soothe French irritation every time he passed a paper written in English to Louis's commissioners. De Vic was forced to admit that treating in English was a great advantage, but feared that it risked losing much by irking the French, 'there beinge nothinge that a Minister shoulde more endeauor then to render himself acceptable in the Courte where hee is employed, so farr as it may stande with his Maisters honor and seruice'.[46] If this lesson was not entirely lost on Charles he was not prepared to prejudice his honour and service to any extent, especially while he remained uninterested in a French alliance. Scudamore continued in rendering himself acceptable to Charles rather than to Louis.

Scudamore's actions were carefully calculated, and were part of his ambassadorial responsibilities of presenting his master's image to a foreign court. Père Joseph and others at the French court quickly decided that Scudamore was 'wholy Spanish', and not to be trusted, so well did he seem to be working against better Anglo-French relations.[47] This reputation was later to be exploited by the earl of Leicester to undermine Scudamore, but in the late summer of 1635 it was an image that Charles wanted conveying to the French. At one level Scudamore was doing no more than representing in his carriage the low ebb to which Anglo-French relations had sunk over the matter of Charles's claims to sovereignty of the seas. Père Joseph had been advised by an English spy that pro-Spanish courtiers in England were hoping that the issue would provoke a conflict with France and Holland, and such a conflict nearly ensued.[48] In the summer of 1635, in an attempt to clinch the Spanish alliance he had been pursuing, Charles himself may have tried to precipitate a break with France over the sovereignty of the seas. Sir John Pennington's journal as rear admiral of the 1635 fleet shows that the English ships were under orders 'with the French Kings Fleete, of what strength soever they weare to Fight it out to the Last Man, if they should refuse to doe their duety to his Majestys Shippes'. Perhaps only Richelieu's insistence on the necessity of avoiding a break with England prevented open war. He ordered the French fleet to avoid the English, and Admiral Lindsey spent a fruitless summer sailing up and down the Channel.[49] Nonetheless, the French were incensed at the English protection of Spanish ships, and retaliated by attacking English ships which they suspected of carrying Spanish goods, even repeatedly seizing the king's post barque. An English sailor who was robbed by Frenchmen in August reported that his attackers said 'there was warres between England and France'.[50]

Scudamore may have had the backing of Charles in his first few months as ambassador, but he was otherwise increasingly isolated. Michael Young's suggestion that 'the cosy triumvirate of Windebank, Scudamore, and de Vic prevailed' until May 1636 is wide of the mark. On his appointment in January 1635 Scudamore had immediately established a much warmer relationship with Windebank than with Coke, but that had not automatically brought him close to de Vic, Windebank's ally in the French embassy.[51] An attempt that spring by Windebank to engineer de Vic's promotion from agent to assistant failed but drove a wedge between Scudamore and de Vic, for the newly appointed ambassador would not tolerate such a move.[52] Only his intense rivalry with his fellow agent, Réné Augier, threw de Vic into the arms of Scudamore, and he sought Scudamore's support for his suit to have Augier recalled. The agents' differences were partly personal and partly ideological: Augier seemed pro-French and pro-Dutch whilst de Vic suspected the French; Augier was close to Coke, de Vic to Cottington and Windebank.[53] On Scudamore's arrival in Paris de Vic very quickly felt unsure about his new superior, perhaps because Scudamore had brought over a warrant for Augier's continuation as joint agent, and he set about undermining Scudamore's credit with Windebank and the English court. When de Vic felt his own position secure he could write of the viscount to Windebank in glowing terms, but when he felt insecure he turned against his superior, alleging to Windebank that 'the Lord Skudamore is in no good predicament with these ministers' and that he was 'weake in experience ... reserved and formall all which are compounde contrary to what is required in an ambassador he as Deuic feares he will not be very acceptable'.[54] De Vic may have felt particularly vulnerable as the French were trying to use Scudamore's outwardly strange and cold behaviour to drive a wedge between the ambassador and him. De Vic later warmed to Scudamore when he realised that Augier's position was in much greater doubt than his own, for Scudamore's use of English meant that he, and not Augier, would act as interpreter. The twists and turns of the relationship between de Vic and Scudamore baffled many. The French *conductuer des ambassadeurs* Berlize believed de Vic governed Scudamore 'absolutely', while Scudamore seemed oblivious to de Vic's treachery, telling Windebank that 'Monsieur De Vic beares himself with very good respect towards mee'.[55]

Scudamore had, furthermore, adversaries at the English court, especially among the followers of the queen. Since the beginning of 1635 Henrietta Maria had ventured back into politics, fallen out with Laud once more and greatly increased her influence. The queen and those in her circle were playing a complicated game, and Scudamore had no part in it. As early as the beginning of October there were strong rumours that Charles was on the point of sending the earl of Holland, a confidant of the queen, as extraordinary ambassador to France to try to arrange the return of the queen mother to France. No ambassador was sent, but at the end of October Wat Montagu came to Paris, bearing letters from Henrietta Maria. Montagu ignored Scuda-more and negotiated directly with the French, even visiting Richelieu, something that Scudamore was forbidden to do. Scudamore felt snubbed. Montagu had presented two proposals from Henrietta which the French thought reasonable. First, that the French and Dutch should make no peace with the emperor without restitution of the Palatinate and revocation of the imperial ban, with the question of the electoral title being remitted to a meeting of all the electors provided that Louis promised to use his influence in favour of the Palatine. Second, and in return, Charles would declare himself completely neutral until after the Palatine was restored.[56]

Scudamore had been effectively bypassed only three months after his arrival in France. He was saved by the intransigence of Senneterre, the French extraordinary ambassador in England. Senneterre was quickly disillusioned with negotiations, concluding that Charles was unlikely to grant much more than a few levies, and wondering whether it was worth keeping the negotia-tions going for such a small advantage. Charles meanwhile was under strong pressure from his wife and her circle to join with France and summon a parliament.[57] His response, in contrast, was to suggest a reciprocal restoration of Lorraine by the French and of the Palatinate by the Habsburgs. It was, in many ways, a clever move, for it delayed any possibility of an alliance with France, and therefore, of the calling of a parliament, whilst at the same time seizing the initiative from the French for the first time in many years. Senneterre declined to entertain Charles's suggestion and refused to promise an answer from France, suggesting that the charge be referred to Scudamore. The scene of the main Anglo-French negotiations consequently shifted from London to Paris, and Scudamore had a positive mission to undertake.[58]

Fresh instructions were sent in November, and in accordance with these Scudamore formally proposed that the best way to obtain a general peace was for Louis to return Lorraine to Duke Charles and for Ferdinand II to return the Palatinate and electoral title to Charles-Louis. If Louis agreed to return Lorraine then Charles promised 'to declare Warre' in alliance with the French king against those who opposed the restoration of the Palatinate. As befitting the serious nature of this proposal, and to remove any French jealousies, Scudamore gave in this proposition in Latin.[59]

It was reported that the French laughed at the proposal, and Senneterre believed that its only purpose was delay while the English continued their negotiations with the Habsburgs.[60] The comte de Chavigny replied to Scudamore that there was a great inequality in the proposition: Lorraine had cost much French blood, the Palatinate very little English, yet now Charles expected that the two would be exchanged with no further effort on his part. Furthermore, Lorraine could not be yielded, for it had been seized legitimately as the punishment of a rebellious subject, Duke Charles. Finally, though Chavigny did not say so openly, Louis refused to be separated from Germany, and Lorraine was an important bridgehead in this respect.[61] Charles almost certainly knew that the French would not agree to the suggestion, and had already received intelligence of their refusal to surrender Lorraine, but the proposal did have a realistic basis.[62] Despite all their protestations over a dozen years and more, the French did relinquish most of Lorraine in 1648; there seemed good reasons for them to do so in 1635, good reasons which Scudamore pressed upon the French, particularly that the seizure of Lorraine had driven Bavaria closer to the emperor (for Duke Maximilian's first wife was Elizabeth of Lorraine). Louis XIII's own propaganda repeatedly stressed that he went to war for two reasons only, to protect and conserve the liberties of German princes, and to make peace. Charles's proposition seemed to encompass these two points.[63] Charles's proposal was one of his few diplomatic masterstrokes, allowing him to occupy the moral high ground and pose, as his father had tried, as the British Solomon.

If Charles could briefly revel in his honour and judgement, Scudamore's experience was less fortunate. The French resorted to delaying tactics and kept him waiting for an answer. He found great difficulty even in meeting with the French. In his judgement the secret of foreign business was known only to four men: Louis, Richelieu, Père Joseph and Chavigny. He was prevented from seeing the cardinal by his instructions. Père Joseph was a slippery fish, and could be treated with only as a private individual, as he had no official commission from the king. Chavigny made appointments for meetings and then excused himself. Scudamore told Coke that to speak with him was 'always a worke of time and difficultie'; later, when the French were trying to evade signing a treaty, Leicester too found Chavigny 'as hard to be found as a mouse in a barne'. The king could be seen only at formal audiences, where his practice was never to give a direct answer but to refer the viscount back to the elusive Chavigny. De Vic contrasted this limited access to Louis with the much freer access the French ambassadors had to Charles when they hoped to catch the English king off guard and ill prepared.[64] Henrietta Maria allowed the French and Savoyard ambassadors, as representatives of her brother Louis and sister Christina, 'domestic access' to come and go as they pleased as members of her own household. In 1634 the French ambassador was requested not to use this privilege to 'surprise' Charles by conversing with him 'without the presence of his lords to assist ... with their counsell', but the privilege remained and was exploited by the French.[65] Charles and Louis both used court ritual to enforce and enhance their power, and both eagerly watched the other for innovations and new tricks. De Vic's advice to follow the French in being more formal with ambassadors is ironic, given Richelieu's earlier advice to Louis to model his proceedings on the formality of Charles's court. Scudamore's experience contrasted with that of the French ambassadors and showed how much more adept Richelieu and Louis were in manipulating ceremony to their own ends. Second, it was a further instance of the complications Charles faced from his wife's court and household, especially as she was now bent on reversing her husband's policy, as Wat Montagu's mission testified.[66]

Scudamore was convinced that the French would not part with all of Lorraine and that their only purpose in negotiating with him was to spur the Spanish to a general peace, a prospect he and de Vic thought every day more likely in the early months of 1636, before the campaigning season began. If so, he wrote, 'there will bee had no respect at all to the Interests of the Prince Elector Palatine', and he informed Coke that 'I am nott able to discerne, that France will doe any thinge at all for the Prince Elector Palatine, butt as they are mouued by his Majesty of Greate Britaine'. His message seemed to be reinforced by the intermittent refusal of the French to address Charles-Louis with the electoral title.[67]

For five months Scudamore had demanded a formal answer from the French, and for five months he had been disappointed; after Easter he asked Coke whether it stood with Charles's dignity to carry on importuning so. Just when he was about to give up all hope a reply was made, but it was hardly one to hearten the English. Louis repeated his belief that only force would restore the Palatine, force that Charles, as the prince's nephew, was bound to contribute. No mention was made of either the electorate or what force France would contribute. Five months earlier the English had had great hopes of the success of their proposal, Charles asking every day what response the French had made; now the French did not even say what they would do about Lorraine.[68]

It is hardly surprising, then, that Charles was not dissuaded from his Spanish counsels. His decision seemed confirmed by the weekly pessimistic despatches from Scudamore in Paris and the optimistic ones from Taylor in Vienna and Aston in Madrid.[69] When Charles received what looked like a firm offer from Vienna, Ferdinand promising to lift the imperial ban and to treat of the restitution of the Lower Palatinate now and the electoral title on the death of the duke of Bavaria, he immediately decided to send the earl of Arundel as extraordinary ambassador to confirm the proposals and, if possible, to treat and conclude an alliance.[70]

Scudamore's reputation at home was at a low ebb, driven down by the poor state of Anglo-French relations, which seemed to grow more strained every day, with fresh reports of French attacks on British shipping.[71] An English captain was killed when his ship, the *Pearl*, was seized off North Africa by a French admiral. English indignation was exacerbated by the report that the French ship was on a mission to make peace with the Barbary States, and soon stories began circulating of French assistance to Turkish pirates and even of English sailors being driven across France in chains by infidel Turks. The case of the *Pearl* in particular took up much of Scudamore's time early in 1636 (as it would do for several years to come), mostly fruitlessly.[72] Scudamore's failures, over the Lorraine proposal and his inability to obtain redress for English merchants, greatly dissatisfied some at the English court. His methods were inflexible, he stuck to his instructions to demand nothing less than justice in the return of seized ships, and he refused any compromises, boasting, 'That which I demanded was justice. I desired nott, I declined grace.' It was a way of proceeding calculated to appeal to Charles's sense of his own honour rather than to achieve success with the French. He defended his lack of success with the thought that his duty was not to achieve ends but only to represent the truth and justice of British claims and demands, a defence as disingenuous as it is revealing about Scudamore and his master the king.[73]

Soon after Christmas 1635 the English court was again filled with rumours that Scudamore was about to be replaced, or at the very least seconded by an extraordinary ambassador. In April 1636 the rumours turned into reality when Henrietta Maria secured the appointment of Robert Sidney, earl of Leicester, as ambassador extraordinary. Only the queen's desire to have her man in Paris, and perhaps Charles's wish to balance Arundel's mission to Vienna so that he could once more claim evenhandedness in his dealings with Bourbon and Habsburg, could justify Leicester's mission. His instructions contained nothing that could not have been conducted through Scudamore, and there was no indication that Leicester would be any more successful than the ordinary ambassador.[74] Indeed, although it was common diplomatic practice to employ two ambassadors to one court, experience showed that the two often fell out; Wicquefort thought that in such situations 'Contestation is inevitable'. In Paris in 1636 the lack of any clear purpose to Leicester's mission, and the failure of the English government to demarcate clear boundaries between his orders and Scudamore's, quickly aggravated a tense situation between the two ambassadors.[75]

The French tried to drive a wedge between the two, but they need not have tried; the four English diplomats in Paris – Leicester, Scudamore, de Vic and Augier – were more than capable of arguing amongst themselves without outside assistance.[76] Leicester had been in Paris only three days when Scudamore rushed an express to Windebank, Laud and Charles complaining of his colleague for threatening to write separate despatches, not joint ones, and for saying that Scudamore would be excluded from all negotiations unless the French specifically requested his presence. None of this seemed to Scudamore to agree with Coke's reassurance to him that Leicester's mission was 'not at al to interrupt or preiudice your Commission'. If it was Charles's pleasure that he should be excluded from negotiation, Scudamore asked to be recalled.[77] Many thought Scudamore's position was in question that summer. Rumours once again circulated at the English court that he would be recalled, and Hamilton for one thought it likely: Scudamore is 'found by experiens no fit mann [f]or that place' he told Viscount Feilding, Charles's ambassador in Italy, assuring him that he was working hard for Feilding to be appointed in Scudamore's place. Windebank ordered Scudamore to stop his pleas for revocation. Windebank had established no positive contact with Leicester, and at this juncture his relations with the queen were little better, and presumably he did not wish to lose his finger in the French pie. Scudamore, meanwhile, believed that his enemies at court wanted him to remain in Paris but incapable of doing anything, to reflect badly on those who thought him fit to be sent as ambassador in the first place.[78]

As Scudamore suggested, their differences were partly rooted in faction at the English court. Leicester professed himself the queen's 'Slave' and was firmly a part of the Percy connection with her court, whereas Scudamore could never penetrate the queen's circle, despite trying hard. Scudamore remained too close to Laud ever to be favoured by the queen, her brief reconciliation with the archbishop in 1634 long forgotten. Moreover, he was unlikely to support the calling of a parliament (the goal of the French and many of the queen's courtiers) which would be likely to attack Laud. Apart from the king himself, Scudamore was reliant on Windebank and Laud only, and it was to these alone that he revealed his wish to be recalled. He did have other friends at court who had their important uses (such as ensuring the payment of his expenses), but none was powerful enough to protect his position in Paris.[79]

Throughout his embassy Scudamore had grave problems with his image and reputation at the English court. He had been able to deploy and manipulate the rhetoric and imagery of loyal service to the crown and his 'country' in the previous fifteen years, when royal and conciliar demands on issues such as knighthood fines or the militia had presented a relatively united front, and he had only to negotiate between central government and the locality, and between local jealousies and rivalries. To the practised, such negotiations left plenty of scope for fashioning one's own favourable image. In Paris, however, his task was much more difficult because of the way that competing interests within the privy council and at the heart of the English government pulled in different ways over foreign policy. Presenting himself as a loyal servant of Charles's wish for a pro-Spanish and anti-French policy left Scudamore exposed to the attacks of those around the queen who wanted a French alliance; it also left him isolated if Charles changed his policy.

Like most ambassadors, Scudamore was almost obsessively concerned about his standing back home,[80] but in relying on Laud and Windebank to promote his interests at court Scudamore did not have the best of masters. Laud was genuinely devoted to Scudamore but was not well liked and was, as we have seen, a poor lord and patronage master.[81] Windebank, meanwhile, and unbeknown to Scudamore, had his own agenda of advancing his own influence in foreign affairs.

Scudamore had written to one of the courtiers closest to the queen, the earl of Holland, offering his service, but his letter was ignored; it was obvious to his brother-in-law John Scudamore of Ballingham when he came to court in August 1637 that Holland disliked Scudamore. Scudamore tried another overture to the queen in August 1637, but once again the project miscarried. The letter fell into the hands of Henry Percy, who joked to Leicester that 'after supper, the letter it selfe was our farse, for I neuer sawe such a one'.[82] The grave, insecure, slightly haughty viscount was not likely to meet with a favourable reception from the wits and gallants who graced Henrietta Maria's court. Leicester particularly took an instant disliking to his colleague, and passed over no opportunity to denigrate him. He ridiculed Scudamore to Henry Percy:[83]

> He hath no Manner of Respect here, nor is esteemed for any more than a formal Pedante, neither is well able to make that good; for when his Knowledge, in speculative Things, comes in Discours to be examined, he is no more a Gyant, then in the Practical. I must confess, I thinke him throughout a very simple Man, unless it be in some Tricks ... He discourses of all Things, and hath neither Reason to argue, nor Power to conclude. He speaks French, as if he had learn'd it in

Herefordshire, and would shew by that his good Breeding. He thinkes he never hath Respect enough, and yet endeavors not at all to deserve any ... the Duke of Chevreuse professed, that if he had not bin le plus grand sot du monde [the greatest blockhead in all the world], he would have complained to our King of him, for the Incivility which he shewed unto him ... he is a ridiculous Creature, and hath no Esteeme here at all

The code which Leicester and Percy used for their correspondence, employing mythical figures for the main actors, revealed their thoughts. Leicester himself was Apollo, symbol of reason and manly beauty; Charles was Arviragus, a fabled British king and terror of the Romans; Wat Montagu, so often sent on errands by the queen, was Mercurius, messenger of the gods. Scudamore was Vulcan, a ridiculous figure, lame, ugly, ill-tempered, and the special patron of cuckolds.[84]

Scudamore, thought Leicester, 'is jealous if me, and thinks that I have come to supplant him in his Imployment', which was, of course, just Leicester's intention.[85] The contest between the two men was unequal, for the earl was much the better politician. Scudamore admitted defeat very early on, asking Windebank in June 1636 for leave to take the waters at Pougues; he was away for a month in August and September, abandoning everything just at the crucial point when negotiations between Leicester and the French were beginning to pick up.[86] In October Scudamore's final comfort was removed, with de Vic's recall to England. The two had drawn closer shortly before Leicester's arrival, and had conspired for Augier's recall. De Vic tried hard to restore Scudamore's credit in England, reminding Windebank that the viscount had 'both spoken lowde and stood out stoutly ... in the defence of his Majesty's honor' and countering rumours that the French despised Scudamore; on the contrary, they compared him favourably with Sir Isaac Wake, the previous ordinary ambassador. The Francophile Augier, however, secured the support of Leicester and the queen's faction, and early in 1637 was rewarded with promotion as secretary of Leicester's extraordinary embassy.[87]

At their heart the dissensions and mistrust between Scudamore and Leicester were ideological, reflecting not just the differences between their patrons and those they supported, but their own attitudes to France, war and English policy, and their own conceptions of what their duties were. Leicester feared Scudamore's close relationship with Windebank and especially Laud, and he warned Henry Percy 'to be beware of Vulcan [Scudamore], who will betray all to the Spaniards', by whom he meant Laud and Windebank, both opposed to a French alliance and war with Spain.[88] Leicester, by contrast, was much more pro-French and did all that he could to shunt Charles into a closer alignment with Louis. In pursuit of this he was much more creative than Scudamore in his use of his instructions, prepared to twist words and even act directly contrary to his orders. Coke complained to Leicester that he attempted 'to straine al woords and clauses you find dispersedly in my letters, to a sense directly contrarie to those cawtions I set down'. Leicester had changed Coke's words that Charles would aid France 'without entring into warre and breach of peace' to 'without entring into open warre'; he had also changed the English negotiating position that the French could use the English fleet 'as ther shal bee cawse' to 'as they [i.e. the French] shal see cawse', which was quite a different offer.[89] Scudamore, on the other had, stuck very closely to the wording of his instructions, almost obsessively so, too closely even for de Vic's liking, who moaned that 'in all things his Lordship is to[o] exact not to say punctuall that as hee doth not take any liberty himself to vary from his instructions'; 'he will not exceede one title or doe or say any thinge then what hee shall haue warranted ... by the Letter of his instructions.' In part this must have reflected his own insecurity and lack of diplomatic experience: Scudamore's early despatches show him edging forward very nervously, unsure of what to do, demanding reassurance on even the smallest points of procedure and protocol.[90] Leicester, by contrast, was an experienced diplomat, the veteran of a mission to Denmark in 1632.[91]

The difference also arose also from their very different conceptions of their mission. Leicester came to Paris with a hidden agenda of securing closer Anglo-French relations and a joint alliance, and behind him stood courtiers in the queen's circle hoping that a war against Spain would bring a parliament and thrust them to power. Scudamore, on the other hand, saw his role as ambassador in the more limited terms of his instructions and the ambassadorial treatises: to represent his king at the court of another, and to defend Charles's honour. Since Charles seemed set on a course of peace (albeit pro-Spanish), Scudamore probably saw no need to try to influence the direction of policy. Where Leicester mocked Scudamore as one who 'affects Ceremony extremely' and who 'thinkes he never hath Respect enough', Scudamore believed that he was carrying out the essence of his responsibilities, ensuring that in the many small ceremonies and elements of protocol that were seen as adding up to a measure of esteem and respect Charles received no affront from a perfidious nation. To protect his master's honour Scudamore would not even yield the place of honour to the *conducteur des ambassadeurs* as others did.[92] Where Scudamore warned of difficulties in the negotiations and repeated his belief that France and Spain might make peace at any moment to the exclusion of Palatine interests, Leicester played down the differences between England and France, even over the sovereignty of the seas, and stressed how willing the French were to come to an accommodation with England; he even told Coke that he could not see how the French could offer more than they already had.[93] Scudamore and Leicester did almost everything differently, from employing different solicitors in merchants' cases to going to different services: the earl to Charenton and the viscount to his own chapel.[94]

Charles tried to soothe relations between the two ambassadors. He ordered Leicester to 'communicat all his negotiations' with Scudamore, and told both ambassadors 'to cooperat as it is fitt in my seruice'. Nonetheless, as was typical with Charles, what he seemed to offer with one hand he took back with the other. He confirmed the liberty of treating individually that he had given Leicester before his departure, provided that it did 'not primalie proceed from you, but from the Ministers there'; in other words, if the French 'shall offer discourses or propositions to you in particular, that they will not willinglie haue imparted to him [Scudamore], you may conceale such things from him, if you fynd thereby, that ye may doe mee the better seruice'. In the same breath that Charles professed to support Scudamore, he undermined him.[95] Leicester lost no time in exploiting this caveat, justifying himself to Coke that 'The Lord Scudamor is thought here to betray all that he knows vnto the enimyes of the Cause', so much so, he claimed, that the French ministers 'auoyd him as much as they can, yet not out of feare of his strength'. Leicester continued to ignore Scudamore, who was left bemoaning that 'I know as little from his Lordship as hee that liues at Jerusalem'.[96]

Scudamore was learning, rather late, the difficult lesson that his sovereign was not to be trusted, and that it was politically inexpedient to rely too heavily on the king for one's credit and position. Deceit ran through Charles's veins. Moreover, it was necessary to Charles's strategy for both Scudamore and Leicester to remain in Paris, but for Leicester's negotiations to remain separate from Scudamore's. The king, who had sent Scudamore to Paris merely to delay negotiations and hide his true intentions from France, was in the summer of 1636 being slowly forced to rethink his attitude to the Habsburgs. The fruit of Arundel's embassy to Vienna was to limit Charles's options. Arundel, who left England a firm partisan of Spain, soon realised that little could be expected from the imperialists. Forced by Arundel's arrival to make a firm decision between Bavaria and England, Ferdinand chose the former, and Duke Maximilian was not prepared to surrender the Upper Palatinate on any conditions. The offer of accommodation over the Lower Palatinate and imperial ban fell far short of the full restitution Arundel had been charged to demand, and in September 1636 he asked for his revocation, there being no further hope of success in his negotiations.[97] Charles slowly began to realise that if he wanted the Palatinate restored he would have to draw closer to France. In July 1636 Charles-Louis was ordered by the king to keep secret the disappointments received from the emperor lest the French offer harsher terms 'seeing we come not to them out of love, but for want of other means'; the king would, the prince said, continue to negotiate with the emperor 'till he had made himself and his party strong, to make war against him'. In the late summer and early autumn of 1636 various observers, including Sir Thomas Roe and the earl of Dorset (but not the French ambassador), foresaw the change of policy.[98] To keep such a change of heart at least partly hidden from the Habsburgs, and the French, it was necessary for both Leicester and Scudamore to continue their negotiations separately, and so Charles followed a characteristically double-dealing path, publicly ordering Leicester to act jointly with Scudamore, but sending instructions about these negotiations to Leicester alone.[99] When, in pursuit of his new course, Charles drew up powers to treat and conclude with the French, they were addressed to both ambassadors but sent to Leicester only, who decided to keep them secret from his colleague and antagonist; Scudamore found out only through Windebank.[100]

Further evidence of the king's support for Leicester came in December 1636 when, after months of pleading from Leicester's friends, the countess of Leicester and the earl of Holland especially, his allowance was raised from the £6 a day (£2,190 p.a.) that both he and Scudamore had received previously to £400 a month (£4,800 p.a.). The earl had claimed that it was intolerable that he should receive no more than the colleague he despised. Furthermore, for the first year only, Charles agreed that Leicester should have £7,700 (£641 13s. 4d. per month). These were clear and extraordinary marks of favour to the earl; moreover, he later admitted that with such a large allowance he was able to live in greater splendour than other ambassadors and without increasing his own debts.[101] Scudamore's allowance remained at £6 a day, and it was usually further in arrears than Leicester's money.[102]

Leicester's negotiations progressed much more promisingly than had Scudamore's. The summer of 1636 was a time of military disaster for France, with a Spanish invasion of the north. In August the loss of the fortress of Corbie on the Somme seemed to leave the way open to Paris, causing panic in the capital and making the French more willing to negotiate.[103] Charles, growing disenchanted with the Habsburgs, very quickly dropped the Lorraine proposal which had prevented Scudamore from achieving much else. He began to restate the terms by which he would offer assistance to France, promising levies, not to aid enemies, the help of the navy in securing the French coast, and co-operation in strengthening the Protestant party in Germany, but refusing to declare open war. These terms were restated several times in the late summer and autumn of 1636 in letters from Coke to Leicester (but never to Scudamore), always with the proviso that Charles was not to be committed to 'entring into warre and breach of peace'.[104] The French too restated their position, but moved significantly over their previous attitude to Bavaria (for Bavarian cavalry formed part of the army threatening Paris), adding the duke to the list of enemies and seeming to grant Charles's wishes over the electoral title.[105]

The negotiations were also kept going by Leicester himself, who was always trying to push Charles faster than the king wanted to go. In particular

Leicester constantly advised that England should join with France in open and declared war: 'nothing can be more glorious,' he told Coke in August, 'nor more religious in the sight of God and man then such a war.' He complained that Charles did not offer Louis enough and added that nothing would be achieved until Charles showed himself 'in an actuall and vigorous way', thereby earning a stern rebuke from Coke.[106] Leicester's words caused some stir in London. Northumberland was reported as saying that he was 'more inclinable to France then is well thought on hear' while Laud was more forthright: 'in mye judgment he wrights more like a counselour of France then an embassador of England'. Nonetheless, Leicester persisted in his belief that 'the diseases of Christendome are not to be cured like the King's euill with touching, but with striking'.[107] The negotiations might not have progressed so far under a less independent ambassador like Scudamore, but he was deliberately kept in the dark. Until November Leicester told him nothing about the treaty. Thereafter he was occasionally informed, and invited to one joint conference but, as he told both secretaries, his 'concurrence euen in this little is rather like a wittnesse then a partner', expected only as and when Leicester needed it to fulfil his instructions.[108]

Despite Leicester's best efforts, opinion in England at the end of December was that the treaty was no nearer a conclusion than when first propounded two years earlier: Charles would not break with Spain, and the French had 'frosen up' negotiations, perhaps because they were more hopeful of a peace with the Habsburgs.[109] The arrival of Arundel at court at the beginning of January, hot-foot from Germany, changed the situation dramatically. His mission had converted him from a friend of Spain to a zealous advocate of the French alliance. As soon as he arrived at court he had a long interview with Charles, who was noted afterwards to be loud and angry in his dissatisfaction with the Austrians. Laud thought that 'it will in time growe into a war'.[110]

Dr Sharpe has suggested that at this point Richelieu changed tack; not so, it was Charles himself who shifted, spurred by the smarting Arundel and the slight to his honour offered by the Habsburgs. The king put the French proposals into two treaties, an auxiliary treaty which he agreed to now, and an offensive and defensive league which he promised to ratify later. These he returned to Leicester, not Scudamore, on 18/28 February 1637. Scudamore was informed by Coke that Leicester would impart the details to him, but Coke's letter to the earl said nothing about this or about acting jointly.[111]

Now that the treaty seemed concluded Leicester was anxious to include Scudamore in his negotiations. Scudamore, however, was not so keen; furthermore, he had been taking lessons in politicking from his colleague and began to take a more independent line, acting on his own initiative. He deliberately left Paris when he should have been at a conference with the French ministers in what looks like an attempt to delay the treaty. If so, he miscalculated, for Charles was now firmly behind the French alliance, and the countess of Leicester gloated at Scudamore's mistake.[112]

By the auxiliary treaty Charles promised not to assist the Habsburgs, to allow Louis to levy 6,000 infantry from his kingdoms, to employ an English fleet of at least thirty ships to blockade Spain and Flanders, and to assist Charles-Louis in setting to sea with twelve or fifteen English ships. Neither Charles nor Louis was to treat for or make peace without the consent of the other. Finally, and most important, friends (in particular Sweden, Denmark, the United Provinces, Venice and Hesse-Cassel) were to be invited to a conference to agree on terms and conditions for peace and the restoration of the Palatine; these were then to be put to the Habsburgs by Charles in the name of all. Only if the emperor refused such terms would Charles have to sign the offensive and defensive league with France and the other confederates promising military action. In such a case, Charles proposed that he and Louis would make 'open Warre' by sea on Spanish and imperial ships, and both kings would 'do what they may' to hinder Habsburg communications between Spain and the Indies, between Flanders and Italy, and between Italy and Germany. In other words, if war ensued, Charles would be tied to no more than a naval war.[113]

Charles's true intentions were hidden to most of his contemporaries and have remained so to most historians, who have focused, then and since, on the question of whether Charles was really willing to break with Spain and go to war. Opinion at the time was divided: Laud, Windebank and Philip IV all thought war likely, and the English court buzzed with expectation. As Dorset wrote in February 1637, 'Here are warrs and rumors of warrs.'[114] It was in Charles's interests to foster this opinion to frighten the Habsburgs and encourage the French. He promoted such rumours, fulfilling minor obligations under the auxiliary treaty (such as sending six ships against the Sallee pirates) and ordering Aston to warn British merchants to be prepared for a breach with Spain.[115]

The king's intention, however, was to plunge his kingdoms not into the European war, but into the expected European peace. War was not ruled out, but it was not the centrepiece of his policy. According to Roe, Charles had said that

> he would neyther doe, nor suffer, nor auow, any action that might directly brake his treaties, and Leagues with Spayne, and force him to a sudden war ... But that he was not so in loue with peace, as that he would suffer any indignitye or Injurye.

The prince elector's English fleet would set sail; in European waters Charles expected to be able to disavow his actions, in the New World, where there were no peace and no binding treaties with Spain, he could avow and protect his nephew. The English, as Coke had explained five years earlier, understood a difference between, on the one hand, an offensive and defensive league, which entailed a breach of peace, and on the other, leagues of 'Amitie and alliance' and 'Aid and assistance' – 'neither of theis breaketh peace, nor giueth iust offence to anie', or so they hoped.[116] Charles seems to have considered the auxiliary treaty as a league of aid and assistance to which the Habsburgs should take no great offence. If there were to be a war, Charles expected it to be a minor affair. He wrote to Wentworth, 'what great Inconvenience this War can bring to me ... I cannot imagine, except it be in Ireland; and there too, I fear not much'. Wentworth, though, was sufficiently concerned to rush a long memorandum to the king advising against any war. The king's reply reveals his true plans, calming Wentworth with his strategy that no war was intended unless the Austrians broke with him by refusing the confederates' terms. Wentworth, he wrote, had mistaken the question:

> For it is not whether I should declare war to the House of Austria or not, but whether I shall join with France and the rest of my friends to demand of the House of Austria my nephew's restitution, and so hazard (upon refusal) a declaration of war.

Any war, therefore, was expected to be a minor affair, limited to the sea, quite possibly mainly in American waters, carrying the faint possibility of a few minor engagements in Ireland, and anyway not until some time in the future, after the confederates' conference.[117]

The entry of France into the Thirty Years' War seemed to many contemporaries to bring peace nearer, and a successful peace conference was expected to start at any time. To the English this opened up the possibility of restoring the Palatine by means of a negotiated peace rather than by force of arms. This was the importance of the auxiliary treaty, as a pretext to secure English involvement in the peace process, for Charles and Scudamore believed only they, and certainly not France or Spain, could be trusted to include Charles-Louis's interests in the peace.[118] Philip IV's secret correspondence along with events in Westphalia a decade later bore out English mistrust of Spain and France, for the Palatine secured even a partial restoration only through Swedish and Dutch pressure. It was therefore vital for the treaty to be agreed and the conference at Hamburg to begin.[119] Consequently, Charles was prepared to make further concessions in the summer of 1637 in the face of French foot-dragging over the auxiliary treaty. In June he conceded all outstanding French demands: he no longer insisted that captured Flemish towns should be given to the prince elector (despite persistent English fears about French designs on Flanders); he accepted a secret article obliging him to assist the Palatine's naval force (rather than merely permitting it to set sail) on Leicester's assurance that this did not mean a breach of peace. Despite a treaty more ambiguous than ever, shot through with significant differences between its

French and Latin copies, Charles again accepted the treaty on 12/22 June.[120] Nonetheless, he immediately set about trying to have it changed, his acceptance notwithstanding. It was entirely typical of Charles that he should immediately try to restrict a promise once it was granted. What was more surprising therefore was his order to Leicester, communicated by Coke on 19/29 July, to proceed to the signing of the secret articles 'without further protraction'.[121]

The French ministers, alone in Europe, had however realised Charles's true intentions. Richelieu understood that Charles's design 'leads to no other end, than to take part in the treaty of peace without doing anything for the war', and he analysed the likely outcome of the confederates' conference. The Habsburgs would forestall further proceedings by promising to return the Palatinate if France returned Lorraine; the English, unlike the French, would consider this arrangement just and, he continued, in place of winning over the English by the treaty, 'we will, in effect, lose them'.[122] The Lorraine proposal, put by Scudamore to the French ministers in 1635, was not dead after all.

The French had been offering Charles terms since 1634 in an attempt to stop him joining with Spain (a prospect that had then seemed likely) and to prevent further English convoys of Spanish men and money to Flanders. Louis judged it 'absolutely necessary' to have England neutral.[123] Beyond this the French held out little hope of anything from their negotiations with England. Senneterre's despatches in the spring of 1637 consistently stressed that Charles and his ministers favoured Spain and the Austrians.[124] Even when Charles seemed more inclinable to France the prospect of an English alliance seemed to offer little to the French. In September 1636 Richelieu sent Bullion a memorandum setting out the advantages and disadvantages of an alliance with England; the latter far outweighed the former. An English alliance would prevent a similar Anglo-Spanish alliance and might close the Channel to Spain, but tying the peace to the re-establishment of the Palatinate would make that peace far harder to obtain: Bouthillier feared that English demands for the restoration of the Palatine would make peace 'almost impossible'. Making peace harder to obtain would endanger France's alliances with Sweden and Holland: Sweden in particular was known to be exhausted and considering peace with the empire. Furthermore, the French feared that if they insisted on the restoration of the Palatinate they would lose their right to Lorraine and Sweden her right to Pomerania. Given French determination to hold on to Lorraine, this reason alone would seem to prevent an alliance with England under the present terms.[125] The cardinal's conviction that little could be expected from the English negotiations is clearly shown in a note he passed to Chavigny during the negotiations with Leicester in the autumn of 1636:

I have seen the papers which you had sent me concerning England; I do not see how one can hope for a conclusion. However, I find the reply to be good, because it does not commit the king and continues negotiations with persons with whom it is always necessary to negotiate.

Richelieu continued the negotiations largely for the sake of negotiating itself, something at which he was a past master, and a tactic whose importance he stressed in his *Testament Politique*.[126] Nevertheless, the French hoped that they might be able to lead Charles on, engaging him by degrees, as Roe put it, and provoke a breach between England and Spain; hence their insistence that the wording of the auxiliary treaty must be changed to tie Charles to assisting his nephew with ships, in the hope that this would provoke Spain to break with England.[127]

The aims of the French and those of Charles were diametrically opposed. Both sides were playing poker. The French hoped to trap Charles into a war he did not want. Charles hoped to entrap Louis into a treaty to restore the Palatine: France would be tied to carry on fighting while Charles, at peace with all, would arbitrate the fate of Europe. Charles's acceptance of the auxiliary treaty seemed to spring the trap in his favour. Tied to no peace without Charles's consent and the restoration of the Palatinate, the French realised they were bound to a perpetual war at the whim of the English king, or they would have to give up Lorraine. As Bernard of Saxe Weimar remarked to Leicester in April 1637, 'you haue them in your hands, and they cannot get out unlesse they will ruine themselues'. Scudamore too sensed the difficulties facing the French, who, 'finding themselues in a Streight ... struggle all they can to remitt the conclusion of this treatie to the Assembly of the Confederates at Hamborough'. All the French could do was wriggle and procrastinate, Charles's own favourite tactics, remitting the treaty to Hamburg and losing Charles's advantage in the diplomatic morass.[128]

That Charles's plan did not work in his favour was not entirely his fault. No one in 1637 expected peace in Germany to wait another eleven years and that between France and Spain twenty-two years. The negotiations for peace at Hamburg went nowhere, the only result being a commercial treaty between Denmark and England, two crowns that were already at peace with everyone, a treaty between Sweden and France to continue, not end, the war, and a host of frustrated diplomats.[129]

Charles's policy explains why it was necessary to keep Scudamore in Paris, even though he had little to do. Scudamore and Leicester were unwitting pawns in the king's game of duplicity. Leicester was needed to push the treaty forward and to try to convince the French that Charles would break with Spain. Scudamore was there to keep Leicester in check and reassure those in England like Laud who did not want war. Scudamore was a vital sign that the pro-Spanish councillors had not been entirely abandoned, although his isolation and treatment could also be read as a metaphor for their lack of influence in the spring of 1637.[130] Scudamore probably little realised how important he was to the king's plans. However, with the treaty remitted to the Hamburg peace conference it becomes harder to understand just what Scudamore's role was.

Richelieu had predicted 'only disorder and confusion as the end of such a treaty with the English'. That he was proved right was partly down to his own efforts: the French were determined that their treaty with the English should not bear the fruit Charles desired. As soon as Charles accepted their demands in July 1637 they raised further objections, and refused to sign the very same secret articles that they had pressed so strongly only a month earlier.[131] The matter was not settled by November, by which time fresh difficulties had driven further wedges between England and France. Despairing of justice over the English ship the *Pearl*, captured by the French nearly two years previously, letters of marque had been granted to the son of its late captain. He seized a French ship; the French complained, terming it 'an act of hostility', and put an embargo on all British ships. Towards the end of 1637 the situation threatened to escalate into war. Anglo-French relations had not been so strained since the peace of 1629. Even Scudamore was temporarily more frustrated with the negotiations than with the affronts he continued to receive from his colleague, bemoaning to Windebank, 'O that the affaire of the Palatinate were settled, that wee mought haue nothing to do wth these Dons or Monsieurs!'[132]

In the summer of 1637, once the two ambassadors were no longer busy with negotiating the treaty, fresh disputes began, or rather they found a new occasion for the same old dispute. This time it was over Philip Burlamachi, who was quarrelling with Claude Voile over payment of the remainder of Henrietta Maria's dowry, still outstanding from the previous decade. Charles had recommended the affair to Scudamore early in 1636; Windebank added that the cause was just but the man impudent. Scudamore had jealously guarded this business from Leicester as one of the few commissions his colleague had not encroached upon. When Burlamachi's suit came to a hearing in July 1637 Scudamore thought he ought to show Leicester the relevant papers (carefully concealing the dates). He had taken Burlamachi's part but Leicester, whom Scudamore described as using 'every new occasion as of a naile in a wound which will keepe it from healing', immediately took Voile's.[133] The mudslinging began all over again. Scudamore sent his secretary Richard Browne to London to complain that he was still kept ignorant over most of the negotiations. This Leicester denied, retorting that Scudamore never helped or visited him, that the viscount's advice was worthless anyway, and that Scudamore spent most of his time taking the air or sleeping, accusations

Scudamore called 'farther from truth then Earth from Heaven'. Both ambassadors denounced the other for seeking not the king's but private interest.[134] Once more Charles tried to calm the situation, telling Leicester, through Coke, that 'you haue much forgotten the respect dew to your fellow Ambassador' and ordering him to concur with Scudamore's proceedings in Burlamachi's case. Scudamore too promised 'to bee freinds' and follow Windebank's advice and be silent.[135]

Once again Scudamore had relied on Windebank and Laud;[136] he seemed not to realise that he could no longer count on the secretary as a trusted confidant and opponent of Leicester. He continued as before to favour Windebank with titbits not sent to Coke; he involved Windebank alone in his French edition of Laud's speech at Prynne's trial; and he carried on sending Windebank details of his quarrel with Leicester and what he hoped would be information to damage Leicester at court.[137] The viscount's reliance on two men once friends but now enemies might surprise historians. Laud had procured the secretaryship for Windebank in 1632, but never forgave him for what he saw as his desertion in joining Cottington in 1634.[138] The viscount's surviving correspondence, especially his use of Windebank to carry important messages to the archbishop, gives no indication that he was aware of these very public rifts. Scudamore had built his house on sand. Of Windebank's relationship with the archbishop (whom the viscount described as 'that Incomparable Freinde') Scudamore wrote that 'no man vnderstands better and loues more the inestimable' Laud than Windebank himself. Without a hint of irony Scudamore reminded Windebank of Laud's virtues as friend and patron, 'For his Grace knowes not onely how to direct and comfort, but how to bee so kind as to chide his servants when they neede it.' Windebank had no doubt received rather more chiding than comfort of late.[139]

In the second half of 1637 the ordinary ambassador was even more isolated than before. His efforts to find new patrons at court failed. His attempts to break into the queen's circle continued, but with no more success than before. He was friendly with Sir Kenelm Digby, who had fallen out with Leicester; in return Digby supported Scudamore against Leicester, but Digby was out of favour with the king for converting to Rome.[140] Scudamore's regular and friendly correspondence with Sir John Finet offered a contact with Finet's patron the earl of Salisbury, especially as Salisbury was sending his two sons to Paris for their education;[141] when they arrived Scudamore showed them all possible respect, and Lord Cranborne stood as godfather and gave his name to the viscount's eighth but short-lived son Charles. Salisbury was rather a political lightweight in the 1630s but, as father-in-law to the earl of Northumberland, offered a potential way into the Percy connection. Nothing concrete, however, seems to have emerged from Scudamore's favours to Salisbury's sons.[142] Scudamore was well placed to do favours for the sons of the political elite as they passed through Paris on the grand tour. He worked hard to earn a reputation for giving them a much warmer reception than Leicester, and met, for example, Thomas Hobbes (tutor to the Cavendish family, earls of Devonshire), as well as John Milton, whom he introduced to Hugo Grotius.[143] The contacts thus established were not, however, immediately useful in improving his credit at a court, where, according to the countess of Leicester, he was 'uerie litle considered hear; for I selldome heare him named; and when he is, it is with Contemt'.[144] Moreover, Scudamore had not been sent to Paris only to act as a society host.

In the autumn of 1636 Leicester had tried, and failed, to establish a better correspondence with Windebank, spurred in part by his shaky relationship with Coke.[145] He tried again in July and August 1637, through the agency of Henry Percy, this time with greater success: in the autumn they exchanged a cipher for their secret correspondence.[146] Leicester was not just swopping horses for form's sake. His friendship with Windebank was engineered as part of a new direction in English foreign policy and even more so in the queen's circle. With the treaty remitted to Hamburg the question of forming an alliance with France to recover the Palatinate became less important, though it remained a priority to see the treaty secured by France signing the secret articles; this would prevent the French negotiating with Spain elsewhere without British representation. The Spanish had tried hard to frustrate Charles's treaty with France, in particular by offering him negotiations in Brussels, Philip giving his brother full powers to conclude an alliance there. Charles may not have been immediately tempted, but he was soon conducting highly secret and unofficial talks in Brussels for the restoration of the Palatinate.[147]

Within the queen's circle there was also a change away from a pro-French position. The papal envoy, George Conn, set about creating a party of Catholics and crypto-Catholics around the queen, effecting a rapprochement between her and Windebank before that between Leicester and Windebank. Plotting against Richelieu was renewed at the queen's court. Feelers were put out and Habsburg agents came to London in the summer of 1637 to try to involve Charles in an anti-Richelieu conspiracy including the French queen mother Marie de Medici, her court in exile in Brussels and her daughter-in-law Anne of Austria, the French queen. Richelieu's uncovering of this plot in August, the celebrated La Porte affair, also revealed the English involvement. Anne was corresponding with both the Spanish ambassador in Brussels and the Cardinal Infante and discussing attempts to frustrate the Anglo-French treaty. The letters were sent in English packets between Augier in Paris and Balthazar Gerbier, Charles's resident in Brussels.[148] Leicester's involvement is implied rather than explicit by his continued support for Augier. Perhaps he was drawn in by Wat Montagu, who returned to England in April 1637 as an enemy of the cardinal; he had been staying in Leicester's house before his return.[149]

Whether previously involved or not, Leicester was soon drawn into Charles's secret negotiations on behalf of members of the queen mother's circle in Flanders, and this would seem to be the reason for the engineering of the new relationship between him and Windebank.[150] In the autumn of 1637 Windebank asked the earl to probe Richelieu, secretly and delicately, to discover Louis's conditions for the return of his mother to France. Leicester had strict orders from both Charles and Henrietta Maria not to tell Scudamore; Coke too was to be kept ignorant. Scudamore, however, became suspicious as the secret leaked out.[151] The French were intercepting Leicester's post (even a letter from Henrietta Maria to him) and were prepared, insisting that this was a domestic affair that did not concern Charles or England.[152] Meanwhile letters continued to pass from Flanders to France via Gerbier, Augier and Leicester, sometimes secretly, sometimes more openly.[153] In the spring of 1638 Charles entrusted another delicate negotiation to Leicester, that of seeking a marriage between Prince Rupert and the French heiress, Margaret, daughter of the late duc de Rohan, which needed Louis's approval. The negotiations were stillborn when Richelieu refused to involve himself. Once again Scudamore was formally excluded.[154]

Both Scudamore and Leicester had little to do throughout 1638, with all eyes turned to Hamburg, 'the place', Scudamore wrote to Sir Thomas Roe, Charles's ambassador to the conference, 'where this Treatie is to expect Life or Death. And heere we stand at gaze in the meane time expecting what will fall from you.'[155] Scudamore admitted he could do little but watch, and even in this he was edged out by Leicester. With the extraordinary ambassador Roe discussed in long letters the state of the negotiations in great detail. Roe confessed to Leicester that 'I write to my Lord Scudamore, but not in this stile': in only short letters to the ordinary ambassador Roe recounted general news, mentioning the treaty only briefly.[156]

Excluded from negotiating in person, excluded from the details of other people's negotiations, Scudamore bemoaned that all he was left to do 'is but to write occurrences' and feared that he was merely 'a chargeable Cypher'. His instructions charged him with two constant duties, intelligence gathering and protecting British merchants.[157] The protection of British merchants remained an onerous task, for the French continued to harry shipping in the Channel and to deny Charles's claims to the sovereignty of the seas or what the French called 'une Empire imaginaire de la Mer'. Scudamore moaned, however, that Augier and Leicester excluded him even from matters relating to British merchants; when tackled Augier told him 'that the Ordinary Ambassador had nothing to doe in it, but that the Extraordinary and Hee were sufficient'. Leicester and his secretary were not motivated merely by their usual desire to make Scudamore look ridiculous; there was money involved. Merchants would usually pay to have their suits presented through an ambassador: it was rumoured that the earl of Bristol, while ambassador to Spain, had received at least £30,000 for soliciting just two such suits.[158] Despite his hard work on behalf of merchants, especially before Leicester's arrival, Scudamore had little success. Leicester himself fared no better. Most of the cases concerned British merchants trading in Canada, which the French interpreted as piracy, claiming all Canada for themselves, or merchants trading with Spain and Flanders, little short of an act of war in French eyes. British merchants found that redress was more likely through direct action (obtaining letters of marque) than through the mediation of the two ambassadors in Paris. Merchants' cases became pawns in the diplomatic games between the two crowns and a barometer of Anglo-French relations. Although Scudamore's enemies tried to use his inability to solve merchants' cases against him, his failings were more an indication that he was ambassador during troubled times.[159]

Scudamore's final duty, that of intelligence gathering, is by its very nature much harder to assess: the most successful spies leave no trace in written records. It was one of the most important charges of an ambassador: his instructions called it his 'most substantial dutie'. When, a decade earlier, Sir Edward Barrett had hoped to go as ambassador to Paris most of Sir William Boswell's advice to him had concerned how and from whom he could gather regular intelligence.[160] Like any other ambassador Scudamore had four main sources of information: he listened for it, he bought it, he traded it, and occasionally he despatched specific 'spies'. As he was leaving Paris in 1639 Windebank asked him to pass on his regular contacts to Leicester; Scudamore's reply detailing his methods shows that he had learned the rules of the intelligence game.[161]

> Sir, cleerly, the best Intelligence that I haue ever sent, hath beene such as my self and my Secretary haue pick'd up, a word heere, a circumstance there, by discourse with diuerse persons, wherof some, little dreamt of the use made of what they said, some, dealt out by way of exchange, and others, in speciall confidence and particular inclination of good-will, entrusted. These, you see, are not such as doe for money, neither is it possible for mee to transmitt these helps of Intelligence.

The formal side of information gathering and processing, the collecting of news, published and, more important, unpublished, and the forwarding of these newsletters or advices, and summaries distilled from them, was a time-consuming task. Information flooded into the embassy from contacts all over France and beyond, and from thence to London. In the years 1636 and 1637 advices were sent to London from at least twenty-six places in and around

France, in addition to the weekly (or more frequent) advices from Scudamore, Leicester, de Vic and Augier. How useful all this was, and to what extent it informed policy decisions taken, is impossible to judge, but it was read in London: most of the letters received were endorsed by the secretaries or their staff, and sometimes a summary of their contents was made on the back.[162] Scudamore was as insatiable for further sources of information in Paris as he had been in England. As part of his duties he swopped newsletters with Charles's other ambassadors across Europe. In addition he sought out less formal contacts. When his brother-in-law John Scudamore of Ballingham passed through Paris on his way to Turin the viscount commanded him to find an informant at the Savoyard court; he was unable to do so, but instead found one Maillot, muster master of the French army in Italy.[163]

The ambassadors of other countries in Paris could also be informants, but usually their information was divulged only for a purpose. The Venetian ambassador supplied occasional scraps in the hope of seeing closer Anglo-French co-operation against the republic's traditional enemies the Habsburgs, as when Contarini gave Scudamore a mangled version of the treaty of Rivoli.[164] Grotius, the Swedish ambassador in Paris who was on friendly terms with Scudamore, gave him more information than any other ambassador. Some of Grotius's information was designed to make Charles incline more to a Swedish alliance (in particular an English subsidy for Swedish arms); at other times the benefit to Charles was more immediately apparent, as when Grotius sent Scudamore a Huguenot from the household of the French ambassador in London who he thought might be useful as a spy.[165]

Perhaps Scudamore's greatest *coup* was to procure a weekly letter from the household of the comte d'Avaux, French ambassador to the Hamburg conference. The man was persuaded to write by one of the viscount's Parisian friends, thinking that his letters went to Duke Bernard of Saxe Weimar, not King Charles. From this source Scudamore learnt that d'Avaux was deliberately hindering proceedings and trying to convince the Swedes that Charles was tricking them.[166]

Occasionally Scudamore employed people more recognisable as 'spies'. In March 1638 he obtained a copy of the Franco-Swedish treaty of Wismar of March 1637, copied secretly from the original 'in hast and feare'. Securing accurate and full copies of treaties was a constant preoccupation of governments concerned to discover whether they were being dealt with openly and honestly.[167] The French fleet was another constant worry to the English, concerned that the French might attempt to seize the Flemish coast or fight Charles's navy for the sovereignty of the seas. Scudamore was never able to secure a constant intelligencer within the French navy, and had to rely instead on agents sent out specially. He sent a man to Brest but he was seized as a suspected Spanish spy until he proved that he was French; Scudamore had to despatch him to England for his own safety.[168] Early in 1638 the French threat seemed more immediate than before, and there were fears of war and a French attack on the Channel Isles or the Isle of Wight. Scudamore employed a Jersey spy and sent his most experienced French spy to La Rochelle, St Malo, Bayonne and Le Havre, at a total cost of over £181, before concluding that Richelieu had no such design against Britain.[169]

No sooner had the threat passed than it looked as if the French were encouraging the Scottish covenanters; such rumours were already circulating in April 1638, made all the more plausible by the recent scares of a French invasion of the south coast. A month later a story that 50,000 Scots were in arms ready to march on London and follow Laud, Conn and Father Philips, chaplain to the queen, prompted Scudamore to an immediate investigation.[170] The English government was convinced that the French were fomenting the Scots' rebellion, and kept on at the two ambassadors in Paris to discover more. Scudamore boasted that he had laid 'ginns' to capture the truth. The viscount suspected that the Scots had been given money or advice from Senneterre's household: he was informed that Senneterre's secretary had said in secret that the Scots would choose a new king if they could get no satisfaction from Charles. Scudamore had no doubt that the French were glad to see Charles embroiled in Scotland, and doubted only that they had the present means to assist the Scots on a large scale. Recent historians, however, have been less certain of French involvement, stressing that the Scottish rebellion hindered French attempts to levy troops in Scotland. Bellièvre, Senneterre's replacement as French ambassador in London, meanwhile believed that rumours of French involvement in the Scottish rebellion were deliberately spread by 'the partisans of Spain'.[171]

Those employed by Scudamore in his intelligence gathering came from a variety of backgrounds. Most are completely untraceable, such as the 'man of Inteligence' to whom he once gave twenty livres, or Monsieur E.P., who sent him information every month. Of the rest, many were British merchants who either wrote regularly from towns across France or who, like one Mr Crew, were able to procure Frenchmen for more dangerous exploits such as spying on the fleet.[172] Traditionally the English had found many sources within the Huguenot community: in Leicester's opinion these were 'our best frends and intelligencers' but were now 'lost'; Leicester no doubt had in mind not only Charles's lack of concern for the Huguenots since 1629 but also Scudamore's refusal to worship with them at Charenton. The contrast between Scudamore's limited contact with French Protestants (disputing with Jean Daillé, pastor at Charenton, about lay elders, for example) and the high profile previous English ambassadors had adopted within the Huguenot community is very marked.[173] Nevertheless, Scudamore was able to find Frenchmen (such as Monsieur Fernand of Lyon) willing to spy on their own country.[174]

The final source of intelligence was the British Catholics: the priests Father Talbot, Father Barnard (probably an alias), Peter Fitton (*vere* Biddulph) and Thomas Chambers all acted as his informants. Fitton was the agent at Rome of Richard Smith, bishop of Chalcedon (from 1625 to 1631 the senior Roman Catholic clergyman in England but thereafter in exile in Paris); Fitton wrote to Scudamore from Rome. Chambers is the most interesting of the four. He was in contact with Scudamore as early as January 1636, when he suggested that if Scudamore wrote occurrences of Paris to George Conn (Latin secretary to Cardinal Barberini, the Pope's nephew, and later papal agent at Henrietta Maria's court), Conn would send notices of French negotiations in Rome. Nothing came of this proposed bartering of information, and instead Scudamore used Conn's nephew, who was going to Rome as confessor to Colonel Hepburn. Chambers later sent Scudamore reports from the French army in Flanders in 1636 and the next year wrote from the court at Ruel. After Scudamore had returned to England in March 1639 he met Chambers in secret.[175] In the case of Chambers the problems of this kind of intelligence gathering were clear. Chambers was Richelieu's almoner and later thought the man most likely to be fomenting the Scots; the Scots also tended to use him, rather than Scudamore or Leicester, as unofficial ambassador for Scotland. It is not clear on what terms, if any, Chambers provided information to Scudamore or, in this exchange, who got the better of whom.[176]

Overall it is very difficult to judge Scudamore as an intelligence gatherer. It is clear, however, that the French were better informed than the English. They were regularly intercepting the posts, and though the English suspected this, they were unaware of the extent. De Vic complained that the French ministers were 'too well acquainted' with Charles's counsels and often knew his resolutions before the English ambassadors.[177] There must be doubts about Augier's actions. Both Scudamore and de Vic suspected him of betraying secrets to the French and Dutch, and by 1640 Leicester and Windebank also were convinced that he could not be trusted.[178] Finally, the French had a spy at the heart of the English court, Forster, who could not be rivalled.[179] Yet the English government thought Scudamore's activities in this field valuable. The viscount had greater success in spying than some others. For example, in July 1635 Admiral Lindsey sent a fishing smack to Brest to spy on the French fleet; as soon as it arrived it was seized by the French, its crew were forced to divulge what they knew of the English fleet, and then it was returned.[180] Nor was Scudamore corrupt, like Balthazar Gerbier, Charles's agent at Brussels, who betrayed English secrets to the Infanta for 20,000 crowns.[181] The field of intelligence gathering was an opportunity for Scudamore to recoup some political capital and to try to improve his reputation and image at the English court. It was one area that Leicester had not encroached upon, it being a duty more appropriate to an ordinary ambassador. Moreover, Leicester's allowance, although much greater than Scudamore's, was meant to cover all expenses: unlike Scudamore he could not claim extra expenses for intelligence, so, with typical economy, he employed no spies. When, in the summer of 1638, Leicester was pressed by the English government for intelligence about the suspected French involvement in the Covenanters' rebellion, he disclaimed all knowledge, admitting that he was as ignorant of Scottish affairs 'as if I liued in Tartary'.[182]

Towards the end of 1637, however, the situation began to change and Scudamore was slowly eclipsed in the field of intelligence gathering, first by Windebank, then by Leicester. The secretary was extending his empire and began to develop his own intelligence network. Previously he had received French news only from Scudamore, but at the end of 1637 he received news of the French court from a certain 'DB', possibly des Bardes, one of Bouthillier's servants who had passed information to de Vic in 1636. Early in 1638, having established a better correspondence with Leicester, Windebank began receiving regular advices from the extraordinary ambassador.[183] He was also in receipt of information via Philip Burlamachi, who used his agencies across Europe to raise both finance and information. In March 1638 Leicester began to create his own intelligence network for Windebank's use, seeking a correspondent in Marseilles; previously this had been the preserve of the ordinary ambassador or Augier. The invasion of Scudamore's duties was now complete: even in writing occurrences he was rivalled by his colleague.[184]

As we have seen, Scudamore had never been able to secure his position in France, and the loss of Windebank's support did nothing to bolster his embassy. Viscount Feilding and his friends had long been looking for something greater than his embassy in Italy; in March 1638 it looked as if they had found it, in the shape of Scudamore's recall and Feilding's appointment to France. Windebank supported Feilding as, probably, did Henrietta Maria. There were even rumours that Scudamore had asked for his own return, which is not impossible. By May it looked as if Scudamore would continue as ambassador, although Feilding persisted in his hopes of employment in France.[185] It was probably the Scottish crisis that saved Scudamore for a further year, for never had the English government's craving for intelligence been so great, and it did not wish to lose Scudamore and his informants.

Anglo-French relations, which had briefly improved in the spring of 1638, were ambushed by the arrival of the duchesse de Chevreuse in England in April. Richelieu had already warned Louis that she 'would again create difficulties in England and lead the English according to her will and always find a cause for new trouble'. An inveterate plotter against the cardinal, she had fled France after the La Porte affair. She was also an old friend of Henrietta Maria and was immediately granted a number of favours, including a loan and a pension. Most symbolic of all, she was granted the *tabouret*, the right to sit in the queen's presence.[186] The favour was normally granted to ambassadors' wives in Paris but had not previously been used in the English court. The French interpreted it as a great snub that a conspirator and fugitive was allowed to sit before the English queen while the wife of their ambassador Bellièvre had to stand. On Bellièvre's complaint the *tabouret* was withdrawn in May 1638 from Elizabeth, Viscountess Scudamore, who was about to visit Anne of Austria; the visit was immediately cancelled by the English.[187] The affair of the *tabouret* hijacked relations between the two crowns, with Coke left to lament to the two ambassadors that what 'is most considerable is: that their contestations are now made the business of your imploiments whilst the treatie which is the maine woorke seemeth to bee laid on sleep'. Leicester was a little more light-hearted, remarking to Henrietta Maria that 'I perceive there is a strange Fatality in it that Madam de Chevereuse and my Lady Scudamore, must never sit both at one Time'. No doubt he was cheered by the thought that the differences between France and England could be blamed on the Scudamores (for he had left his wife in England).[188] The only solution proved to be the return of the viscountess to England in September.[189] Her return, however, brought no improvement in affairs, for at the same time the queen mother, an exile from France condemned to wander around Europe as an all-too-often unwelcome guest, landed in England. The French accounted her 'wholly Spanish' and were convinced that she would poison relations between the two crowns yet further. Charles had tried to prevent her visit, but Richelieu for one believed that she came to England with Charles's explicit permission.[190] London was now the centre of anti-Richelieu plotting. Although the scheming against the cardinal did nothing to improve the state of Anglo-French relations, the Scottish revolt had effectively killed off the French treaty. Charles's Scottish troubles had made him incapable of fulfilling any league with France. When additional instructions were penned for Leicester after Easter 1639 they ordered him to press the French over the treaty they had yet to ratify after two years but also, 'by your dexteritie mesnage the proceedings by such degrees, that you cum to no conclusion til wee bee freed from our trobles at home'.[191]

Before this Scudamore had come home. In November 1638, perhaps because he missed his wife more than for any other reason, he had asked for his recall. He gave as his reasons that he saw no prospect of Leicester's return, 'the business your Majestie sent him for training it self out into vncertaine length' and that one ambassador was sufficient to discharge all the present duties in Paris, 'besides the addition of other private occasions which grow vrgent vpon mee'. Even in the business of his return Scudamore was unable to preserve his reputation at the English court unspotted. The countess of Leicester spread the unlikely rumour that he had been recalled at the behest of the French, who refused to make a proposition concerning the prince elector while Scudamore remained in Paris.[192] Scudamore had borne the insults and humiliation from his colleague for nearly two and a half years until nothing was reserved to him save manuscript collecting, a private commission laid upon him by Laud – and in this, as in so much else, he had little success and was bested by Richelieu.[193] The viscount had served over three years, thought by some to be the standard length of an embassy, and it is doubtful if he could have gone on bearing the cost of his post indefinitely. In his last seven months as ambassador he borrowed £3,475 from Edward Ashe, the London merchant and moneylender. It was not a situation that could last for long.[194]

Charles agreed to Scudamore's request and returned his letters of revocation by Coke, who added, 'Your fower yeares employment, and the memorie of your good seruice will honour you and yours.'[195] January and February 1639 were taken up with his final audiences, where Scudamore found that he was treated with more respect than he expected. Louis, Anne, the prince of Condé, all expressed their esteem and Chavigny added:[196]

> they had received relations concerning mee before my coming over, and that they had found them true and had found more then was related; that I had carried myself in my employment no otherwise than as a good Minister having sustained avec fermeté the interests of the King my master ... Hee assured mee that both the King and Cardinal were satisfied wth mee.

Scudamore left Paris on 20 February/2 March 1639 and arrived at the English court on Saturday 2/12 March; the following day he had a two-hour audience with Charles and by kissing the king's hand formally ended his appointment as ambassador.[197] One of the last things that the prince of Condé had said to him was that Charles should 'cutt off 3. or 4. Heads, and then hee shall haue peace' in Scotland, for 'these Puritans if they had their Will, they would neither haue King, nor Bishop, nor Great one, but all Equall'.[198] It was an unusually prescient prediction.

Viscount Scudamore had spent three and a half years representing the king's wishes, and three and a half years embodying the failings of Charles's strategy. The fatal flaw in the king's policy was that neither France nor Spain wanted Charles-Louis restored. Scudamore repeated that the Bourbons would do nothing for the Palatinate unless pressed by England; the realisation that the same was true of the Habsburgs seems to have come later and been harder for Charles and his pro-Spanish councillors to accept fully. This meant that Charles would have to offer something really tempting to induce either side to do something for his nephew, but that he could not do. The Spanish valued the assistance of the English navy highly, but they were already receiving it without having to make any further promises for the Palatine. The French wanted an English commitment to the land war, a commitment which Charles was not prepared to give. This loophole in his strategy was uncovered in the summer of 1637: when the French refused to ratify the treaty Charles had no means of coercing or persuading them except by sending troops to Flanders, the very measure he was trying by diplomacy to avoid. He had baited his trap and the French had nearly fallen for it, but he had no fall-back position, no second chance. Here is where Charles came unstuck. As the civil wars were to demonstrate, Charles was not a master tactician. Rather he was a one-move chess player and, when outflanked, he had no reply.

Scudamore was far from being the perfect ambassador. Chosen at Laud's behest to uphold the honour and reputation of both Charles and the church of England abroad, and as a sop to the French rather than a flexible negotiator, he was not the man to mollify the French when the treaty with Spain failed, and the king realised he had no option other than to incline to France. Scudamore was too inflexible a man to change with English policy, and was left behind twice with two major policy shifts, first towards a French alliance in 1636, then again the following year when the queen's party began to change from a Francophile one following an anti-Habsburg alliance to a crypto-Catholic one seeking once more to overthrow Richelieu. Meanwhile, Charles could not afford to ditch him entirely, fearing the message such a decision would send both to his Hispanophile councillors such as Cottington and Laud whom he needed, and his Francophile courtiers whom he wanted to keep in check. So Charles seconded Scudamore with Leicester rather than recall him, and thereby all but paralysed the French embassy. Scudamore was never able to shake off the rumours that the French believed him 'partiall and vntrue'. His standing on ceremony quickly convinced the French that he was 'Spanish' and opposed to closer Anglo-French co-operation.[199] His friendship with Laud and his alliance with Windebank meant that he was unlikely to support the parliament the French hoped Charles would be forced to call. Leicester was able to exploit these beliefs and rumours in order to exclude Scudamore from all business. The last thirty months of Scudamore's embassy are a story of the gradual assumption by the extraordinary ambassador of all the ordinary's duties, with the king's connivance. Scudamore was left with little to do but grumble at his eclipse. When English policy changed Scudamore was unable to change with it.

Scudamore was too uncertain to exploit his position to his own advantage, too isolated back at court to be adequately supported, too rigid to be flexible in changing times, and too faithful to his own view of his duties as representing the honour of his king ever to find favour with the French. He seems never to have realised that he was little more than the tool of the king and of Spanish courtiers like Windebank, the latter especially concerned to use him only to prevent the conclusion of a treaty with France. He possessed enough of the virtues of reserve, honesty and caution to prevent him from rushing headlong into disaster, but perhaps too much of them to make an adept diplomat. In de Vic's words, 'the Lord Scudamore doth proceede so slowly and is extremely formall and iealous as he doth spoyle busines'. 'Concerning Lord Scudamore it coulde neuer be expected that a person of his waz and humor shoulde reuisser [succeed] in Courte of France where grauitie sparengnes formallity retirednes are so odious.'[200] A decade later many were thinking much the same things about King Charles himself. According to Torquato Tasso's work on diplomacy, 'To have the perfect ambassador you must first have the perfect prince.'[201] If Scudamore was not the former, Charles was certainly not the latter.

NOTES

1 PRO, SP78/97, fol. 11; Bodleian, MS Carte 77, fol. 390v; G. Wall, *A Sermon at the Lord Archbishop of Canterbury his Visitation Metropoliticall* (London, 1635), sig. A3r.

2 M. S. Anderson, *The Rise of Modern Diplomacy 1450–1919* (Harlow, 1993), pp. 26, 45; BL, Add. MS 11044, fol. 57r.

3 Anderson, *Rise of Modern Diplomacy*, pp. 26–7; G. Mattingly, *Renaissance Diplomacy* (Harmondsworth, 1965), pp. 201–12.

4 Anderson, *Rise of Modern Diplomacy*, pp. 6, 12, 16–17.

5 J. Hotman, *The Ambassador*, trs. J. Shaw (London, 1603), sigs. C2, C3r; J. Howell, *A Discourse concerning the Precedency of Kings … A Distinct Treatise of Ambassadors* (London, 1664), p. 189.

6 Hotman, *Ambassador*, sig. C3r; Mattingly, *Renaissance Diplomacy*, p. 207.

7 T. Webster, *Godly Clergy in Stuart England: The Caroline Puritan Movement c. 1620–1643* (Cambridge, 1997), pp. 102, 104; J. Fisher, *The Priest's Duty and Dignity* (London, 1636), p. 49; Wall, *Sermon*, sig. A2v, pp. 21–4.

8 Mattingly, *Renaissance Diplomacy*, p. 208; Howell, *Treatise of Ambassadors*, p. 191; W. Roosen, 'Early Modern Diplomatic Ceremonial: A Systems Approach', *Journal of Modern History*, 52 (September 1980), p. 457; FSL, Va 147, fol. 38r.

9 D. Starkey, 'Representation through Intimacy: A Study in the Symbolism of Monarchy and Court Office in Early Modern England', in I. Lewis, ed., *Symbols and Sentiments* (London, 1977), pp. 188–9, 201–2; BL, Add. MS 11044, fols 57–9; Bodleian, MS Clarendon 7, no. 567, fols 205–7; Anderson, *Rise of Modern Diplomacy*, p. 10.

10 Mattingly, *Renaissance Diplomacy*, p. 205; Howell, *Treatise of Ambassadors*, pp. 190–1.

11 Starkey, 'Representation through Intimacy', p. 191; G. Goodman, *The Court of King James the First*, ed. J. Brewer (2 vols, London, 1839), I, p. 185.

12 Hotman, *Ambassador*, following sig. G4v; Anderson, *Rise of Modern Diplomacy*, p. 57; BL, Add. MS 11044, fol. 57r; PRO, SP78/98, fol. 86r.

13 PRO, SP78/101, fol. 86v; T. and D. Godefroy, *Le Ceremonial François* (2 vols, Paris, 1649), II, p. 781; Christ Church, Oxford, Browne Misc. I, 'Notes concerning my Lord of Leicester'; Roosen, 'Early Modern Diplomatic Ceremonial', p. 469.

14 PRO, C115/N8/8798–8828; Christ Church, Oxford, Browne Misc. I; Staffordshire RO, D988; A. J. Loomie, ed., *Ceremonies of Charles I: The Note Books of John Finet 1628–1641* (New York, 1987); J. Finet, *Finetti Philoxenis* (London, 1656); Godefroy, *Ceremonial*; A. de Wicquefort, *The Embassador and his Functions*, trs. J. Digby (London, 1716).

15 PRO, SP78/103, fols 78–83; Howell, *Treatise of Ambassadors*, pp. 97–8, 218.

16 PRO, SP78/98, fol. 279Av, SP78/99, fol. 89.

17 PRO, SP78/102, fols 277v–8v.

18 PRO, SP78/103, fols 78–83.

19 M. B. Young, *Servility and Service: The Life and Work of Sir John Coke* (Woodbridge, 1986), pp. 229–52; M. B. Young, *Charles I* (Basingstoke, 1997), p. 93.

20 R. M. Smuts, 'The Puritan Followers of Henrietta Maria in the 1630s', *English Historical Review*, 93 (1978), pp. 24–45; PRO, SP78/99, fol. 115r.

21 Young, *Charles I*, p. 92; HMC, *Report on the Manuscripts of Lord De L'Isle and Dudley* (6 vols, London, 1925–66), VI, p. 77.

22 S. R. Gardiner, *History of England from the Accession of James I. to the Outbreak of the Civil War, 1603–1642* (new edition, 10 vols, London, 1893–96), VII, pp. 169, 391; Young, *Charles I*, p. 89; Atherton, thesis, pp. 241–2.

23 For a fuller consideration of Charles's foreign policy and the ways in which historians have understood it see Atherton, thesis, ch. 5.

24 BL, Add. MS 11044, fol. 65v.

25 B. W. Quintrell, 'Charles I and his Navy in the 1630s', *Seventeenth Century*, 3:2 (1988), pp. 159–79; J. H. Elliott, *The Count-Duke of Olivares* (New Haven and London, 1986), p. 464; G. Parker, *The Army of Flanders and the Spanish Road* (Cambridge, 1972), pp. 55, 61, 76, 84.

26 A. Leman, 'Urbain VIII et les origines du Congrès de Cologne', *Revue d'Histoire Ecclésiastique*, 19 (1923), pp. 370–83; Elliott, *Olivares*, pp. 491, 521–3, 533.

27 For example: H. Taylor, 'Trade, Neutrality, and the "English Road", 1630-1648', *Economic History Review*, 2nd series, 25:2 (1972), pp. 236–60; J. S. Kepler, *The Exchange of Christendom* (Leicester, 1976).

28 F. S. Boase, ed., *The Diary of Thomas Crosfield* (London, 1973), p. 75; PRO, SP16/287/35, fol. 73r; *CSPV 1632–36*, p. 329; Young, *Charles I*, p. 199 n. 92.

29 BL, Add. MS 11044, fol. 58v; Richelieu, *The Political Will and Testament*, trs. T. E. H. (2 parts, London, 1695), II, p. 24.

30 PRO, PRO31/3/68, fols 6–10, also printed in D. L. M. Avenel, ed., *Lettres, instructions diplomatiques et papiers d'état du Cardinal de Richelieu* (8 vols, Paris, 1853–77), IV, pp. 559–66; C. J. Burckhardt, *Richelieu and his Age: III, Power Politics and the Cardinal's Death*, trs. B. Hoy (London, 1971), p. 62; V.-L. Tapié, *France in the Age of Louis XIII and Richelieu*, trs. D. McN. Lockie (Cambridge, 1988), pp. 329–30; Richelieu, *Mémoires*, in J. F. Michaud and J. J. F. Poujoulat, eds, *Nouvelle collection des mémoires relatifs à l'histoire de France* (new edition, 34 vols, Paris, 1854–57), XXII, pp. 590–2.

31 R. Scrope and T. Monkhouse, eds, *State Papers collected by Edward, Earl of Clarendon* (3 vols, Oxford, 1767–86), I, pp. 74–85, 100–26, 226–30, 291–3; Bodleian, MSS Clarendon 5–6; BL, Add. MS 32093, fols 63–91; A. J. Loomie, 'The Spanish Faction at the Court of

Charles I, 1630–38', *Bulletin of the Institute of Historical Research* 59:139 (May 1986), pp. 38–42.

32 Bodleian, MS Clarendon 6, nos. 449–50, fols 203–6; PRO, SP78/98, fol. 215r; Atherton, thesis, pp. 170–3.

33 H. Grotius, *Briefwisseling van Hugo Grotius* vol. VI *1635–1636*, ed. B. L. Meulenbroek ('s-Gravenhage, 1967), p. 197, no. 2260; BL, Add. MS 11407; Bodleian, MS Rawl. D.924, fol. 238; PRO, SP78/98, fols 215r, 223r, SP16/397/57, fols 98–9, SO3/11; Atherton, thesis, p. 349. Manfeild was back in England by May 1636: PRO, C115/N17, C115/N9/8860.

34 PRO, SP78/98, fols 247–8, 261v; Godefroy, *Ceremonial*, II, p. 781; Wicquefort, *Embassador*, p. 131.

35 K. Sharpe, *The Personal Rule of Charles I* (New Haven and London, 1992), pp. 74–5, 96, 509–19.

36 BL, Add. MS 11044, fols 57–9; PRO, SP78/98, fols 175–6; Young, *Coke*, ch. 14.

37 Bodleian, MS Clarendon 7, nos. 522–3, fols 76r, 78r, 90v.

38 PRO, SP78/98, fols 215–22, 261r, SP103/11.

39 *CSPV 1632–36*, pp. 456, 459, 464; Edward Hyde, earl of Clarendon, *The History of the Rebellion and Civil Wars*, ed. W. D. Macray,(6 vols, Oxford, 1888), II, pp. 418–19; PRO, SP78/98, fol. 298r.

40 *CSPV 1632–36*, pp. 459, 464.

41 R. W. Blencowe, ed., *Sydney Papers* (London, 1825), pp. 261–3; *Gentleman's Magazine*, 25 (1755), p. 70.

42 P. Heylyn, *Cyprianus Anglicus* (London, 1668), pp. 274–6; corroboratory evidence of Heylyn's claims has not been found.

43 BL, Add. MS 11044, fol. 57v; *CSPV 1632–36*, pp. 456, 459; Wicquefort, *Embassador*, pp. 166, 234, 302.

44 BL, Add. MS 11044, fol. 82r; PRO, SP78/98, fol. 247v.

45 PRO, SP78/98, fols 269v–71v, 298r, SP78/99, fols 85r, 102r, 185r, SP78/104, fol. 297r; *Gentleman's Magazine*, 25 (1755), p. 70; *CSPV 1632–36*, p. 464.

46 PRO, SP78/98, fols 261, 279A.

47 BL, Add. MSS 4168, fol. 149v, 4169, fol. 39r.

48 T. W. Fulton, *The Sovereignty of the Sea* (Edinburgh and London, 1911), pp. 209–337; PRO, SP16/293/12, fol. 22, SP78/98, fols 94–7; 1635, Avenel, *Lettres*, V, p. 69 n. 1.

49 National Maritime Museum, Greenwich, MS JOD/1/1, 5 and 7 June 1635; Avenel, *Lettres*, V, pp. 66–70; PRO, SP16/291/58–9, fols 115r, 117r.

50 PRO, SP16/293/12, SP16/293/20, SP16/293/49, SP16/293/71, SP16/293/95, SP16/294/54, SP16/295/44V, SP16/295/63–5; National Maritime Museum, MS JOD/1/1, 12 and 20 October 1635; Bodleian, MS Bankes 5/68.

51 Young, *Coke*, p. 243; Atherton, thesis, pp. 164–5.

52 PRO, SP78/97, fols 50, 67r, SP16/289/59, fol. 117; *CSPV 1632–36*, pp. 388–9, 391–2, 418; Bodleian, MS Rawl. D.918, fols 88r, 136v.

53 PRO, SP78/100, fol. 48r, SP78/101, fols 234r, 336r, SP78/97, fol. 69r; HMC, *De L'Isle*, VI, p. 79; Young, *Coke*, pp. 242–3; L. M. Baker, ed., *The Letters of Elizabeth Queen of Bohemia* (London, 1953), pp. 102–3.

54 PRO, SP78/98, fols 279Ar–279Bv, SP78/99, fols 18v, 57v. De Vic's use of the cipher, or Windebank's deciphering of it (the key is missing), was often hasty, making the English especially poor.

55 PRO, SP78/98, fol. 270v, SP78/99, fols 38r, 89; Godefroy, *Ceremonial*, II, p. 795.

56 Smuts, 'Puritan Followers', pp. 35–7; *CSPV 1632–36*, pp. 463–4, 466, 469; Avenel, *Lettres*, V, pp. 353–5; PRO, PRO31/3/68, fol. 18r, SP78/99, fols 114r, 115r, 143r; BL, Egerton MS 1673, fol. 375v.

57 PRO, PRO31/3/68, fols 134, 137r; Smuts, 'Puritan Followers', p. 37.

58 PRO, SP78/99, fol. 91r, PRO31/3/68, fol. 136r; *CSPV 1632–36*, p. 492.

59 PRO, SP78/99, fols 149–50, 201–2; Bodleian, MS Clarendon 7, no. 567 fols 205–7; BL, Add. MS 11044, fols 65r–7v.

60 PRO, SP16/311/22, fol. 49r, PRO31/3/68, fol. 158r.

61 PRO, SP78/99, fol. 207; H. Weber, 'Richelieu at le Rhin', *Revue Historique*, 239 (1968), pp. 265–80; K. Repgen and M. Braubach, eds, *Acta Pacis Westphalicae. Serie I. Band 1* (Münster, 1962), no. 3 pp. 45–6.

62 PRO, SP78/98, fol. 280r.

63 PRO, SP78/99, fol. 208v; BL, Add. MS 11044, fol. 66; Elliott, *Olivares*, p. 520; W. F. Church, *Richelieu and Reason of State* (Princeton, 1972), pp. 298, 414, 431–6.

64 PRO, SP78/100, fols 50, 223, 225, 255r, SP78/104, fol. 212r. Claude de Bullion, superintendent of finance, who later played an important mediating role, was more of an Anglophile.

65 Loomie, *Ceremonies*, pp. 30 and n. 69, 33, 168, 178, 188–9; Gédéon Tallemant (sieur des Réaux), *Historiettes*, ed. A. Adam (2 vols, Paris, 1960–61), II, p. 884; PRO, C115/N8/8811.

66 Richelieu, *Testament*, I, p. 165; K. Sharpe, 'The Personal Rule of Charles I', in H. Tomlinson, ed., *Before the English Civil War* (London, 1983), pp. 59–60; O. A. Ranum, 'Courtesy, Absolutism, and the Rise of the French State, 1630–1660', *Journal of Modern History*, 52 (1980), pp. 426–51.

67 PRO, SP78/99, fol. 278r, SP78/100, fols 139v, 160–1, 191v, 246–7, 318v–19r; *CSPV 1632–36*, pp. 486–7, 490, 503.

68 PRO, SP78/99, fol. 317v, SP78/100, fols 339r, 351, 345–8; *CSPV 1632–36*, pp. 494, 518.

69 Bodleian, MSS Clarendon 7, no. 586 fol. 249v, Clarendon 8, no. 678 fols 243–4.

70 PRO, PRO31/3/69, fols 33, 36; Arundel Castle Archives, G1/88–89; T. Rymer, *Foedera* (3rd edition, 10 vols, The Hague, 1739-45), IX, part ii, p. 3.

71 PRO, SP78/100, fols 262–3, 351v, SP78/101, fol. 7v; *CSPV 1636–39*, pp. 5–6; *CSPD 1635–36*, pp. 392–3.

72 PRO, SP78/99, fols 333–4, 345, SP16/298/26, fol. 48r, SP16/298/76, fols 167–8, SP16/321/84, fols 171–2, SP16/328/191, fol. 5, SP16/330/13, fols 22–3, SP16/341/6, fol. 8r, SP16/536/80, fols 222–5, PRO31/3/69, fols 1–20; Bodleian, MSS Bankes 44/28,

Carte 1, fol. 133r; Arundel Castle Archives, 'Autograph letters 1632 to 1723', nos. 360, 365.

73 PRO, SP78/102, fol. 283v, SP78/100, fols 23r, 323r; BL, Add. MS 11044, fol. 59r.

74 Collins, *Letters*, II, p. 387; PRO, SP78/101, fols 31–8.

75 HMC, *Sixth Report* (London, 1877), p. 277; *CSPV 1632–36*, pp. 331, 354–5, 371; Wicquefort, *Embassador*, p. 237.

76 PRO, SP78/101, fols 83r, 114r, 133r, 134r, 70, 85–6, 103r; Collins, *Letters*, II, p. 388.

77 PRO, SP78/101, fols 43–8, 99–100.

78 *CSPV 1632–36*, p. 543; Warwickshire RO, CR2017/C1/60–2; PRO, SP78/101, fols 161v–2r; Atherton, thesis, p. 190.

79 Collins, *Letters*, II, p. 387; PRO, SP78/101, fol. 161r; Atherton, thesis, p. 191; Bodleian, MS Rawl. D.859, fol. 28.

80 For example, PRO, C115/M13/7264.

81 Clarendon, *Rebellion*, I, p. 131; H. R. Trevor-Roper, *Archbishop Laud 1573–1645* (London, 1940), p. 335.

82 PRO, SP78/104, fol. 15r, C115/M13/7264; Collins, *Letters*, II, pp. 514–15.

83 Collins, *Letters*, II, p. 387. Others had a much higher opinion of Scudamore's intellect: above, pp. 51–2.

84 Collins, *Letters*, II, pp. 387–8, 506–8, 515; Atherton, thesis, pp. 191, 193.

85 Collins, *Letters*, II, p. 387.

86 PRO, SP78/101, fols 181–2. 253r, 403r, SP78/102, fols 16r, 24–5.

87 PRO, SP78/99, fols 191r, 276r, SP78/101, fols 214r, 330r, 411r, SP78/102, fol. 146, E403/2568, fol. 25v, SP16/347/20, fol. 57r; Berkshire RO, Trumbull MSS, miscellaneous correspondence LXI (Weckherlin's diary), 12/22 November 1637; Bodleian, MS Clarendon 10, no. 797 fol. 65.

88 Collins, *Letters*, II, pp. 387–8; HMC, *Sixth Report*, p. 281; W. Laud, *Works*, ed. W. Scott and J. Bliss (7 vols, Oxford, 1847–60), VI, p. 516, VII, pp. 319, 335–6, 366–7.

89 PRO, SP78/102, fols 204v–5r.

90 PRO, SP78/97, fol. 185v, SP78/99, fols 241–2. 246r.

91 R. Cant, 'The Embassy of the Earl of Leicester to Denmark in 1632', *English Historical Review*, 54 (1939), pp. 252–62.

92 Smuts, 'Puritan Followers', pp. 36–9; Collins, *Letters*, II, p. 387; Godefroy, *Ceremonial*, II, pp. 781, 794–5; Wicquefort, *Embassador*, p. 177.

93 PRO, SP78/100, fols 317–19, SP78/101, fols 253r, 399r, SP78/102, fols 219–20.

94 PRO, SP78/101, fol. 121r; BL, Add. MS 11044, fol. 83r; Blencowe, *Sydney Papers*, pp. 261–2.

95 Bodleian, MS Clarendon 9, no. 730 fol. 97r; BL, Add. MS 24023, fol. 12r. The king's letter to Leicester gave the earl greater leeway than his summary of it to Windebank and Scudamore implied.

96 PRO, SP78/101, fol. 271v, SP78/102, fol. 323r, SP78/103, fol. 191r.

97 P. Haskell, 'Sir Francis Windebank and the Personal Rule of Charles I' (Southampton University Ph.D. thesis, 1978), pp. 107–8; F. C. Springell, *Connoisseur and Diplomat: The Earl of Arundel's Embassy to Germany in 1636* (London, 1963), pp. 25–35; Bodleian, MS Clarendon 10, nos. 786 fols 39–41, 795 fol. 61, 802 fols 73–4, 806 fols 82–7, 830 fol. 134.

98 G. Bromley, ed., *A Collection of Original Royal Letters* (London, 1787), pp. 55 (date should be 16/26 September 1636), 81; PRO, SP16/329/21, fol. 30r, PRO31/3/69, fol. 84r; HMC, *Fourth Report* (London, 1874), p. 291.

99 BL, Add. MS 24023, fols 12–14; PRO, SP78/101, fols 302–8.

100 Berkshire RO, Trumbull MSS, miscellaneous correspondence, XIX, 1630–37, no. 108; PRO, SP78/101, fols 430–3, SP78/102, fols 5–6, 109v, 206r, 266r; BL, Harl. MS 7001, fol. 100.

101 PRO, E403/2567, fols 102v–3r, E403/2568, fols 5v, 19v, SP78/101, fol. 267v; HMC, *De L'Isle*, VI, pp. 54–60, 62–3, 66–7, 554; BL, Egerton MS 807, especially fols 7r, 9r, 45r, 49r, 55r.

102 PRO, E403/1749–53; Atherton, thesis, p. 198.

103 Tapié, *France*, pp. 351–2; Marquis de Fontenay-Mareuil, *Mémoires*, in Michaud and Poujoulat, *Nouvelle collection des mémoires*, XIX, pp. 254–6.

104 PRO, SP78/101, fols 305, 430–1, SP78/102, fols 80–1.

105 PRO, SP78/10, fols 399v–400r, SP103/11, draft treaty of 4/14 October 1636.

106 PRO, SP78/101, fol. 400, SP78/102, fols 172–5, 203–5.

107 Collins, *Letters*, II, pp. 451–2; HMC, *De L'Isle*, VI, p. 67; Laud, *Works*, VII, p. 297; PRO, SP78/102, fol. 279r.

108 PRO, SP78/102, fols 125–6, 281, 287, 338–9, SP78/103, fol. 9.

109 PRO, SP78/102, fols 275r, 305r; Laud, *Works*, VII, pp. 301, 306; Collins, *Letters*, II, p. 453.

110 Bromley, *Original Royal Letters*, pp. 96–9; *CSPV 1636–39*, pp. 126–9, 146–7; Laud, *Works*, VII, p. 319.

111 Sharpe, *Personal Rule*, p. 529; Berkshire RO, Trumbull MSS, miscellaneous correspondence LXI, 12/22–18/28 February 1637; PRO, SP78/103, fols 101–4.

112 PRO, SP78/103, fols 126v–7r, PRO, PRO31/3/70, fol. 7r; HMC, *De L'Isle*, VI, p. 92.

113 PRO, SP103/11, draft auxiliary treaty, 17/27 February 1637, and draft league, SP78/103, fols 103v, 375v, SP99/40, fol. 128v; Wiltshire RO, 413/498.

114 Laud, *Works*, VII, pp. 319, 342, 366–7; HMC, *Sixth Report*, p. 281; H. Lonchay, J. Cuvelier and J. Lefèvre, eds, *Correspondance de la cour d'Espagne sur les affaires des Pays-bas au XVIIe siècle* (6 vols, Brussels, 1923–37), III, p. 148 no. 433; W. Knowler, ed., *The Earl of Strafforde's Letters and Dispatches* (2 vols, London, 1739), II, pp. 48–9; Sharpe, *Personal Rule*, pp. 533, 535–6; Young, *Charles I*, pp. 90–1; Kent Archives Office, uncatalogued Cranfield papers, Dorset to Cranfield, 7/17 February 1637.

115 BL, Egerton MS 2716, fol. 270r; HMC, *Fourth Report*, p. 278; Knowler, *Strafforde's Letters*, II, p. 50; PRO, SP78/103, fol. 172r; Bodleian, MS Clarendon 12, no. 938 fol. 23r.

116 PRO, SP16/350/16, fol. 33r, SP81/38, fols 181v–2r.

117 Knowler, *Strafforde's Letters*, II, pp. 53, 60–4, 78.

118 PRO, SP78/100, fols 191v, 246r, 319r.

119 Lonchay et al., *Correspondence*, III, no. 603 pp. 219–20, no. 807 p. 277; J. W. Stoye, *Europe Unfolding 1648–1688* (London, 1969), p. 16; BL, Add. MS 38091 O, fols 224–6.

120 PRO, SP78/103, fols 279r, 343–5, 347–8, 375, 402, SP103/11, memo of differences between the two translations; HMC, *Supplementary Report on the Manuscripts of his Grace the Duke of Hamilton* (London, 1932), p. 41.

121 PRO, SP78/103, fols 441–4, SP78/104, fols 41–2.

122 Avenel, *Lettres*, V, p. 818, VI, p. 136; PRO, PRO31/3/70, fol. 20r.

123 Bodleian, MS Clarendon 6, no. 439, fols 176–7; PRO, SP103/11, proposed treaties; PRO, PRO31/3/68, fols 6r–10v, 30–5; Avenel, *Lettres*, IV, pp. 559–66; Richelieu, *Mémoires*, in Michaud and Poujoulat, *Nouvelle collection des mémoires*, XXII, p. 592; *CSPV 1632–36*, pp. 328–9; BL, Egerton MS 1673, fol. 360v.

124 PRO, PRO31/3/69, fols 36v, 84r, 100v, PRO31/3/70, fol. 20r.

125 Avenel, *Lettres*, V, pp. 592–7; PRO, PRO31/3/70, fol. 20r; M. Roberts, *Sweden as a Great Power, 1611–1697* (London, 1968), pp. 148–54; Repgen and Braubach, *Acta Pacis Westphalicae*, I, i, no. 3, pp. 45–6, 55.

126 O. A. Ranum, *Richelieu and the Councillors of Louis XIII* (Oxford, 1963), p. 96; Richelieu, *Testament*, II, p. 24.

127 BL, Add. MS 4169, fol. 44v; PRO, SP78/103, fols 304r, 426r, SP78/104, fol. 3r.

128 Avenel, *Lettres*, V, pp. 595–6 n. 2; PRO, SP78/103, fols 195r, 219v.

129 E. A. Beller, 'The Mission of Sir Thomas Roe to the Conference at Hamburg, 1638–40', *English Historical Review*, 41 (1926), pp. 61–77; M. Strachan, *Sir Thomas Roe* (Salisbury, 1989), pp. 232–43; Tapié, *France*, p. 381; BL, Add. MSS 4168–9; Richelieu, *Mémoires*, in Michaud and Poujoulat, *Nouvelle collection des mémoires*, XXIII, pp. 323–4; G. H. Bougeant, *Histoire des guerres et des negociations* (3 vols, Paris, 1751–67), I, p. 332.

130 Laud, *Works*, VII, p. 334; C. M. Hibbard, *Charles I and the Popish Plot* (Chapel Hill, 1983), p. 74.

131 Avenel, *Lettres*, VI, pp. 136–7; PRO, SP78/104, fols 80–1, 116v.

132 PRO, SP16/352/7, SP16/130, pp. 1–3, SP16/372/56, SP16/372/59, SP16/373/69, SP16/374/66, SP78/104, fols 268, 272r, 309, 351r, 365r.

133 PRO, C115/N4/8605, SP78/100, fols 83–5; SP78/102, fol. 298r, SP78/103, fols 426–32; BL, Add. MS 15857, fols 163–6.

134 PRO, SP78/103, fols 361–6, SP78/104, fols 5v–6r, 19–24, 105–6.

135 PRO, SP78/103, fol. 419, SP78/102, fols 90, 144–5, 164r; Berkshire RO, Trumbull MSS, miscellaneous correspondence LXI, 25 June/5 July 1637.

136 PRO, SP78/103, fol. 111r, SP78/104, fols 49r, 164r.

137 PRO, SP78/104, fols 403, 412–13, SP78/105, fols 51–2, 119r, 171r, 178r, 223–4, 442r; W. Laud, *Harangve Prononcee en la Chambre de l'Estoille* ([Paris], 1637[8]).

138 Laud, *Works*, III, p. 223, VII, pp. 176–7, 198, 201, 217, 231, 277.

139 PRO, SP78/101, fol. 161v, SP78/104, fols 49r, 430r.

140 Collins, *Letters*, II, p. 515; PRO, SP78/104, fol. 15r, SP78/105, fol. 287, SP101/12, bundle 3, letter to Windebank of 7/17 May 1638, C115/M13/7264; Sheffield University Library, Hartlib papers, 31/22/19B; Hibbard, *Popish Plot*, pp. 52–3; HMC, *De L'Isle*, VI, pp. 355–8.

141 PRO, C115/N8/8798–800, C115/N8/8812, C115/N8/8818, C115/N8/8822; Loomie, *Ceremonies*, pp. 8–10.

142 PRO, SP78/105, fol. 134v; Atherton, thesis, pp. 218–19.

143 HMC, *Report on the Manuscripts of the Earl of Denbigh (Part V)* (London, 1911), p. 49; PRO, SP78/106, fol. 94r, SP16/357/90, fol. 146r; BL, Add. MS 11044, fols 180–1; A. B. Grosart, ed., *The Lismore Papers (Second Series)* (5 vols, privately printed, 1887–88), III, p. 278, IV, pp. 6–7; J. M. French, *The Life Records of John Milton* (5 vols, New Brunswick, 1949–58), I, pp. 367–9.

144 Collins, *Letters*, II, p. 494.

145 Young, *Coke*, pp. 245–7; PRO, SP78/102, fols 74, 103–4.

146 Collins, *Letters*, II, pp. 507, 509, 511; PRO, SP16/366/8, fol. 14r; Bodleian, MS Clarendon 19, no. 1486, fols 232–3.

147 Lonchay *et al.*, *Correspondence*, III, pp. 156–7 nos. 455–6, 458, p. 167 no. 485, p. 204 no. 581; Bodleian, MS Clarendon 12, nos. 965 fols 113–14, 986, fol. 174v; BL, Add. MS 36324, fols 46–8; Hibbard, *Popish Plot*, pp. 76–7, 86; Young, *Coke*, pp. 236–8 PRO, SP81/44, fol. 22.

148 Smuts, 'Puritan Followers', p. 40. Hibbard, *Popish Plot*, pp. 76–7, 268–9 nn. 37–9; Laud, *Works*, VII, p. 390; Richelieu, *Mémoires*, in Michaud and Poujoulat, *Nouvelle collection des mémoires*, XXIII, pp. 222–4; *CSPV 1636–39*, p. 260; Tapié, *France*, pp. 365–9; M. Carmona, *Marie de Médicis* (Paris, 1981), pp. 530–1.

149 Hibbard, *Popish Plot*, p. 77; Smuts, 'Puritan Followers', pp. 40–1; Westminster Diocesan Archives, MS XXIX, no. 12 p. 25.

150 PRO, SP78/104, fols 74r, 96r.

151 PRO, SP78/104, fols 210, 374r, 345r, PRO31/3/70, fol. 53; Collins, *Letters*, II, p. 516.

152 Deputy Keeper of the Public Records, *Thirty-ninth Annual Report* (London, 1878), appendix 8, p. 680; PRO, PRO31/3/70, fol. 53, SP78/103, fol. 52r, SP78/104, fols 257–8, 289, 306–8.

153 PRO, SP78/104, fols 345r, 377r, 396v–7r, SP105/14–15, Gerbier's letters to Leicester of 18/28 November, 25 November/5 December, 9/19 December 1637 and 12/22 January 1638.

154 PRO, SP78/105, fols 277–80, PRO31/3/70, fol. 75r; Collins, *Letters*, II, pp. 545–6, 548, 551–2; Richelieu, *Mémoires*, in Michaud and Poujoulat, *Nouvelle collection des mémoires*, XXIII, p. 301.

155 PRO, SP81/44, fol. 151r, SP78/105, fols 369r, 371r.

156 BL, Add. MS 4168, fol. 37v; compare fols 37–8, 43–4, 68–9, 87–8.

157 PRO, SP78/101, fol. 386v, SP78/103, fol. 56r; BL, Add. MS 11044, fols 58v–9r.

158 PRO, PRO31/3/70, fol. 48, SP78/105, fols 47v–8r, SP78/106, fols 309–10; Goodman, *Court of King James*, I, pp. 185–6; Christ Church, Oxford, Browne Misc. I; BL, Egerton MS 807, fol. 65.

159 PRO, SP16/269/51, fol. 98, SP78/101, fols 11–13, SP16/333/65, fols 177–8, SP16/329/70, fol. 121, SP16/347/21–2, fols 57–61, SP16/350/77, fols 171–4, SP16/353, fol. 3v; *Calendar of State Papers, Colonial Series, 1574–1660*, ed. W. N. Sainsbury (London, 1860), p. 219; Rymer, *Foedera*, IX, part ii, pp. 49–50, 79–80; Atherton, thesis, p. 226.

160 BL, Add. MS 11044, fols 58r, 59r, Harl. MS 1579, fols 56-8. Barrett never got to Paris.

161 PRO, SP16/537/5, fols 6–7, SP78/107, fol. 23r.

162 PRO, SP101/11.

163 BL, Add. MSS 45140–1; PRO, C115/M13/7256; Atherton, thesis, pp. 227–8, 445–52, for a list of these.

164 PRO, SP78/98, fol. 313r.

165 PRO, SP78/104, fols 284, 412–13; BL, Add. MS 11044, fols 96–105.

166 PRO, SP78/105, fols 380, 456v–7r, SP78/106, fol. 76r.

167 PRO, SP78/105, fols 203–4, SP103/11, treaty of Wismar.

168 PRO, SP78/100, fols 270v–1r, SP78/99, fol. 319r, SP78/101, fols 379–80, SP78/106, fols 79–80, SP101/11, 30 March/9 April 1636.

169 HMC, *Fifteenth Report, Appendix, Part II. The Manuscripts of J. Elliot Hodgkin* (London, 1897), pp. 44–5; PRO, SP78/105, fols 42r–3r, 115v (the enciphered passage means 'iersy or gernsey'), 220–1, 244, 289–92, 308, SP78/106, fol. 87.

170 P. H. Donald, 'The King and the Scottish Troubles, 1637–1641' (Cambridge University Ph.D. thesis, 1987), p. 162; PRO, SP78/105, fols 414–24, 437–8, SP78/106, fols 74v–5r.

171 PRO, SP78/105, fols 475, 476v, SP78/106, fols 13r, 34r, 74r, PRO31/3/71, fol. 16v; Hibbard, *Popish Plot*, pp. 77–8; Donald, 'Scottish Troubles', pp. 170–6, 220.

172 HCL, MS L.C.647.1, 'Scudamore MSS: Accounts 1635–37[8]', fols 16r, 53r, 57; PRO, SP78/100, fol. 271r, SP78/106, fols 99–100.

173 PRO, SP78/105, fol. 43r; BL, Add. MS 11044, fol. 83v; G. Serr and D. Ligou, 'Henri de Rohan: son rôle dans le parti protestant. Tome II 1617–1622', *Divers aspects de la réforme aux XVIe et XVIIe siècles: études et documents* (Société de l'Histoire du Protestantisme Français, supplement, Paris, 1975), pp. 326–7; Atherton, thesis, p. 232.

174 PRO, C115/N5/8653–69; HCL, MS L.C.647.1, 'Scudamore MSS: Accounts 1635–37[8]', fol. 57r.

175 PRO, SP78/100, fol. 95r, SP78/101, fol. 284r, SP78/104, fol. 345r; C115/N5/8634–42, C115/N9/8861–70; HCL, MS L.C.647.1, 'Scudamore MSS: Accounts 1635–37[8]', fols 59–61; BL, Add. MS 11044, fol. 85v.

176 Hibbard, *Popish Plot*, p. 269 n. 43; PRO, SP78/105, fol. 475v; Collins, *Letters*, II, p. 646.

177 PRO, SP78/101, fol. 103v, SP78/104, fols 257–8.

178 PRO, SP78/98, fol. 124v, SP78/101, fols 234r, 309r, SP78/102, fol. 242r; Haskell, 'Windebank', p. 158; HMC, *De L'Isle*, VI, p. 225.

179 Hibbard, *Popish Plot*, pp. 268 n. 30, 294 n. 79; PRO, PRO31/3/70, fol. 51r.

180 National Maritime Museum, MS JOD/1/1, 2 and 11 July 1635; PRO, SP16/294/21, fols 52–3.

181 *DNB* (Gerbier).

182 PRO, SP78/105, fols 106–7, 475r, E403/2567, fols 102v–3r, E403/2568, fol. 19v.

183 PRO, SP101/10, SP101/12, DB to Windebank, 15/25 December 1637, SP101/12, 'January: 1637[8] Newes: France', and *passim*, SP78/100, fols 139, 143–4.

184 PRO, SP101/96, Burlamachi to Windebank, 27 October/6 November 1638, SP78/105, fol. 195r; A. V. Judges, 'Philip Burlamachi: A Financier of the Thirty Years' War', *Economica*, 6 (1926), pp. 290–1.

185 HMC, *Sixth Report*, p. 283; *CSPV 1636–39*, pp. 363, 398–9, 411, 417, 421. 468; Warwickshire RO, CR2017/C72/1, CR2017/C47/114C, CR2017/C47/118A; PRO, SP92/22, fols 208v, 246v; Atherton, thesis, p. 236.

186 M. Prawdin (*vere* Charol), *Marie de Rohan, Duchesse de Chevreuse* (London, 1971), pp. 80–107; *CSPV 1636–39*, pp. 404, 407–8, 410.

187 PRO, SP78/105, fols 335r–8r; *CSPV 1636–39*, p. 414; Bougeant, *Histoire des guerres*, I, p. 331.

188 PRO, SP78/105, fols 365, 451r; HMC, *De L'Isle*, VI, pp. 143–8; Collins, *Letters*, II, pp. 558–9; *CSPV 1636–39*, pp. 420–2.

189 PRO, SP78/105, fol. 476v, SP78/106, fols 81, 158r, 180r; *CSPV 1636–39*, pp. 437–8.

190 *CSPV 1636–39*, pp. 468, 471, 475; Richelieu, *Mémoires*, in Michaud and Poujoulat, *Nouvelle collection des mémoires*, XXII, p. 232; Avenel, *Lettres*, VI, pp. 115–17; Bodleian, MS Clarendon 12, no. 962 fol. 108r.

191 PRO, SP78/107, fol. 154.

192 PRO, SP78/106, fol. 303r; HMC, *De L'Isle*, VI, p. 156; Atherton, thesis, p. 239.

193 PRO, C115/M12/7223; *Notes and Queries*, 1st series, 8:207 (1853), p. 367; Atherton, thesis, p. 239.

194 Warwickshire RO, CR2017/C39/1, p. 3; FSL, Vb 2(18).

195 BL, Add. MS 11044, fols 79–81; PRO, SP78/106, fol. 342.

196 PRO, SP78/107, fols 27r, 56–7, 81v, 91–4, BL, Add. MS 11044, fols 82–3; Scudamore's relation, now lost, but excerpted in Sotheby's sale catalogue, *Bibliotheca Phillippica. Catalogue of ... Sir Thomas Phillipps. 10 June 1896* ([London, 1896]), lot 1052, p. 187 (copy in Bodleian, MS Phillipps-Munby d.16).

197 PRO, SP78/107, fol. 97r; HMC, *De L'Isle*, VI, pp. 161–2; Loomie, *Ceremonies*, p. 258.

198 BL, Add. MS 11044, fols 82v–3r.

199 PRO, SP78/103, fol. 364r.

200 PRO, SP78/100, fols 107r, 162v.

201 Mattingly, *Renaissance Diplomacy*, p. 212.

Chapter 7

Scudamore as a royalist leader

I n the summer of 1642, as the royalists secured Herefordshire, the king and many of the gentry and people of the shire looked to Viscount Scudamore to provide local leadership of the royalist party. They were disappointed. He did not show his hand fully in the county until September 1642. Weeks later Hereford fell to parliamentarian forces under the earl of Stamford, and the royalist leaders, Scudamore included, fled. Stamford withdrew to Gloucester in December and the royalists returned. From then until April 1643 Scudamore did assert himself in Hereford, but at the end of April another disaster struck, and Hereford fell once again to a parliamentary army, this time under Sir William Waller. Scudamore was captured and sent to London as a prisoner, where he remained until March 1647, placed by the sergeant-at-arms under house arrest in St Martin's in the Fields, contemplating his short and inglorious career as a royalist leader.[1]

In February and May 1643 all of Scudamore's money, plate, household goods and furniture in London, both those at his house in Petty France, Westminster, and those he had hidden in the Inner Temple chambers of his servant and legal adviser Richard Seaborne, were seized by the parliament; they were later all sold.[2] The raiding and ransacking of their London house, their main residence for the past three years, were a personal and financial disaster for the viscount and viscountess: he reckoned that they had lost property worth £700, although the official valuation of the goods was only £176 15s.[3] The loss was also a historical misfortune (if not quite a disaster), for among the goods seized were almost all the viscount's papers relating to the past four years since his return from Paris; we are left with only a few fragments (mostly three account books) produced by Scudamore himself from which to piece together his actions and motivation.[4] Scudamore speaks to us directly only once, in a series of notes he wrote on the solemn league and covenant and the negative oath, and whether it was lawful to take them,[5] compiled between his capture and his taking of both early in 1647.[6] Instead, we have to see Scudamore though the eyes of others. We have two principal types of source. First, there are the letters and papers of the parliamentary Harley family, which have been the subject of an excellent study of the outbreak of the civil war in Herefordshire and which provide much of the local context for Scudamore's action and inaction in 1642.[7] Second, especially for the spring of 1643, are the surviving papers of the royalist council of war which sat to determine culpability in the fall of Hereford in April 1643;[8] parts of these papers have several times been printed.[9] From these we can build up a detailed picture of the royalist administration in the county in the first four months of 1643, and Scudamore's part in it.[10] The vicissitudes of the survival of the evidence determine the sorts of questions we can ask about Viscount Scudamore between his return from Paris in March 1639 and his capture in April 1643. We can know very little about his actions from 1639 to the summer of 1642. Thereafter we often have to judge his motivation from what we know of his actions as observed by others. We can know little of Scudamore's royalism, but much of Scudamore as a royalist.

Had Scudamore's papers survived from the early 1640s we would know more of what the viscount was up to, but it is probable that we would not know much more about his inner motivation, about what made him a royalist leader. Few royalists penned clear, reasoned and individual statements of belief; for many their politics were, as Paul Seaward has suggested, a matter of private counsel.[11] It is clear that for many 1642 represented an agony of decision making. John Morrill has vividly described the nerve-racking weeks in the early summer of 1642 from the point of view of the moderates and the undecided. Henry Oxinden famously described himself as caught between the Scylla of the king's commission of array and the Charybdis of the parliament's militia ordinance; the petition of the Devon quarter sessions to the king in August lamented their unhappy state: 'In how hard a Condition are we, whilst a Twofold Obedience, like Twins in the Womb, strives to be borne to both!'[12] For others the choice of sides was clear but the decision to act no less agonising; nevertheless, P. R. Newman's description of the 'self-evident rightness' and 'obviously sensible' nature of their views does not do justice to the complexities of choosing to be a royalist.[13] That choice dictated a sometimes anguished restriction on one's public image or pronouncements. Swift intellectual footwork and clearsightedness (not always qualities readily found in a crisis) were needed to conform oneself with the public propaganda of the chosen side. We can see such processes at work in a number of royalists. Lord Spencer of Wormleighton expressed his doubts about the royalist cause in a *private* letter in September 1642: 'How much I am unsatisfied with the proceedings here, I have at large expressed.' Nevertheless, he felt bound by a duty of honour to fight for the king.[14] Self-fashioning as a royalist, even for the committed, was often not an easy process, and must, at least in the initial stages, have involved some ingenuity and disingenuity, some masking of true beliefs rather than internalising of the message. Perhaps that is why so many royalists chose rather to express their motivation in terms of their personal loyalty to a personal monarch.[15] Yet royalism itself was not so simple, and consisted of a shifting *mélange* of different ingredients – loyalty to the king, defence of the church and the ancient constitution, anti-puritanism, fear of unrest. The case of Viscount Scudamore and the other royalist leaders in Herefordshire illustrates many of these points.

At the Epiphany sessions in January 1642 a pro-episcopacy petition was brought before the bench by two clergymen, Dr William Sherbourne of Pembridge and Mr Mason of Yazor and Hereford. Viscount Scudamore was the first to put his hand to it, Sir William Croft spoke enthusiastically in favour of it, and all the JPs signed it bar two, James Kyrle and Edward Broughton, both godly JPs who later supported the parliament.[16] A month later Fitz-william Coningsby and Wallop Brabazon pressed the petition on the corporation of Leominster. Scudamore's avowal of the petition was clearly meant to be a public act of defending the church, a role, as we have seen, he had so often and so successfully played in the 1630s. His action is all the more remarkable in that it is his first direct act in county politics for which we have evidence since 1635, and it is likely that he had returned to Herefordshire especially to defend the bishops; rumours that such a petition would be presented had been circulating since the middle of December 1641.[17]

Sir Robert Harley, the godly senior knight of the shire and future parliamentarian, refused to present the petition to the Commons, but it probably circulated widely in manuscript – an almost identical petition was disseminated in Staffordshire – and it was later printed in Sir Thomas Aston's *Collection*.[18] It asked for the prayer book to be re-established and confirmed; for cathedrals, 'the Monuments of our Forefathers Charity, the reward of present Literature and furtherance of Pietie', to be continued; and for episcopacy, 'the Ancient and Primitive Government of the Church, Renowned for Successes, Victorious against Schismes', to be maintained 'for the glory of God, preservation of Order, Peace, and Unity, the Reformation and suppression of wickednesse and vice, and the mature prevention of Schismes, Factions, and Seditions'. With all this Scudamore, doubtless, wholeheartedly agreed. In one point, however, the petition deviated from Scudamore's private opinions, for it closed with a guarded admission that the church had been beset with 'Excesses, Exorbitances, and Encroachments', although these had issued 'not from any poyson in the nature of the Discipline, but rather from the infirmitie and corruption of the Persons', and asked the parliament to regulate and correct them.[19] One is left wondering what, in the church policy of the 1630s, Scudamore regarded as an excess or an exorbitance.

It was not only Scudamore who had, early in 1642, to adopt a posture of enthusiasm for the non-Laudian church which ran counter to an earlier image of support for Laudianism. Brabazon, and especially Coningsby, were both adept at moulding their public religious image. In March 1642 they commended the purging of Hereford Cathedral of 'Copes, Candlesticks, Basons, Altar with bowing and other Reuerence vnto it', claiming that these had been introduced against the wishes of the dean and chapter by a former bishop (probably Matthew Wren); but they also made plain their support for episcopacy and common prayer. At the same time they refused to take the Protestation and made their opposition to its enforcement in the county plain; yet ten months earlier Coningsby, then one of the county's MPs (he was expelled from the Commons in October 1641 as a monopolist, but replaced by his son Humphrey) had commended the Protestation to the sheriff and justices.[20] In the 1630s both Brabazon and Coningsby had presented themselves as ceremonialists. Brabazon, the brother of an Irish earl, had himself made churchwarden of Leominster in order to set the communion table there altar-wise and introduce rails and an organist.[21] Coningsby set up some remarkable stained glass in the chapel at Hampton Court, depicting the Deposition from the Cross, and sought Laud's advice in preventing a friend's conversion to Rome.[22] Unless we are to posit a damascene conversion as the Laudian scales fell from their eyes, it would appear that the dictates of public propaganda in 1642 required some nimble presentation and trimming of views.

As quickly as Viscount Scudamore appeared in January 1642, he disappeared again, to take no further recorded part in local politics for another four months. His absence is significant, for it was between March and May 1642 that the leaders of the Herefordshire royalists emerged. He was not one of the nine justices who wrote two letters to Harley in March and April 1642.[23] The letters were deliberate statements of the emerging royalist cause, and they circulated widely as propaganda: copies survive from Shropshire, Staffordshire, Nottinghamshire and Kent.[24] The same nine JPs were also almost certainly behind the printed *A Declaration, or Resolution of the County of Hereford* issued at the end of June 1642;[25] it too reached a wide audience, and several manuscript copies are also extant, perhaps because the parliament complained so bitterly of its publication, calling it in a rage of hyperbole 'the foulest and most scandalous Pamphlet that ever was raised or published against the Parliament'.[26] The two letters and the *Declaration* developed a fourfold case against the parliament and in favour of the king. Firstly, the church, now purged of Laudianism, should be upheld as the best defence against papists and sectaries. Secondly, although the kingdom was composed of the three estates of king, lords and commons, the king was the dominant partner and any attempt to 'vntwist' the 'triple cord', as the parliament was now attempting, would be dangerous. Thirdly, the king, having acknowledged his past mistakes, could now be trusted, so that, fourthly, the current threat to the kingdom was not princely but parliamentary tyranny. In the *Declaration* the Herefordshire royalists professed that they and the king stood for four pillars: the Protestant religion, the king's just power, the laws of the land and the liberty of the subject.

These nine justices – Sir William Croft (1593–1645), Wallop Brabazon (*c.* 1585–*c.* 1675), William Smallman of Kinnersley (*c.* 1615–43), Thomas Wigmore of Shobdon (*c.* 1605–*c.* 1653), Thomas Price of Wisterton in Marden (1582–1654), Fitzwilliam Coningsby (*c.* 1595–1666), Henry Lingen (1612–62), William Rudhall (*c.* 1590–1651), and John Scudamore of Ballingham (1600–45) – became the royalist leadership in the county in the summer of 1642. All were named as commissioners of array, and all were active for the king in 1642–43.[27] They became known locally as the 'nine worthies', and the *Declaration* was known as 'the nine worthies' resolution'. At the execution of the commission of array in July 1642 the cry was 'God bless the 9 wortheys of Hereford-sheire'. It was as if they were the physical embodiment of those nine heroes of popular myth, usually thought of as Hector, Alexander, Julius Caesar, Joshua, David, Judas Maccabaeus, Arthur, Charlemagne and Godfrey of Bouillon. Their soubriquet likened the Herefordshire royalist leaders with these military champions of old.[28] It had further advantages, too. The royalists could hide behind the name, an anonymity useful when the parliament sought to discover the true identity of the authors of the *Declaration*, and considerable confusion reigned over who the authors were.[29] Concealing their true identity may have made the royalists appear more powerful, as the leaders of popular unrest were often kept secret behind nicknames such as 'Lady Skimmington' or, in France, 'Jean Nu-pieds'. Moreover, their title drew on extra legitimation for their actions by linking them with past heroes, and extra legitimation may have been just what they needed, given that the traditional leader of the country, Viscount Scudamore, was not of their number and had barely shown himself in the local strife.

Lord Scudamore's actions between February and September 1642, as the royalist party in Herefordshire first formed and then crystallised, are hard to fathom. One act (his intervention in the bye-election for Hereford) and one failure to act (at the execution of the commission of array in July) are especially puzzling. Richard Weaver, MP for Hereford, died in the middle of May 1642 after several months of illness; rumour had already buried him in March, and the scramble to replace him began in April.[30] One of the points at issue in the correspondence between the nine justices and Harley at that time was the extent to which Harley truly represented the shire, and so various people saw in the Hereford bye-election the opportunity to seek through victory public legitimation of their stand. Seven people were named as possible candidates in Brilliana Harley's letters, our main source for the contest.[31] Croft, the acknowledged leader of the nine justices, was rumoured to be gathering support, as was Price, another of the nine worthies. Brilliana sought support for her son Edward, whose agent in Hereford, Dr Nathaniel Wright, earned abuse, criticism, threats and new enemies in seeking voices for Harley. Croft was clearly a key figure in the canvassing, and his opposition to his former allies the Harleys provoked Brilliana to describe him as 'quite turned abowute'.

The second key figure in the contest was Viscount Scudamore, who was high steward of the city. No one could be elected without being a freeman of the city, for which the assistance of either Scudamore or his deputy Richard Seaborne, the surviving MP for the city, was vital. In April it was rumoured that Scudamore was backing Robert Whitney, his lieutenant in the county troop of horse. Brilliana thought Whitney a moderate royalist in August 1642, but he was sufficiently loyal to the king to be added by Charles to the commission of the peace the following June.[32] At the end of May 1642 Viscount Scudamore put forward his son James as a candidate; it was an unbeatable combination. Edward Harley instantly withdrew, and the others probably did likewise. Neither Scudamore was in any hurry, partly because they had to wait until James's eighteenth birthday at the end of June before he could be sworn a freeman of the city. The king issued the writ for the election from York on 6 June, and James was elected on 26 July.[33] He never took his seat at Westminster, though he did later attend the royalist Oxford parliament.[34] The viscount had confirmed his power base in Hereford. The earl of Pembroke, the electoral patronage manager *par excellence* of the early seventeenth century and the previous high steward, had never secured direct influence over the city's two seats. The election of Lord Scudamore's son in 1642 meant the end of the city's previous and jealously guarded electoral independence, and it marked a key stage in the conversion of Hereford into the safe seat for outside candidates that it had become by the turn of the century.[35] In the spring of 1642 James Scudamore prevented Harley from securing a victory for the Roundheads (a term first recorded in Herefordshire in June),[36] but his father had forestalled the attempts of Croft and Price to win for the king and the nine worthies.

A second occasion when Scudamore's motivation is perhaps surprising to historians, as it was to contemporaries, was his failure to act in the execution of the commission of array in July 1642. Scudamore was listed as one of the three members of the quorum of the commission issued in the summer of 1642, along with Prince Charles (probably as prince of Wales) and Wallop Brabazon. Since there was a feeling that the commission should be executed by a nobleman (and Scudamore was the only peer with a residence in

Herefordshire), the viscount's action was clearly expected by the king and other royalists.[37] They were to be disappointed in Herefordshire, as in so many other counties.

The commission had arrived in Herefordshire by the beginning of July, and a grand, set-piece muster was planned for Hereford on the 14th; the warrants to the constables summoning the trained soldiers of every township were sent out on the 8th.[38] On the morning of 14 July the commission was read aloud under the town hall (being in Latin, it was alleged, few understood it). The trained bands were then reviewed outside the city. James Barroll, a former mayor, led 150 volunteers out of the city crying, 'God save the Kinge,' 'for the Kinge for the Kinge' and 'God-bless the 9 wortheys of Hereford-sheire.' A letter from the king was read welcoming the county's loyalty and appointing Robert Croft, a younger brother of Sir William, to command whatever horse the county sent to York; Coningsby had already raised 100 volunteers. The *Declaration* was acclaimed by all. The day ended with the volunteer band re-entering the city, their hats held high on their sticks (few had any arms) in a great acclamation for the king.[39]

In almost all respects the day was a great triumph. The muster at Hereford was a visible demonstration of the power and extent of active support for the king and an intimidation of anyone else: many had cried that they would have torn Sir Robert Harley in pieces had he been present. The trained bands had been secured for the king. The parliament's rival militia ordinance remained a dead letter in the county. The foot bands of captains John Scudamore of Ballingham, George Slaughter and Richard Wigmore all appeared 'very fully'. Even Harley's own foot band put in a show: fifty or sixty of the soldiers appeared, along with two of the officers. Harley was deposed as its captain and the band was given to Coningsby. With Viscount Scudamore's county troop of horse, however, the story was very different. Only about thirty of the ninety-two horse appeared, and 'few or none' of the officers. The viscount stayed away.

Scudamore's absence perplexed contemporaries. He did not return to Herefordshire until 2 September, when Brilliana announced to her husband that 'my Lord Scidamore is Come downe'.[40] The following year, when Coningsby prepared his defence of his own actions for the royalist court of war, he railed against Scudamore's inactivity in the summer of 1642, on which he blamed many of the subsequent problems of the royalist war effort in the area.[41]

> I vnderstood my selfe diligent in his Majesties Service, in the Execucion of the said Comission, the effect whereof might have beene as Conspicuouse in that County as in any of this Nation, if the Coldnes and slow apparance of the Lord Scudamore had not damped the Countreys zeale, he being the Prince in Quality of that Countrey, and regardfully lookt vpon by reason of his former State Employment and of the Quorum in that Comission, elevated or depressed the people according to his

accesse or recesse, to or from that soe Concernable affaire. His Lordshipps secret likeing, had noe such influence on them, as his too apparent Absence, they who know his face, if he had beene in presence Countenanceing the Action, not knowing his Meaneing, and thinkeing it neyther wise nor safe, to be Overt in that, in which soe late a minister of State, and so interessed in his Majesties Service, walked so obscurely.

Scudamore, who had so skilfully manipulated his image in the 1620s and early 1630s, had lost his touch.

Why did Scudamore walk so obscurely? One possible answer, that he was a moderate, has a long and respectable pedigree dating back to the nineteenth century, but it must be dismissed. The nineteenth-century historian John Webb saw Scudamore as a 'a quiet, but it may be believed, not an unconcerned observer of what was going on around him', yet still a county leader who 'conducted himself with that dignified moderation that became his wisdom and experience' and who 'won for him the respect of persons whose principles were opposed to his own'. Webb assumed that Scudamore, 'respected by all', was 'probably in daily intercourse with members of both Houses'. There is no evidence whatsoever for Webb's assumptions. Like so many others who have studied the Scudamores, Webb's account is a mixture of hagiography and back-projection of the attributes the author values most highly himself. Webb's picture of Scudamore as a respected moderate befitted a historian who believed that all the royalists, and especially the Scudamores, exhibited the most noble virtues of loyalty and devotion, but it cannot be allowed to stand.[42]

Ronald Hutton and Jacqueline Eales have both, more recently, described Scudamore as a moderate, yet the evidence they produce does not stand up to close scrutiny. Hutton thinks that Scudamore showed a pronounced mildness to parliamentarians. His one example is that of Thomas Hitchman, one of Sir Samuel Luke's scouts, who was imprisoned as a spy in royalist Oxford but whose release was procured by Scudamore. Thomas Hitchman the parliamentarian scout who was able to visit Hereford unsuspected as Waller drew near must be none other than Thomas Hitchman the servant of Scudamore who had accompanied the viscount to Paris and relative of the viscount's trusted and loyal servant Edward Hitchman. In procuring Thomas's release Scudamore was guilty, not of moderation, but of good lordship, and perhaps naivety, showing how, in the early stages of the fighting, pre-war social bonds could cut across more recently formed allegiances.[43]

To Jacqueline Eales the viscount 'was at best a moderate Royalist' who was 'very lukewarm in his commitment to the king', and she cites two pieces of evidence in support of her view. First is a letter from Scudamore to Sir Robert Pye in May 1643, in which he excused his involvement in the defence of Hereford as unavoidable and a case where 'I knew not how in honor to run away'.[44] But the letter was drafted while Scudamore was held a prisoner by the parliament and feared vengeance on himself, his wife and his estates, so it is hardly surprising that he tried to diminish his support for the king. Moreover, the letter was never sent. Scudamore completely redrafted his plea and the letter he sent to Pye made no such excuses for his royalism.[45] Dr Eales's second piece of evidence is an appeal Brilliana Harley made to Lord Scudamore on 27 December 1642 for the release of some of her servants imprisoned in Hereford on the grounds that they were parliamentarian agents. The letter itself was a model of studied disingenuity and restraint, and a rhetorical appeal to pre-war ideals of charity, kinship and the country. In Dr Eales's view it was evidence that Brilliana 'was shrewd enough to know that Scudamore was a moderate, who might be more sympathetic to her plight than the more committed Royalists in the county'. In contrast, I would say that the letter shows Harley playing with images and rhetorics to construct an ideal image to suit the moment in exactly the same way that we have seen Scudamore and others engaging in this creative bricolage.[46] Brilliana did not see Scudamore as a moderate. She sent a similar letter to both Croft and Coningsby (whom no one has ever thought to portray as anything other than committed royalists), and as she candidly admitted to her husband about all three, 'I can not say that any one of them showes me a Comon kindines.' Moreover, she did not include Scudamore on her list of moderate royalists in August 1642.[47] In whatever way we may analyse Scudamore's royalism, he was not a moderate.

Nor can we portray Scudamore as a neutral in the summer of 1642, reluctantly forced into royalism by the autumn. A few years later, reflecting on whether to take the solemn league and covenant, he ruled out neutralism as a political stance:

> Wee shall not shew ourselues indifferent or neutrall when wee shall bee required to any action which our duty expects from us and the conscience of the lawfullness and necessitie therof shall iustifie us in performance (in our places and callings).

Scudamore's calling was as a local governor, 'a Prince in Quality of that Countrey', in Coningsby's words. By nature Scudamore was cautious, even timid; he was not acting out of character in 1642. His two closest patrons during his embassy were Laud and Windebank: one was in the Tower, the other in hiding in France. He was timid, but he was not a neutral.[48]

Furthermore, in the summer of 1642 Scudamore was preparing for armed conflict. His accounts show that expenditure on arms and armour was a continuing charge, so that it is difficult to separate regular maintenance from preparations for war. In April 1642 his steward Thomas Manfeild went to Llanthony to view the armour there, and on 5 May it was brought to Holme Lacy. From 23 June 'Armes and Ammunition' are for the first time allotted their own section in the account books; by 28 September, the end of the accounting year, £52 16s. 3d. had been spent. These were preparations for war: money was spent on lead, armourers, saddlers, bandoleers, coats of mail, and on four barrels of powder brought from Bristol and Gloucester to Holme Lacy.[49] As soon as the viscount had been captured in April 1643 his wife Elizabeth produced a deed dated 20 June 1642 by which he claimed to have made over most of his estate to four trustees for ninety-nine years. Such trusts were common royalist devices to try to evade the worst consequences of sequestration and composition. It seems unlikely that it was a later forgery, however. If it was fraudulent, it was remarkably incompetent, for why date it so late? The Commons resolved that any contractual changes on delinquents' estates made after 20 May 1642, the day it resolved that the king intended to wage war against the parliament, were invalid. The deed suggests that Scudamore, however reluctantly or eagerly, had realised by the middle of June 1642 that he would soon be involved in armed conflict on the king's side.[50]

It is hard to know what the most important spring of Scudamore's royalism was. Defence of the church was clearly a key ingredient, as he had shown in January 1642, but it should not be overplayed. The church to which Scudamore was committed, the church of Laud and Wren, of ceremonies and cathedrals, had been repudiated by Charles. It is possible that Scudamore shared with Laud and Charles a view of the dangers of a populist, puritan plot. He had translated into French Laud's speech at the trial of Bastwick, Burton and Prynne, a classic exposition of the conspiracy theory that the puritans 'have no other purpose, than to stirre up sedition among the people', and he defended it at the French court, but, as we shall see, his view of politics, especially popular political participation in elections, was far from Charles's fear of popularity.[51]

Defence of the ancient constitution, the king-in-parliament, may have been important for Scudamore as it was for some of the other royalist leaders in Herefordshire, but he had shown in the 1620s and 1630s, in his work in businesses such as privy seals, the forced loan, knighthood fines and the collection for St Paul's, a view of the constitution which seemed to allow for prerogative taxation quite different from that envisaged in the king's moderate propaganda of 1642. Scudamore had, in the Commons in 1628, briefly outlined a vision of the working of the English constitution which stressed the subject's duty of aiding the king above that of the king's duty to his subjects. His speech in 1628 had a particular purpose, to move the granting of subsidies and deflect the Commons from its attacks on the duke of Buckingham, but its sentiments were as applicable in 1642 as they were in 1628.

> The question is what is to be done that is most wise. The church and common-wealth are now in apparent danger. Necessity is the cause of our calamities. Let us remove this necessity. There are two causes of this: war abroad and misunderstandings at home. Will you have your liberties secured? Remove this necessity; labor to bring

the King in love with parliaments ... The King is tied to ease the subject of his grievances, and the subject is tied to relieve the King in his necessity. Let us conjoin our hearts and purses to serve the King.

Two other diarists' versions of the same speech ended with Scudamore saying of the duties of subject and king to aid one another, 'Let the subject begin first,' or 'Let us perform our duty to our sovereign so we may expect right from him.'[52] In the summer of 1642 Scudamore's duty to his sovereign was to support him against the parliament, and at some point before the autumn of 1643 (and probably in the summer of 1642) Scudamore sent the king £225.[53]

Scudamore's speeches in 1628 may, I think, be taken as representative of his beliefs, and not merely designed to protect the duke. If I am right, then Scudamore's view laid great emphasis in the role and person of the king. In his notes on the covenant, for example, the example of the king was a persuasive argument, as it had been in his reasons to induce the taxpayers of Herefordshire to contribute to St Paul's.[54] He was unpersuaded by the parliament's arguments that sovereignty could be divided between the king and the parliament. Considering England, Scotland and the covenant, he wrote, 'The peace of these two Kingdomes, hath been by vnion vnder one King. That bond being taken away, and the Soueraingty placed in divided bodies wee may not long rest secure of that happines'.[55]

The stress on the king may have been the most important strand of Scudamore's royalism in three further ways: trust, the supreme governorship, and personal loyalty. First, Charles was a man who could be trusted. Scudamore had said in 1628, 'let us trust him that God has trusted with us', and there is no sign in any of the records that he had any doubts about the king (though such negative evidence has to be treated very cautiously).[56] The issue of whether the king could be trusted was at the heart of political debate at the outbreak of the civil war.[57] Another of Scudamore's speeches in the Commons fourteen years earlier, this time on the petition of right, had resonances in 1642:

Behold, our Sovereign is ready to declare our liberties, our goods, and persons; that he will govern us by his laws, whereby we claim our rights. Besides, we have his word that we shall not have cause hereafter to complain ... I see not how I can answer my country that we refused to supply the King. And to end, in this parliament we have gained ground ... Why should we not be contented with the King's promise?[58]

The second way that the person of the king was important was in the monarch's role as supreme governor. Discoursing on the covenant, Scudamore wrote, 'That which the King forbids is unlawfull because hee the supreme gouernour.' Scudamore may have limited his thoughts to the church, but other royalist propaganda suggests that the moral force of the supreme governorship extended beyond the ecclesiastical settlement. Sir Francis Wortley wrote that one of the hallmarks of the true Cavalier was that he 'conceives the King to be the Head of the Church, as it is personall, not spirituall, and hath sworne him God's Deputy in Government'. When Sir Charles Dallison explained the reasons underpinning his royalism, he 'resolved the Laws of England ought to be my guide': England was governed by a known law expounded by the judges, 'Those Judges appointed and authorised by the King our only Supreme Governor, unto whom alone all the people of England are obliged ... to submit themselves'.[59]

The third and final way in which the king may have been important to Scudamore's royalism was the issue of the personal obligation and commitment owed to the king, which a number of historians have stressed as lying at the heart of royalism. In Dr Newman's view 'the idea of service' more clearly conveyed the thinking of the royalists than any other.[60] Scudamore had kissed his king's hand on quitting his service as ambassador and, more important, as ambassador had been Charles's personal representative, the embodiment of his wishes. As we have seen, his image in the 1620s was grounded in the rhetoric of loyal and effective service to the king.[61] Arguments such as these were not lightly to be traduced. Sir Edward Verney found the arguments that he had eaten the king's bread and served him nearly thirty years unanswerable.[62] Nevertheless, it was pointed out at the time how few of the king's servants became royalists, and historians have noted that many of the king's leading courtiers and councillors were parliamentarians in 1642–43, as if too much service to Charles, or seeing too much of the king, warts and all, undermined the ties of personal loyalty.[63] In Scudamore's case, however, this was clearly not the case. The most famous statement of the ties of personal loyalty to the king came not from 1642 but three years earlier; on leaving to join Charles's army in the bishops' wars Sir Bevil Grenville wrote that he could not 'contain himself within my doors when the King of England's standard waves in the field'.[64] In 1642 Charles set up his standard on 22 August; eleven days later Scudamore had returned to Herefordshire to take up a leading role in the king's cause.

Scudamore's royalism was founded on principle – loyalty to the king, defence of his view of the constitution, defence of the church – but there was one further element – self-interest. We have already seen that his intervention in the bye-election in Hereford in the spring of 1642 was designed in part to bolster his position in the city. The timing of his return to the county in September may have been influenced also by a desire to maintain his authority within the structures of local government. On 18 August 1642 the king's appointment of Fitzwilliam Coningsby as high sheriff of the county (replacing the equivocating Isaac Seward, who had attempted to obey both king and parliament) was certified to the commissioners of array; two weeks later Scudamore was back in the county.[65]

In order to understand why Coningsby's appointment as sheriff may be seen as threatening to Scudamore, we need to return to the late sixteenth century, when Herefordshire was racked by a struggle for supremacy between the Crofts (and their allies the Holme Lacy Scudamores) and the Coningsbys. The animosities had died down by the 1620s as the leadership of each house passed to a new generation.[66] Sir Herbert Croft had fled abroad in 1617, leaving his son Sir William as his heir, but Sir William spent part of the 1620s abroad and did not play a leading role in the county until the later 1630s. Moreover, he had links with Viscount Scudamore through the Danvers family and seems to have co-operated with Scudamore rather than threatened his position. In early April 1642 rumour named Robert Whitney as the viscount's candidate in the Hereford bye-election, with Croft his manager in the city.[67] Sir Thomas Coningsby died in 1625. The career of his eldest surviving son Fitzwilliam had not, before 1640, lived up to its early promise. He was junior knight of the shire in 1621, in which service, a friend remarked, 'you haue ... taken exceedinge payens for the good of your countrey, and therby gayned yourself the intire and harty love of all honest herefsheer men', but he was not elected again until 1640. Some of his problems were of his own making. Everything he touched turned to dust: the project to navigate the river Wye; the soap monopoly; his own estates. His father commented on Fitzwilliam's 'owne facilitie to intangle himselfe to all our detriments'. He was forever heavily in debt, and one of his creditors called him 'powerful and dilatory'. His grandson called him a 'man of great extravagance and expense, as well as beyond description negligent in the management of his affairs'.[68] In the early 1640s, however, Fitzwilliam's star was rising. He was elected to the Long Parliament as junior knight of the shire, and although disabled as a monopolist, his son Humphrey succeeded to the seat. In 1642 he emerged as one of the leading royalists, and in the summer he concentrated power in his hands. He raised volunteers and money for the king. He was made a captain in the trained bands, with his son as his lieutenant. The king appointed him a commissioner of array and then, in August, sheriff.[69]

In the summer of 1642, and in the absence of Lord Scudamore, Coningsby's rise did not disturb the ranks of the royalists because it was matched by the growth of Sir William Croft's power. In September Brilliana described Coningsby as 'the Instrument' and Croft 'the Contriuer' of royalist plans. Moreover, one of the first things the commissioners of array did was to bind themselves to co-operate in the service of the king: Coningsby, Croft and Scudamore of Ballingham all buried the hatchet, laying aside private quarrels in the interest of the king's service. Brilliana reported that 'all thoes Commissioners haue tiyed themselfes on to another by a deepe protestation that what the on does the other will doo, so Sir William Croft whoo once did not loue Mr Cunnisbe nor Mr Scidmore is now theire mighty frinde'.[70] Viscount Scudamore, however, was not in the county and did not take this protestation, so he did not feel himself bound to Coningsby. His struggle to wrest power from Coningsby was to take three months, and to prove disastrous for the royalist cause in Hereford, and even more so for his own position.

In September 1642, before Scudamore could move against his rival, fate struck a blow against all the royalists. The armies of the king and the earl of Essex shadowed one another across Midlands in September 1642, each seeking the advantage but shying away from a pitched battle. Since August the commissioners of array had been busy in Herefordshire raising men and money for the king, levying a rate on Hereford to buy armour and weapons, strengthening the city's defences, and training the militia.[71] Commissioners of array could secure the trained bands for the king, but they were an ineffective means of raising an army. Dr Hutton has emphasised that the armies which fought for the king were created not by the commissions of array but by commissions given to individuals as colonels; troops had been raised in Herefordshire by at least one such royalist colonel, but they had then been marched out of the county to join the king.[72] When Essex marched towards Worcester (he occupied the city on 24 September 1642), many people in Hereford panicked and fled.[73] Scudamore was in Hereford on 28 September, where he entertained the whole of the common council to dinner. The mayor was making preparations to defend the city against a siege, but Scudamore's advice was probably flight. He left for Llanthony later that same day and sent his valuable horses into hiding in Wales.[74] Two days later the earl of Stamford and a column of troops detached from Essex's army at Worcester took Hereford without a fight, and garrisoned the city for the parliament. Stamford's rule in Hereford was to last until mid December.[75]

Once again, Scudamore's actions are puzzling. Not his flight, for that was understandable. None of the commissioners of array gave a lead in defence of the county. Most left to join the king (John Scudamore of Ballingham, Henry Lingen, Thomas Price, Sir Walter Pye and Sir William Croft), while Fitz-william Coningsby joined the marquis of Hertford in Wales.[76] What looks odd is the evidence from Scudamore's account books that he went to Llanthony, only yards beyond the walls of parliamentarian Gloucester, and stayed there until at least 25 November. His servants at Holme Lacy sent money 'to your Lordship at Lanthonie' on 2, 3, 17 and 25 November 1642.[77] Gloucester had a radical tradition which was converted to parliamentarianism. Troops were raised for the parliament in August 1642; the militia ordinance was executed the following month and the deputy lieutenants began meeting weekly in the city. By 10 November Gloucester was securely under the parliament's control under its governor, Colonel Thomas Essex.[78] There are three possibilities for Scudamore's action. The first is that he left his wife in Llanthony and then fled elsewhere, but kept his servants in the dark about his true movements, perhaps out of fear that they would reveal his location to the parliament's forces. This seems unlikely, for the continued traffic between Holme Lacy and Llanthony would surely have meant that any secret that his lordship was not, after all, at Llanthony would have been impossible to keep.[79] The second possibility is that Scudamore felt that his two houses at Llanthony were in greater danger of plunder than Holme Lacy, and his presence might afford them some protection. Holme Lacy was indeed visited by Stamford's troops, but there is no record of any loss or plunder beyond a few fish and some arms.[80] Llanthony did not suffer until Christmas 1642, by which time the viscount was back in Hereford, but when it was plundered, it suffered indeed.[81] The third, and perhaps most likely, possibility is that Scudamore felt safer in a county where he had no formal role in government or the royalist administration. The radicalism of the city of Gloucester has tended to blind historians to the royalism of the county's gentry. Corbet praised the city for its adherence to the parliament but contrasted and criticised the county gentry for their 'inclinations to the contrary Faction'. Until Christmas 1642 the hold of the parliamentarian deputy lieutenants over the county was weak, and royalists were able to meet at Over, less than two miles to the west of Gloucester. As late as 22 December 1642 one of Scudamore's servants was able to travel, unhindered, from Holme Lacy to Llanthony and return with a box of pistols.[82] Moreover, Scudamore had friends in Gloucester.[83] Stamford's rule in Hereford, by contrast, was harsher to people, if not to property: he sent out raiding parties and imprisoned delinquents.[84] Until Stamford quit Hereford, Scudamore was probably safer lying low at Llanthony.

Stamford, increasingly isolated in Hereford, retreated to Gloucester on 11 December 1642, and the royalists reoccupied the city five hours later.[85] They spent the next month rebuilding their control of the city and county, raising money for the king (a monthly contribution of £3,000 was agreed upon in January), harassing their opponents and sequestering their estates, planning to besiege the Harleys' castle at Brampton Bryan, which Brilliana Harley had turned into a parliamentarian garrison, and securing the grand jury's support for the king.[86] Their success in all but the capture of Brampton Bryan (which held out until April 1644) can be seen in the letters of Brilliana Harley.[87]

There is, however, another story to be told of the months from December 1642 to April 1643, one that stresses not the struggle between royalist and parliamentarian in the county, but the contest for supremacy within the royalist command in Hereford. The four months from the royalist recapture of Hereford saw a bitter and ultimately crippling struggle between Fitzwilliam Coningsby and Viscount Scudamore for leadership in Hereford.

Scudamore had three power bases: his status as the leading commissioner of array, confirmed when the commission was remodelled early in January

1643; his position within Hereford as high steward and member of the common council;[88] and he had friends at the royalist headquarters in Oxford, firends who were never named in the sources but who probably included the secretary, Sir Edward Nicholas, to whom he had professed his love in 1629.[89] Coningsby's power was fourfold. He was a commissioner of array. He had been named sheriff by the king in August 1642. In December he was made governor of the city and commissioned as a colonel to raise a foot regiment. According to Coningsby it was the power that these positions gave him which lay at the root of the quarrel, for 'The Lord Scudamore look't with an euill Eye vpon these powers vnited in me'.[90] Coningsby's powers were, on paper, the greater, but he had two disadvantages compared with Scudamore. First, he could not command the support at Oxford that the viscount had. When, for example, Coningsby wrote to Lord Falkland the letter went unanswered. Second, Coningsby's power in Hereford was contingent only on his position as governor, granted to him by the simple accident that he was the first local royalist to return to the city after Stamford's retreat. Coningsby's ties were with Leominster, not Hereford, and he could not command the support of the Hereford corporation in the way that Scudamore could.[91] Third, it seems likely that the powers united in Coningsby as sheriff and governor were sufficiently great to exacerbate tensions between soldiers and citizens in general, and not just between him and Scudamore. Such seems to have been the judgement in Oxford, anyway, for in the summer of 1643 the governorship and shrievalty were separated: Henry Lingen was made sheriff and an outsider, Sir William Vavasour, made colonel-general. When the two positions of sheriff and governor were once more united in 1644, in the person of Barnaby Scudamore, the viscount's brother, tension between the garrison and the countryfolk exploded in a rising of Clubmen.[92] Lord Scudamore's powers as high steward were settled and known powers, unlike those of Coningsby as governor, and perhaps, therefore, more likely to command the respect of the citizens. They were not, however, such powers as to enable Scudamore effectively to organise the defence of a town during civil war, as was to be shown in April 1643. 'And hence was the spring head,' wrote Coningsby, 'of all the Envie that produced, Thwartings and disturbances to the weakening his Majesties Service, and Ruining our Countrey.'[93]

On 8 January 1643 Charles commanded the Herefordshire justices to assist Coningsby in raising and arming a regiment to defend the county. Scudamore immediately raised objections to the power this would give Coningsby: he did not want Coningsby's troops paid out of the county's monthly contribution. He tried to undermine local support for the regiment by suggesting that, like earlier bodies of troops, it might be ordered out of the county to join the king.[94] If he could triumph in his claim that the commissioners of array could and should secure the county without resorting to Coningsby's dual commission as governor and colonel, he could assert his power over that of Coningsby.

In order to stop what Coningsby called these 'jealousies tending to the Ruine of my Regiment', Coningsby procured further letters from Charles, promising that the king had no intention of withdrawing the regiment from the county and requiring the raising of money to maintain Coningsby's troops. So armed, on 28 January 1643 Coningsby mustered his 685 soldiers, along with their officers, before Edward Somerset, Lord Herbert, whom the marquis of Hertford had appointed as commander in south Wales and the southern marches. Scudamore was undeterred. He continued his opposition by 'fomenting Jealousies and passages of dislike', none of which can have helped in the execution of Coningsby's other orders to besiege Brampton Bryan Castle. The attack was stillborn, and though it was not Scudamore's fault the viscount's whisper campaign produced an ugly confrontation with Coningsby's lieutenant-colonel, Richard Wigmore.[95]

Entwined in the power struggle between Coningsby and Scudamore was a secondary dispute about the cost of the royalist forces. Coningsby was almost certainly attempting to defraud the county of money, claiming £1,643 3s. 6d. a month in pay for his regiment of 685 men plus their officers; by comparison Edward Harley reckoned to pay his parliamentarian regiment of 1,200 foot and their officers only £1,312 a month. Sir William Russell, royalist governor of Worcester, was also accused by some of the commissioners of array of irregularities concerning the excessive payment of soldiers.[96] In addition to detecting Coningsby's attempted fraud, Scudamore proposed a further way of reducing the cost of the royalist military establishment. If Coningsby is to be believed, Scudamore proposed 'hireing men like Covenaunted servants'. Perhaps Scudamore was thinking of a troop similar to the company of his own trained men – his household servants and retainers – that he had commanded in 1627. In 1644, while the viscount languished in captivity, the viscountess leased out the Holme Lacy estates with the proviso that the lessees 'be not retayned, or serve vnder ane person, or persons other then the Kings Majestie, or the said Viscount, and his Heires'.[97] Behind Coningsby's claim we may detect an echo of the viscount's military image two decades earlier, when he refused to pay the muster master and instead offered to train and lead the militia himself.[98] Scudamore may also have been exploiting the king's rhetoric about the commissions of array to aggrandise himself. One of the king's motives behind the issuing of the commissions was a financial one, for they were an economical measure. The king's instructions to his Northampton-shire commissioners, for example, had stressed that the trained bands were not to be assembled permanently, nor to be augmented, in order to allay fears about their expense.[99] Scudamore's proposal played with the duty of the commissioners not to burden the people with extra expense. It also was a means to increase his own power. Its military value was less obvious.

The king had instructed the Herefordshire commissioners to conclude with Lord Herbert 'what summes of money are to be Raysed for the supporting and weekely payment of the forces raised and to be Raysed ther vnder his Commaund' and to pay them over to Herbert or his appointee. Scudamore persuaded the commissioners that these orders should be inter-preted to mean that the whole of the monthly contribution should be delivered to Herbert, forcing Coningsby to arm and pay his regiment at his own expense and from borrowed money. In four months his regiment received only one and a half weeks' pay. The earl of Coningsby later boasted proudly of the regiment which his grandfather 'raised, clothed and armed at his own Expence', but this was making a virtue of Fitzwilliam's necessity.[100]

Not satisfied with the diversion of the monthly contribution alone, Scuda-more went on to insist that no public money whatsoever should pass into Coningsby's control. No doubt he was able to manipulate the image of Coningsby as financially untrustworthy, unable even to manage his own estates. Rather than accede to the governor's demand that the clergy dues, which were separate from the contribution, should be used to fortify Here-ford, the viscount persuaded his fellow commissioners that they should be used to raise another horse troop under his brother-in-law, John Scudamore of Ballingham. Instead, Charles ordered the money to be paid to Colonel Herbert Price of Brecon, who had command in the southern marches and was closely related to the Herefordshire commissioner of array Thomas Price. Viscount Scudamore had been overruled, but his primary purpose of undermining Coningsby was achieved nevertheless.[101]

Scudamore's actions emasculated Coningsby. They also, inadvertently, weakened the royalist war effort in Herefordshire: the city went unfortified, and the only professional troops in the area went unpaid. Scudamore had isolated Coningsby from Herbert, the senior royalist commander in the southern marches who had formerly backed Coningsby and, by granting Herbert the county's monthly contribution, ensured his support for Scudamore.[102] The viscount had yet fully to isolate Coningsby from Charles, however. To this end he travelled to Oxford in February 1643, where he saw his brother-in-law John Scudamore of Ballingham knighted. More important, he procured an order preventing Coningsby from raising further troops on the pretext that there were insufficient arms to supply to them. There may have been some truth in the claim about the lack of weapons, for Scudamore's accounts show that his servants were busy making clubs between December 1642 and April 1643, a sure sign that more sophisticated weapons were in short supply.[103]

One of Coningsby's allies, Lieutenant Colonel Richard Wigmore, was so exasperated with the viscount that he threatened to raise further troops at his own expense and march away with them to the king, leaving the county naked. It was a threat designed to silence opposition but, if Coningsby is to be believed, Scudamore called Wigmore's bluff. Now secure of Herbert's support, Scudamore was alleged to have asked him to allow Wigmore's troops to depart. Coningsby's version of Scudamore's words is worth quoting fully:

> I pray my Lord take Lieutenant-Collonel Wigmore at his word, and we will secure the Contrey; yet were we comanded by hundreds to the Frontiers, neyther suffred to raise our numbers for the Service of the Countrey, nor to serve his Majestie out of it.[104]

Scudamore's words, as reported by Coningsby, were the classic localist and civilian reaction to the demands of the military, betraying jealousies and rivalries between soldiers and civilians that were to bedevil the royalists later, but which were present from the start of the war. Such sentiments were widespread. The English civil war may be remarkable for the extent to which local susceptibilities were overcome or local concerns welded together to establish a national struggle, but there were many incidents when local forces refused to move out of their locality: Cornish royalists refused to cross into Devon; Stockport parliamentarians declined to come to the defence of Manchester; the Radnorshire trained bands refused to leave their county to attack Brampton Bryan.[105] Nevertheless, Coningsby's version of Scudamore's words does not ring true. The commission of array did not merely command the militia to defend the county borders; its great advantage was, as had been pointed out in Hampden's ship money case in 1638, that by it the king could order the militia out of the county, a power lacking under the lieutenancy.[106] Moreover, Scudamore had no objection to the removal of Coningsby's troops from the county to either Oxford or Monmouth, and he co-operated with Lord Herbert, whose command spanned several counties. Coningsby's version of the viscount's interpretation of the commission of array is strikingly similar to the statements and actions of some of the neutralist pacts of 1642.[107] It looks as if Coningsby, in his defence designed for the royalist high command in Oxford, was trying to manipulate images and rhetorics in order to undermine the credit of the viscount with the king and to portray him as a neutral in royalist's clothing. The attempt failed, for Scudamore remained trusted by the king even while he was imprisoned by the parliament, and continued to be named to royalist commissions.[108]

It was not Scudamore, but Herbert, who dealt the final blow against Coningsby. Herbert drew off 400 of Coningsby's men, and all his arms, to the siege of Gloucester. All were lost when Sir William Waller surprised the royalists at Highnam on 25 March 1643.[109] Coningsby lost his regiment and his last supporter, Richard Wigmore, who was captured. Herbert lost his nerve: his family prepared to take ship, and he ceased to be an effective leader.[110] Coningsby was left with no arms, no money and few men, 'rather like a Constables watch then a Garrison'. Defeated by his own side, he resolved to quit, but his letter of resignation sent to Oxford went unanswered.[111]

Waller was pursued westwards by Prince Maurice, who sent Sir Richard Cave to Hereford as his temporary commander-in-chief in Herefordshire, Monmouthshire and Glamorganshire. Cave sized up the situation in Hereford and sided with Scudamore, recognising where the real power lay. Cave and Scudamore became 'most inward' with one another; Coningsby was excluded. Scudamore did not complain when Cave removed the companies of Coningsby and Colonel Herbert Price to Monmouth. They soon returned, but Coningsby had lost further troops, and was down to only eighty men.[112]

The debacle at Highnam had dealt a crippling blow to royalist morale. On 18 April a muster was held at Hereford before Lord Herbert. The following morning perhaps 150 of his own men deserted. Three days later the as yet undefeated parliamentary commander Sir William Waller, 'William the Conqueror', the terror of the Welsh, advanced out of Gloucester. Immediately Herbert fled. That same day Maurice, unaware of recent events in the area, recalled Cave.[113] Cave was, however, persuaded to stay by Scudamore, Croft, Pye and Herbert Price. Coningsby was not party to the decision. The decision-making process was symptomatic of the exclusion of the city's governor from the government of the city.[114] It was also typical of the confused nature of the royalist command in Hereford and the whole of the southern marches, which was racked with problems. The marquis of Hertford, Charles's supreme commander in the area, and Lord Herbert, his deputy, quarrelled openly and bitterly. Herbert had problems with his subordinates, some of whom baulked at following a Catholic commander.[115] In Hereford itself it was an open question who exercised overall command. On this point turned most of the later proceedings in Cave's trial before the court of war. When asked 'who had the Comand in Chiefe of the Towne', Colonel Herbert Price, one of the senior royalist officers in Hereford in April 1643, had to admit that 'hee doeth not knowe'.[116] The accounts of all the protagonists are full of examples of orders refused, commanders bickering with one another, and decisions taken by small cliques, particularly Cave and Scudamore.[117] Ann Hughes has argued that, whereas local in-fighting could be harnessed by the parliament and work to its ultimate advantage, such local disputes tended to have a negative and destructive effect on the royalist cause: the case of Herefordshire in 1642–43 is a clear example of the latter proposition.[118]

On the news of Waller's advance, belated efforts were made to fortify Hereford, left without complete earthworks thanks to Scudamore's machinations. The mayor was summoned and the common bell rung, 'the strictest summons that can be given to the cittizens, and upon which they are bound by oath to appear'. The call had failed when Stamford had attacked, and with the extinction of the governor's authority by Scudamore, it failed again: 'very few or none' of the citizens appeared. Proclamation was made that all should appear as pioneers 'vnder paine of present plund'ring and the vtmost Perill that can be incurred and instantly inflicted vpon them', but so few showed themselves that only one earthwork was begun, which reached no more than knee high. The city was also chronically short of powder. Scudamore's examination of the mayor, magistrates and the comptroller of the magazine could not add to the mere five barrels in the magazine.[119] The mayor, William Price, suspected by the royalists but allowed to continue in office, later claimed that he had hidden six or seven barrels of gunpowder, but the claim was made in 1646 to impress the new parliamentarian rulers of the city.[120] The arms and munitions of the city had all been lost at Highnam. On Sunday 23 April the council of war appealed to Worcester for assistance, but no help was forthcoming. Hereford was alone. Morale was low. Jealousies between local troops and professional soldiers were rampant. Cave valued his veterans above the raw and untested trained bands, and ordered the fresh horses of the county troop to be shared out among his own eighty cavalry and 100 dragoons. Disheartened, the county troop refused to muster when so ordered on the night of Monday 24th. As Cave's closest adviser, civilian leader of the local royalists, high steward of the city and former captain of the county horse, these were rivalries and jealousies that Scudamore should have prevented. Morale among the foot was no better. Cave estimated that there were between 700 and 800 foot in Hereford, but they were raw, undisciplined, unled and demoralised. On the night of Monday 24th they deserted their posts and returned to their lodgings. The city was 'Plundred, disarmed, vnmagazin'd, destitute of all helps, much awed by the vicinity of a powerfull Enemy, and the unrepairable wants for its defence, from no place, nor for any price to be supplied'.[121]

The opportunities to stop Waller and his 2,500 troops as they advanced on Hereford were thus lost. He reached the city in the early morning of Tuesday 25 April, blew in Widemarsh gate on the north side of the city, and captured St Owen's church, just to the east of the city, from which he could scour the walls.[122] Waller had no troops to the south of the city on the right bank of the Wye, but Cave and Scudamore considered Hereford lost. The veteran horse and dragoons were sent away at noon to save them for the king. Scudamore's first reaction was flight, just as it had been in the autumn when Stamford had advanced. The viscount's general attitude of easy submission sat uneasily with the military image he had deployed in the 1620s. Then he had declared that he would rather die than live under Spanish tyranny; now he would rather flee than fight against parliamentary tyranny.[123] He was, however, persuaded to stay and call a parley. In a moment of supreme disgrace and dishonour, Scudamore's handkerchief was held out as a flag of truce; it was exposed to the contempt of the besiegers, and 'one of the rebells turn'd his back, and in scorne clap't his hand on his Breech, and a Musquett was shot at the Captain of the watch'.[124] The easy capitulation of Scudamore and the other royalists meant that Hereford became a laughing stock. The following month, when Waller summoned Worcester, it was reported that Waller was rebuked by Colonel Sandys 'that he was not now at Hereford, and bad him be gone'. At Oxford they suspected treachery in the surrender at Hereford, and held a court of war to investigate the matter.[125] In the image of the viscount's white hand-kerchief and the besieger's obscene gesture we have an eloquent judgement on Scudamore's short career as a royalist.

While the negotiations continued the foot slipped over the Wye to safety. Only the royalist officers and commissioners remained, a sacrifice to prevent the sacking and firing of the city. The royalist leaders surrendered Hereford and themselves in return for quarter for the remaining soldiers and officers, 'civill' or 'honourable vsuage', and freedom from plunder for the citizens and clergy.[126] For the loss of one man, with three or four injured, Waller had captured almost the entire royalist administration of the county. Scudamore, the officers and the other commissioners were confined to their lodgings. There Waller visited Scudamore, as the viscount later explained:

> hee desir'd mee to consider him as the Centurions seruant who was to doe as hee was comaunded, that he was governd by instructions, and according unto them was to intreat mee to apply my self with what conuenience I might to goe to London to the Parliament. The answere I made him was, that I should bee ready to obey his comaundments.[127]

Cave escaped to Oxford. Fitzwilliam and Humphrey Coningsby, Croft, Pye, Herbert Price, Thomas Price and others were imprisoned, first at Gloucester and then at Bristol.[128]

Waller lacked the troops to secure Hereford and retreated within a fortnight, stripping the city and county of whatever wealth he could lay his hands on – at least £600 from Hereford and more from elsewhere. When his soldiers came to Holme Lacy they were given £10 15s., euphemistically des-cribed as 'Gifts' in the steward's accounts.[129] Waller, who had been short of money at the beginning of the month, had been on no more than a smash-and-grab raid, but he brought about the complete reorganisation of the royalist administration in the southern marches.[130] Most of the royalist leadership returned to Herefordshire in June 1643, but the structures of command were quickly reshaped. The Herefordshire commission of the peace was remodelled, a new sheriff was appointed, the commissions of array were supplemented by commissions of safeguard in Herefordshire, Monmouthshire, Breconshire and Radnorshire, and Sir William Vavasour, an experienced soldier, was made colonel-general in the same four counties.[131]

The only local royalist leader not to return was Viscount Scudamore. Having given the word of a gentleman to Waller that he would surrender himself before the parliament, he had, for once, not tried to escape but meekly went up to London offering to treat of a ransom for his liberty.[132] Scudamore sought to use his friend Sir Robert Pye, MP (1584–1662), as an intermediary with the House of Commons, and in his letter to Pye, and in the quite different draft, he sought to present an image of himself that he hoped would appease the Commons.[133] He described himself as a sufferer and victim. His possessions in Westminster and Gloucestershire had been seized; his houses at Llanthony had been plundered and defaced; his trees had been felled; his rents had been sequestered; his wife was made a hostage for the safety of Brilliana Harley. He described himself as a victim of 'malice' and 'the abuse of the Parliaments' authority, for surely no order had passed for the extreme carriage used against his houses. In both letters he tried to present his own actions as deriving from his own interpretation of the public good and his desire to serve the commonwealth, and not arising out of any malice or hope of private gain. In the draft he described his actions as 'onely such as haue expressed conscientiousnes of duty according to my vnderstand[ing] without bitternes of mind towards persons or sinister designes upon things'. In the letter he sent he continued the same theme, drawing on pre-war types of public service contrasted with private greed:

> And I hope further that when a thorough search shall haue been made of mee it will be found that neither bitternes of mind against persons, nor greedy desire of any worldly thing[134] haue moued mee to or fro in the carriage of my self amidst these dismall distractions and diuine iudgments upon my deare mother England, but that I haue desird and laboured to keep a good conscience according to the best of my understanding, and though it should prooue to be an erring conscience, yet it had been sinne in mee to goe against it being mine.

Moreover, he elaborated in the draft, his sufferings were not proportionate with his deeds, for he disingenuously described himself as 'but a Volunteer' with no command, in Hereford 'casually', only as a 'sworn citizen and Steward of the town', so that he 'knew not how in honor to run away ... when a force appeared before it'. Such an explanation of his royalism was omitted from the letter he sent to Pye. In that he made no mention of his role as a royalist leader, but tried instead to present himself as a citizen of the city, pointing to his service as an MP for Hereford in the 1620s, for by article six of the treaty of surrender of Hereford the citizens of the town were to be saved free from plunder and were granted immunity for any past deeds.[135]

It was an image born of desperation, an attempt to fashion some of the discourses of pre-war political rhetoric about service to the commonwealth and the duties of a citizen to a very different end. It was also an image with which he persisted. When, over three years later, he petitioned to compound for his sequestration he continued to present himself as 'a great Sufferer by long Imprisonment Sequestracion and Destruccion of his Estate', as one who was in Hereford as its high steward and a member of the common council, avoiding the issue of whether he had been in arms.[136] The extent of Scudamore's failure to convince others of the reality of this image can be judged by the reaction of the Commons. He was regarded as a great catch and four senior MPs – John Pym, Sir Robert Harley, Sir Henry Vane and Oliver St John – were appointed to treat with him 'upon his ransome'. Pym and Harley met with him but the Commons rejected the terms they agreed, and Scudamore remained in custody until 20 March 1647, when his composition fine was set at £2,690. The ordinance of his pardon was passed in September 1648.[137]

At the end of 1646 Scudamore described himself as one who 'hath endured much, done little, and been in hold almost from the beginning of this warre'.[138] His short, inglorious career as a royalist contrasted dramatically with that of his only surviving brother, Barnaby (1609–52). Barnaby's situation before 1640 had been the classic paradigm of the younger son in early modern England, left only five small pieces of plate by his father and an estate worth a mere £50 a year by his grandfather. Truly he was described as 'a man of noe fortune'.[139] Though we know nothing of Barnaby's motivation, he had military experience in the Low Countries and the bishops' wars, and he declared himself for the king early on.[140] He was already with Charles on 20 August 1642, two days before the raising of the king's standard at Nottingham, when the royal army unsuccessfully besieged Coventry. Barnaby was seriously wounded in the encounter, shot in the hand and the arm; he was left behind as a prisoner when the royalists retired, and for a time there were fears that his arm would have to be amputated. Barnaby escaped to Shrewsbury and marched to Edge Hill as a sergeant-major in Colonel Thomas Blagge's foot regiment. There he was again wounded.[141] In the spring of 1643 he was serving as sergeant-major to Colonel Henry Hastings, operating in Leicestershire and Staffordshire, and he was at the battle of Hopton Heath in March and the siege of Lichfield in April.[142]

Thereafter, Barnaby disappears from view, resurfacing only a year later in Herefordshire, as major-general to Nicholas Mynne, Vavasour's successor as royalist governor of Hereford.[143] Mynne was killed in August 1644, and on 10 September Barnabas succeeded him as governor. He had the support of his brother's allies on the city corporation, testimony to the great power of Lord Scudamore in Hereford. In December he augmented his power with the shrievalty of Herefordshire and a colonel's commission to raise a foot regiment.[144] He set about restoring the garrison of Hereford and raising men, money and munitions with such vigour that he was at least partly responsible for provoking a rising of Clubmen in Herefordshire in March 1645. Barnaby had no experience of peacetime government. He found the king's commitment to govern by what he called 'the rules of a peacable Government' restrictive and proposed sweeping them away. He was one of those whom John Morrill has characterised as 'royalist hard men' who 'believed in the efficacy of looting to instil obedience or at least acquiescence from the country'.[145] In the summer of 1645 the Scots besieged Hereford for five weeks;[146] Barnaby won numerous accolades for his defence of the town. He was knighted by the king, who may also have intended to ennoble him, for there were stories that his peerage passed the privy seal but progressed no further because Barnaby lacked the money to prosecute the matter. To the royalists Barnaby was 'a vigilant and faithful Commander'; to the inhabitants of Hereford he was 'Caesar's great rival', subduer of the Scots, whom even the Roman emperors had not conquered; to his distant cousins he was 'soe generous and remarkable for his sweetnesse and curtesie'; to the parliamentarian newsbooks he was 'mad Scudamore'; to the anti-royalist author of 'Certain Observations' he was a committer of 'many desperate actions' and a gambling, wenching drunkard and renegade.[147]

The Scots withdrew from outside Hereford in September 1645. Three months later Hereford fell to a surprise attack by Colonel Thomas Morgan and Colonel John Birch, probably assisted by some turncoat officers within the garrison.[148] In an episode strikingly similar to the fall of Hereford in 1643, Barnabas escaped but was suspected of treachery and imprisoned by his own side. Unlike Cave in 1643, however, Barnabas was never tried before a court of war, for the first civil war ended before one could be convened.[149] Barnabas's royalism was not dulled, however. He was briefly active in June 1648 during the second civil war, raising forces for the king before he was captured at Newmarket, and he was arrested as a suspected royalist in the summer of 1651.[150] He died, heavily in debt, in February or March 1652.[151]

There is a strange mixture of symmetry and diversity in the civil war careers of the two Scudamore brothers. The elder had a short and fairly disastrous passage as a royalist leader, while the younger was both more successful and active for longer as an armed partisan of the king. Yet both were associated with separate falls of Hereford to parliamentary armies, and both were tainted with suspicions of perfidy. The viscount was never openly accused of treachery, both his status as a peer and his imprisonment by the parliament no doubt protecting him, but Fitzwilliam Coningsby came close in his own defence, and he clearly laid the blame for the fall of Hereford at the door of Lord Scudamore. Three years later Barnabas was imprisoned on suspicion of betraying Hereford, and one (false) report had him condemned in Oxford and executed for the loss of the city. His case never came to trial, which meant that he was never formally acquitted, and though he published his own *Defence* in vindication of his name, he was never fully able to clear himself of the charge of selling the town to the parliament. Although some doubted not of his integrity and innocence, the author of 'Certain Observations' thought that all Hereford would remain convinced of his guilt 'though he should swear the contrary upon a book'.[152]

The two brothers finally redeemed themselves through two processes. First, the stories of the capture of Hereford in 1643 and 1645 and the roles of John and Barnaby tended to become intermingled and confused, lessening the force of either. In the early eighteenth century, for example, the earl of Coningsby wrote that Hereford was captured in April 1643 'by the Desertion of one Barnaby Scudamore, who was in some Command likewise in the Garrison'; it is not clear whether Coningsby was thinking of Viscount Scudamore in 1643 or Barnaby in 1645. Second, and more important in removing what Barnaby called in 1646 'the blemishing of that honourable Profession of a Soldier ... and the stayning of the Family whereof I am descended', were their later sufferings and conduct. Barnaby continued a zealous royalist until his death. The viscount endured nearly four years' imprisonment 'with great sicknes', two of his houses (at Llanthony) were ruined, two more (Holme Lacy and Petty France) plundered of their household furniture, books and horses. He computed his losses at £19,460.[153] By his conduct in the 1650s too, especially his charity to distressed divines, he won further honour which eliminated any suspicions about his conduct in 1642–43. In November 1660 Sir John Scudamore of Ballingham (1630–84) could commend his uncle Viscount Scudamore 'for the seruice of his Majestie who as I dare say no man has beene more faithfull to his seruice so I am confident hee is as able and as fitt a person to be employed as most are in the Nation'. By 1662 Lord Scudamore's 'secret Loyalty to his Sovereign' during 'the Tyranny of the Protectorian times' was held up approvingly to public approbation.[154] By the early eighteenth century the reassembled image of Lord Scudamore's loyalty was complete, his reputation fully repaired. He was accounted one of the greatest sufferers in the civil wars. Stories were told of how he secretly sent money to the exiled king. To non-jurors he became the model of how to behave under a pretended power, living 'quietly and peaceably at last, under an irresistible Power' but, it was alleged, never entering into 'Obligations against his natural Allegiance': 'These were the Principles and Practices of that noble Lord,' proclaimed Theophilus Downes, a deprived fellow of Balliol. 'They are the same with those of the Non-abjurors at present, and it is not in the Power of Subtility to distinguish them.'[155] Readers may judge for themselves how far the image of Viscount Scudamore as a royalist leader had diverged from the less than happy days of April 1643.

NOTES

1 FSL, Vb 2(27).

2 FSL, Vb 2(22), Vb 3(10), Vb 3(13); PRO, SP20/1, pp. 28, 30, SP19/3, p. 274, SP19/85/5**, fol. 11.

3 PRO, E115/361/99, E115/363/23; BL, Add. MS 11044, fols 49, 193–6, 222r.

4 HCL, L.C. 647.1 'Scudamore MSS: Accounts 1640–42' (disbursements October 1640–September 1641), L.C. 647.1 'Scudamore MSS: Accounts 1641–42' (disbursements September 1641–September 1642), L.C. 647.1 'MSS Scudamore Accounts' (includes disbursements September 1642–September 1643).

5 PRO, C115/M14/7312–14.

6 PRO, SP23/198, pp. 771–2.

7 BL, Add. MSS 70001–523, formerly BL, Loan 29, and especially Add. MSS 70003–4; *LBH*; J. Eales, *Puritans and Roundheads: The Harleys of Brampton Bryan and the Outbreak of the English Civil War* (Cambridge, 1990), chs 5–7.

8 Bodleian, MS Tanner 303, fols 113–25; FSL, Vb 2(4)–(5), Vb 3(1).

9 J. Duncumb, W. H. Cooke *et al.*, *Collections towards the History and Antiquities of the County of Hereford* (6 vols, Hereford, 1804–1915), I, pp. 245–58; *The Annual Register 1805* (London, 1807), pp. [896]–904; *MCW*, I, pp. 274–83; B. Whelan, 'Hereford and the Civil War: Some Original Papers', *Dublin Review*, 179 (1926), pp. 44–72. Because none of the printed versions is perfect I have cited the original manuscripts, but I have added the reference to Webb's more readily available transcription in *MCW* where appropriate.

10 The accounts of Cave, Coningsby and Price are obviously partial and biased; where it has not been possible to corroborate one with another, it has sometimes been necessary to take the views of one without substantiation.

11. P. Seaward, 'Constitutional and Unconstitutional Royalism', *Historical Journal*, 40 (1997), p. 227.

12 J. S. Morrill, *The Revolt of the Provinces: Conservatives and Radicals in the English Civil War, 1630–1650* (London, 1976), pp. 34–42, 139, 162.

13 P. R. Newman, *The Old Service: Royalist Regimental Colonels and the Civil War, 1642–46* (Manchester, 1993), p. 36.

14 Newman, 'The King's Servants: Conscience, Principle, and Sacrifice in Armed Royalism', in J. S. Morrill, P. Slack and D. Woolf, eds, *Public Duty and Private Conscience in Seventeenth-Century England* (Oxford, 1993), p. 230.

15 For the argument of personal loyalty see Newman, 'King's Servants', and Newman, *Old Service*.

16 BL, Add. MSS 70003, fols 195v, 207r, 70004, fols 325r, 327r; Eales, *Puritans*, pp. 109, 129–30, 152.

17 BL, Add. MS 70003, fols 184r, 207r.

18 J. D. Maltby, 'Approaches to the Study of Religious Conformity in late Elizabethan and early Stuart England, with Special Reference to Cheshire and the Diocese of Lincoln' (Cambridge University Ph.D. thesis, 1991), pp. 141–4, 148; T. Aston, *A Collection of*

Svndry Petitions ([London], 1642), pp. 42–3, 69–[71]. I am grateful to the Revd Dr Judith Maltby for guidance on the Herefordshire and Staffordshire petitions.

19   Compare above, pp. 59–80.

20   BL, Add. MS 70003, fols 100r, 226r, 228v–9r; Eales, *Puritans*, p. 100 n. 1.

21   H. Sharpe, *Genealogical History of the Family of Brabazon* (Paris, 1825), pp. xxiv–xxvii; J. Foster, *Collectanea Genealogica Vol. I* (privately printed, 1887), pp. 52–3; BL, Add. MSS 70002, fol. 344r, 70003, fol. 99r, 70086, no. 74, Leominster petition.

22   N. Tyacke, *Anti-Calvinists: The Rise of English Arminianism c. 1590–1640* (Oxford, 1987), p. 219.

23   BL, Add. MS 70003, fols 228–9, 239–40r; also Add. MS 70109, no. 64. Only copies of their letters survive, with one of the signatories named as J. Scudamore. Matthew Gibson and others have been thereby misled into thinking that Viscount Scudamore was one of the nine: Balliol College, Oxford, MS 333, fol. 29r; A. J. Fletcher, *The Outbreak of the English Civil War* (London, 1981), p. 302. It is clear from an examination of the order of signatories, and from the copy of Harley's reply, where J. Scudamore was described as an esquire (BL, Add. MS 70109, no. 64), that this was not the viscount but his brother-in-law John Scudamore of Ballingham. See Atherton, thesis, pp. 271–2.

24   Shropshire RO, 212/364, letters of nine Herefordshire justices to Harley, 5 March and 28 April 1642; Staffordshire RO, D868/2/32; Fletcher, *Outbreak*, pp. 306–7; K. Sharpe, *The Personal Rule of Charles I* (New Haven and London, 1992), p. 717.

25   *A Declaration, or Resolution of the County of Hereford* (London, 1642); *LBH*, p. 182; BL, Harl. MS 163, fol. 26iv.

26   Bodleian, MS Add. c. 132, fols 35–6; Staffordshire RO, D868/2/74; *Commons' Journals*, II, pp. 661, 679; *Lords' Journals*, V, p. 242.

27   Northamptonshire RO, Finch-Hatton MS 133 *sub* Herefordshire; PRO, C115/I26/6511; Atherton, thesis, pp. 271–2.

28   I. J. Atherton, ed., 'An Account of Herefordshire in the First Civil War', *Midland History*, 21 (1996), p. 140; BL, Add. MS 70004, fol. 278v; E. C. Brewer, *Brewer's Dictionary of Phrase and Fable*, ed. I. H. Evans (London, 1977), p. 1167.

29   Atherton, 'First Civil War in Herefordshire', p. 141; *Lords' Journals*, V, p. 242; *LBH*, p. 182.

30   M. F. Keeler, *The Long Parliament, 1640–1641: A Biographical Study of its Members* (Memoirs of the American Philosophical Society, 36, 1954), pp. 381–2; *LBH*, pp. 122, 124 (both wrongly dated 1641).

31   BL, Add. MS 70003, fols 229r, 239r; D. Hirst, *The Representative of the People? Voters and Voting in England under the Early Stuarts* (Cambridge, 1975), p. 185; *LBH*, pp. 124, 154, 156, 162–6, 171.

32   BL, Add. MSS 70004, fols 306–7, 70109, no. 63, muster of 30 October 1640; PRO, C231/3, p. 22.

33   PRO, C219/43/1/200–1; HCL, MS L.C. 647.1, 'Scudamore MSS: Accounts, 1641–42', fol. 23r; HRO, AL17/1, 1624.

34   *A List of the Names of the Long Parliament* (London, 1659), p. 24; *A Catalogue of the Names of the Knights* (London, 1656); FSL, Vb 2(19).

35   R. Johnson, *A Lecture on the Ancient Customs of the City of Hereford* (Hereford, 1845), pp. 62–4; V. A. Rowe, 'The Influence of the Earls of Pembroke on Parliamentary Elections', *English Historical Review*, 50 (1935), pp. 242–56; Atherton, thesis, pp. 79–80; G. Davies, 'The Election at Hereford in 1702', *Huntington Library Quarterly*, 12:3 (1949), pp. 322–7.

36   *LBH*, p. 167.

37   Northamptonshire RO, Finch-Hatton MS 133, *sub* Herefordshire; M. Bennett, 'Between Scylla and Charybdis: The Creation of Rival Administrations at the Beginning of the English Civil War', *Local Historian*, 22:4 (November 1992), p. 194. Brilliana Harley's correspondent added the earl of Bridgewater, lord president of the council of Wales and the marches, to the other three members of the quorum: HMC, *The Manuscripts of his Grace the Duke of Portland* (10 vols, London, 1891–1931), III, pp. 90–1.

38   BL, Add. MS 70004, fols 269r, 270v; Nottinghamshire RO, DD4P/66/11.

39   HMC, *Portland*, III, pp. 90–2; BL, Add. MS 70004, fols 277r, 278.

40   HCL, MS L.C. 647.1 'Scudamore MSS: Accounts 1641–42', fol. 20r; BL, Add. MS 70004, fol. 310r.

41   Bodleian, MS Tanner 303, fol. 113.

42   *MCW*, I, pp. 81, 240–1. At another point (I, p. 5), Webb wrote that Scudamore's 'attachment to his native land was equalled only by his virtues and talents and sufferings in the royal cause'.

43   R. Hutton, *The Royalist War Effort 1642–1646* (London, 1982), p. 53; I. G. Philip, ed., *Journal of Sir Samuel Luke* (Oxfordshire Record Society, 1950–53), pp. 13–14, 61; HCL, MSS L.C. 647.1 'Scudamore MSS: Accounts 1635–37[8]', fol. 73r, L.C. 647.1 'MSS Scudamore Accounts' 1642–43, *sub* 'Stable'.

44   Eales, *Puritans*, pp. 154, 156, 163; FSL, Vb 2(2), copied in *MCW*, I, p. 265.

45   FSL, Vb 2(6), copied in *MCW*, I, pp. 263–4.

46   Eales, *Puritans*, p. 163; PRO, C115/N2/8521.

47   BL, Add. MS 70004, fols 307r, 1 (second series of foliation), Brilliana's letters of [11] August 1642 and 17 January 1643.

48   PRO, C115/M14/7313, fol. 3v; Bodleian, MS Tanner 303, fol. 113.

49   HCL, MS L.C. 647.1, 'Scudamore MSS: Accounts 1641-42', fols 14r, 15r, 34r.

50   PRO, SP20/1/63, 2 June 1643, SP20/3, fol. 94r, SP23/198, p. 779, C115/M14/7280, C115/M14/7283–5; FSL, Vb 2(10), Vb 3(8)–(9); BL, Add. MS 11044, fols 188r, 192v, 211r; H. J. Habakkuk, 'Landowners and the Civil War', *Economic History Review*, 2nd series, 18 (1965), p. 132 and n. 2. The deed itself has not been found.

51   W. Laud, *A Speech Delivered in the Starr-Chamber* (London, 1637), especially pp. 8–9; W. Laud, *Harangve Prononcee en la Chambre de l'Estoile* ([Paris], 1637[8]); BL, Add. MS 11044, fols 82v–3r; below, pp. 260–4.

52   R. C. Johnson *et al.*, eds, *Proceedings in Parliament 1628* (6 vols, New Haven and London, 1977–83), IV, pp. 116, 120, 126.

53   J. Ashburnham, *A Narrative*, ed. George, earl of Ashburnham (2 vols, London, 1839), II, appendix, p. vii.

54   PRO, C115/M14/7312–13; BL, Add. MS 11044, fols 247–9.

55 PRO, C115/M14/7212, fol. 2v. For the parliament's arguments see C. Russell, *The Causes of the English Civil War* (Oxford, 1990), pp. 157–60, and C. Russell, *The Fall of the British Monarchies, 1637–1642* (Oxford, 1991), pp. 505–9.

56 Johnson, *Proceedings in Parliament 1628*, III, p. 202.

57 BL, Add. MSS 70003, fol. 240r, 70004, fol. 33v; *A Plaine Case* ([Oxford], 1643); G. E. Aylmer, 'Collective Mentalities in Seventeenth-Century England: II. Royalist Attitudes', *TRHS*, 5th series, 37 (1987), p. 16.

58 Johnson, *Proceedings in Parliament 1628*, III, p. 194, VI, p. 82.

59 Newman, *Old Service*, pp. 29, 39.

60 Newman, *Old Service*, especially p. vii; Newman, 'King's Servants'; Aylmer, 'Royalist Attitudes'; J. G. Marston, 'Gentry Honor and Royalism', *Journal of British Studies*, 13 (1973), pp. 39–43.

61 See above, chapters 4–5.

62 Newman, 'King's Servants', p. 226.

63 BL, Add. MS 70003, fol. 237v; Russell, *Causes*, pp. 5, 7, 188–91.

64 Newman, 'King's Servants', p. 232.

65 Bodleian, MS Tanner 303, fol. 113r; Eales, *Puritans*, p. 132.

66 Above, pp. 28–9.

67 BL, Add. MS 37999, fol. 57; PRO, E372/474–80, IND1/6746, June 1623; *LBH*, p. 124.

68 HRO, W15/2, Henry Vaughan to Coningsby, 14 November 1621; PRO, C24/937/23, PROB11/148/38, fol. 292v; Keeler, *Long Parliament*, pp. 139–40; T. Coningsby, *Marden* (2 vols, London, 1722–27), I, p. 467.

69 BL, Add. MS 70004, fols 277r, 278r, 285r, 300r, 309v; HMC, *Portland*, III, pp. 90–3.

70 BL, Add. MS 70004, fols 280r, 309v.

71 BL, Add. MS 70105, Gower to Harley, 5 September 1642, Egerton MS 3054, fol. 50v; *A Perfect Diurnall of the Passages in Parliament*, no. 15, 19–26 September 1642; Nottinghamshire RO, DD4P/66/12; *A Catalogue of the Moneys, Men, and Horse, Already Subscribed ... for His Majesteyes Service* (London, 1642); Atherton, 'First Civil War in Herefordshire', pp. 141–2.

72 Hutton, *Royalist War Effort*, p. 22; Atherton, 'First Civil War in Herefordshire', p. 140.

73 Bodleian, MS Carte 103, fol. 94r; BL, Egerton MS 3054, fol. 51r.

74 HCL, MS L.C. 647.1 'Scudamore MSS: Accounts 1641–42', fol. 23r, MS L.C. 647.1 'MSS Scudamore Accounts', 1642–43, *sub* 'Stable'; Atherton, 'First Civil War in Herefordshire', p. 142.

75 PRO, SP16/492/32; Atherton, 'First Civil War in Herefordshire', p. 142.

76 Bodleian, MS Tanner 303, fols 113v–14r; I. Roy, ed., *Royalist Ordnance Papers* (2 vols, Oxford Record Society, 43, 49, 1963–73), I, p. 176, II, p. 491; D. Lloyd, *Memoires* (London, 1668), p. 673.

77 HCL, MS L.C. 674.1 'MSS Scudamore Accounts', 1642–43, 'Moneyes returned to your Lordship'. The claim in *DNB* (Scudamore) and J. Foster, *Alumni Oxonienses 1500–1714* (4 vols, Oxford, 1891–92), IV, p. 1327, that Viscount Scudamore was in Oxford on 1 November 1642 to receive an M.A., is incorrect: Atherton, thesis, pp. 294–5.

78 P. Clark, '"The Ramoth-Gilead of the Good": Urban Change and Political Radicalism at Gloucester, 1540–1640', in P. Clark, A. G. R. Smith and N. Tyacke, eds, *The English Commonwealth* (Leicester, 1979), pp. 167–87; G. A. Harrison, 'Royalist Organisation in Gloucestershire and Bristol 1642–1645' (Manchester University M.A. thesis, 1961), pp. 43–6; PRO, SP28/154, accounts of Nurse, Hill and Webb, 1642; Gloucestershire RO, GBR/G3/SO/2, fols 24–7r, GBR/B3/2, pp. 210, 220–36, D2510/21, D2510/24, D2510/26.

79 FSL, Vb 2(2); BL, Add. MS 70106, Scudamore to Harley, Vaughan and Kyrle, 13 January 1643; HCL, MS L.C. 647.1 'MSS Scudamore Accounts', 1642–43, *sub* 'Moneyes returned to your Lordship' and 'Messengers'.

80 HCL, MS L.C. 647.1, 'MSS Scudamore Accounts', 1642–43, *sub* 'Pettie perticulars. Homelacie', a payment on 13 October 1642 of 8*d*. to 'Ball drawing the poole for carpes for the Earle of Stamforde'; FSL, Vb 2(2).

81 Atherton, thesis, pp. 298, 379–80.

82 J. Washbourn, ed., *Bibliotheca Gloucestrensis: A Collection of Scarce and Curious Tracts, relating to the City and County of Gloucester* (2 vols, Gloucester, 1823–25), I, pp. 16–17; Harrison, 'Royalist Organisation', pp. 44–6, 55–7; HCL, MS L.C. 647.1, 'MSS Scudamore Accounts', 1642–43, *sub* 'Messengers'.

83 BL, Add. MS 11044, fols 207–8, 215; PRO, C115/M14/7297–8.

84 *Lords' Journals*, V, pp. 452–3, 475.

85 Staffordshire RO, D868/2/39; Gloucestershire RO, GBR/G3/SO/2, fol. 26v; Atherton, 'First Civil War in Herefordshire', pp. 142–3 (putting the retreat on 10 December); *LBH*, p. 186.

86 Atherton, thesis, pp. 296–300.

87 *LBH*, pp. 186–98; BL, Add. MS 70004, fols 1–18 (second series of foliation); Eales, *Puritans*, pp. 163–7; C. Hopkinson, *Herefordshire under Arms: A Military History of the County* (Bromyard, 1985), p. 88.

88 PRO, C115/I26/6511; FSL, Vb2(2).

89 PRO, SP16/149/10, fol. 12r; Bodleian, MS Tanner 303, fol. 115r.

90 Northamptonshire RO, Finch-Hatton MS 133, *sub* Herefordshire; BL, Harl. MS 6851, fol. 243r; Bodleian, MS Tanner 303, fols 113r, 114.

91 Bodleian, MS Tanner 303, fols 114r, 115v; Atherton, 'First Civil War in Herefordshire', pp. 143–4.

92 PRO, C231/3, p. 22; Hutton, *Royalist War Effort*, p. 112; B. Scudamore, *Sir Barnabas Scvdamore's Defence*, ed. I. J. Atherton (Akron, 1992), pp. 7–11.

93 Bodleian, MS Tanner 303, fol. 114r.

94 Bodleian, MS Tanner 303, fol. 114.

95 Bodleian, MS Tanner 303, fol. 114v; BL, Add. MS 70107, no. 3, Charles I to Coningsby, 26 January 1643; Eales, *Puritans*, p. 165.

96 Bodleian, MS Tanner 303, fols 113–15r; Atherton, thesis, p. 305; P. Styles, 'The Royalist Government of Worcestershire during the Civil War', *Transactions of the Worcestershire Archaeological Society*, 3rd series, 5 (1976), pp. 28–9.

97 Bodleian, MS Tanner 303, fol. 114; FSL, Vb 3(2); PRO, C115/I2/5617.

98 See above, chapter 4.

99 M. Bennett, *The Civil Wars in Britain and Ireland, 1638–1651* (Oxford, 1997), p. 122; Bennett, 'Creation of Rival Administrations', p. 193.

100 BL, Harl. MS 6804, fol. 133; Bodleian, MS Tanner 303, fols 113r, 114v–15r; HCL, FLC 942.44 MS, no. 23133 'Civil War Assesments relating to William Price, mercer', Coningsby's receipt for £60 borrowed from Price, Evans and Cooper; T. Coningsby, *The Case of the right honourable Thomas Earl Coningsby* ([?London, ?1722]), p. 46.

101 Bodleian, MS Tanner 303, fol. 120r; B. D. Henning, ed., *The House of Commons 1660–1690* (3 vols, London, 1983), III, pp. 285–6, 289–90.

102 Bodleian, MS Tanner 303, fols 113v, 114v.

103 Bodleian, MS Tanner 303, fol. 115r; Philip, *Journal of Luke*, pp. 13–14; HCL, MS L.C. 647.1, 'MSS Scudamore Accounts', 1642–43, *sub* 'Pettie perticulars. Homelacie': 'Gifts by your Lordships extraordinarie directions' and 'Armes and Ammunition'; W. A. Shaw, *The Knights of England* (2 vols, London, 1906), II, p. 215.

104 Bodleian, MS Tanner 303, fol. 115r.

105 A. Hughes, 'Local History and the Origins of the Civil War', in R. P. Cust and A. Hughes, eds, *Conflict in Early Stuart England* (Harlow, 1989), p. 228; E. A. Andriette, *Devon and Exeter in the Civil War* (Newton Abbot, 1971), pp. 63, 71; Eales, *Puritans*, p. 165.

106 J. Rushworth, *Historical Collections* (7 vols, London, 1659–1721), III, appendix, p. 229; Morrill, *Revolt*, p. 40.

107 Morrill, *Revolt*, pp. 112–13; Bennett, *Civil Wars*, p. 129; J. L. Malcolm, *Caesar's Due: Loyalty and King Charles, 1642–1646* (London, 1983), p. 36.

108 W. H. Black, ed., *Docquets of Letters Patent and other Instruments passed under the Great Seal of King Charles I. at Oxford* (privately printed, 1837), p. 49.

109 Bodleian, MS Tanner 303, fol. 115r; Washbourn, *Bibliotheca Gloucestrensis*, I, p. 29; *MCW*, I, pp. 235–7.

110 *The Copy of a Letter sent from Bristoll* (London, 1643), p. 5, printed in J. R. Phillips, *Memoirs of the Civil War in Wales and the Marches* (2 vols, London, 1874), II, pp. 62–5; Hutton, *Royalist War Effort*, p. 57.

111 Bodleian, MS Tanner 303, fol. 115v.

112 Hutton, *Royalist War Effort*, p. 55; FSL, Vb 3(1), also *MCW*, I, pp. 274–5; Bodleian, MS Tanner 303, fols 115v, 116v, 118v.

113 FSL, Vb 3(1), also *MCW*, I, pp. 275–6 (where the date is incorrectly rendered as the 15th).

114 FSL, Vb 3(1), also *MCW*, I, p. 276; Atherton, thesis, pp. 309–10.

115 Rushworth, *Collections*, part 3, vol. I, pp. 672–4; Bodleian, MS Carte 4, fol. 145r; B. E. G. Warburton, *Memoirs of Prince Rupert and the Cavaliers* (3 vols, London, 1849), II, p. 161.

116 FSL, Vb 2(5).

117 FSL, Vb 2(4)–(5), Vb 3(1), also *MCW*, I, pp. 275–7, 279–80, 282–3; Bodleian, MS Tanner 303, fols 116–17r, 118–19r, 120r, 123v–4v. Confusion has reigned over historians too.

Duncumb made unacknowledged additions to Cave's account to the effect that Herbert Price was governor; Webb innocently repeated these, adding that perhaps Price was Coningsby's deputy, a suggestion followed by Hutton: Duncumb, *Collections*, I, pp. 248, 251; *MCW*, I, pp. 275, 277; Hutton, *Royalist War Effort*, p. 57.

118 A. Hughes, 'The King, the Parliament and the Localities during the English Civil War', in R. P. Cust and A. Hughes, eds, *The English Civil War* (London, 1997), pp. 261–87.

119 FSL, Vb 3(1), also *MCW*, I, pp. 276–7; Atherton, 'First Civil War in Herefordshire', p. 142; Bodleian, MS Tanner 303, fol. 118.

120 Atherton, 'First Civil War in Herefordshire', p. 143; HCL, FLC 942.44 MS, no. 23133, 'Papers relating to William Price, mercer', Price's account of his sufferings.

121 FSL, Vb 2(4), Vb 3(1), also *MCW*, I, pp. 276, 278–80; Bodleian, MS Tanner 303, fol. 114v.

122 FSL, Vb 2(5), Vb 3(1), also *MCW*, I, pp. 279–81; Bodleian, MS Tanner 303, fols 121–4; Washbourn, *Bibliotheca Gloucestrensis*, I, pp. 35–6.

123 FSL, Vb 2(5), Vb 2(24); PRO, SP23/198, p. 775.

124 Bodleian, MS Tanner 303, fol. 123; FSL, Vb 2(5).

125 *Mercurius Aulicus*, 22nd week, 28 May–4 June 1643, p. 288; Bodleian, MS Carte 5, fol. 204r; *The Iudgement of the Court of Warre upon the Charge laid against Sir Richard Cave, for the Delivery up of Hereford* (Oxford, 1643).

126 FSL, Vb 2(3), Vb 2(5), Vb 3(1), also *MCW*, I, pp. 257–8, 281–2.

127 *Mercurius Bellicus. The Fourth Intelligence from Reading* (London, 1643); FSL, Vb 2(6), Vb 3(1), also *MCW*, I, pp. 263, 282; Acts 10:1–23.

128 FSL, Vb 3(1), also *MCW*, I, p. 282; BL, Add. MS 70004, fol. 247r (wrongly dated and bound as 1642); *Mercurius Bellicus*; *Speciall Passages and Certaine Informations*, no. 38, 25 April–2 May 1643, p. 313; *A Continuation of Certaine Remarkable Passages*, no. 43, 27 April–4 May 1643; *A Most True Relation of Divers Notable Passages* (London, 1643); *Mercurius Civicus*, no. 2, 11–18 May 1643; *Certaine Informations*, no. 18, 15–22 May 1643, p. 140.

129 Atherton, 'First Civil War in Herefordshire', p. 144; HCL, FLC 942.44 MSS, nos. 23132, 'Civil war Assesments relating to William Price, mercer', assessment for Waller, 23133, 'Papers relating to William Price, mercer', Price's account of his sufferings, MS L.C. 647.1 'MSS Scudamore Accounts', 1642–43, 'Gifts soldiers'.

130 Bodleian, MS Carte 103, fol. 95r; Hutton, *Royalist War Effort*, p. 58.

131 *LBH*, p. 205; BL, Add. MS 70004, fol. 33r (second series of foliation); PRO, C231/3, pp. 22, 24, Black, *Docquets of Letters Patent*, pp. 44, 46–50, 52; Hutton, *Royalist War Effort*, p. 112.

132 FSL, Vb 2(2), Vb 2(6), Vb 2(20).

133 FSL, Vb 2(2), Vb 2(6), also in *MCW*, I, pp. 263–5.

134 These words erased at this point: 'hath had dominion ouer mee in the gouernment of my self'.

135 BL, Add. MS 70106, Scudamore to Harley, Vaughan and Kyrle, 13 January 1643; FSL, Vb 2(3), also in *MCW*, I, pp. 257–8.

136 PRO, SP23/198, p. 774, C115/M14/7280, fol. 1r, C115/M14/7316.

137 PRO, C115/M14/7287, C115/M14/7291–2, C115/M14/7294, C115/M14/7308, SP23/ 198, pp. 759–62.

138 PRO, C115/M14/7287.

139 L. Pollock, 'Younger Sons in Tudor and Stuart England', *History Today*, 39 (June 1989), pp. 23–9; J. Thirsk, 'Younger Sons in the Seventeenth Century', *History*, 54 (1969), pp. 358–77; PRO, PROB11/133/50, fol. 402v, PROB11/142/84, fol. 138r, C115/M13/7275; BL, Harl. MS 6868, fol. 100. See also Scudamore, *Defence*.

140 PRO, E157/15, fol. 41v, C115/M13/7267; E. Peacock, *The Army Lists of the Roundheads and Cavaliers* (2nd edition, London, 1874), p. 82.

141 A. Hughes, *Politics, Society and Civil War in Warwickshire, 1620–1660* (Cambridge, 1987), pp. 147–8; *Mercurius Aulicus*, 21st week, 19–25 May 1644, p. 992; F. P. Verney, ed., *Memoirs of the Verney Family* (4 vols, London, 1892–99), II, p. 103; P. Young, *Edgehill 1642: The Campaign and the Battle* (Kineton, 1967), pp. 146, 174, 264; *A Most True Relation of the Present State of His Majesties Army* (London, 1642), sig. A3v.

142 S. Shaw, *The History and Antiquities of Staffordshire* (2 vols, London, 1798–1801), I, p. 52; G. M., ed., 'Ottleiana: or Letters, &c. Relating to Shropshire, Written during and subsequent to the Civil War', 3 parts, *Collectanea Topographica et Genealogica*, 6 (1839), pp. 23–4, 37, and 7 (1840), pp. 85–6, 91–2; W. Phillips, ed., 'The Ottley Papers relating to the Civil War', *Transactions of the Shropshire Archaeological and Natural History Society*, 2nd series, 7 (1895), pp. 291–3, 295–6, 315.

143 *Mercurius Aulicus*, 21st week, 19–25 May 1644, pp. 991–2.

144 BL, Add. MS 11043, fols 14–17; Atherton, 'First Civil War in Herefordshire', p. 146; Scudamore, *Defence*, pp. 7–9; PRO, C115/I2/5624–5.

145 Scudamore, *Defence*, pp. 10–16, 22–3; BL, Add. MS 18982, fol. 33r; Atherton, 'First Civil War in Herefordshire', pp. 146–7; P. Gladwish, 'The Herefordshire Clubmen: A Reassessment', *Midland History*, 10 (1985), pp. 62–71; Morrill, *Revolt*, p. 84; *Mercurius Veridicus*, no. 26, 18–25 October, 1645.

146 B. Scudamore, *A Letter sent to the Right Honourable the Lord Digby* (Oxford, 1645); Scudamore, *Defence*, pp. 17–20.

147 *The Kingdomes Weekly Intelligencer*, no. 131, 16–23 December 1645, p. 1053; *A Diary, or an Exact Iournall*, no. 84, 18–24 December 1645, p. 6; *A Continuation of Certaine Speciall and Remarkable Passages*, no. 14, 19–26 December, 1645, p. 6; E. Walker, *Historical Discourses upon Several Occasions* (London, 1705). p. [137]; BL, Add. MS 45714, fol. 71; *The Citie Scout*, no. 6, 2 September 1645, p. 1; Atherton, 'First Civil War in Herefordshire', p. 146.

148 Scudamore, *Defence*, pp. 25–6, 44–56.

149 Scudamore, *Defence*, pp. 28, 44.

150 B. Whitelocke, *Memorials of the English Affairs* (London, 1682), p. 308; PRO, SP18/16/7, fol. 10r. A. Everitt, *The Community of Kent and the Great Rebellion* (Leicester, 1973), p. 252, has Barnaby in Kent in June 1648.

151 BL, Add. MS 11044, fol. 229r; PRO, PROB6/27, fols 117v–19r, SP23/12, p. 297, SP23/ 116, p. 295.

152 *The Cities Weekly Post*, no. 7, 27 January–3 February 1646, p. 3; W. Sanderson, *A Compleat History of the Life and Raigne of King Charles* (London, 1658), pp. 824, 839; Walker, *Historical Discourses*, p. 150; Atherton, 'First Civil War in Herefordshire', p. 146.

153 Coningsby, *Case*, p. 46; Scudamore, *Defence*, p. 44; PRO, C115/M14/7282, C115/M14/7289, SP19/90/29–30, fols 55–7; BL, Add. MS 11044, fol. 222r.

154 BL, Add. MS 15858, fol. 142; T. Fuller, *The History of the Worthies of England* (3 parts, London, 1662), II, p. 47.

155 M. Gibson, *A View of the Ancient and Present State of the Churches of Door, Home-Lacy, and Hempsted* (London, 1727), pp. 109–10; A. Collins, *The Baronetage of England* (2 vols, London, 1720), II, pp. 175–6; Balliol College, Oxford, MS 333, fol. 57r; FSL, Va 147, fol. 36v; T. Downes, *Mr. Downs's Letter to Lord Scudamore*, in *Plain Truths: or, A Collection of Scarce and Valuable Tracts* ([?Edinburgh, ?1716]), p. 61; *DNB* (Downes).

Chapter 8

Honour, politics, ambition
and Scudamore

Honour spoke in many tongues in Stuart England, a diversity of voices which allowed a gentleman to fashion assorted images of himself. Such images varied. Some were superficial, having little connection with action, while most were internalised in the actor's self-understanding and so defined what they also described. They were as much creative as descriptive. Self-mastery and an internalising of the code of honour were acts of self-definition of masculinity and gentility, the very being of a gentleman. In these pages we have met various Lord Scudamores, and we have met only one. We have encountered Scudamore the Laudian, furthering the 'catholic sacramentalist adventure' in the southern marches and advancing the claims of the church of England abroad. We have seen Scudamore the protector of the church and defender of the clergy, paying his tithes and restoring churches. We have observed the learned Scudamore, a friend of philosophers and an experimental agriculturalist, and we have glimpsed Scudamore the dullard, his learning no more than formal pedantry, at least in the eyes of his adversary the earl of Leicester. We have come across Scudamore the loyal servant of the king, solicitous to do Charles service by advancing the subsidy and perfecting the militia, and we have investigated Scudamore the local governor, some-times zealously executing royal policy, sometimes equivocating, sometimes refusing. We have beheld Scudamore the perfect ambassador and the image of his king, and we have experienced Scudamore the imperfect ambassador, frustrated, ineffectual, squeezed out by more adept and more powerful politicians. We have spied Scudamore the suffering royalist, loyal to his king in adversity, and we have confronted Scudamore the failed royalist, crippling the king's cause by seeking his own power against that of a rival. We have witnessed Scudamore the heroically virtuous and we have discovered Scudamore the man. We have seen Scudamore through various eyes: his own; those of his contemporaries, family, friends and foes; our own.

It is tempting to think that we started with Scudamore the myth and uncovered Scudamore the reality, but that is far too simple, and too bold, a claim to make. For, in some respects, all these descriptions of Scudamore are true. The Scudamore who in 1622 over the benevolence for the Palatinate preferred parliamentary taxation,[1] and the Scudamore who conscientiously collected the unparliamentary forced loan, knighthood fines and collections for St Paul's, were one and the same. Glenn Burgess has recently criticised the depiction of Sir Thomas Wentworth by Richard Cust. Where earlier accounts claimed that Wentworth 'changed sides' from country to court, Dr Cust emphasises the ways that Wentworth constructed his own images as crown servant, honest patriot, forced loan refuser, and courtier. To Dr Burgess this is toying with postmodernism: 'In reply to Russell's revisionist assertion that there were no sides to change, Cust appears to assert that there were perhaps sides but no Wentworth to do the changing.'[2] Postmodern and feminist critics of biography have denied the reality of consistency in actors' lives; nevertheless, there are consistencies in people's lives and it is possible to detect them. Most people now, as they did in the seventeenth century, expect to be able to uncover patterns in the lives and characters of those whom they know. Some degree of consistency is expected, and the possibility of identifying it lay behind the popularity in the seventeenth century of 'character books' which sought to expose a series of ideal types against which people could be measured.[3] Moreover, not all images were the same. Some were prudential, some contingent, some short-lived; others were deep-seated and internalised. Seventeenth-century folk took much delight in attempting to unmask actors and reveal the hypocrite, activities which suggested that some coherence of character was expected to underlie the public presentations of a political actor. We have seen how Scudamore hastily constructed some of the depictions of himself, as in the defence of the non-Laudian church in 1642, or in portraying his actions as a royalist before parliament, and how some, especially the latter, failed to convince. Finally, all the images and rhetorical and presentational strategies were linked in one person, Viscount Scudamore, and what united them, I aver, were a number of coherences and consistencies of character and action.

So we are justified in seeking some degree of consistency in Scudamore and the various images and rhetorics with which his actions were described and defined. If we have found it in the pursuit of ambition, honour and service, that is not to descend to some cynical ultimate cause that the pursuit of power, subconscious or otherwise, was the only begetter of his actions. It is the curse of the ambitious to be judged by the basest of motives. As we have seen in the analysis of early modern depictions of ambition, very often ambition was cast as a falling sin, a temptation which gentlemen had to strive hard to avoid and, consequently, the refuge of the rogue, the scoundrel and the dishonourable. Echoes of such a view can still be detected today. David Underdown, for example, has recently described Sir Edward Sawyer, who rose from comparative obscurity to become master of requests in 1628, as a 'careerist' who 'conformed to the stereotype of the courtier as the ambitious social climber, supporting arbitrary courses in order to advance himself'. The alternatives, that Sawyer had less base or self-seeking motives, that he was a reformer animated by an ideological commitment to strong government and service to the crown, or that he was fulfilling his duty under the code of honour of realising and extending his honour not as personal aggrandisement but as the most valuable possession of his family and descendants, are not contemplated.[4] The pursuit of power must not be under-rated or ignored, but honour was an energising and constructive force in early modern England, giving meaning to people's lives and actions and the way they understood their world. Honour conferred power, and with power came honour, but there was far more to honour than potency or naked aggression.

Scudamore, 'the Floorishinge Braunche of so Renowned an Offspring' in John Gwillim's phrase, was ambitious to turn his 'Sparkes of Honor ... Into Flames'.[5] In the 1620s and 1630s he sought advancement and court office. In some degree he succeeded. He was ennobled in 1628, and made ambassador to Louis XIII in 1635. He maintained his local power against challengers until 1643, and was able to restore his position in the 1660s. From his grandfather in 1623 he had inherited a powerful and honourable position at the apex of local society and administration and, despite a major crisis in the mid 1620s, he was able to consolidate that position. Furthermore, by strengthening and extending his sway within Hereford city as its MP and high steward, and over its electoral politics, he emerged with a stronger power base in the city than any of his forebears had enjoyed. In 1641 John Tombes thought that Scudamore shone like 'a star of the first magnitude'. In 1670, at the very end of Scudamore's life, it was said that it was not possible to get justice at law against Lord Scudamore, he 'being a person of great Honour and potency in those partes'. Fitzwilliam Coningsby, even while paying Scudamore a backhanded compliment in 1643, acknowledged that the viscount was 'the Prince in Quality of that Countrey, and regardfully lookt vpon', with a power that 'elevated or depressed the people according to his accesse or recesse'.[6] Such were Lord Scudamore's successes. There were also great failures. He proved that he was no match for the two great challenges in his public career, the embassy to France and his role as a royalist leader. He was unable to pass on to his grandson Jack all his power and position at his death in the way that he had inherited them from his grandfather half a century before. The second viscount's power in the southern marches was considerably less than his grandfather's. The office of *custos rotulorum*, the most prestigious position that the first viscount had, went in 1671 not to the second viscount but to Henry

Somerset, third marquis of Worcester; for the first time since 1574, barring the 1640s and 1650s, a Scudamore was not *custos* of Herefordshire.[7]

Judging by the comments of his contemporaries, Scudamore was adept at moulding himself to, and internalising many of the dictates of, contemporary notions of honour and gentility. He was helped by his birth, as Robert Tetlow, in a Latin epistle to the viscount, recounted in rhetorical style:[8]

> For do we possess a family more ancient or celebrated than that of the Scudamores, who themselves recognise you as their leading light and chief? Has the county of Hereford ever given birth to, or nourished with its own milk, any other man distinguished with the title of viscount, besides you alone, its honour and sweet glory?

On these foundations Scudamore built an honourable life, expressive in his actions of the notions of honour and virtue. A number of later accounts of Viscount Scudamore have depicted him withdrawing from the world at crucial points in the 1620s and 1630s, especially after the assassination of Buckingham in 1628, neglecting the service of king and commonwealth.[9] Such depictions not only greatly exaggerate the extent of Scudamore's retirement, they also mistake the means for the end. Scudamore's withdrawal was only a means to prepare himself for further service to the commonwealth and as a gentleman. The couplet on Scudamore recorded by William Higford made the point: 'By divine inspiration often I used to go into retirement / Retiring I yield, yet conquer as Monarch of myself.' Conquering as monarch of oneself meant self-fashioning as a gentleman, self-mastery through reason and the conquest of the passions essential to prepare a man for his God-given duty to rule. The precept that active involvement in public affairs was preferable to withdrawal and philosophical contemplation was endorsed by Scudamore in the education of his son and grandson. Even during his enforced retirement during the Interregnum Scudamore pursued his agricultural pursuits to the benefit of the wider commonwealth, as John Beale made plain.[10] Scudamore fashioned a life that expressed charity, wisdom, learning, and service to church and crown. Martin Johnson contrasted Scudamore's sober zeal, didactic and inspirational, with the destructive zeal 'spouted out' by Hobbes and Pym. The 'God Dam-mees of the Ranting Age', the blasphemers, cursers, atheists, deriders of learning, and addicts of fashion and drink could, thought Johnson, learn much from the life of Scudamore; his was true gentility where they were no more than 'stately Clownes' and 'Dam-destroying Cuckows in silke Gownes'.[11] To Rowland Watkyns Scudamore's 'pious mind' was a 'sea of vertues' with justice, religion and wisdom fixed at its centre, and his every action bore 'a Stamp Divine'.[12] Such accounts made Scudamore the epitome of the perfect gentleman and they suggest Scudamore's success in living out the early modern code of honour.

The emphases on consistency and self-fashioning in Scudamore's life and actions are important, for here we can cut to the quick in some of the current debates between revisionists and post-revisionists about the nature of politics in seventeenth-century England. Dr Burgess has recently and trenchantly restated the revisionist case for 'broad consensus and agreement in fundamental issues in early Stuart England', and central to his arguments is the assertion that potentially competing and antagonistic languages and discourses were restricted to separate spheres, thereby preventing, or at least minimising, opportunities for conflict.[13]

> If there was a 'consensus' in early Stuart political and constitutional discourse, it lay here: not in the existence of only one political language, but in the maintenance of defined roles for, and boundaries between, a variety of such languages. The language of divine right was not inherently 'opposed' to the language of common law or the language of consent, because each had its own sphere within which it could be used uncontroversially.

The existence of these separate spheres seems far from clear. We have seen that political actors like Scudamore were able to present diverse images of themselves on different stages, and use varying rhetorics and languages at different times – horses for courses, we might say – but we have also seen that such strategies worked only if there were some consistency and connection between the images and languages. If they were hermetically sealed, closed off one from another, the actor would be open to charges of hypocrisy and dissimulation. Moreover, we have also seen that the discourses of honour and gentility were multi-vocal, spilling out into different areas, without defined roles, implicitly holding within themselves seeds of contradiction and discord which were not always easily contained. The languages of honour, usually held in creative tension, could be used against one another, as when the English nobility challenged the position of Englishmen like Scudamore who held Scottish or Irish titles. The skill of politicians like Scudamore lay in blending and separating the varying elements, and in exploiting the margins, gaps and interstices between the differing languages and symbols to fashion images for their own ends, sometimes consensual, sometimes conflictive. The normative rules about the use of such images were not fixed, the languages were neither clearly bounded nor rigidly defined.

What did the political world look like to Lord Scudamore, in his varying roles as Christian, Laudian, royal servant, diplomat, ambitious politician, gentleman of honour? Clearly, we are in no position to present a complete or holistic picture, but a number of partial views can be described. First, in contrast both to traditional views of Scudamore himself, and to recent delineations of royalism, there was a robust and authoritarian strand in the viscount's thinking and actions.[14] We cannot say whether Scudamore was an absolutist, but his stress on the trust that could and should be placed in Charles I is similar to Anthony Milton's recent portrayal of Wentworth and his attitude to parliament, revealing a lord deputy with 'a more "absolutist" style within apparently traditional language'. It is, moreover, unlikely that Scudamore the ceremonialist, friend of William Laud and restorer of Dore would have regarded the prospect of a parliament with any enthusiasm after the experience of the parliaments of the later 1620s.[15] Scudamore's attitude to the forced loan, knighthood fines and the collections for St Paul's Cathedral all show an enthusiastic supporter of Caroline policy, while his religious views show that he was by no means one to walk a middle, consensual way, avoiding conflict.

Scudamore was adept at taking the commonplaces of contemporary political discourse and adapting them to his own ends and to the ends of royal policy. What is particularly interesting is that many of the images and languages he appropriated are those which historians have previously depicted as the hallmarks of the godly or those less enthusiastic about the personal rule. In the 1620s Scudamore took the notion that gentry honour resided in martial prowess and blended it with anti-Spanish feeling to fashion a military image for himself and to appeal to the gentry of Herefordshire to improve the standard of the county militia. Like other Laudians he deployed ideas of reforming the church and settling it according to tradition and custom, but his vision of the church of England, as acted out at Dore and in his embassy chapel, was far removed from what many of his contemporaries recognised as Protestantism.[16] Viscount Scudamore's language may suggest Kevin Sharpe's picture of the Laudians as churchmen of a moderate, irenicist, conventional and conformist stamp, but his actions reveal that Dr Sharpe's characterisation of the Laudians is seriously misleading.

Three further examples are worth exploring in some depth because they not only touch on previous views of Scudamore but also remain at the heart of revisionist and post-revisionist debate: Scudamore's view of the role of freeholders in the political process, his use of the rhetoric of the 'country', and his attitude to consensus. Revisionist historians have privileged consensus and agreement as the hallmarks of early modern political attitudes. Post-revisionists, meanwhile, have seen the language of free elections and the independent choice of the voters as typical of the godly gentry, they being guarantees against the election of court candidates and popish fellow-travellers, and they have described how the image of the 'country' often implied staunch Protestantism, adherence to the rule of law and support for the centrality of parliament in the process of government, and how an upright and honest country was often contrasted with a corrupt court, tinged with popery and inimical to parliaments.[17] Scudamore's deployment of these discourses and images suggest that both revisionist and post-revisionist views are incomplete, for once again he claimed them for himself and for his service to the crown.

Although Scudamore's vision of the political process was a top-down one, with the gentry firmly holding the reins of power locally, he was adept at manipulating the language of freeholder independence and the public good. In 1661 he proposed that the Herefordshire election agreement of 1620, by which the senior gentry would agree on two candidates to be proposed to the assembled electors, should be reinstated. The agreement of 1620 had been cast as an instrument for the public peace, a means of avoiding faction in elections, language that Scudamore's 1661 agreement picked up. He described the ill effects on the country if there was dissension among its gentry, including miscarriages of justice and unfair tax assessments. The 'proper cure of these euills', opined Scudamore, was 'the vnion and agreement of the Gentry':

> it is the order which the wisdome of the Creator and supreme Providence hath thought good to fix in nature, namely, that inferiors are to receiue from their superiours, that participation of knowledge and light, by which their resolutions and actions are to bee guided and deliuerd from Error.

Nevertheless, pre-selection of candidates by the gentry did not preclude the electorate's involvement in the decision-making process. The good of the commonwealth required that the freeholders should participate; they were not merely to receive instructions from the senior gentry. Scudamore warned against neglecting the 'liberty of the Freeholder': 'For the Gentry is not to impose upon, but only to recommend unto the Freeholder their iudgment and opinion.' The electoral agreement, he claimed, was designed to assert, not restrict, the freeholders' 'Legall and Just Liberty of Electing'.[18] On other occasions Scudamore used a similar rhetoric of the importance to the common-wealth of the free assent of freeholders and others in government. 'Vse your own reason,' he told the taxpayers when recommending the collection for St Paul's, and he went on to show how human reason demonstrated the importance of contributing to the cathedral. Likewise, when communicating the king's instructions concerning the militia, he took great pains in pointing out the reason behind these orders[19]

> And for that those operations which are most free, are ever best; I will endevour to lay before you, not only that which is comaunded as requisite to this end, but the reason of that which is expected: the minde of Man being more delighted to bee led by persuasion of reason, then to bee drawen by force of authority.

Scudamore's rhetoric on these occasions differed greatly from the fears of popularity expressed by Charles I and Laud, and it can be contrasted with the horror of the Laudian Lord Maynard at 'popular assemblies where fellowes without shirts challenge as good a voice as myselfe'.[20] Like other local governors Scudamore was aware of the dangers of popularity, and according to Rowland Watkyns, he capped his honour by remaining 'Deaf to Applause, averse to empty Names'; he also played upon Charles's fears of disloyalty, portraying himself as being 'zealously deuoted' to Charles and the means whereby others in parliament and in Herefordshire 'weare the more willing and forward to be well accommodated, in his majesties service'.[21] Nevertheless, Scudamore's language suggested neither the obsessive concern for loyalty nor the fear of a populist-puritan plot felt by Charles and Laud.

In Scudamore's use the term 'country' not only meant, as it did to others, a shifting kaleidoscope of local area, the county, the commonwealth and the kingdom; it was also a metaphorical construct, a locus of honour. On one occasion, for example, he wrote of 'my deare mother England'. To all of them a special debt of service was owed; to one's countryfolk special reverence and honour should be paid. The term was deliberately ambiguous; in this lay its rhetorical force. Sometimes that ambiguity led to confusion, as when Scudamore told the two sons of Richard Boyle, earl of Cork, that 'he was bound to loue vs aboue others, because we were his lordships contrymen', which brought a blank response from the elder to his father: 'How his lordship meant itt, I know not.' He had forgotten what Scudamore had not, that the Boyles were descended from an old Herefordshire family.[22] Not the least advantage of the language of the country was that it allowed actors, by seeking self-advancement and the pursuit of personal and family honour through service to the wider commonwealth, to avoid charges of ambition.

Scudamore emptied the rhetoric of the country of all association with godly Protestantism and resistance to taxation, and of all contrast with the king or the court. Instead, he firmly yoked it to the service of the king. At the election to the Cavalier Parliament in March 1661, for example, while proposing his son James for senior knight of the shire, he spoke of 'The deuoting of my Sonne to the service of the King, and in particular of this county' as 'this ioynt end, the serving the King and this countrey'. Only once in the record did Scudamore link the language of the country with the rhetoric of Hispanophobia, manipulating commonplace anti-Spanish themes in his speech to the county horse, and that was in the later 1620s when his king was fighting a war against Spain. In the Commons in 1628 he pressed for a grant of subsidies as in the interests of the king and the country. MPs were generally unenthusiastic about granting taxation, couching their reluctance in terms of their responsibility to the electorate. Scudamore neatly reversed the rhetoric, telling members, 'I see not how I can answer my country that we refused to supply the King.' The following month Scudamore could be heard in the Commons defending the duke of Buckingham as a 'cause of good to this kingdom'. On each occasion the language of the country and the language of the public good were pressed into the service of the king.[23] Scudamore was using the rhetoric of consensus and was continuing to stress the congruity of country and court in the 1620s and 1630s when others believed that evil counsellors were seeking to drive them apart. We should, nevertheless, be careful of accepting Newton Key's recent judgement that Lord Scudamore was a natural con-sensualist, filled with 'comprehensive inclinations', the 'architect of the local consensus'.[24] Scudamore's speeches were oratorical exercises and though, as we have seen, they had to have a connection with his other actions and beliefs as perceived by his audience to carry weight and authority, they were also designed to reinforce his power and that of the crown. The advantage to Scudamore, the senior justice in the county and the only resident peer in Herefordshire, of a political process which stressed consensus, social prestige and the lead of the gentry was obvious. To say that early modern people assumed that politics would be conducted through consensus and agreement – expectations that Scudamore's rhetoric played upon – is not, however, to presuppose that the political process was always carried on by consensus. It is a distinction which some revisionist scholars have missed. The low level of conflict in many stages of Scudamore's career should not beguile us into positing an absence of conflict in political life generally. Scudamore was wily enough to know that there were occasions when he had to make concessions in order to transact smoothly the enforcement of royal policy, allowances such as how many to excuse from the forced loan on the grounds of poverty, who to summon and who to fine for distraint of knighthood, and whether to levy the muster master rate. These examples suggest areas of genuine conflict, some-times ideological, and it was precisely the reality of conflict and disagreement in the political process, not their absence, that forced Scudamore's hand in certain ways and determined his course of action. Unlike Charles I, he was wise enough to realise that he had sometimes to bend to achieve a longer-term goal.

Through Scudamore many of the recent perspectives on the political culture of the gentry and nobility thrown up by the researches of scholars such as Thomas Cogswell, Richard Cust, Jacqueline Eales and Anthony Milton[25] can be rescued from the claim that they have revived a Whiggish, puritan constitutional opposition in postmodern guise.[26] Scudamore is in many ways a familiar figure, comparable to others such as Sir Robert Phelips, Sir Richard Grosvenor, Sir Edward Dering or Sir Robert Harley, all better known to historians. Yet Scudamore is also distinctively different. In his case many of the cultural forms, institutional contexts and locales that feature so centrally in the careers of men such as Phelips, Grosvenor and Harley are found operating in a career of a very different ideological, theological and political timbre.

Scudamore's vision of politics skilfully blended images of the country, the assent of the freeholders, the good of the commonwealth, and the exercise of reason, in a whole which nevertheless stressed Scudamore's own power and prestige and the execution of royal policy. It was a vision of the political process which suggested the reality of conflict whilst not denying the desire for consensus. It was also one in which that conflict was not between two sides which historians may conveniently label crown and opposition, court and country, or Laudians and puritans, but in which conflict was a shifting kaleidoscope of clashes involving the appropriation of language, forms and symbols on many sides and for varied ends. It was a political process in which a convinced Laudian and proponent of the crown's military and financial policies could nevertheless be described as an 'Honourable and much lamented Patriot of our Country' and an Elijah, 'the Glory of our Countrey'.[27]

Ultimately it was only one aspect of Scudamore's difference which came to be celebrated and upon which his fame and reputation rested. Part of the rhetorical force of Martin Johnson's elegy was that Scudamore had been out of tune with the times, a moral man surrounded by rakes, a representative of a former, better age. Above all his virtues and deeds, it was for his munificence to the church that Scudamore was remembered. In 1635 George Wall wrote that Scudamore had made himself 'beloved by God and good Men, *particularly* by Rescuing the Revenues that were Dedicated to God's Worship from the hands of Avarice and Oppression'. Other attributes, such as his wisdom as a local governor or his royalism, were less important in constructing the image of Scudamore, while some were forgotten altogether: his service as ambassador, for example, ultimately mattered in Herefordshire only in that he had been chosen as the king's envoy, and not for what he achieved or failed to achieve in Paris. Such was the message of Tetlow's epistle in 1639 and Johnson's elegy in the 1670s.[28] Reputations could be maintained in a variety of ways, by service to the commonwealth as JP or MP, by conformity to the notions of gentility, by self-fashioning, by litigation to defend one's name, but probably the most important was by the support of the local clergy. They were the key to shaping local opinion, and they were vital for the spread of an honourable image beyond the immediate locality. Clergy were the most prolific of publishers, and in the pages and dedications of their books they could spread the fame and honour of their patrons. One example illustrates the point. In the 1660s one of Viscount Scudamore's deputy estate stewards was the Herefordshire lawyer Thomas Carpenter, and one of Carpenter's near relations, William Carpenter, minister of Staunton-on-Wye in Herefordshire, published in 1661 a defence of clerical incomes and power entitled *Jura Cleri* under the pseudonym Philo-Basileus Philo-Clerus. In a marginal note Carpenter praised Viscount Scudamore as a restorer of church lands, 'a Worthy Copy for others to write after'. Leonard Wastell, minister of Hurworth-on-Tees in County Durham at the Restoration, read Carpenter's work and copied down in his own notebook the passage referring to Scudamore. Over

200 years later George Ross-Lewin, curate of Hurworth, came across Wastell's notes, saw the passage about Scudamore and, intrigued, set off on his own researches into the viscount, which he published in 1900.[29]

Ever since Scudamore made the public protestation about paying his tithes that George Wall commended, clergymen have been in the vanguard of extolling his praises and helping to fashion his image. With one exception, what they concentrated on was Scudamore's munificence to the church. Other more controversial aspects of his Laudianism such as his ceremonialism tended to get left out. Only Tetlow mentioned the 'rich ornaments' of Dore and its consecration 'with such great ceremony'. Elsewhere, if Scudamore's Laudianism drew any comments, they were negative, as in the judgements of Clarendon and an anonymous parliamentary memorandum found among the papers of the Buller family of Cornwall.[30] In Scudamore's lifetime the clergymen George Wall, Robert Tetlow, John Tombes, Rowland Watkyns and John Gregory were all instrumental in fashioning and publicising the image of Scudamore as pious and religious, a defender and, as he was later styled, a 'nursing Father' of the church.[31] Since his death other clergymen have taken up the task of praising Scudamore in successive ages: John Newton and Martin Johnson in the later seventeenth century;[32] Theophilus Downes and Matthew Gibson in the eighteenth;[33] Mark Noble, John Webb and George Ross-Lewin in the nineteenth;[34] Anthony Russell in the twentieth.[35] It is appropriate, therefore, that the last word should go to a churchman. On the lintel of the new parsonage house of Hempsted, built at Scudamore's expense, John Gregory, the rector there, inscribed the following lines in golden letters, an enduring encomium that can still be seen today above the door of the old rectory in Hempsted:[36]

> Who'ere doth dwell within this door
> Thank God for Viscount Scudamore.

NOTES

1 PRO, SP14/132/40, fol. 59; J. Eales, *Puritans and Roundheads: The Harleys of Brampton Bryan and the Outbreak of the English Civil War* (Cambridge, 1990), p. 85.

2 G. Burgess, review in *History*, 82:267 (1997), p. 499.

3 B. Boyce, *The Theophrastan Character in England to 1642* (Cambridge, 1947); B. Boyce, *The Polemic Character 1640–1661: A Chapter in English Literary History* (Lincoln, 1955).

4 D. Underdown, *A Freeborn People? Politics and the Nation in Seventeenth-Century England* (Oxford, 1996), pp. 20–3.

5 Beinecke Library, Yale, Osborn MS b.28.

6 J. Tombes, *Christs Commination against Scandalizers* (London, 1641), sig. *4r; PRO, C5/56/38, bill of complaint; Bodleian, MS Tanner 303, fol. 113.

7 PRO, C231/7, p. 394; Atherton, thesis, p. 402.

8 BL, Add. MS 11044, fol. 89r.

9 M. Gibson, *A View of the Ancient and Present State of the Churches of Door, Home-Lacy, and Hempsted* (London, 1727), p. 70; MCW, I, p. 5.

10 R. P. Cust, ed., *The Papers of Sir Richard Grosvenor, 1st Bart. (1585–1645)* (Record Society of Lancashire and Cheshire, 134, 1996), p. xxxvi; BL, Add. MS 45714, fol. 71r; J. Beale, *Herefordshire Orchards, a Pattern for all England* (London, 1724), p. 22.

11 FSL, Va 147, fols 36–9.

12 R. Watkyns, *Flamma sine Fumo*, ed. P. C. Davies (Cardiff, 1968), pp. 24–5, the second verse translated in Gibson, *View*, pp. 47–8.

13 G. Burgess, *Absolute Monarchy and the Stuart Constitution* (New Haven and London, 1996), p. 2; G. Burgess, 'The Divine Right of Kings Reconsidered', *English Historical Review*, 107 (1992), p. 861.

14 See appendix for traditional views of Scudamore and for royalism see C. Russell, *The Fall of the British Monarchies 1637–1642* (Oxford, 1991), and D. L. Smith, *Constitutional Royalism and the Search for Settlement, c. 1640–1649* (Cambridge, 1994).

15 R. C. Johnson et al., eds, *Proceedings in Parliament 1628* (6 vols, New Haven and London, 1977–83), III, pp. 193–4, 200, 202, 204, VI, p. 82; A. Milton, 'Thomas Wentworth and the Political Thought of the Personal Rule', in J. F. Merritt, ed., *The Political World of Thomas Wentworth, Earl of Strafford, 1621–1641* (Cambridge, 1996), pp. 147–8.

16 For other Laudians see A. Milton, *Catholic and Reformed: The Roman and Protestant Churches in English Protestant Thought, 1600–1640* (Cambridge, 1995), and Milton, 'Wentworth and Political Thought', pp. 155–6.

17 R. P. Cust and A. Hughes, 'Introduction: After Revisionism', in R. P. Cust and A. Hughes, eds, *Conflict in Early Stuart England* (Harlow, 1989), pp. 19–21; R. P. Cust, 'Politics and the Electorate in the 1620s', in Cust and Hughes, *Conflict in Early Stuart England*, pp. 138–43.

18 FSL, Vb 2(21); BL, Add. MS 11051, fols 227–8, 253–4; M. Kishlansky, *Parliamentary Selection: Social and Political Choice in Early Modern England* (Cambridge, 1986), pp. 26, 129–30.

19 BL, Add. MS 11044, fols 247–9; FSL, Vb 2(24).

20 Cust, 'Politics and the Electorate', p. 139.

21 Watkyns, *Flamma sine Fumo*, pp. 24–5; Gibson, *View*, pp. 47–8; PRO, C115/N5/8632.

22 BL, Add. MS 11044, fols 253r, 254r; FSL, Vb 2(6); R. P. Cust and P. Lake, 'Sir Richard Grosvenor and the Rhetoric of Magistracy', *Bulletin of the Institute of Historical Research*, 54 (1981), pp. 40–54; A. B. Grosart, ed., *The Lismore Papers (Second Series)* (5 vols, privately printed, 1887–88), III, p. 278; C. J. Robinson, *A History of the Manors and Mansions of Herefordshire* (London and Hereford, 1873), pp. 90, 94–5.

23 BL, Add. MS 11044, fols 253v–4r; Johnson et al., eds, *Proceedings in Parliament 1628*, III, p. 194, IV, pp. 116, 120, 126, 266, 277; D. Hirst, *The Representative of the People?: Voters and Voting in England under the Early Stuarts* (Cambridge, 1975), pp. 166–77.

24 N. E. Key, 'Politics beyond Parliament: Unity and Party in the Herefordshire Region during the Restoration Period' (Cornell University Ph.D. thesis, 1989), pp. 127, 159,

250, 253–8, 281–7, 305; N. E. Key, 'Comprehension and the Breakdown of Consensus in Restoration Herefordshire', in T. Harris, P. Seaward and M. Goldie, eds, *The Politics of Religion in Restoration England* (Oxford, 1990), pp. 193–4.

25 T. Cogswell, *The Blessed Revolution: English Politics and the Coming of War, 1621–1624* (Cambridge, 1989); R. P. Cust, 'Wentworth's "Change of Sides" in the 1620s', in J. F. Merritt, ed., *The Political World of Thomas Wentworth, Earl of Strafford, 1621–1641* (Cambridge, 1996), pp. 63–80; Eales, *Puritans*; Milton, 'Wentworth and Political Thought'.

26 Burgess, *Absolute Monarchy*, p. 2; Burgess, review in *History*, 82:267 (1997), p. 499.

27 J. Newton, *The Compleat Arithmetician* (London, 1691), sig. [A5].

28 G. Wall, *A Sermon at the Lord Archbishop of Canterbury his Visitation Metropoliticall* (London, 1635), sig. A2; BL, Add. MS 11044, fol. 89r; FSL, Va 147, fols 36–9.

29 PRO, C8/130/113, m. 1; PROB11/336/96, fol. 332r; W. Carpenter, *Jura Cleri: or An Apology for the Rights of the Long-despised Clergy* (Oxford, 1661), p. 11; G. H. Ross-Lewin, *Lord Scudamore a Loyal Churchman and a Faithful Steward of God's Bounty* (Edinburgh, 1900).

30 BL, Add. MS 11044, fol. 89r; E. Hyde, earl of Clarendon, *The History of the Rebellion and Civil Wars in England*, ed. W. D. Macray (6 vols, Oxford, 1888), II, pp. 418–19; R. N. Worth, ed., *The Buller Papers* (privately printed, 1895), p. 128.

31 Wall, *Sermon*, sig. A2; BL, Add. MS 11044, fol. 89r; Tombes, *Christs Commination*, sig. *4r; Watkyns, *Flamma sine Fumo*, pp. 24–5; Gloucestershire RO, PMF 173; Gibson, *View*, pp. 235–8.

32 Newton, *Compleat Arithmetician*, sig. [A5]; FSL, Va 147, fols 36–9.

33 T. Downes, *Mr. Downs's Letter to Lord Scudamore*, in *Plain Truths: or, A Collection of Scarce and Valuable Tracts* ([?Edinburgh, ?1716]), pp. 61–2; Balliol College, Oxford, MS 333; Gibson, *View*.

34 M. Noble, 'Memoirs of the Illustrious Family of Scudamore' (1816), HCL, 929.2; *MCW*; Ross-Lewin, *Lord Scudamore*.

35 A. Russell, *The Country Parish* (London, 1986), pp. 206, 210.

36 Gibson, *View*, pp. 173–4.

Appendix

—◆—

The image of the Scudamores

'There is something so peculiarly pleasing and extraordinary in the History of the Family of Scudamore that I could not resist committing to paper all that my Books could furnish me relative to this ennobled race.'[1] So wrote Mark Noble in 1816, introducing his account of the Scudamores of Holme Lacy. Noble's work shares two characteristics with much else that has been written about the Scudamores. First, it is unreliable, confusing and conflating different generations and branches of the Scudamore family (most of them inconveniently christened James or John). Indeed, Noble's obituary remarked that 'his works have procured for him the reputation of industry and application, if not of perspicuity and correctness'.[2] Second, it is little more than an exercise in hagiography, recycling the plaudits of earlier works ready for them to be repeated by later generations. Hugh Trevor-Roper's judgement on the biographers of Archbishop William Laud is applicable equally to many who have previously written about Laud's friend the first Viscount Scudamore: he seems like a giant 'since they approach him on their knees'.[3]

The myth of the Scudamores began in the decade before John, the first viscount (1601–71), was born with Edmund Spenser's *Faerie Queene*, in which Sir Scudamore is portrayed as the pattern and type of chivalry. Spenser's model was probably the viscount's father Sir James Scudamore, although some scholars think that it was the latter's father, Sir John Scudamore.[4] Further praise was heaped upon the first viscount during his life, but the real boost to the extraordinary praise heaped upon him and the rest of the family was the impending extinction of the family line in the early eighteenth century. The sole heir of James, the third viscount (1684–1716), was a daughter, Frances, and though the line was to last another century it was as if pen and paper had now to preserve what flesh and bone might not. In 1716 Theophilus Downes depicted the first viscount as the paradigmatic loyal sufferer for the Stuart cause.[5] Four years later Arthur Collins held him up as a paragon of all true virtues:[6]

> No good Thing can be said of any Man which may not justly be said of him, who liv'd a rare Example of *Piety* towards God, *Loyalty* to his Prince, Love to his Country, *Hospitality* to his Friends, *Economy* in his Family, *Charity* to the Poor, and great *Munificence to the Church.*

Shortly thereafter Matthew Gibson, rector of the Scudamores' living of Dore, Herefordshire, took up his pen to honour and spread the fame of 'the good old Lord Scudamore'.[7] Gibson recorded his praise of the first viscount in three media: manuscript, print and stone. He began in 1722 with a manuscript account of Scudamore's embassy to France and his sufferings in the civil war;[8] five years later he expanded his account in print;[9] and he recorded Scudamore's piety and benefactions in a stone inscription in Dore church.[10] Throughout, Gibson's subtext was his assertion that 'Never surely was the memory of so great a Patron of Learning and Religion, so much and so long neglected, as that of this Noble Lord!' and his determination to right such a wrong.[11] Thomas Hearne denounced Gibson's *View* as 'a weak shallow Thing' and its author 'crazed ... conceited and opiniative'.[12] Certainly it is not a work without faults, relying in places on unsupported family tradition, but used carefully it is enormously valuable, resting on an examination of the Holme Lacy muniment room and printing some documents that have since disappeared. All later works on the Scudamores use it extensively; the fault of most is to have copied it uncritically, inflating its praise of the first viscount in the process. This trend is particularly noticeable at the beginning of the nineteenth century. Just as the death of the third Viscount Scudamore in 1716 started the craze for Scudamorean praise, so the death of the last of the line, Frances, duchess of Norfolk (1750–1820) a century later was a further spur to eulogising the now defunct family. Frances Scudamore, granddaughter of the third Viscount Scudamore, had married Charles Howard, later eleventh duke of Norfolk, in 1771 but went mad soon after; the couple had no children, and he died in December 1815. One encomium, published in 1817, begins, 'the memory of the good and wise ought not to die while it is in the power of any one to prevent it'.[13]

The fame of the first Viscount Scudamore has twin facets. On one the picture of Scudamore has not changed since the early eighteenth century. Collins's account, for example, was reprinted in the 1930s with neither addition nor subtraction; the most recent account of Holme Lacy House bristles with tales of the family's loyalty and the 'stout Scudamorean spirit'.[14] The constant rehearsal of the same pieties has too often stood in the place of original documentary research. In part this has been because a large cache of family papers, the so-called duchess of Norfolk deeds, remained closed to public inspection from their removal to Chancery in 1816 until 1928, when they were made available in the Public Record Office. Another portion of the Holme Lacy archive made its way to the British Museum in the mid nineteenth century but, until recently, was little used.[15] Mark Noble candidly admitted, 'My relation of the Family of Scudamore is derived from Books. How much would deeds, Wills, Parish Registers etc have added?'[16]

On the second facet the myth of 'Good Old Lord Scudamore' is constantly appropriated to other ends. Most commonly he is cast as a saviour of the church, an archetype of the pious and loyal benefactor and patron, an encouragement to others to perform similar feats. This is as true in the Restoration judgement that Scudamore was 'a Worthy Copy for others to write after' as it is in the bishop of Dorchester's recent impression of Scudamore as a model Anglican.[17] Scudamore, who developed the redstreak cider apple, is also cast as the saviour of the cider industry. When cider was threatened with an increase in excise duty in the mid eighteenth century, the figure of Lord Scudamore the cider pioneer was used to send a warning to the government from beyond the grave.[18] The fullest printed account of the viscount after Gibson came in a work devoted to Herefordshire cider apples.[19] Recently, Scudamore has become the hero of those who wish to rescue 'real cyder' – strong, flat and wine-like – from its weaker and gaseous commercial cousin.[20] Paradoxically, his heritage is also claimed by the commercial cider companies: Bulmer's of Hereford, for example, borrowed his portrait to illustrate a promotional exhibition in the 1970s.[21]

Viscount Scudamore is constantly being remade in the image of the writer. To the late nineteenth-century cleric George Ross-Lewin he was the perfect Victorian, the 'manly high-spirited' and 'high-minded Englishman'.[22] To the Herefordshire patriot Harry Fletcher he was the epitome of 'all good Herefordshire men'.[23] While this historical reinvention of Viscount Scudamore over more than 350 years, from the early eighteenth century to the late twentieth, is interesting in itself and says much about his encomiasts, it does tell us something about the man himself. For such high praises were sung of him during his life and immediately after his death. In 1656 John Beale sent Samuel Hartlib a list of 'a great number of admirable Contrivers for the publick good':[24]

> The Lord *Scudamore* may well begin us; a rare Example, for the well-ordering of all his Family, a great preserver of woods against the Day of *England's* need, maintaining laudable hospitality regularly bounded with due sobriety, and always keeping able servants to promote the best expediences of all kinds of Agriculture.

Martin Johnson's 'Elegie on the Death of the Right Honorable the Lord Viscount Scudamore', written in or shortly after 1671, expresses many of the themes taken up by later writers: his piety, beneficence to the established church, charity to the poor, loyal service to the crown, and learning.[25] It is this mutability of Scudamore's image, that in life as in death he could be all things to all people, which is one of the reasons that make him so interesting.

NOTES

1. M. Noble, 'Memoirs of the Illustrious Family of Scudamore' (1816), HCL, 929.2, p. 1.

2 *Gentleman's Magazine* (1827), II, p. 278.

3 H. R. Trevor-Roper, *Archbishop Laud 1573–1645* (London, 1940), p. 6.

4 E. Spenser, *Faerie Queene*, ed. J. C. Smith (2 vols., Oxford, 1909); A. C. Hamilton, *The Spenser Encyclopedia* (London, 1990), pp. 634–5.

5 T. Downes, *Mr. Downs's Letter to Lord Scudamore*, in *Plain Truths: or, A Collection of Scarce and Valuable Tracts* ([?Edinburgh, ?1716]), p. 60.

6 A. Collins, *The Baronetage of England* (2 vols, London, 1720), II, p. 176.

7 Bodleian, MS Tanner 342, fol. 30r.

8 Balliol College, Oxford, MS 333; for its authorship see Atherton, thesis, p. 26 n. 4.

9 M. Gibson, *A View of the Ancient and Present State of the Churches of Door, Home-Lacy, and Hempsted* (London, 1727).

10 Copied in HRO, F88/1, p. 78.

11 Balliol College, MS 333, fol. 71r.

12 T. Hearne, *Remarks and Collections*, ed. C. E. Doble *et al.* (11 vols, Oxford History Society, 1885–1921), IX, p. 325, X, p. 13.

13 W. Skidmore, *Thirty Generations of the Scudamore/Skidmore Family in England and America* (Akron, 1991), p. 57; O. Y., 'Memoir of John first Viscount Scudamore', *Gentleman's Magazine*, 87 (1817), I, p. 99.

14 *Early History of the Scudamore Family (Reprinted from an Ancient Book)* (London, [c. 1931]); Warner Holidays Ltd, *Holme Lacy House: A History* (n.p., 1995), especially pp. 7–10. In 1995 the house opened as a hotel.

15 Atherton, thesis, pp. 16–24.

16 Noble, 'Memoirs of the Illustrious Family of Scudamore', HCL, 929.2, p. 1.

17 W. Carpenter, *Jura Cleri: or An Apologie for the Rights of the long-despised Clergy* (London, 1661), p. 11; A. Russell, *The Country Parish* (London, 1986), pp. 206, 210.

18 *An Epistle from Lord Scudamore in the Elysian Fields* (London, [c. 1740]); there is a copy at Bodleian, G. Pamph. 1744(20).

19 H. G. Bull, 'A Sketch of the Life of Lord Viscount Scudamore', in H. G. Bull, ed., *The Herefordshire Pomona*, volume I (Hereford, 1876–85).

20 R. K. French, *The History and Virtues of Cyder* (London, 1982), pp. 3, 81, 103, 175.

21 'Bulmer's Raise their Eighteenth-Century Cider Glasses', *Art and Antiques*, 18 October 1975.

22 G. H. Ross-Lewin, *Lord Scudamore a Loyal Churchman and a Faithful Steward of God's Bounty* (Edinburgh, 1900), p. 5.

23 H. L. V. Fletcher, *Portrait of the Wye Valley* (London, 1948), p. 130; also H. L. V. Fletcher, *Herefordshire* (London, 1948), p. 174; compare *MCW*, I, p. 5.

24 J. Beale, *Herefordshire Orchards, a Pattern for all England* (London, 1724), p. 22.

25 FSL, Va 147, fols 36–8.

Bibliography

MANUSCRIPTS

ARUNDEL CASTLE ARCHIVES

'Autograph letters 1632 to 1723'.

G1/88–9   Earl of Arundel's commission to treat with the emperor.

'Howard Letters and Papers 1636–1822 II Various'   Howard and Scudamore papers.

BATH CITY ARCHIVES

Furman catalogue   Bath city papers.

BERKSHIRE RECORD OFFICE

D/A1/119/18a   Will and inventory of Mary Scudamore, 1632.

Trumbull papers:.

     Trumbull Add. MS 31   Plan to restore impropriations to the church, 1629.

     Miscellaneous correspondence   G. R. Weckherlin's papers.

BIRMINGHAM CITY ARCHIVES

Coventry MSS:

     602427   Patents of creation, 1626–38.

     602725   Licences to eat flesh, 1627–39.

     603503   Commissions of the peace, 1626–40.

BRISTOL RECORD OFFICE

DC/F/1/1   Benefactions to Bristol Cathedral, 1630–33.

CAMBRIDGE UNIVERSITY LIBRARY

Add. MS 41   Notes on Peter Gunning.

Add. MS 2956   Matthew Wren's will.

Add. MS 6863   Sir Richard Hutton's journal, 1622–38.

DORSET RECORD OFFICE

D53/1   Denis Bond's chronology.

ESSEX RECORD OFFICE

D/DBa o1   Sir Thomas Barrington's papers as commissioner for the repair of St Paul's Cathedral.

D/DGd F88   James Scudamore to his father-in-law, 10 April 1654.

GLOUCESTERSHIRE RECORD OFFICE

D327	Archdeacon Furney's history of Gloucester.
D678	Sherborne House papers.
D2510	Civil war papers.
D3117/1	Tuffley (Sheephouse) deeds.
GBR/B3/2	Gloucester common council minute book, 1632–56.
GBR/G3/SO/2	Gloucester quarter sessions order book, 1633–71.
GBR/F1/11	Printed receipts for monies for the repair of St Paul's Cathedral.
PMF 173	Hempsted register, 1558–1710.

HAMPSHIRE RECORD OFFICE

21M65/A1/31	Register of the bishop of Winchester, 1632–42.
44M69/G3/199/1–16	Papers of the Hampshire commissioners for the repair of St Paul's Cathedral.

HEREFORD CATHEDRAL ARCHIVES

2382	Donors to the repair of Hereford Cathedral, 1664–65.
2761–2	Sir John Scudamore's papers as steward of the dean and chapter, 1601, 1619.
4681	Papers relating to the tithes of Sellack.
6417	Scudamore accounts, 1632.
R820	Woolhope manor court rolls, 1625–35.
R1042	Canon Pyon manor court rolls, 1626–42.
R1045–6	Canon Pyon manor court rolls, 1661–62.

Dean and chapter act book, vol. 3, 1600–1712.

HEREFORD CITY LIBRARY

631.16	'Scudamore papers. Farm accounts of Holm Lacy'. Weekly disbursements, 1667–68.
929.2	Mark Noble, 'Memoirs of the Illustrious Family of Scudamore, Viscounts Scudamore in Ireland', 1816.
FLC 924.44	MS 'Civil war Assesments relating to William Price, mercer' (no. 23132).
FLC 924.44	MS 'Papers relating to William Price, mercer' (no. 23133).
L.C. 647.1	'Scudamore MSS: Accounts 1635–37[38]'. Disbursements, 1635–38.
L.C. 647.1	'Scudamore MSS: Accounts 1640–42'. Disbursements 1640–41.
L.C. 647.1	'Scudamore MSS: Accounts 1641–42'. Disbursements 1641–42.
L.C. 647.1	'Scudamore MSS: Accounts'. Disbursements ?1631x35 and 1642–43.
L.C. 647.1	'Scudamore MSS: Accounts 1643–44'. Disbursements 1643–44.

Bibliography

L.C. 647.1   'Scudamore MSS: Accounts 1661'. Receipts at Holme Lacy, 1661–62.

pLC 726.7   'Abbeydore plan and drawing of the great window'.

L.C. 929.2   'Webb MSS: Pengelly and Scudamore Papers'.

HEREFORD RECORD OFFICE

A29/1–5   Wormelow court records, 1601–63.

A31/2–4   Maund Bryan manor court records, 1623–60.

AA20   Hereford diocese probate records.

AG64/1   Little Birch register, 1557–1741.

AL17/1   Holme Lacy register, 1561–1727.

AL19/16–18   Hereford bishops' registers, 1610–77.

AT24/1   Bosbury register, 1558–1708.

BE7/1   Sellack register, 1566–1678.

D55/1   Robert Jackson's genealogical notes.

D71/5   Agreement between Viscount Scudamore and Richard Phelps concerning Craddock Court, 1639.

F88/1   Nineteenth-century Herefordshire antiquarian notebook.

Hereford City Records: bound volumes I–IX.

Hereford City Records: law day papers, 1655–71.

Hereford City Records: mayors' accounts, box 1: 1533–1695.

Hereford City Records: quarter sessions papers, 1624–68.

MX 186   Much Dewchurch register.

Q/SO/1–2   Quarter sessions order books, 1665–89.

R93   Hopton papers.

S33   Croft of Croft papers.

W15/2   Coningsby papers.

KENT ARCHIVES OFFICE

Uncatalogued Cranfield papers.

BRITISH LIBRARY, LONDON

Additional MSS:

4168–9   Sir Thomas Roe's negotiations at Hamburg, 1638–39.

4464   Extracts from the earl of Leicester's commonplace book.

5482   Robert Knight's historical and heraldic notes.

6693   Collections relating to Herefordshire.

11042–56   Scudamore papers.

11407   Viscount Scudamore's journey to France, 1635.

11689–90   Scudamore papers.

11816	Scudamore papers.
15552	Sidney papers.
15645	Consecration of Abbey Dore, 1635.
15857–8	Correspondence of Richard Browne and John Evelyn.
15914	Sydney papers, 1550–1709.
18982	Prince Rupert's correspondence.
21567	Survey of the river Wye and the river Lugg, *c.* 1700.
24023	Correspondence of the earl of Leicester.
28326	Thomas, first Baron Fairfax, 'The High way to Hedelbergh', 1621x25.
32093	State papers, 1625–60.
32324	Papers of Sir Julius Caesar.
34013–14	Major-generals' returns of suspected persons, 1655–56.
34079	Original letters and papers, 1513–1839.
35097	Viscount Scudamore's despatches from Paris, 1635–39.
36324	Venezuela papers.
38091	Papers relating to the Palatinate.
38915	Consecration of Abbey Dore, 1635.
40730	Sidney papers, 1637.
45140–8	Scudamore papers.
45714	Copy of William Higford's 'Institutions'.
61989	Harley papers.
64890	Coke papers, 1626–27.
64898	Coke papers, 1628–29.
70001–6	Harley papers, 1582–1652.
70010	Harley papers, 1663–66.
70086	Harley papers.
70105–9	Sir Robert Harley's letters and papers.
70123	Sir Edward Harley's letters.

Additional charters:

1926	Scudamore charter.
1953	Scudamore charter.

Burney MSS:

368	Copy of Bishop Richard Corbet's speech concerning St Paul's Cathedral, 1634.

Cotton MSS:

Julius CIII	Papers of Sir Robert Cotton.

Bibliography

Cotton charters:

    i 14   Huntingdonshire papers for the collection for St Paul's Cathedral.

Egerton MSS:

    807   William Hawkins's correspondence with the Sidneys.

    1673   Lepré Balain, 'Supplement à l'histoire de France', 1624–38.

    2552   Collection of copies of warrants and commissions.

    2714–16   Gawdy papers, 1599–1649.

    2882   Register of the council of Wales and the marches, 1586–1644.

    3054   Account book of Joyce Jefferies.

Harleian MSS:

    163   Sir Simonds D'Ewes's journal, 1641–42.

    188   William Tucker's discourse on the subsidy.

    476   John Moore's parliamentary journal.

    750   Copy of Bishop Richard Corbet's speech concerning St Paul's Cathedral, 1634.

    1579   Papers of Edward, Lord Barrett of Newburgh.

    1581   Letters to George, first duke of Buckingham.

    6804   Papers of Edward Walker.

    6851   Papers of Edward Walker.

    6868   Silas Taylor's collections.

    6942   Henry Hammond's correspondence with Gilbert Sheldon.

    7001   Letters of state, 1633–1724.

    7039   Notes on Peter Gunning.

    7189   Account of the first civil war in Herefordshire.

Lansdowne MSS:

    255   Heraldic and historical collections.

    987   Notes on Thomas Lockey.

    989   Bishop White Kennett's collections.

Microfilms:

    M285   Percy correspondence.

    M772(52)   Dudley and De L'Isle papers.

Sloane MSS:

    2596   William Smith, 'The Particuler Description of England', 1588.

COLLEGE OF ARMS, LONDON
I.25   Earl marshal's book.

CORPORATION OF LONDON RECORD OFFICE
City cash accounts, vols I–III, 1632–40.

GREATER LONDON RECORD OFFICE
WCS 37–8   Westminster commission of sewers.

GUILDHALL LIBRARY, LONDON
25474/1–6   Accounts of collections for St Paul's Cathedral.
25475/1–2   Accounts of receipts and expenditure for St Paul's Cathedral.
25478   Accounts of collections for St Paul's Cathedral.
25490   Survey of St Paul's Cathedral, 1620.

HOUSE OF LORDS RECORD OFFICE
L.P. 181/23   'An Act for the making voyd of divers Judgments and
                                 Conveyances, obtained from James Scudamore Esq. by
                                 George Colt and Thomas Colt and their Trustees', en-
                                 grossed copy of this failed bill.

Main Papers   Papers of the House of Lords.
Original Acts:
    13 & 14 Car. II no. 44   'An Act for the endowment of severall Churches by the
                                 Lord Scudamore of Sligo in the Realm of Ireland'.

LAMBETH PALACE LIBRARY
COMM.XIIa/10   Survey of Hereford diocese, *c.* 1658.

NATIONAL MARITIME MUSEUM, GREENWICH
JOD/1/1   Sir John Pennington's journal, 1632–36.

PUBLIC RECORD OFFICE, LONDON
ASSI5/1/3   Hereford assize papers, 1660.
ASSI5/2   Hereford assize papers, 1666.
Bishops' institution books   Index of patrons and presentees.
C2/JAMESI   Chancery proceedings, James I.
C2/CHASI   Chancery proceedings, Charles I.
C5/56/38   Chancery: James and Thomas Jancey *v.* Lord Scudamore,
                                 1670.
C22/171/31   Chancery: James Scudamore *v.* Thomas Colt, 1667.
C24/937/23   Chancery: Coningsby Hospital *v.* Humphrey and Lettice
                                 Coningsby, 1668.
C66   Patent rolls.
C115   Duchess of Norfolk deeds: Scudamore papers.
C142/374/85   Inquisition *post mortem* of Sir James Scudamore, 1619.

Bibliography

C142/404/114	Inquisition *post mortem* of Sir John Scudamore, 1623.
C181/2-5	Entry books of commissioners, 1606–46.
C181/7	Entry book of commissioners, 1660–73.
C192/1	Entry book of commissioners for charitable uses, 1629–42.
C193/12/2	List of forced loan commissioners, 1626–27.
C193/13/1	Liber pacis, 1621–22.
C219	Parliamentary writs and election returns.
C231/3–5	Docket books of letters patent, 1615–46.
C231/7	Docket book of letters patent, 1660–79.
E115	Subsidy, certificates of residence.
E134/4 W&M/Easter 16	Exchequer: William Watts *v.* parishioners of Dore.
E157/15	Register of persons passing overseas.
E178/5333	Commissions and returns for knighthood fines in Herefordshire.
E178/7154	Returns for knighthood fines.
E179/118–19	Herefordshire subsidy rolls.
E179/283	Books and rolls of subsidy collectors.
E359/62–8	Enrolled accounts, pipe office.
E359/70	Enrolled accounts, pipe office.
E372/464–86	Pipe rolls, 1618–41.
E401/1906–20	Pells receipt books, 1621–34.
E401/2313–26	Abbreviates of pells receipt books, 1622–29.
E401/2586	Assessments for privy seal loans, 1625.
E401/2590	Papers relating to loans.
E403/1749–53	Pells issue books, 1635–40.
E403/2567–8	Auditor's privy seal books, 1632–41.
E407/35	Knighthood fines.
IND1/4224	Docket book of warrants for the great seal, 1631–38.
IND1/6746–8	Privy seal office docket books 1618–37.
IND1/23396	Schedule of the duchess of Norfolk deeds (C115).
KB27/1771	King's bench, coram rege roll, Hilary 1654.
KB27/1780	King's bench, coram rege roll, Michaelmas 1655.
PC2	Privy council registers.
PRO31/3/68–72	Baschet's transcripts of diplomatic despatches in Paris archives.
PRO31/9/17B	Panzani to Barberini, November 1635.
PROB6/27	Prerogative court of Canterbury, act book of administrations, 1652.

PROB11	Prerogative court of Canterbury, copy wills.
SO1/1–3	Signet office, 'Irish letter books', 1627–42.
SO3/5–11	Signet office docket books 1610–38.
SP14	State papers, domestic: James I.
SP16	State papers, domestic: Charles I.
SP18	State papers, domestic: Interregnum.
SP19	Papers of the committee for advance of money.
SP20	Papers of the committee for sequestrations.
SP23	Papers of the committee for compounding with delinquents.
SP28	Commonwealth exchequer papers.
SP29	State papers, domestic: Charles II.
SP78	State papers, foreign: France.
SP81	State papers, foreign: Germany, States.
SP84	State papers, foreign: Holland.
SP92	State papers, foreign: Savoy.
SP99	State papers, foreign: Venice.
SP101	State papers, foreign: newsletters.
SP103/11	State papers, foreign: treaty papers, France, 1632–37.
SP105/12–16	Gerbier's entry books, 1635–40.
STAC8/181/13	Star chamber: John Hewson *v.* Sir James Scudamore, 1614.
WARD5/15ii/2783	Feodary's survey of Sir Arthur Porter's estate, 1631.
WARD5/16	Feodaries' surveys, Herefordshire.
WARD7/68/122	Inquisition *post mortem* of Sir John Scudamore.
WARD7/80/12	Inquisition *post mortem* of Sir Arthur Porter.
WARD9/93	Court of wards, entry book of decrees, 1616–19.
WARD9/205	Court of wards, entry book of contracts for wardship and leases, 1616–22.
WARD9/217	Court of wards, entry book of petitions for composition, 1617–20.
WARD9/538	Court of wards, entry book of orders, 1621–22.

SOCIETY OF ANTIQUARIES, LONDON

790/7	William Higford's 'Institutions'.

WESTMINSTER ABBEY LIBRARY

Register of leases and grants made by the dean and chapter, 1662–66.

WESTMINSTER CITY ARCHIVES

E23	St Margaret's Westminster, churchwardens' accounts 1640–41.
E154–84	St Margaret's Westminster, overseers' accounts 1637–72.

Bibliography

E2413	St Margaret's Westminster, vestry minutes, 1591–1662.
E2568A	St Margaret's Westminster, miscellaneous parish affairs, 1579–1751.

WESTMINSTER DIOCESAN ARCHIVES

XXVIII–XXIX	Letters and papers, 1635–40.

NORTHAMPTONSHIRE RECORD OFFICE

Finch Hatton MS 133	Commissions of array.
Temple (Stowe) Box 40/11	Grant of rectory of Dore by the crown to earl of Lincoln, 1578.
XYZ 1596	Papers relating to Henry, Lord Danvers, 1598–1611.

NOTTINGHAM UNIVERSITY LIBRARY

Pw 2 Hy	Harley papers.

NOTTINGHAMSHIRE RECORD OFFICE

Portland collection:

DD4P/66/11–12	Warrants, 1642.
DD4P/66/25	Military rates of pay.
DD4P/73/2	Inquisition under commission of sewers about river Wye, 1621.

BODLEIAN LIBRARY, OXFORD

Add. A.40	John Blaxton, 'The English Appropriator, or, Sacriledge condemned'.
Add. c.132	Miscellaneous English state papers, 1617–89.
Ashmole 818	Heralds' papers.
Ashmole 857	Elias Ashmole's collections relating to the office of arms.
Bankes	Papers of Sir John Bankes.
Bodley 323	Committee for plundered ministers minute book, 1646.
Carte 1	Ormonde papers, 1577–1641.
Carte 4–5	Ormonde papers, 1642–43.
Carte 77	Papers of the earls of Huntingdon.
Carte 103	Wharton, Huntingdon, Montagu and Carte papers.
Clarendon	Clarendon state papers.
Don. f.5	Book of poetry and devotions.
Eng. hist. b.205	Papers of Bishop John Warner of Rochester.
Eng. hist. e.309	Roger Whitley's notebook.
Eng. misc. b.193–4	Papers of Bishop John Warner of Rochester.
North a.2	Sir Julius Caesar's state papers, 1603–25.

North b.1	Papers of the earl of Down.
North c.4	Letters to Sir Dudley North, 1635–72.
North c.7	Papers of the earl of Downe.
Rawlinson D.191	Notes on education by John Shipman, 1669–71.
Rawlinson D.807	Viscount Scudamore's embassy bill, April 1637.
Rawlinson D.859	Hannibal Baskervile's collections.
Rawlinson D.918	Warrants for grants.
Rawlinson D.924	Viscount Scudamore's draft passport, 1635.
Tanner 60	Lenthall papers, 1645.
Tanner 121	Militia returns, 1591.
Tanner 303	Fitzwilliam Coningsby's defence, 1643.
Tanner 342	Matthew Gibson's letters to Thomas Hearne, 1727–28.
Tanner 465	Seventeenth-century verse.
Top. Glouc. c.3	Abel Wantner, 'The History of Gloucester', 1714.
Top. Glouc. e.1	Archdeacon Richard Furney's notes on Llanthony.
Top. Herefs. d.2	Digest of the Hereford dean and chapter act book, vol. 1, 1512–66.
J. Walker c.1–7	Collections for John Walker's Sufferings.

BALLIOL COLLEGE, OXFORD

333	Life of Viscount Scudamore.

CHRIST CHURCH, OXFORD

Browne Letters, A–W	Sir Richard Browne's letters.
Browne Misc. I	Fragment of Richard Browne's notebook.

CORPUS CHRISTI COLLEGE, OXFORD

C206	Survey of the Herefordshire ministry, 1640.

MAGDALEN COLLEGE, OXFORD

350	Walter Stonehouse's sermons.

BIBLIOTHÈQUE NATIONALE, PARIS

MS Fonds Français 15916	Letters to Pompone II de Bellièvre, 1637–40.

HUNTINGTON LIBRARY, SAN MARINO, CALIFORNIA

Ellesmere MSS	Papers of the council of Wales in the marches.
H.A. Personal Box 15, no. 8	The earl of Huntingdon's advice to his son, *c.* 1614.

SHEFFIELD ARCHIVES

EM 1284(b)	List of baronets, 1616–42.
EM 1331	Pye family estate book.
Str. P. 34	Miscellaneous Strafford papers.

Bibliography

SHEFFIELD UNIVERSITY LIBRARY

Hartlib papers:

31/22	Samuel Hartlib's 'Ephemerides', 1648.
31/1/51–8	John Beale's papers.

SHROPSHIRE RECORD OFFICE

212/364	Earl of Bridgewater's correspondence.
356/278	Papers of the council of Wales in the marches.

SOMERSET RECORD OFFICE

DD/PH	Phelips papers.
D/P/Tims 2/1/1	Timsbury parish register.

STAFFORDSHIRE RECORD OFFICE

D868/2	Sir Richard Leveson's papers, 1623–61.
D988	Sir Walter Aston's commonplace book.
Q/SR/214	Quarter sessions roll, 1634.

SURREY (GUILDFORD) RECORD OFFICE

LM 1327/9	Sir George Chaworth's diary, 1621–30.
LM 1758	Roll of absentees from county quarter sessions and assizes, 1624–28.

WARWICKSHIRE RECORD OFFICE

CR2017	Papers of Basil, Viscount Feilding.

FOLGER SHAKESPEARE LIBRARY, WASHINGTON

Va147	Theophilus Alye's commonplace book.
Vb2–3	Scudamore papers.

WILTSHIRE RECORD OFFICE

413/498	Letter from Charles I to the landgrave of Hesse-Cassel, 1637.
865/392	Bullen Reymes's diary, 1632.

WORCESTER (ST HELEN'S) RECORD OFFICE

705: 423 BA 3164/7	Covenant to levy fines on the lands of Sir John Scudamore, 1623.

BEINECKE LIBRARY, YALE UNIVERSITY

Osborn MS b.28	John Gwillim, 'Famous Funerals'.

PRINTED PRIMARY SOURCES

Acts of the Privy Council of England. 1542–1631 (46 vols, London, 1890–1964).

Adams, Thomas, *The Sovldiers Honovr* (London, 1617).

Alison, Richard, *An Howres Recreation in Musicke* (London, 1606).

Andrewes, Lancelot, *Ninety-six Sermons* (5 vols, Oxford, 1851–53).

Andrewes, Lancelot, *XCVI. Sermons* (London, 1629).

An Answer of Truth to a Scandalous and False Pamphlet (London, 1661). There is a copy at HCL, 324.242.

Ashburnham, John, *A Narrative by John Ashburnham of his Attendance on King Charles the First*, ed. George, earl of Ashburnham (2 vols, London, 1830).

Aston, Sir Thomas, ed., *A Collection of Svndry Petitions* ([London], 1642).

Atherton, I. J., ed., 'An Account of Herefordshire in the First Civil War', *Midland History*, 21 (1996), pp. 136–55.

Aubrey, John, *Brief Lives*, ed. A. Clark (2 vols, Oxford, 1898).

Aubrey, John, *Brief Lives*, ed. O. L. Dick (Harmondsworth, 1976).

Austin, Ralph, *A Treatise of Frvit-Trees* (Oxford, 1653).

Austin, Ralph, *The Spirituall Vse, of an Orchard* (Oxford, 1653).

Avenel, D. L. M., ed., *Lettres, instructions diplomatiques et papiers d'état du Cardinal de Richelieu* (8 vols, Paris, 1853–77).

Babington, Gervase, *Workes*, ed. T. Charde and M. Smith (London, 1615).

Bacon, Francis, *The Essays*, ed. S. H. Reynolds (Oxford, 1890).

Baker, L. M., ed., *The Letters of Elizabeth Queen of Bohemia* (London, 1953).

Bannister, A. T., *Diocese of Hereford. Institutions, etc. (A.D. 1539–1900)* (Cantilupe Society, Hereford, 1923).

Barksdale, Clement, *Memorials of the Life and Death of H. Grotius* (London, 1654).

Barksdale, Clement, *Nympha Libethris, or The Cotswold Muse* (London, 1816).

Barksdale, Clement, ed., *The Illustrious Hugo Grotius* (London, 1655).

Baxter, Richard, *Autobiography*, ed. N. H. Keeble (London, 1974).

Beale, John, *Herefordshire Orchards, a Pattern for all England* (London, 1724).

Best, Henry, *The Farming and Memorandum Books of Henry Best*, ed. D. Woodward (British Academy Records of Social and Economic History, new series, 8, London, 1984).

Bettey, J. H., *Calendar of the Correspondence of the Smyth Family of Ashton Court 1548–1642* (Bristol Record Society, 35, 1982).

Birch, T., and Williams, R. F., eds, *The Court and Times of Charles the First* (2 vols, London, 1848).

Birch, T., and Williams, R. F., eds, *The Court and Times of James the First* (2 vols, London, 1848).

Black, W. H., ed., *Docquets of Letters Patent ... Passed under the Great Seal of King Charles I at Oxford* (n.p., 1837).

Blencowe, R. L., ed., *Sydney Papers* (London, 1825).

Bibliography

Boase, F. S., ed., *The Diary of Thomas Crosfield* (London, 1973).

Bourchier, E., ed., *The Diary of Sir Simonds D'Ewes* (Paris, [1974]).

Brathwait, Richard, *The English Gentleman* (London, 1630).

Brerewood, Edward, *A Learned Treatise of the Sabbath* (Oxford, 1630).

Brerewood, Edward, *A Second Treatise of the Sabbath* (Oxford, 1632).

A Brief Declaration of the State of the Accompt of all Monies received and paid, as well for and towards the Reparation of the Cathedral Church of St. Paul, London ([London, 1685]). There is a copy at Cambridge University Library, Broadsides, A.68.7.

Brigden, S., ed., 'The Letters of Richard Scudamore to Sir Philip Hoby, September 1549– March 1555', *Camden Miscellany XXX* (Camden, 4th series, 39, 1990), pp. 67–148.

Bromley, G., ed., *A Collection of Original Royal Letters* (London, 1787).

B[rouncker], E[dward], *The Cvrse of Sacriledge* (Oxford, 1630).

Browning, A., ed., *English Historical Documents 1660–1714* (London, 1953).

Bryskett, Lodowick, *A Discovrse of Civill Life* (London, 1606).

Buckeridge, John, *A Sermon Preached at the Fvneral of ... Lancelot late Lord Bishop of Winchester* (London, 1629).

Butler, A. T., *The Visitation of Worcestershire 1634* (Harleian Society, 90, 1938).

Calendar of State Papers and Manuscripts, relating to English affairs, existing in the Archives and Collections of Venice, and in other Libraries of Northern Italy (38 vols, London, 1864–1947).

Calendar of State Papers, Colonial Series, 1574–1660, ed. W. N. Sainsbury (London, 1860).

Calendar of State Papers, Domestic Series, 1547–1685 (75 vols, London, 1856–1939).

Carpenter, William, *Jura Cleri: or An Apologie for the Rights of the long-despised Clergy* (Oxford, 1661).

Carte, T., ed., *A Collection of Original Letters and Papers, concerning the Affairs of England, from the Year 1641 to 1660. Found among the Duke of Ormonde's papers* (2 vols, London, 1739).

A Catalogue of the Moneys, Men, and Horse, already subscribed unto by severall Counties of this Kingdome, and undertaken for His Majesteyes Service (London, 1642).

A Catalogue of the Names of the Knights, Citizens, and Burgesses, that have Served in the last Four Parliaments (London, 1656), BL, Thomason Tract E1602(6).

[Cayet, Pierre Victor], *Chronologie novenaire, contenant l'histoire de la guerre, sous le regne du ... Henri IIII* (3 vols, Paris, 1608).

Certaine Informations from severall parts of the Kingdome, no. 18, 15–22 May 1643.

Chamberlain, John, *The Letters of John Chamberlain*, ed. N. E. McClure (2 vols, Memoirs of the American Philosophical Society, 12, 1939).

Charles-Louis, Elector Palatine, *A Protestation* (London 1637).

Charles-Louis, Elector Palatine, *The Manifest* (London, 1637).

Charrier, F., *Magnae Britanniae auster Iknographicus ad illustriss. generasissimumq; dominum domin. I. Vicecomitem Scudamoreum* ([Paris], 1637).

The Citie Scout, no. 6, 2 September 1645.

The Citties Weekly Post, no. 7, 27 January–3 February 1646, BL, Thomason Tract E320(6).

Cleland, James, *The Institvtion of a Yovng Noble Man* (Oxford, 1607).

Collins, A., ed., *Letters and Memorials of State* (2 vols, London, 1746).

A Continuation of Certaine Speciall and Remarkable Passages (1643–45).

Cooper, J. P., ed., *Wentworth Papers 1597–1628* (Camden, 4th series, 12, 1973).

The Copy of a Letter sent from Bristoll (London, 1643), BL, Thomason Tract E94(30).

Cosin, John, *Works* (5 vols, Oxford, 1843–55).

Cuming, J., ed., 'Mr. Henry Yelverton (afterward Sir Henry) his Narrative of what Passed on his being Restored to the King's Favour in 1609', *Archaeologia*, 15 (1806), pp. 27–52.

Cust, R. P., ed., *The Papers of Sir Richard Grosvenor, 1st Bart. (1585–1645)* (Record Society of Lancashire and Cheshire, 134, 1996).

Davies, Edward, *The Art of War, and Englands Traynings* (London, 1619).

Davies, Edward, *Military Directions, or The Art of Trayning* (London, 1618).

Day, Angel, *The English Secretorie* (London, 1586).

A Declaration, or Resolution of the County of Hereford (London, 1642).

Dee, John, *The Private Diary of Dr. John Dee*, ed. J. O. Halliwell (Camden Society, 1st series, 19, 1842).

A Diary, or an Exact Iournall, no. 84, 18–24 December 1645.

Dingley, Thomas, *History from Marble*, ed. J. G. Nichols, (2 vols, Camden Society, 2nd series 94, 97, 1867–68).

Doddridge, John, *A Compleat Parson* (London, 1630).

Downes, Theophilus, *Mr. Downs's Letter to Lord Scudamore*, in *Plain Truths: or, A Collection of Scarce and Valuable Tracts* ([?Edinburgh, ?1716]), pp. 56–64.

Ellis, H., ed., 'Compositions for Knighthood, temp. Charles I', *Sussex Archaeological Collections*, 16 (1864), pp. 45–51.

An Epistle from Lord Scudamore, in the Elysian Fields, to Velters Cornwall (London, [c. 1740]).

An Essay of a King (London, 1642).

Evelyn, John, *Sylva ...To which is annexed Pomona* (2nd edition, London, 1670).

Fage, Mary, *Fames Rovle* (London, 1637).

Fairholt, F. W., ed., *Poems and Songs relating to George Villiers, Duke of Buckingham* (Percy Society, 1850).

Faraday, M. A., ed., *Herefordshire Militia Assessments of 1663* (Camden, 4th series, 10, 1972).

Farley, Henry, *The Complaint of Pavles* ([London], 1616).

Farley, Henry, *Portland-stone in Paules-Church-Yard* (London, 1622).

Farley, Henry, *St. Pavles-Chvrch her Bill for the Parliament* ([London], 1621).

Farnaby, Thomas, *Florilegium Epigrammatum Graecorum* (London, 1629).

Finet, John, *Finetti Philoxenis* (London, 1656).

Fisher, J., *The Priest's Duty & Dignity* (London, 1636).

Fleming, Gyles, *Magnificence Exemplified: and, The Repaire of Saint Pauls exhorted unto* (London, 1634).

Bibliography

French, J. M., ed., *The Life Records of John Milton* (5 vols, New Brunswick, 1949–58).

Fuller, Thomas, *The History of the Worthies of England* (3 parts, London, 1662).

G., H., 'Sepulchral Memorials of the Scudamore Family at Home-Lacy, co. Hereford', *Collectanea Topographica et Genealogica*, 4 (1837), pp. 256–9.

Gainsford, Thomas, *The Secretaries Stvdie* (London, 1616).

Gardiner, S. R., ed., *The Fortescue Papers* (Camden Society, 2nd series, 1, 1871).

Gibson, T. E., ed., *Crosby Records: A Cavalier's Note Book, being Notes, Anecdotes and Observations of William Blundell* (London, 1880).

Godefroy, Theodore, and Godefroy, Denys, *Le Ceremonial François* (2 vols, Paris, 1649).

Godwin, Francis, *Annales of England. Containing the reignes of Henry the Eighth. Edward the Sixt. Queene Mary*, trs. Morgan Godwin (London, 1630).

Goodman, F. R., ed., *The Diary of John Young S.T.P. Dean of Winchester, 1616 to the Commonwealth* (London, 1928).

Goodman, Godfrey, *The Court of King James the First*, ed. J. S. Brewer (2 vols, London, 1839).

Gregory, John, *A Discourse of the Morality of the Sabbath* (London, 1681).

Gregory, John, *Novum Testamentum una cum Scholiis Graecis* (Oxford, 1703).

Grosart, A. B., ed., *The Lismore Papers* (10 vols, privately printed, 1886–88).

Grotius, Hugo, *Briefwisseling van Hugo Grotius* vol. VI *1635–1636*, ed. B. L. Meulenbroek ('s-Gravenhage, 1967).

Grotius, Hugo, *Epistolae* (Amsterdam, 1687).

Grotius, Hugo, *The Truth of the Christian Religion*, ed. J. Le Clerc, (London, 1711).

Gwillim, John, *A Display of Heraldrie* (London, 1611).

Hammond, Henry, *Miscellaneous Theological Works*, ed. N. Pocock (Oxford, 1847).

Hartlib, Samuel, ed., *A Designe for Plentie, by an Vniversall Planting of Frvit-Trees* (London, [1652]).

Hearne, Thomas, *Remarks and Collections*, ed. C. E. Doble, D. W. Rannie and H. E. Salter (11 vols, Oxford History Society, 1885–1921).

Herbert, Edward, *The Autobiography*, ed. S. Lee (2nd edition, London, 1907).

Herbert, George, *Works*, ed. F. E. Hutchinson (Oxford, 1941).

Herbert, H., *Dramatic Records*, ed. J. Q. Adams (New Haven and London, 1917).

Heylyn, Peter, *Cyprianus Anglicus* (London, 1668).

Higford, William, *Institutions or Advice to his Grandson* (London, 1658).

Higford, William, *The Institution of a Gentleman* (London, 1660).

Historical Manuscripts Commission, *Third Report* (London, 1872).

> *Fourth Report* (London, 1874).
>
> *Fifth Report* (London, 1876).
>
> *Sixth Report* (London, 1877).
>
> *Seventh Report* (London, 1879).
>
> *Eighth Report* (London, 1881).

Calendar of the Manuscripts of the most honourable the Marquis of Salisbury (24 vols, series 9, London, 1883–1976).

Tenth Report, Appendix, Part IV. The Manuscripts of the Earl of Westmorland ... and Others (series 13, London, 1885).

Eleventh Report, Appendix, Part I. The Manuscripts of Henry Duncan Skrine, esq. Salvetti Correspondence (series 16, London, 1887).

Supplementary Report on the Manuscripts of his Grace the Duke of Hamilton, ed. J. H. McMaster and M. Wood (series 21, London, 1932).

Twelfth Report, Appendix, Parts I–III. The Manuscripts of the Earl Cowper (3 vols, series 23, London, 1888–89).

Twelfth Report, Appendix, Part IX. The Manuscripts of the Duke of Beaufort (series 27, London, 1891).

The Manuscripts of his Grace the Duke of Portland (10 vols, series 29, London, 1891–1931).

Thirteenth Report, Part IV. MSS of Rye and Hereford Corporations (series 31, London, 1892).

Fifteenth Report, Appendix, Part II. The Manuscripts of J. Elliot Hodgkin (series 39, London, 1897).

Report on the Manuscripts of the Duke of Buccleuch and Queensberry (3 vols, series 45, London, 1899–1926).

Calendar of the Manuscripts of the Marquis of Bath (5 vols, series 58, London, 1904–81).

Report on the Manuscripts of the Earl of Denbigh (Part V), ed. S. C. Lomas (series 68, London, 1911).

Report on the Manuscripts of Lord De L'Isle and Dudley (6 vols, series 77, London, 1925–66).

A Calendar of the Shrewsbury and Talbot Papers in Lambeth Library and the College of Arms, ed. C. Jamison and G. R. Batho (2 vols, London, 1966–71).

Hobbes T., *The Correspondence*, ed. N. Malcolm (2 vols, Clarendon Edition of the Works of Thomas Hobbes, vols VI–VII, Oxford, 1994).

Hobbes, Thomas, *Die neue Wissenschaft des Thomas Hobbes*, ed. F. O. Wolf (Stuttgart, 1969).

Holles, G, *Memorials of the Holles Family 1493–1656*, ed. A. C. Wood (Camden, 3rd series, 55, 1937).

Hooker, Richard, *Of the Lawes of Ecclesiastical Politie* (London, 1622).

[Hotman, Jean], *The Ambassador*, trs. J. Shawe (London, 1603).

Howell, James, *A Discourse concerning the Precedency of Kings ... also adjoyned a Distinct Treatise of Ambassadors* (London, 1664).

Hughes, John, ed., *A Complete History of England* (3 vols, London, 1719).

The Humble Representation of his late Majesties and Princes Domestick Servants ([London], 1655), BL, Thomason Tract 669f19(75).

Hyde, Edward, earl of Clarendon, *The History of the Rebellion and Civil Wars in England*, ed. W. D. Macray (6 vols, Oxford, 1888).

The Iudgement of the Court of Warre upon the Charge laid against Sir Richard Cave, for the Delivery up of Hereford (Oxford, 1643), BL, Thomason Tract 669f7(26).

Jansson, M., and Bidwell, W. B., eds, *Proceedings in Parliament 1625* (New Haven, 1987).

Johnson, R. C., Keeler, M. F., Cole, M. J., and Bidwell, W. B., eds, *Proceedings in Parliament 1628* (6 vols, New Haven and London, 1977–83).

Journals of the House of Commons, 1547–1732 (21 vols, [London, 1742–]).

Journals of the House of Lords, 1515–1731 (23 vols, [London, 1767–]).

Journals of the House of Lords [of Ireland] vol. I. *From 10 Car. I 1634 to 10 Gul. III 1698* (Dublin, 1779).

Kekewich, M. L., ed., *Princes and Peoples: France and the British Isles, 1620–1714: An Anthology of Primary Sources* (Manchester, 1994).

Kempe, A. J., ed., *The Loseley Manuscripts* (London, 1836).

Kenyon, J. P., ed., *The Stuart Constitution 1603–1688: Documents and Commentary* (Cambridge, 1966).

King, John, *A Sermon at Paules Crosse, on behalfe of Paules Church, March 26. 1620* (London, 1620).

The Kingdomes Weekly Intelligencer, no. 131, 16–23 December 1645.

Kitto, J. V., ed., *The Register of St. Martin-in-the-Fields London 1619–1636* (Harleian Society, register section, 66, 1936).

Knowler, W., ed., *The Earl of Strafforde's Letters and Dispatches* (2 vols, London, 1739).

Langenes, Bernardt, *The Description of a Voyage made by certaine Ships of Holland into the East Indies*, trs. W. Phillip (London, 1598).

Larkin, J. F., and Hughes, P. L., eds, *Stuart Royal Proclamations* (2 vols, Oxford, 1973–83).

Laud, William, *Harangve Prononcee en la Chambre de l'Estoille, la Mercredy XIV. de Iuin, de l'Anné M.DC.XXXVII. a la Censvre, de Iehan BastWick Henry Burton, & Guillaume Prinn, touchant les Pretenduës Innouations en l'Eglise*, trs. John Scudamore ([Paris], 1637[8]). There is a copy in Canterbury Cathedral library, press mark W/H–4–16.

Laud, William, *The History of the Troubles and Tryal* (London, 1695).

Laud, William, *A Relation of the Conference betweene William Lawd ... and Mr. Fisher the Jesuite* (London, 1639).

Laud, William, *A Speech delivered in the Starr-Chamber* (London, 1637).

Laud, William, *Works*, ed. W. Scott and J. Bliss (7 vols, Oxford, 1847–60).

Legg, J. W., ed., *English Orders for Consecrating Churches in the Seventeenth Century* (Henry Bradshaw Society, 41, 1911).

Legg, L. G. W., ed., 'A Relation of a Short Survey of the Western Counties made by a Lieutenant of the Military Company in Norwich in 1635', *Camden Miscellany XVI* (Camden, 3rd series, 52, 1936), pp. 1–128.

Leland, John, *Itinerary*, ed. T. Hearne (2nd edition, 9 vols, Oxford, 1744–45).

Lewis, T. T., ed., *Letters of the Lady Brilliana Harley* (Camden Society, 1st series, 58, 1854).

A List of the Names of the Long Parliament, Anno 1640. Likewise of the Parliament holden at Oxford (London, 1659), BL, Thomason Tract E1836(4).

Lloyd, David, *Memoires of the Lives, Actions, Sufferings & Deaths of those Noble, Reverend, and Excellent Personnages, that Suffered ... in our late Intestine Wars* (London, 1668).

Lonchay, H., Cuvelier, J., and Lefevre, J., eds, *Correspondance de la cour d'Espagne sur les affaires des Pays-bas au XVIIe siècle* (6 vols, Brussels, 1923–37).

Loomie, A. J., ed., *Ceremonies of Charles I: The Note Books of John Finet 1628–1641* (New York, 1987).

M., G., ed., 'Ottleiana: or, Letters, &c. Relating to Shropshire, Written during and subsequent to the Civil War', 3 parts, *Collectanea Topographica et Genealogica*, 5 (1838), pp. 291–304; 6 (1839), pp. 21–37; 7 (1840), pp. 84–110.

Maclean, J., and Heane, W. C., eds, *The Visitation of the County of Gloucester, taken in the Year 1623* (Harleian Society, 21, 1885).

Macray, W. D., ed., *Annals of the Bodleian Library* (2nd edition, Oxford, 1984; first published, 1890).

Markham, Gervase, 'The Muster-master', ed. C. L. Hamilton, *Camden Miscellany XXVI* (Camden, 4th series, 14, 1975), pp. 49–76.

Markham, Gervase, *The Souldiers Accidence, or An Introduction into Military Discipline* (London, 1625).

Marlowe, Christopher, *Tamburlaine the Great*, ed. U. Ellis-Fermor (2nd edition, London, 1951).

Martin, C. T., ed., *Minutes of Parliament of the Middle Temple* (4 vols, London, 1904–05).

Mercurius Aulicus (1643–44).

Mercurius Bellicus. The Fourth Intelligence from Reading (London, 1643), BL, Thomason Tract E100(7).

Mercurius Civicus, no. 2, 11–18 May 1643.

Mercurius Veridicus, no. 26, 18–25 October, 1645, BL, Thomason Tract E307(7).

Mersenne, M, *Correspondence*, ed. C. de Waard *et al.* (12 vols, Paris, 1932–72).

Metcalfe, W. C., ed., *The Visitations of Essex* (2 vols, Harleian Society, 13–14, 1878–79).

Michaud, J. F., and Poujoulat, J. J. F., eds, *Nouvelle collection des mémoires relatifs a l'histoire de France* (new edition, 34 vols, Paris, 1854–57).

Morden, R., and Lea, P., *A Prospect of London and Westminster* (London, 1682).

Morgan, F. C., 'Bosbury Tithes and Oblations 1635–1641', *Transactions of the Woolhope Naturalists' Field Club*, 38:2 (1965), pp. 140–8.

Morgan, F. C., ed., 'The Steward's Accounts of John, First Viscount Scudamore of Sligo (1601–1671) for the Year 1632', *Transactions of the Woolhope Naturalists' Field Club*, 33 (1949–51), pp. 155–84.

Morgan, P., 'Churchwardens' Accounts of Pembridge, Herefordshire, for the Years 1642 and 1643', *Transactions of the Woolhope Naturalists' Field Club* (1939–41), pp. 156–60.

A Most True Relation of Divers Notable Passages &c of Divine Providence (London, 1643), BL, Thomason Tract E100(12).

A Most True Relation of the Present State of His Majesties Army (London, 1642), BL, Thomason Tract E244(2).

Mountagu, Richard, *Appello Caesarem* (London, 1625).

Mountagu, Richard, *Diatribae vpon the First Part of the late History of Tithes* (London, 1621).

Mountagu, Richard, *A New Gagg for the Gospell?* (London, 1624).

Bibliography

Newdigate, B. H., 'Mourners at Sir Philip Sidney's Funeral', *Notes and Queries*, 180 (January–June 1941), pp. 398–401.

Newton, John, *The Compleat Arithmetician* (London, 1691).

Notestein, W., Relf, F. H., and Simpson, H., eds, *Commons Debates in 1621* (7 vols, New Haven, 1935).

Oldenburg, Henry, *Correspondence*, ed. A. R. and M. B. Hall (13 vols, Madison, Milwaukee and London, 1965-86).

[Oxford University], *Academiae Oxoniensis Fvnebra Sacra aeternae Memoriae serenissimae Reginae Annae* ([Oxford], 1619).

Paulet, William, *The Lord Marqves Idelnes* (London, 1586).

Peacock, E., *The Army Lists of the Roundheads and Cavaliers* (2nd edition, London, 1874).

A Perfect Diurnall of the Passages in Parliament, no. 15, 19-26 September 1642.

Philip, I. G., ed., *Journal of Sir Samuel Luke* (2 vols, Oxfordshire Record Society, 1950–53).

Philips, John, *Cider: A Poem in Two Books*, ed. C. Dunster (London, 1791).

Phillimore, W. P. W., and Fry, G. S., eds, *Abstracts of Gloucestershire Inquisitiones Post Mortem. Part I: 1625–1636* (British Records Society, 1893).

Phillips, W., ed., 'The Ottley Papers relating to the Civil War', *Transactions of the Shropshire Archaeological and Natural History Society*, 2nd series, 7 (1895), pp. 241–360.

Pierce, Thomas, *The New Discoverer Discover'd* (London, 1659).

A Plaine Case, or, Reasons to Convince any (that would be Honest or Thrive in the World) which Side to take in this Present Warre ([Oxford], 1643), BL, Thomason Tract E56(14).

Powell, W. S., *John Pory, 1572–1636: The Life and Letters of a Man of Many Parts* (Chapel Hill, 1977).

Prynne, William, *Canterburies Doome* (London, 1646).

Prynne, William, *Hidden Workes of Darkenes brought to Public Light* (London, 1645).

Repgen, K., and Braubach, M., eds, *Acta Pacis Westphalicae. Serie I: Instruktionen. Band 1: Frankreich, Schweden, Kaiser* (Münster, 1962).

[Reynolds, John], *Vox Coeli, or Newes from Heaven* ('Elisium', 1624).

Richelieu, Armand Jean du Plessis de, *The Political Will and Testament*, trs. T. E. H. (2 parts, London, 1695).

Rimbault, E. F. ed., *The Old Cheque-book, or Book of Remembrance, of the Chapel Royal, from 1561 to 1744* (Camden Society, 2nd series, 3, London, 1872).

Rogers, Henry, *An Answer to Mr. Fisher the Jesvite* (London, 1623).

Rogers, Henry, *The Protestant Church existant, and their Faith professed in all Ages, and by whom* (London, 1638).

Romei, Annibale, *The Courtiers Academie*, trs. I. K. ([London, 1598]).

Roy, I., ed., *The Royalist Ordnance Papers 1642–1646* (Oxfordshire Record Society, 43, 49, 1963–64, 1971–73).

Royal Commission on Historical Monuments, England, *Herefordshire* (3 vols, London, 1931–37).

Royal Society, *Philosophical Transactions* (London, 1665–).

Rushworth, John, ed., *Historical Collections* (7 vols, London, 1659–1721).

Russell, J. F., ed., *The Form and Order of the Consecration and Dedication of the Parish Church of Abbey Dore* (London, 1874).

Rymer, T., *Foedera* (3rd edition, 10 vols, The Hague, 1739–45).

Sanderson, W., *A Compleat History of the Life and Raigne of King Charles* (London, 1658).

Scrope, R., and Monkhouse, T., eds, *State Papers collected by Edward, Earl of Clarendon* (3 vols, Oxford, 1767–86).

Scudamore, Barnabas, *A Letter sent to the Right Honourable the Lord Digby* (Oxford, 1645), BL, Thomason Tract E303(4).

Scudamore, Barnabas, *Sir Barnabas Scvdamore's Defence*, ed. I. J. Atherton (Akron, 1992).

Scudamore, James, trs., *The Sixty Sixe Admonitory Chapters of Basilius, King of the Romans, to his Sonne Leo, in Acrostick Manner* (Paris, 1638).

Searle, A., ed., *The Barrington Family Letters 1628–1632* (Camden, 4th series, 28, 1983).

Seddon, P. R., ed., *Letters of John Holles 1587–1637* (3 vols, Thoroton Society record series, 31, 35–6, 1975, 1983, 1986).

Segar, W., *Honor Military, and Ciuill* (London, 1602).

[Silhon, Jean de], *The Minister of State*, trs. H. Herbert (London, 1658).

Silhon, Jean de, *The Second Part of the Minister of State*, trs. H. Herbert (London, 1663).

Simpson, W. S., ed., *Documents Illustrating the History of S. Paul's Cathedral* (Camden Society, 2nd series, 26, 1880).

Slingsby, Henry, *Diary*, ed. D. Parsons (London, 1836).

Sorbière, S., *A Voyage to England* (London, 1709).

Speciall Passages and Certaine Informations, no. 38, 25 April–2 May 1643.

A Speech delivered by the right honourable William Lord Marquesse Hartford (London, 1643), BL, Thomason Tract, E85(31).

Spelman, Henry, *De Non Temerandis Ecclesiis. A Tract of the Rights and Respect due vnto Churches* (2nd edition, London, 1616).

Spelman, Henry, *The History and Fate of Sacrilege* (London, 1698).

Spelman, Henry, *The Larger Treatise concerning Tithes* (London, 1647).

Spenser, Edmund, *Faerie Queene*, ed. J. C. Smith (2 vols, Oxford, 1909).

Squibb, G. D., ed., *Reports of Heraldic Cases in the Court of Chivalry 1623–1732* (Harleian Society, 107, 1956).

Staley, V., ed., *Hierurgia Anglicana: Documents and Extracts illustrative of the Ceremonial of the Anglican Church after the Reformation* (new edition, 3 parts, London, 1902–03).

Stanhope, B. S., and Moffatt, H. C., *The Church Plate of the County of Hereford* (London, 1903).

Steer, F. W., *The Ashburnham Archives: A Catalogue* (Lewes, 1958).

Steer, F. W., *A Catalogue of the Earl Marshal's Papers at Arundel Castle* (Harleian Society, 115–16, 1964).

Bibliography

Sturgess, H. A. C., ed., *Register of Admissions to the Honourable Society of the Middle Temple from the Fifteenth Century to the year 1944*, vol. I, *1501–1781* (London, 1949).

Symonds, Richard, *Diary of the Marches of the Royal Army during the Great Civil War*, ed. C. E. Long (Camden Society, 1st series, 79, 1859).

T., R., *De Templis, a Treatise of Temples* (London, 1638).

Tallemant, Gédéon (Sieur des Réaux), *Historiettes*, ed. A. Adam (2 vols, Paris, 1960–61).

Taylor, Jeremy, *The Whole Works*, ed. R. Haber (15 vols, London, 1828).

Thompson, R., ed., *Samuel Pepys' Penny Merriments* (London, 1976).

Thorndike, Herbert, *The Theological Works* (6 vols, Oxford, 1844–56).

Tighe, W. J., 'William Laud and the Reunion of the Churches: Some Evidence from 1637 and 1638', *Historical Journal*, 30:3 (1987), pp. 717–27.

To the Honorable the Knights Citizens and Burgesses of the Commons House assembled in Parliament the Humble Petition of the High Sheriffe and Divers of the Gentrey, Ministers, Freeholders, and Inhabitants of the County of Hereford ([London, 1642]), BL, Thomason Tract 669f6(16).

Tombes, John, *Christs Commination against Scandalizers* (London, 1641).

Tombes, John, *Fermentum Pharisaeorum* (London, 1643).

Townshend, Henry, *Diary of Henry Townshend of Elmley Lovett, 1640–1663*, ed. J. W. Bund (2 vols, Worcestershire Historical Society, 1920).

Traherne, T., *Centuries, Poems, and Thanksgivings*, ed. H. M. Margoliouth (2 vols, Oxford, 1958).

Trapp, John, *Mellificium Theologicum, or, The Marrow of Many Good Authors* (London, 1647), issued as part of John Trapp, *A Commentary or Exposition upon all the Epistles* (London, 1647).

Trevor-Roper, H. R., 'Five Letters of Sir Thomas Bodley', *Bodleian Library Record*, 11 (1941–49), pp. 134–9.

Two Petitions. The One, presented to the Honourable House of Commons, from the Countie of Hereford May the Fourth, 1642 (London, 1642).

[Udall, Ephraim], *Noli Me Tangere is a Thinge to be Thought on* (London, 1642).

Vaughan, R., ed., *The Protectorate of Oliver Cromwell* (2 vols, London, 1838).

Vaughan, Rowland, *Most Approved, and Long Experienced Water-workes* (London, 1610).

Verney, F. P., ed., *Memoirs of the Verney Family* (4 vols, London, 1892–99).

Walker, Edward, *Historical Discourses, upon Several Occasions* (London, 1705).

Walker, William, *A Sermon Preached in St. Pauls-Church in London, in the Course of the Divinity Lecture there. Novemb. 28 1628* (London, 1629).

Wall, George, *A Sermon at the Lord Archbishop of Canterbury his Visitation Metropoliticall, held at All-Saints in Worcester* (London, 1635).

Waller, Edmund, *Poems*, ed. G. T. Drury (London, 1893).

Walsingham, Francis, *Sir Francis Walsingham's Anatomizing of Honesty, Ambition, and Fortitude*, in Robert Cotton, *Cottoni Posthuma*, ed. J. Howell (London, 1672), pp. 329–40.

Wandesford, Christopher, *A Book of Instructions*, ed. T. Comber (Cambridge, 1777).

Ward, Samuel, *Woe to Drvnkards* (London, 1622).

Warner, R., ed., *Epistolary Curiosities; Series the First: Consisting of Unpublished Letters, of the Seventeenth century, Illustrative of the Herbert family* (Bath, 1818).

Warwick, Philip, *Memoires of the Reigne of King Charles I* (London, 1701).

Washbourn, J., ed., *Bibliotheca Gloucestrensis: A Collection of Scarce and Curious Tracts, relating to the County and City of Gloucester* (2 vols, Gloucester, 1823–25).

Watkyns, Rowland, *Flamma sine Fumo*, ed. P. C. Davies (Cardiff, 1968, first published 1662).

Webb, J., 'Some Passages in the Life and Character of a Lady resident in Herefordshire and Worcestershire during the Civil War', *Archaeologia*, 37 (1857), pp. 189–223.

The Welchmens Lamentation and Complaint, for te Losse of her great Towne and City of Hereford ([London], 1643).

Whelan, B., ed., 'Hereford and the Civil War: Some Original Papers', *Dublin Review*, 179 (1926), pp. 44–72.

Whitelocke, Bulstrode, *Memorials of the English Affairs* (London, 1682).

Wicquefort, Abraham de, *The Embassador and his Functions*, trs. J. Digby (London, 1716).

Williams, Gryffith, *The True Church* (London, 1629).

Witty Apophthegms delivered at Several Times, and upon Several Occasions, by King James, King Charls, the Marquess of Worcester, Francis Lord Bacon, and Sir Thomas Moor (London, 1669).

Wood, A., *Fasti Oxonienses*, ed. P. Bliss (2 vols in 1, London, 1815–20).

Woodruff, C. E., ed., 'Notes on the Municipal Records of Queenborough', *Archaeologia Cantiana*, 32 (1897), pp. 169–85.

Worth, R. N., ed., *The Buller Papers* (privately printed, 1895).

Wren, Christopher, *Parentalia: or, Memoirs of the Family of the Wrens* (London, 1750).

Wren, Matthew, *Articles to be Inquired of within the Diocesse of Hereford* (London, 1635).

[Younge, Richard], *Philarguromastix. or, The Arraignment of Covetouseness, and Ambition* (2 vols, London, 1653).

[Tract beginning] 'You perceive by His Majesties Letters Patents for rebuilding the Cathedral Church of St Pauls ...' ([London], 14 June 1678). There is a copy at Cambridge University Library, Syn 4.67.6.

Zagorin, P., 'Thomas Hobbes's Departure from England in 1640: An Unpublished Letter', *Historical Journal*, 31:1 (1978), pp. 157–60.

SECONDARY SOURCES

Adams, S., 'Early Stuart Politics: Revisionism and After', in J. R. Mulryne and M. Shewring, eds, *Theatre and Government under the Early Stuarts* (Cambridge, 1993), pp. 29–56.

Adamson, J. S. A., 'The Baronial Context of the English Civil War', *Transactions of the Royal Historical Society*, 5th series, 40 (1990), pp. 93–120.

Bibliography

Adamson, J. S. A., 'Chivalry and Political Culture in Caroline England', in K. Sharpe and P. Lake, eds, *Culture and Politics in Early Stuart England* (Basingstoke, 1994), pp. 161–97.

Addleshaw, G. W. O., and Etchells, F., *The Architectural Setting of Anglican Worship* (London, 1948).

Alexander, M. A. van C., *Charles I's Lord Treasurer: Sir Richard Weston, Earl of Portland (1577–1635)* (London, 1975).

Alldridge, N., 'Loyalty and Identity in Chester Parishes 1540-1640', in S. J. Wright, ed., *Parish, Church and People: Local Studies in Lay Religion, 1350–1750* (London, 1988), pp. 85–124.

Anderson, M. S., *The Rise of Modern Diplomacy 1450–1919* (Harlow, 1993).

Andriette, E. A., *Devon and Exeter in the Civil War* (Newton Abbot, 1971).

The Annual Register 1805 (London, 1807).

Anstruther, G., *A Hundred Homeless Years: English Dominicans 1558–1658* (London, 1958).

Anstruther, G., *The Seminary Priests: A Dictionary of the Secular Clergy of England and Wales* (4 vols, Ware, Ushaw and Great Wakering, 1969–77).

Ashton, R., *The City and the Court 1603-1643* (Cambridge, 1979).

Askew, R., 'Faith in the Theological Countryside', *Theology*, 94:759 (May/June 1991), pp. 195–8.

Atherton, I. J., 'The Itch Grown a Disease: Manuscript Transmission of News in the Seventeenth Century', in J. Raymond, ed., *News, Newspapers, and Society in Early Modern Britain* (London, 1999).

Atherton, I. J., 'Viscount Scudamore's "Laudianism": The Religious Practices of the first Viscount Scudamore', *Historical Journal*, 34:3 (1991), pp. 567–96.

Aylmer, G. E., 'Collective Mentalities in mid Seventeenth-Century England: II. Royalist Attitudes', *Transactions of the Royal Historical Society*, 5th series, 37 (1987), pp. 1–30.

Baker, T., *History of the College of St John the Evangelist, Cambridge*, ed. J. E. B. Mayor (Cambridge, 1869).

Barnes, T. G., *The Clerk of the Peace in Caroline Somerset* (Leicester University, Department of English History, occasional papers, 14, Leicester, 1961).

Barnes, T. G., *Somerset 1625–1640: A County's Government during the 'Personal Rule'* (London, 1961).

Bayliss, D. G., 'The Effect of Bringewood Forge and Furnace on the Landscape of Part of Northern Herefordshire to the End of the Seventeenth Century', *Transactions of the Woolhope Naturalists' Field Club*, 45 (1985–87), pp. 721–9.

Beaven, A. B., *The Aldermen of the City of London temp. Henry III.–1912* (2 vols, London, 1908–13).

Beller, E. A., 'The Mission of Sir Thomas Roe to the Conference at Hamburg, 1638–40', *English Historical Review*, 41 (1926), pp. 61–77.

Bennett, M., 'Between Scylla and Charybdis: The Creation of Rival Administrations at the Beginning of the English Civil War', *Local Historian*, 22:4 (November 1992), pp. 191–202.

Bennett, M., *The Civil Wars in Britain and Ireland, 1638–1651* (Oxford, 1997).

Bernard, G. W., 'The Church of England, *c*. 1529–*c*. 1642', *History*, 75 (1990), pp. 181–206.

Bigland, R., *Historical, Monumental and Genealogical Collections, relative to the County of Gloucester* (3 vols, London, 1786–1838).

Bindoff, S. T., ed., *The House of Commons, 1509–1558* (3 vols, London, 1982).

Bosher, R. S., *The Making of the Restoration Settlement: The Influence of the Laudians 1649–1662* (London, 1951).

Bougeant, G. H., *Histoire des guerres et des negociations qui précédèrent le traité de Wetphalie, sous le regne de Louis XIII* (3 vols, Paris, 1751–67).

Boyce, B., *The Polemic Character 1640–1661: A Chapter in English Literary History* (Lincoln, 1955).

Boyce, B., *The Theophrastan Character in England to 1642* (Cambridge, 1947).

Boynton, L. O. J., *The Elizabethan Militia 1558–1638* (London, 1967).

Birch, T., *The History of the Royal Society* (4 vols, London, 1756–57).

Braddick, M. J., *Parliamentary Taxation in Seventeenth-Century England: Local Administration and Response* (Woodbridge, 1994).

Brooke, J., 'Namier and Namierism', *History and Theory*, 3:3 (1963–64), pp. 331–47.

Bull, H. G., 'A Sketch of the Life of Lord Viscount Scudamore', in H. G. Bull, ed., *The Herefordshire Pomona*, vol. I (Hereford, 1876–85).

'Bulmer's raise their Eighteenth-century Cider Glasses', *Art and Antiques*, 18 October 1975.

Bund, J. W. W., *The Civil War in Worcestershire, 1642–1646* (Gloucester, 1979, first published 1905).

Burckhardt, C. J., *Richelieu and his Age:* vol. III. *Power Politics and the Cardinal's death*, trs. B. Hay (London, 1971).

Burgess, G., *Absolute Monarchy and the Stuart Constitution* (New Haven and London, 1996).

Burgess, G., 'The Divine Right of Kings Reconsidered', *English Historical Review*, 107 (1992), pp. 837–61.

Burgess, G., 'On Revisionism: An Analysis of Early Stuart Historiography in the 1970s and 1980s', *Historical Journal*, 33:3 (1990), pp. 609–27.

Burgess, G., 'Revisionism, Politics and Political Ideas in Early Stuart England', *Historical Journal*, 34:2 (1991), pp. 465–78.

Butler, M., *Theatre and Crisis 1632–1642* (Cambridge, 1984).

Calder, I. M., *Activities of the Puritan Faction of the Church of England 1625–33* (London, 1957).

Cant, R., 'The Embassy of the Earl of Leicester to Denmark in 1632', *English Historical Review*, 54 (1939), pp. 252–62.

Carlisle, N., *An Inquiry into the Place and Quality of the Gentlemen of His Majesty's most honourable Privy Chamber* (London, 1829).

Carlton, C., *Archbishop William Laud* (London and New York, 1987).

Carlton, C., *Charles I: The Personal Monarch* (London, 1983).

Carmona, M., *Marie de Médicis* (Paris, 1981).

Carter, D. P., 'The "Exact Militia" in Lancashire, 1625–1640', *Northern History*, 11 (1976 for 1975), pp. 87–106.

Chaney, E., *The Grand Tour and the Great Rebellion: Richard Lassels and 'The Voyage of Italy'* *in the Seventeenth Century* (Geneva, 1985).

Charles, A. M., 'Sir Henry Herbert: The Master of the Revels as a Man of Letters', *Modern Philology*, 80 (1982–83), pp. 1–12.

Church, W. F., *Richelieu and Reason of State* (Princeton, 1972).

Clark, Peter, '"The Ramoth-Gilead of the Good": Urban Change and Political Radicalism at Gloucester 1540–1640', in P. Clark, A. G. R. Smith and N. Tyacke, eds, *The English Commonwealth 1547–1640: Essays in Politics and Society presented to Joel Hurstfield* (Leicester, 1979).

Cockburn, J. S., *A History of English Assizes 1558–1714* (London, 1972).

Cockburn, J. S., *Calendar of Assize Records: Home Circuit Indictments, Elizabeth I and James I. Introduction* (London, 1985).

Cogswell, T., *The Blessed Revolution: English Politics and the Coming of War, 1621–1624* (Cambridge, 1989).

Cogswell, T., 'Prelude to Ré: The Anglo-French Struggle over La Rochelle, 1624–1627', *History*, 71 (1986), pp. 1–21.

Cokayne, G. E., *Complete Baronetage* (5 vols, Exeter, 1900–09).

Cokayne, G. E., *Complete Peerage*, ed. V. Gibbs *et al.* (2nd edition, 13 vols in 14, London, 1910–40).

Collins, A., *The Baronetage of England* (2 vols, London, 1720).

Colvin, H. M., ed., *The History of the King's Works* (6 vols, London, 1963–82).

Colvin, H. M., 'The Restoration of Abbey Dore Church in 1633–34', *Transactions of the Woolhope Naturalists' Field Club*, 32 (1946–48), pp. 235–7.

Commissioners for Inquiring Concerning Charities, *Reports* (32 vols in 40, London, *c.* 1818–40).

Coningsby, T., *The Case of the right honourable Thomas Earl Coningesby* ([?London, ?1722]).

Coningsby, T., *Marden* (2 vols, London, 1722–27).

Cope, E. S., *The Life of a Public Man: Edward, First Baron Montagu of Boughton, 1562–1644* (Memoirs of the American Philosophical Society, 142, 1981).

Cope, E. S., *Politics without Parliaments, 1629–1640* (London, 1987).

Cope, E. S., 'Politics without Parliament: The Dispute about Muster Masters' Fees in Shropshire in the 1630s', *Huntington Library Quarterly*, 45 (1982), pp. 271–84.

Copinger, W. A., *The Manors of Suffolk: Notes on their History and Devolution* (7 vols, privately printed, 1905–12).

Cottret, B., *The Huguenots in England: Immigration and Settlement c. 1550–1700*, trs. P. and A. Stevenson (Cambridge and Paris, 1991).

Coward, B., *The Stuart Age: England, 1603–1714* (2nd edition, London, 1994).

Croft, P., 'The Religion of Robert Cecil', *Historical Journal*, 34:4 (1991), pp. 773–96.

Cust, R. P., 'Charles I and a Draft Declaration for the 1628 Parliament', *Historical Research*, 63:151 (June 1990), pp. 143–61.

Cust, R. P., *The Forced Loan and English Politics 1626–1628* (Oxford, 1987).

Cust, R. P., 'Honour, Rhetoric and Political Culture: The Earl of Huntingdon and his Enemies', in S. D. Amussen and M. Kishlansky, eds, *Political Culture and Cultural Politics in Early Modern England* (Manchester, 1995), pp. 84–111.

Cust, R. P., 'Humanism and Magistracy in Early Stuart England' (unpublished paper).

Cust, R. P., 'News and Politics in Early Seventeenth-century England', *Past and Present*, 112 (August 1986), pp. 60–90.

Cust, R. P., 'Politics and the Electorate in the 1620s', in R. P. Cust and A. Hughes, eds, *Conflict in Early Stuart England* (Harlow, 1989), pp. 134–67.

Cust, R. P., 'Wentworth's "Change of Sides" in the 1620s', in J. F. Merritt, ed., *The Political World of Thomas Wentworth, Earl of Strafford, 1621–1641* (Cambridge, 1996), pp. 63–80.

Cust, R. P., and Hughes, A., eds, *Conflict in Early Stuart England: Studies in Religion and Politics, 1603–1642* (Harlow, 1989).

Cust, R. P., and Hughes, A., 'Introduction: After Revisionism', in R. P. Cust and A. Hughes, eds, *Conflict in Early Stuart England* (Harlow, 1989), pp. 1–46.

Cust, R. P., and Lake, P., 'Sir Richard Grosvenor and the Rhetoric of Magistracy', *Bulletin of the Institute of Historical Research*, 54 (1981), pp. 40–54.

D., B., 'The Armor of Sir James Scudamore', *Bulletin of the Metropolitan Museum of Art*, 8:6 (June 1913), pp. 118–23.

Davies, E., *A General History of the County of Radnor* (Brecknock, 1905).

Davies, G., 'The Election at Hereford in 1702', *Huntington Library Quarterly*, 12:3 (1949), pp. 322–7.

Davies, J., *The Caroline Captivity of the Church: Charles I and the Remoulding of Anglicanism 1625–1641* (Oxford, 1992).

Dawson, B. S., 'Notes on the Manor and Church of Hempsted', *Transactions of the Bristol and Gloucester Archaeological Society*, 13 (1888–89), pp. 146–54.

Dearmer, P., *Linen Ornaments of the Church* (Alcuin Club tracts, 17, 1929).

Delorme, M., 'A Watery Paradise: Rowland Vaughan and Hereford's "Golden Vale"', *History Today*, 39 (July 1989), pp. 38–43.

Dendy, D. R., *The Use of Lights in Christian Worship* (Alcuin Club collections, 41, 1959).

Dietz, F. C., *English Public Finance 1558–1641* (2nd edition, London, 1964).

Donagan, B., 'A Courtier's Progress: Greed and Consistency in the Life of the Earl of Holland', *Historical Journal*, 19 (1976), pp. 317–53.

Duffy, E., *The Stripping of the Altars: Traditional Religion in England 1400–1580* (New Haven and London, 1992).

Duncan-Jones, K., *Sir Philip Sidney: Courtier Poet* (London, 1991).

Duncumb, J., Cooke, W. H., *et al.*, *Collections towards the History and Antiquities of the County of Hereford* (6 vols, Hereford, 1804–1915).

Eales, J. S., *Puritans and Roundheads: the Harleys of Brampton Bryan and the Outbreak of the English Civil War* (Cambridge, 1990).

Eales, J. S., 'Sir Robert Harley, K.B. (1579–1656), and the "Character" of a Puritan', *British Library Journal*, 15:2 (1989), pp. 134–57.

Bibliography

Earl, D. C., *The Political Thought of Sallust* (Amsterdam, 1966).

Early History of the Scudamore Family (Reprinted from an Ancient Book) (London, [?1931]).

Elliott, J. H., *The Count-Duke of Olivares: The Statesman in an Age of Decline* (New Haven and London, 1986).

Elliott, J. H., *Richelieu and Olivares* (Cambridge, 1984).

Elliott, J. H., 'The Year of the Three Ambassadors', in H. Lloyd-Jones, V. Pearl and B. Worden, eds, *History and Imagination: Essays in Honour of H. R. Trevor-Roper* (London, 1981), pp. 165–81.

Evans, J. T., *Seventeenth-Century Norwich: Politics, Religion, and Government, 1620–1690* (Oxford, 1979).

Everitt, A., *The Community of Kent and the Great Rebellion* (Leicester, 1973).

Fagniez, G., *Le Père Joseph et Richelieu (1577–1638)* (2 vols, Paris, 1894).

Faraday, M. A., 'Ship Money in Herefordshire', *Transactions of the Woolhope Naturalists' Field Club*, 41:2 (1974), pp. 219–29.

Fincham, K., ed., *The Early Stuart Church, 1603–1642* (Basingstoke, 1993).

Firth, C. H., and Lomas, S. C., *Notes on the Diplomatic Relations of England and France 1603–1688* (Oxford, 1906).

Fletcher, A. J., *A County Community in Peace and War: Sussex 1600–1660* (London and New York, 1975).

Fletcher, A. J., *Gender, Sex and Subordination in England, 1500–1800* (New Haven and London, 1995).

Fletcher, A. J., 'Honour, Reputation and Local Officeholding in Elizabethan and Stuart England', in A. J. Fletcher and J. Stevenson, eds, *Order and Disorder in Early Modern England* (Cambridge, 1985), pp. 92–115.

Fletcher, A. J., *The Outbreak of the English Civil War* (London, 1981).

Fletcher, A. J., *Reform in the Provinces: The Government of Stuart England* (New Haven, 1986).

Fletcher, H. L. V, *Herefordshire* (London, 1948).

Fletcher, H. L. V, *Portrait of the Wye Valley* (London, 1968).

Foster, A., 'Church Policies of the 1630s', in R. P. Cust and A. Hughes, eds, *Conflict in Early Stuart England* (Harlow, 1989), pp. 193–223.

Foster, A. 'The Clerical Estate Revitalised', in K. Fincham, ed., *The Early Stuart Church, 1603–1642* (Basingstoke, 1993), pp. 139–60.

Foster, E. R., 'Printing the Petition of Right', *Huntington Library Quarterly*, 38:1 (1974–75), pp. 81–3.

Foster, J., *Alumni Oxonienses: The Members of the University of Oxford, 1500–1714* (4 vols, Oxford, 1891–92).

Foster, J., *Collectanea Genealogica* vol. I (privately printed, 1887).

Fraser, P., *The Intelligence of the Secretaries of State and their Monopoly of Licensed News, 1660–1688* (Cambridge, 1956).

French, R. K., *The History and Virtues of Cyder* (London, 1982).

Fulton, T. W., *The Sovereignty of the Sea: An Historical Account of the Claims of England to the Dominion of the British Seas* (Edinburgh and London, 1911).

Fussell, G. E., *The English Dairy Farmer 1500–1900* (London, 1966).

Gardiner, S. R., *History of England from the Accession of James I. to the Outbreak of the Civil War, 1603–1642* (new edition, 10 vols, London, 1893–96).

Gibson, M., *A View of the Ancient and Present State of the Churches of Door, Home-Lacy, and Hempsted; Endow'd by the right honourable John, Lord Viscount Scudamore. With some Memoirs of that Ancient Family; and an Appendix of Records and Letters relating to the same Subject* (London, 1727).

Gladwish, P., 'The Herefordshire Clubmen: A Reassessment', *Midland History*, 10 (1985), pp. 62–71.

Greenblatt, S., *Renaissance Self-fashioning from More to Shakespeare* (Chicago and London, 1980).

Greenslade, M. W., *The Staffordshire Historians* (Collections for a History of Staffordshire, 4th series, 11, Staffordshire Record Society, 1982).

Gruenfelder, J. K., *Influence in Early Stuart Elections* (Columbus, 1981).

Guy, J. A., 'The Origins of the Petition of Right Reconsidered', *Historical Journal*, 25:2 (1982), pp. 289–312.

Habakkuk, H. J., 'Landowners and the Civil War', *Economic History Review*, 2nd series, 18 (1965), pp. 130–51.

Ham, R. E., 'The Four Shire Controversy', *Welsh History Review*, 8:4 (1977) pp. 381–400.

Hamilton, A. C., ed., *The Spenser Encyclopedia* (London, 1990).

Haller, W., *Liberty and Reformation in the Puritan Revolution* (New York, 1955).

Harrison, G. B., *The Life and Death of Robert Devereux Earl of Essex* (London, 1937).

Hasler, P. W., ed., *The House of Commons 1558–1603* (3 vols, London, 1981).

Hayes, J., *The Garton Collection of English Table Glass* (London, 1965).

Heal, F., *Hospitality in Early Modern England* (Oxford, 1990).

Heal, F., 'Reputation and Honour in Court and Country: Lady Elizabeth Russell and Sir Thomas Hoby', *Transactions of the Royal Historical Society*, 6th series, 6 (1996), pp. 161–78.

Heal, F., and Holmes, C., *The Gentry in England and Wales, 1500–1700* (Basingstoke, 1994).

Heath-Agnew, E., *A History of Hereford Cattle and their Breeders* (London, 1983).

Henning, B. D., ed., *The House of Commons 1660–1690* (3 vols, London, 1983).

Herbert, N. M., ed., *A History of the County of Gloucester*, vol. IV: *The City of Gloucester* (Victoria County History of Gloucestershire, Oxford, 1988).

Herrup, C., '"To Pluck Bright Honour from the Pale-faced Moon": Gender and Honour in the Castlehaven Story', *Transactions of the Royal Historical Society*, 6th series, 6 (1996), pp. 137–59.

Hervey, M. F. S., *The Life, Correspondence and Collections of Thomas Howard, Earl of Arundel* (Cambridge, 1921).

Hibbard, C., *Charles I and the Popish Plot* (Chapel Hill, 1983).

Bibliography

Hill, C., *Economic Problems of the Church from Archbishop Whitgift to the Long Parliament* (Oxford, 1956).

Hill, C., *A Nation of Change and Novelty: Radical Politics, Religion and Literature in Seventeenth-Century England* (1990).

Hirst, D., *Authority and Conflict: England 1603–58* (London, 1986).

Hirst, D., 'Court, Country, and Politics before 1629', in K. Sharpe, ed., *Faction and Parliament* (Oxford, 1978), pp. 105–37.

Hirst, D., 'The Place of Principle', *Past and Present*, 92 (August 1981), pp. 79–99.

Hirst, D., 'The Privy Council and Problems of Enforcement in the 1620s', *Journal of British Studies*, 18:1 (1978), pp. 46–66.

Hirst, D., *The Representative of the People? Voters and Voting in England under the Early Stuarts* (Cambridge, 1975).

Hopkinson, C., *Herefordshire under Arms: A Military History of the County* (Bromyard, 1985).

Hughes, A. 'The King, the Parliament and the Localities during the English Civil War', in R. P. Cust and A. Hughes, eds, *The English Civil War* (London, 1997), pp. 261–87.

Hughes, A., 'Local History and the Origins of the Civil War', in R. P. Cust and A. Hughes, eds, *Conflict in Early Stuart England* (Harlow, 1989), pp. 224–53.

Hughes, A., *Politics, Society and Civil War in Warwickshire, 1620–1660* (Cambridge, 1987).

Hutton, R., *The Rise and Fall of Merry England: The Ritual Year 1400–1700* (Oxford, 1994).

Hutton, R., *The Royalist War Effort 1642–1646* (London, 1982).

Jackson, J. N., 'Some Observations upon the Herefordshire Environment of the Seventeenth and Eighteenth Centuries', *Transactions of the Woolhope Naturalists' Field Club*, 36:1 (1959), pp. 28–41.

Jancey, E. M., *The Royal Charters of the City of Hereford* (Hereford, 1973).

Jenkins, G. H., *The Foundations of Modern Wales: Wales 1642–1780* (Oxford, 1993).

Johnson, R., *The Ancient Customs of the City of Hereford* (London and Hereford, 1868).

Johnson, R., *A Lecture on the Ancient Customs of the City of Hereford* (Hereford, 1845).

Judges, A. V., 'Philip Burlamachi: A Financier of the Thirty Years' War', *Economica*, 6 (1926), pp. 285–300.

Kaufman, H. A., *Conscientious Cavalier: Colonel Bullen Reymes* (London, 1962).

Kearney, H., *Strafford in Ireland 1633–41: A Study in Absoutism* (Manchester, 1959).

Keeler, M. F., *The Long Parliament, 1640–1641: A Biographical Study of its Members* (Memoirs of the American Philosophical Society, 36, 1954).

Kennett, W., *The Case of Impropriations* (London, 1704). Kennett's notes for a proposed second edition are interleaved with the copy at Bodleian Library, Gough Eccl. Top. 47–48.

Kepler, J. S., *The Exchange of Christendom: The International Entrepôt at Dover 1622–1651* (Leicester, 1976).

Kerridge, E., *The Farmers of Old England* (London, 1973).

Key, N. E., 'Comprehension and the Breakdown of Consensus in Restoration Herefordshire', in T. Harris, P. Seaward and M. Goldie, eds, *The Politics of Religion in Restoration England* (Oxford, 1990), pp. 191–215.

Kishlansky, M., 'The Emergence of Adversary Politics in the Long Parliament', *Journal of Modern History*, 49 (1977), pp. 617–40.

Kishlansky, M., *A Monarchy Transformed: Britain, 1603–1714* (Harmondsworth, 1996).

Kishlansky, M., *Parliamentary Selection: Social and Political Choice in Early Modern England* (Cambridge, 1986).

Kleinman, R., *Anne of Austria, Queen of France* (Columbus, 1985).

Lake, P., 'The Collection of Ship Money in Cheshire during the Sixteen-thirties: A Case Study of Relations between Central and Local Government', *Northern History*, 17 (1981), pp. 44–71.

Lake, P., 'Lancelot Andrewes, John Buckeridge, and Avant-garde Conformity at the Court of James I', in L. L. Peck, ed., *The Mental World of the Jacobean Court* (Cambridge, 1991), pp. 113–33.

Lake, P., 'The Laudian Style: Order, Uniformity, and the Pursuit of the Beauty of Holiness in the 1630s', in K. Fincham, ed., *The Early Stuart Church, 1603–1642* (Basingstoke, 1993), pp. 161–85.

Lake, P., 'Retrospective: Wentworth's Political World in Revisionist and Post-Revisionist Perspective', in J. F. Merritt, ed., *The Political World of Thomas Wentworth, Earl of Strafford, 1621–1641* (Cambridge, 1996), pp. 252–83.

Lambley, K., *The Teaching and Cultivation of the French Language in England during Tudor and Stuart times* (Manchester, 1920).

Langston, J. N., 'John Workman, Puritan Lecturer in Gloucester', *Transactions of the Bristol and Gloucestershire Archaeological Society*, 66 (1945), pp. 219–32.

Larminie, V., *The Godly Magistrate: The Private Philosophy and Public Life of Sir John Newdigate, 1571–1610* (Dugdale Society, occasional papers, 28, 1982).

Larminie, V., *Wealth, Kinship and Culture: The Seventeenth-Century Newdigates of Arbury and their World* (Woodbridge, 1995).

Lee, F. G., *A Glossary of Liturgical and Ecclesiastical Terms* (London, 1877).

Lee, S., and Stephen, L., eds, *Dictionary of National Biography* (63 vols, London, 1885–1900).

Lee-Warner, E., *The Life of John Warner Bishop of Rochester 1637–1666* (London, 1901).

Leman, A., 'Urbain VIII et les origines du Congrès de Cologne', *Revue d'Histoire Ecclésiastique*, 19 (1923), pp. 370–83.

Lennard, T. B., *An Account of the Families of Lennard and Barrett* (privately printed, 1908).

Leonard, H. H., 'Distraint of Knighthood: The Last Phase, 1625–41', *History*, 63 (1978), pp. 23–37.

Leslie, M., 'The Spiritual Husbandry of John Beale', in M. Leslie and T. Raylor, eds, *Culture and Cultivation in Early Modern England: Writing and the Land* (Leicester and London, 1992), pp. 151–72.

Levack, B. P., *The Civil Lawyers in England 1603–1641* (Oxford, 1973).

Lloyd, J. E., and Jenkins, R. T., eds, *The Dictionary of Welsh Biography down to 1940* (London, 1959).

Lockyer, R., *Buckingham: The Life and Political Career of George Villiers, first Duke of Buckingham, 1592–1628* (London and New York, 1984).

Bibliography

Loomie, A. J., 'The Spanish Faction at the Court of Charles I, 1630–8', *Bulletin of the Institute of Historical Research*, 59:139 (May 1986), pp. 37–49.

MacDonald, J., and Sinclair, J., *History of Hereford Cattle* (London, 1886).

McGee, J. S., 'William Laud and the Outward Face of Religion', in R. L. DeMolen, ed., *Leaders of the Reformation* (Selinsgrove, 1984), pp. 318–44.

McCoy, R. C., 'Old English Honour in an Evil Time: Aristocratic Principle in the 1620s', in R. M. Smuts, ed., *The Stuart Court and Europe: Essays in Politics and Political Culture* (Cambridge, 1996), pp. 133–55.

MacCulloch, D., 'The Impact of the English Reformation', *Historical Journal*, 38:1 (1995), pp. 151–3.

MacNamara, F. N., *Memorials of the Danvers Family (of Dauntsey and Culworth)* (London, 1895).

Malcolm, J. L., *Caesar's Due: Loyalty and King Charles, 1642–1646* (London, 1983).

Marston, J. G., 'Gentry Honor and Royalism in Early Stuart England', *Journal of British Studies*, 13:1 (1973), pp. 21–43.

Marwil, J. L., *The Trials of Counsel: Francis Bacon in 1621* (Detroit, 1976).

Mathias, R., *Whitsun Riot* (London, 1963).

Matthews, A. G., *Walker Revised, being a Revision of John Walker's 'Sufferings of the Clergy during the Grand Rebellion 1642–60'* (Oxford, 1948).

Mattingly, G., *Renaissance Diplomacy* (Harmondsworth, 1965).

Mayes, C. R., 'The Early Stuarts and the Irish Peerage', *English Historical Review*, 73 (1958), pp. 227–51.

Mayes, C. R., 'The Sale of Peerages in Early Stuart England', *Journal of Modern History*, 29 (1957), pp. 21–37.

Merritt, J. F., ed., *The Political World of Thomas Wentworth, Earl of Strafford, 1621–1641* (Cambridge, 1996).

Milton, A., *Catholic and Reformed: The Roman and Protestant Churches in English Protestant Thought, 1600–1640* (Cambridge, 1995).

Milton, A., 'Thomas Wentworth and the Political Thought of the Personal Rule', in J. F. Merritt, ed., *The Political World of Thomas Wentworth, Earl of Strafford, 1621–1641* (Cambridge, 1996) pp. 133–56.

Morgan, F. C., 'Hereford Cathedral and the Vicars' Choral Library', *Transactions of the Woolhope Naturalists' Field Club*, 35 (1955–57), pp. 222–55.

Morgan, F. C., 'Local Government in Hereford', *Transactions of the Woolhope Naturalists' Field Club*, 31 (1942–45), pp. 37–57.

Morres, H. R., *The History of the Principal Transactions of the Irish Parliament from the year 1634 to 1666*, ed. D. Englefield (2 vols, Shannon, 1971; first published 1792).

Morrill, J. S., 'The Attack on the Church of England in the Long Parliament', in D. Beales and G. Best, eds, *History, Society and the Churches: Essays in Honour of Owen Chadwick* (Cambridge, 1985), pp. 105–24.

Morrill, J. S., *Cheshire, 1630–1660: County Government and Society during the English Revolution* (Oxford, 1974).

Morrill, J. S., 'The Church in England, 1642–9', in J. S. Morrill, ed., *Reactions to the English Civil War* (London, 1982), pp. 89–114.

Morrill, J. S., 'The Making of Oliver Cromwell', in J. S. Morrill, ed., *Oliver Cromwell and the English Revolution* (Harlow, 1990), pp. 19–48.

Morrill, J. S., *The Nature of the English Revolution* (Harlow, 1993).

Morrill, J. S., 'The Religious Context of the English Civil War', *Transactions of the Royal Historical Society*, 5th series, 34 (1984), pp. 155–78.

Morrill, J. S., *The Revolt of the Provinces: Conservatives and Radicals in the English Civil War 1630–1650* (London, 1976).

Morrill, J. S., 'Sir William Brereton and England's Wars of Religion', *Journal of British Studies*, 24:3 (July 1985), pp. 311–32.

Morrill, J. S., 'William Davenport and the "Silent Majority" of Early Stuart England', *Journal of the Chester Archaeological Society*, 58 (1975), pp. 115–29.

Morriss, R. K., and Shoesmith, R., *Caradoc Court: Interim Report* (City of Hereford Archaeology Unit, Hereford, 1989).

Namier, L. B., *Personalities and Powers* (London, 1955).

Namier, L. B., *The Structure of Politics at the Accession of George III* (2nd edition, London, 1957).

Neville, M., 'Dore Abbey, Herefordshire, 1536–1912', *Transactions of the Woolhope Naturalists' Field Club*, 41 (1975), pp. 312–17

Newman, P. R., 'The King's Servants: Conscience, Principle, and Sacrifice in Armed Royalism', in J. S. Morrill, P. Slack and D. Woolf, eds, *Public Duty and Private Conscience in Seventeenth-Century England* (Oxford, 1993), pp. 225–41.

Newman, P. R., *The Old Service: Royalist Regimental Colonels and the Civil War, 1642–46* (Manchester, 1993).

Notestein, W., *The Winning of the Initiative by the House of Commons* (London, 1924).

O'Day, R., and Heal, F., eds, *Continuity and Change: Personnel and Administration of the Church in England 1500–1642* (Leicester, 1976).

[Oldmixon, J.], *The Critical History of England, Ecclesiastical and Civil* (2 vols, London, 1724–26).

Oman, C., *English Church Plate 597–1830* (London, 1957).

Ormond, R., and Rogers, M., *Dictionary of British Portraiture* (4 vols, London, 1979–81).

Oster, M., 'The Scholar and the Craftsman Revisited: Robert Boyle as Aristocrat and Artisan', *Annals of Science*, 49 (1992), pp. 255–76.

Page, W., and Bund, J. W. W., *The Victoria History of the County of Worcester*, vols 2–4, (London, 1906–24).

Parker, G., *The Army of Flanders and the Spanish Road 1567–1659: The Logistics of Spanish Victory and Defeat in the Low Countries' Wars* (Cambridge, 1972).

Parker, G., *The Thirty Years' War* (London, 1984).

Parry, G., *The Golden Age Restor'd: The Culture of the Stuart Court, 1603–42* (Manchester, 1981).

Patterson, C. F., 'Leicester and Huntingdon: Urban Patronage in Early Modern England', *Midland History*, 16 (1991), pp. 45–62.

Pearl, V., *London and the Outbreak of the Puritan Revolution* (Oxford, 1961).

Bibliography

Peck, L. L., *Court Patronage and Corruption in Early Stuart England* (London, 1993).

Peck, L. L., '"For a King not to be Bountiful were a Fault": Perspectives on Court Patronage in Early Stuart England', *Journal of British Studies*, 25:1 (1986), pp. 31–61.

Phillips, J. R., *Memoirs of the Civil War in Wales and the Marches* (2 vols, London, 1874).

Pincus, S. C. A., *Protestantism and Patriotism: Ideologies and the Making of English Foreign Policy, 1650–1668* (Cambridge, 1996).

Pintard, R., *Le Libertinage érudit dans la première moitié du XVIIe siècle* (Paris, 1943).

Pliny the Younger, *Letters*, trs. J. D. Lewis (London, 1879).

Pollock, L., 'Younger Sons in Tudor and Stuart England', *History Today*, 39 (June 1989), pp. 23–9.

Porter, H. B., *Jeremy Taylor, Liturgist (1613–1667)* (Alcuin Club collections, 61, 1979).

Prawdin, M. (*vere* Charol), *Marie de Rohan, Duchesse de Chevreuse* (London, 1977).

Quintrell, B. W., 'Charles I and his Navy in the 1630s', *Seventeenth Century*, 3:2 (1988), pp. 159–79.

Quintrell, B. W., 'The Church triumphant? The Emergence of a Spiritual Lord Treasurer, 1635–1636', in J. F. Merritt, ed., *The Political World of Thomas Wentworth, Earl of Strafford, 1621–1641* (Cambridge, 1996), pp. 81–108.

Rabb, T. K., 'The Role of the Commons', *Past and Present*, 92 (August 1981), pp. 55–78.

Ranum, O. A., 'Courtesy, Absolutism, and the Rise of the French State, 1630–1660', *Journal of Modern History*, 52 (1980), pp. 426–51.

Ranum, O. A., *Richelieu and the Councillors of Louis XIII: A Study of the Secretaries of State and Superintendents of Finance in the Ministry of Richelieu, 1635–1642* (Oxford, 1963).

Rawlinson, R., *The History and Antiquities of the City and Cathedral-Church of Hereford* (London, 1717).

Raylor, T., 'Samuel Hartlib and the Commonwealth of Bees', in M. Leslie and T. Raylor, eds, *Culture and Cultivation* (Leicester and London, 1992), chapter 5.

Reade, C., ed., *Memorials of Old Herefordshire* (London, 1904).

Reeve, L. J., *Charles I and the Road to Personal Rule* (Cambridge, 1989).

Roberts, M., *Sweden as a Great Power, 1611–1697* (London, 1968).

Roberts, S. K., *Recovery and Restoration in an English County: Devon Local Administration 1646–1670* (Exeter, 1985).

Robinson, C. J., *A History of the Castles of Herefordshire and their Lords* (London and Hereford, 1869).

Robinson, C. J., *A History of the Mansions and Manors of Herefordshire* (London, 1873).

Roosen, W., 'Early Modern Diplomatic Ceremonial: A Systems Approach', *Journal of Modern History*, 52 (1980), pp. 452–76.

Roskell, J. S., Clark, L., and Rawcliffe, C., eds, *The House of Commons 1386–1421* (4 vols, Stroud, 1992).

Ross-Lewin, G. H., *Lord Scudamore a Loyal Churchman and a Faithful Steward of God's Bounty* (Edinburgh, 1900).

Rowe, V. A., 'The Influence of the Earls of Pembroke on Parliamentary Elections, 1625–41', *English Historical Review*, 50 (1950), pp. 242–56.

Rowe, V. A., 'Robert, second Earl of Warwick and the Payment of Ship-Money in Essex', *Transactions of the Essex Archaeological Society*, 3rd series, 1:2 (1962), pp. 160–4.

Ruigh, R. E., *The Parliament of 1624* (Cambridge, Mass., 1971).

Russell, A., *The Country Parish* (London, 1986).

Russell, C., 'The British Problem and the English Civil War', *History*, 72 (1987), pp. 395–415.

Russell, C., *The Causes of the English Civil War* (Oxford, 1990).

Russell, C., *The Fall of the British Monarchies 1637–1642* (Oxford, 1991).

Russell, C., 'The Nature of a Parliament in Early Stuart England', in H. Tomlinson, ed., *Before the English Civil War* (London, 1983), pp. 123–50.

Russell, C., *Parliaments and English Politics, 1621–1629* (Oxford, 1979).

Russell, C., 'Sir Thomas Wentworth and Anti-Spanish Sentiment, 1621–1624', in J. F. Merritt, ed., *The Political World of Thomas Wentworth, Earl of Strafford, 1621–1641* (Cambridge, 1996), pp. 47–62.

Russell, C., *Unrevolutionary England* (London, 1990).

Sacks, D. H., 'The Corporate Town and the English State: Bristol's "Little Businesses" 1625–1641', *Past and Present*, 110 (February 1986), pp. 69–105.

Sainty, J. C., *Lieutenants of Counties, 1585–1642* (*Bulletin of the Institute of Historical Research*, special supplement, 8, 1970).

Salt, A. E. W., 'Ironworks at Bringwood', *Transactions of the Woolhope Naturalists' Field Club*, 32 (1946–48), pp. 237–8.

Schofield, R. S., 'Taxation and the Political Limits of the Tudor State', in C. Cross, D. Loades, and J. J. Scarisbrick, eds, *Law and Government under the Tudors: Essays presented to Sir Geoffrey Elton* (Cambridge, 1988), pp. 227–55.

Seaward, P., 'Constitutional and Unconstitutional Royalism', *Historical Journal*, 40 (1997), pp. 227–39.

Serr, G., and Ligou, D., 'Henri de Rohan: son rôle dans le parti protestant. Tome II, 1617–1622', in *Divers aspects de la réforme aux XVIe et XVIIe siècles: études et documents* (Société de l'Histoire du Protestantisme Français, supplement, Paris, 1975), pp. 287–631.

Seymour, I., 'The Political Magic of John Dee', *History Today*, 39 (January 1989), pp. 29–35.

Sharp, B., *In Contempt of All Authority: Rural Artisans and Riot in the West of England, 1586–1660* (Berkeley, Los Angeles and London, 1980).

Sharp, L., 'Timber, Science and Economic Reform in the Seventeenth Century', *Forestry*, 48:1 (1975), pp. 51–86.

Sharpe, H., *Genealogical History of the Family of Brabazon* (Paris, 1825).

Sharpe, K., 'Archbishop Laud', *History Today*, 33 (August 1983), pp. 26–30.

Sharpe, K., 'Crown, Parliament and Locality: Government and Communication in Early Stuart England', *English Historical Review*, 101 (1986), pp. 321–50.

Sharpe, K., 'Faction at the Early Stuart Court', *History Today*, 33 (October 1983), pp. 39–46.

Bibliography

Sharpe, K., 'The Image of Virtue: The Court and Household of Charles I, 1625–1642', in D. Sharkey *et al.*, eds, *The English Court: From the Wars of the Roses to the Civil War* (Harlow, 1987), pp. 226–60.

Sharpe, K., 'Parliamentary History 1603–1629: In or Out of Perspective?', in K. Sharpe, ed., *Faction and Parliament: Essays on Early Stuart History* (Oxford, 1978), pp. 1–42.

Sharpe, K., 'The Personal Rule of Charles I', in H. Tomlinson, ed., *Before the English Civil War* (London, 1983), pp. 53–78.

Sharpe, K., *The Personal Rule of Charles I* (New Haven and London, 1992).

Sharpe, K., 'Private Conscience and Public Duty in the Writings of James VI and I', in J. S. Morrill, P. Slack and D. Woolf, eds, *Public Duty and Private Conscience in Seventeenth-Century England* (Oxford, 1993), pp. 77–100.

Sharpe, K., and Lake, P., 'Introduction', in K. Sharpe and P. Lake, eds, *Culture and Politics in Early Stuart England* (Basingstoke, 1994), pp. 1–20.

Sharpe, K., ed., *Faction and Parliament: Essays on Early Stuart History* (Oxford, 1978).

Shaw, S., *The History and Antiquities of Staffordshire* (2 vols, London, 1798–1801).

Shaw, W. A., *The Knights of England* (2 vols, London, 1906).

Shoesmith, R., and Richardson, R., eds, *A Definitive History of Dore Abbey* (Little Logaston, 1997).

Simpson, J. M., *The Folklore of the Welsh Border* (London, 1976).

Skeel, C. A. J., *The Council in the Marches of Wales* (London, 1904).

Skidmore, W., *The Scudamores of Upton Scudamore: A Knightly Family in Medieval Wiltshire, 1086–1382* (2nd edition, Akron, 1989).

Skidmore, W., *Thirty Generations of the Scudamore/Skidmore Family in England and America* (2nd edition, Akron, 1991).

Skinner, Q., *The Foundations of Modern Political Thought* (2 vols, Cambridge, 1978).

Skinner, Q., 'The Principles and Practice of Opposition: The Case of Bolingbroke versus Walpole', in N. McKendrick, ed., *Historical Perspectives: Studies in English Thought and Society in Honour of J. H. Plumb* (London, 1974), pp. 93–128.

Skinner, Q., 'Thomas Hobbes and his Disciples in France and England', *Comparative Studies in Society and History*, 8 (1965–66), pp. 153–67.

Slack, P. 'The Public Conscience of Henry Sherfield', in J. S. Morrill, P. Slack and D. Woolf, eds, *Public Duty and Private Conscience in Seventeenth-Century England* (Oxford, 1993), pp. 151–71.

Sledmere, E., *Abbey Dore, Herefordshire, its Building and Restoration* (Hereford, 1914).

Smith, D. L., *Constitutional Royalism and the Search for Settlement, c. 1640–1649* (Cambridge, 1994).

Smith, D. L., 'The fourth Earl of Dorset and the Personal Rule of Charles I', *Journal of British Studies*, 30 (July 1991), pp. 257–87.

Smith, L. P., *The Life and Letters of Sir Henry Wotton* (2 vols, Oxford, 1907).

Smuts, R. M., 'The Puritan Followers of Henrietta Maria in the 1630s', *English Historical Review*, 93 (1978), pp. 26–45.

Snow, V. F., *Essex the Rebel: The Life of Robert Devereux, the third Earl of Essex 1591–1646* (Lincoln, Nebr., 1971).

Sommerville, C. J., *The Secularization of Early Modern England: From Religious Culture to Religious Faith* (New York and Oxford, 1992).

Sommerville, J. P., *Politics and Ideology in England, 1603–1640* (Harlow 1986).

Sorrel, T., ed., *The Cambridge Companion to Hobbes* (Cambridge, 1996).

Spaeth, D. A., 'Common Prayer? Popular Observance of Anglican Liturgy in Restoration Wiltshire', in S. J. Wright, ed., *Parish, Church and People: Local Studies in Lay Religion 1350–1750* (London, 1988).

Springell, F. C., *Connoisseur and Diplomat: The Earl of Arundel's Embassy to Germany in 1636* (London, 1963).

Spufford, M., *Small Books and Pleasant Histories: Popular Fiction and its Readership in Seventeenth-Century England* (London, 1981).

Spurling, H., *Elinor Fettiplace's Receipt Book* (Harmondsworth, 1987).

Spurr, J., *The Restoration Church of England, 1646–1689* (New Haven and London, 1991).

Staley, V., *The Ceremonial of the English Church* (Oxford and London, 1899).

Starkey, D., 'Representation through Intimacy: A Study in the Symbolism of Monarchy and Court Office in Early-Modern England', in I. Lewis, ed., *Symbols and Sentiments: Cross-cultural Studies in Symbolism* (London, 1977), pp. 187–224.

Starkey, D. *et al.*, eds, *The English Court: From the Wars of the Roses to the Civil War* (Harlow, 1987).

Stephens, E., *The Clerks of the Counties, 1360–1960* (Society of Clerks of the Peace and of Clerks of County Councils, 1961).

Stone, L., *The Crisis of the Aristocracy 1558–1641* (Oxford, 1966).

Stoye, J. W., *Europe Unfolding 1648–1688* (London, 1969).

Strachan, M., *Sir Thomas Roe* (Salisbury, 1989).

Strong, R. C., *The Cult of Elizabeth: Elizabethan Portraiture and Chivalry* (London, 1977).

Strong, R. C., *The English Icon: Elizabethan and Jacobean Portraiture* (London, 1969).

Stubbs, M., 'John Beale, Philosophical Gardener of Herefordshire'. Part I. 'Prelude to the Royal Society (1608–1663)' and Part II, 'The Improvement of Agriculture and Trade in the Royal Society', *Annals of Science*, 39 (1982), pp. 463–89, and 46 (1989), pp. 323–63.

Styles, P., 'The Royalist Government of Worcestershire during the Civil War, 1642–6', *Transactions of the Worcestershire Archaeological Society*, 3rd series, 5 (1976), pp. 23–39.

Sutherland, J., *The Restoration Newspaper and its Development* (Cambridge, 1986).

Sykes, N., 'The Church of England and Non-episcopal Churches in the Sixteenth and Seventeenth Centuries: An Essay towards an Historical Interpretation of the Anglican Tradition from Whitgift to Wake', *Theology*, occasional papers, new series, no. 11, (London, 1948).

Tapié, V.-L., *France in the Age of Louis XIII and Richelieu*, trs. D. McN. Lockie (Cambridge, 1988).

Bibliography

Taylor, E., 'The Seventeenth-Century Iron Forge at Carey Mill', *Transactions of the Woolhope Naturalists' Field Club*, 45:2 (1986), pp. 450–68.

Taylor, E. G. R., *The Mathematical Practicioners of Tudor and Stuart England* (Cambridge, 1954).

Taylor, H., 'Trade, Neutrality and the "English Road", 1630–1648', *Economic History Review*, 2nd series, 25:2 (1972), pp. 236–60.

Thirsk, J., 'Younger Sons in the Seventeenth Century', *History*, 54 (1969), pp. 358–77.

Thirsk, J., ed., *The Agrarian History of England and Wales*, vol. V.i, 1640–1750. *Regional Farming Systems* (Cambridge, 1984).

Thirsk, J., ed., *The Agrarian History of England and Wales*, vol. V.ii, 1640–1750. *Agrarian Change* (Cambridge, 1985).

Thomas, K., *Religion and the Decline of Magic* (Harmondsworth, 1982).

Tighe, W. J., 'Country into Court, Court into Country: John Scudamore of Holme Lacy (*c.* 1542–1623) and his Circles', in D. Hoak, ed., *Tudor Political Culture* (Cambridge, 1995), pp. 157–78.

Tighe, W. J., 'Courtiers and Politics in Elizabethan Herefordshire: Sir James Croft, his Friends and Foes', *Historical Journal*, 32:2 (1989), pp. 257–79.

Tomlinson, H., ed., *Before the English Civil War: Essays on Early Stuart Politics and Government* (London, 1983).

Townsend, G. F., *The Town and Borough of Leominster* (Leominster and London, 1863).

Trevor-Roper, H. R., *Archbishop Laud 1573–1645* (London, 1940).

Trevor-Roper, H. R., 'The Church of England and the Greek Church in the Time of Charles I', in D. Baker, ed., *Studies in Church History*, 15 (1978), pp. 213–40.

Trow-Smith, R., *A History of British Livestock Husbandry to 1700* (London, 1957).

Turnbull, G. H., *Hartlib, Dury, and Comenius* (London, 1947).

Tyacke, N., *Anti-Calvinists: The Rise of English Arminianism c. 1590–1640* (Oxford, 1987).

Tyacke, N., and White, P., 'Debate: The Rise of Arminianism Reconsidered', *Past and Present*, 115 (1987), pp. 201–29.

Underdown, D., *A Freeborn People? Politics and the Nation in Seventeenth-Century England* (Oxford, 1996).

Underdown, D., *Pride's Purge: Politics in the Puritan Revolution* (London, 1985).

Underdown, D., *Revel, Riot and Rebellion: Popular Politics and Culture in England 1603–1660* (Oxford, 1985).

Underdown, D., *Somerset in the Civil War and Interregnum* (Newton Abbot, 1973).

Upton, A. F., *Sir Arthur Ingram c. 1565–1642: A Study of the Origins of an English Landed Family* (Oxford, 1961).

Venn, J. and J. A., *Alumni Cantabrigienses, a Biographical List of all known Students, Graduates and Holders of Office at the University of Cambridge. I: From the Earliest Times to 1751* (4 vols, Cambridge, 1922–27).

Wall, A., 'Patterns of Politics in England, 1558–1625', *Historical Journal*, 31:4 (1988), pp. 947–63.

Warburton, B. E. G., *Memoirs of Prince Rupert and the Cavaliers* (3 vols, London, 1849).

Warner Holidays Ltd, *Holme Lacy House: A History* (n.p., 1995).

Webb, J., *Memorials of the Civil War between King Charles and the Parliament of England as it affected Herefordshire and the adjacent Counties*, ed. and completed by T. W. Webb, (2 vols, London, 1879).

Weber, H., 'Richelieu et le Rhin', *Revue Historique*, 239 (1968), pp. 265–80.

Webster, C., *The Great Instauration* (London, 1975).

Webster, T., *Godly Clergy in Early Stuart England: The Caroline Puritan Movement c. 1620–1643* (Cambridge, 1997).

Weinbaum, M., *British Borough Charters 1307–1660* (Cambridge, 1943).

Welsby, P. A., *Lancelot Andrewes 1555–1626* (London, 1964).

Whigham, F., *Ambition and Privilege: The Social Tropes of Elizabethan Courtesy Theory* (London, 1984).

Whinney, M., and Millar, O., *English Art 1625–1714* (Oxford, 1957).

White, P., 'The Rise of Arminianism Reconsidered', *Past and Present*, 101 (1983), pp. 34–54.

White, P., 'The *Via Media* in the early Stuart Church', in K. Fincham, ed., *The Early Stuart Church, 1603–1642* (Basingstoke, 1993), pp. 211–30.

Willcox, W. B., *Gloucestershire: A Study in Local Government 1590–1640* (New Haven and London, 1940).

Williams, G., *Renewal and Reformation: Wales c. 1415–1642* (Oxford, 1993).

Williams, P., 'The Activity of the Council in the Marches under the Early Stuarts', *Welsh History Review*, 1:2 (1961), pp. 133–60.

Williams, P., 'The Attack on the Council in the Marches, 1603–1642', *Transactions of the Honourable Society of Cymmrodorion* (1961, part I), pp. 1–22.

Williams, P., *The Council in the Marches of Wales under Elizabeth I* (Cardiff, 1958).

Williams, W. R., *The Parliamentary History of the County of Hereford* (Brecknock, privately printed, 1896).

Woodhouse, A. S. P., ed., *Puritanism and Liberty: Being the Army Debates (1647–49) from the Clarke Manuscripts* (London, 1938).

Wright, P., 'A Change in Direction: The Ramifications of a Female Household, 1558–1603', in D. Starkey *et al.*, eds, *The English Court: From the Wars of the Roses to the Civil War* (Harlow, 1987), pp. 147–72.

Wright, S. J., ed., *Parish, Church and People: Local Studies in Lay Religion 1350–1750* (London, 1988).

Y., O., 'Memoir of John first Viscount Scudamore', *Gentleman's Magazine*, 87:1 (January–June 1817), pp. 99–100.

Young, M. B., *Charles I* (Basingstoke, 1997).

Young, M. B., *Servility and Service: The Life and Work of Sir John Coke* (Woodbridge, 1986).

Young, P., *Edgehill 1642: The Campaign and the Battle* (Kineton, 1967).

Zagorin, P., *The Court and the Country: The Beginning of the English Revolution* (London, 1969).

Bibliography

UNPUBLISHED THESES

Cust, R. P., 'The Forced Loan and English Politics, 1626–8' (London University Ph.D., 1983).

Donald, P. H., 'The King and the Scottish Troubles, 1637–1641' (Cambridge University Ph.D., 1987).

Ham, R. E., 'The Career of Sir Herbert Croft (1564?–1629): A Study in Local Government and Society' (University of California at Irvine Ph.D., 1974).

Harrison, G. A., 'Royalist Organisation in Gloucestershire and Bristol 1642–1645' (Manchester University M.A., 1961).

Haskell, P., 'Sir Francis Windebank and the Personal Rule of Charles I' (Southampton University Ph.D., 1978).

Hughes, A., 'Politics, Society and Civil War in Warwickshire 1620–1650' (Liverpool University Ph.D., 1979).

Key, N. E., 'Politics beyond Parliament: Unity and Party in the Herefordshire Region during the Restoration Period' (Cornell University Ph.D., 1989).

Levy, J. S., 'Perceptions and Beliefs: the Harleys of Brampton Bryan and the Origins and Outbreak of the first Civil War' (London University Ph.D., 1983).

McParlin, G. E., 'The Herefordshire Gentry in County Government, 1625–1661' (University College of Wales, Aberystwyth, Ph.D., 1981).

Maltby, J. D., 'Approaches to the Study of Religious Conformity in late Elizabethan and early Stuart England, with Special Reference to Cheshire and the Diocese of Lincoln' (Cambridge University Ph.D., 1991).

Schofield, R. S., 'Parliamentary Lay Taxation 1485–1547' (Cambridge University Ph.D., 1963).

Tighe, W. J., 'The Gentleman Pensioners in Elizabethan Politics and Government' (Cambridge University Ph.D., 1984).

Wanklyn, M. D. G., 'Landed Society and Allegiance in Cheshire and Shropshire in the first Civil War' (Manchester University Ph.D., 1976).

Xiang, R., 'The Staffordshire Justices and their Sessions 1603–42' (Birmingham University Ph.D., 1996).

Index

Note: 'n.' after a page reference indicates the number of a note on that page.

forced loan 10–11, 16–17, 104, 106–8,
  117, 142, 155, 162, 256, 260, 263
knighthood fines 104, 107–10, 117,
  129nn. 65, 68, 151, 256, 260, 263
privy seal loans 104–6, 109, 129n. 68
ship money 104, 114, 162
subsidy 94, 96–105, 107, 151, 162, 262
see also London: St Paul's Cathedral
Taylor, John (*c.* 1600–55) 186
Tetlow, Robert (*c.* 1585–1659) 121, 258,
  264–5
Thirty Years' War (1618–48) 178, 195
Thurscrosse, Timothy (d. 1671) 67–8
Thynne, Francis (*c.* 1545–1608) 172
Tighe, W. J. 26–7
Tombes, John (*c.* 1603–76) 68, 125, 257,
  265
Tomkins, James (1569–1636) 116
Tomkins, Nathaniel 16–17
Traherne, Thomas (*c.* 1636–74) 58, 85n.
  40
Trapp, John (1601–69) 13
Trehearne, Philip 96, 109, 152
Trevor-Roper, Hugh 136, 144, 163n. 8,
  268
Tripoli 161
Tucker, Mr, newsfactor 153
Tucker, William 10, 95, 103
Turner, Matthew (*c.* 1600–*c.* 1660) 53–4,
  66, 69, 89n. 106, 179

Underdown, David 257
United Provinces *see* Netherlands

Vane, Sir Henry (1589–1655) 243
Vaughan, Edward 121
Vaughan, Hugh 122–3
Vaughan, John 115
Vaughan, Roger 102
Vaughan, Rowland 30, 56
Vavasour, Sir Charles 36
Vavasour, Sir William 235, 241, 243
Venice 161, 194
Verney, Sir Edward (1590–1642) 231
Vic, Henry de 175, 177, 179, 181–3, 185,
  189–90, 205
Voile, Claude 198

Wake, Sir Isaac (*c.* 1580–1632) 157, 189
Walker, Sir Edward (1612–77) 148
Wall, Alison 2
Wall, George, senior 52, 62–3, 65, 70,
  80, 171–2, 264–5
Wall, George, junior 63
Waller, Sir William (1598–1668) 220,
  227, 238–41
Walsingham, Sir Francis (*c.* 1530–90) 13
Wandesford, Sir Christopher (1628–87)
  135
Ward, Samuel (1577–1640) 40
Warner, John, bishop of Rochester
  (1581–1666) 68
Warwick, Sir Philip (1609–83) 80
Warwickshire 4, 128n. 48
Wastell, Leonard 264
Watkyns, Rowland 51, 258, 262, 265
Weaver, Richard (1575–1642) 224
Webb, John 227, 248n. 42, 265
Webtree hundred 98, 101–3, 107, 114, 123
Weckherlin, Georg (1584–1653) 156
Wenman, Richard, Viscount (*c.* 1573–
  1640) 150
Wentworth, Sir Thomas, earl of Strafford
  (1593–1641) 10–11, 14, 151, 195,
  256, 260
Westfaling, Herbert (d. 1638) 121
Westminster *see* London
Weston, Jerome (1605–63) 157
Weston, Sir Richard, *see* Portland, earl of
Whig history 2, 5–6, 263
  see also anti-revisionist history; post-
    revisionist history; revisionist
    history
Whitney, Eustace 121
Whitney, Robert 225, 232
Wicquefort, Abraham de (1606–82) 181,
  187
Wigmore, Richard 226, 236–8
Wigmore, Thomas (*c.* 1605–*c.* 1653) 224
Wigmore hundred 100, 114
Wilcocks, John 96
Williams, John (1582–1650) 95
Williamson, Sir Joseph (1633–1701) 156
Windebank, Sir Francis (1582–1646)
  176, 189, 194, 198–9, 206
  earl of Leicester and 187, 199–201, 206